Selected Reading Lists and Course
Outlines from American Colleges
and Universities

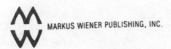
Medieval History

edited by Penelope D. Johnson
New York University

Second updated and expanded edition, 1985

MARKUS WIENER PUBLISHING, INC.

First M. Wiener Publishing Inc. Edition 1983
Second Edition 1985

ISBN 0-910129-42-8
Library of Congress Card No. 83-061358
Printed in America

TABLE OF CONTENTS

i

74034

INTRODUCTION

This volume of course outlines and reading lists represents the second edition of syllabi in medieval history. When I gathered syllabi for the original volume in the spring of 1983, the range and creativity of the submissions struck me as exciting and provocative. Now, two years later, the collection has been substantially revised by many of the contributors who have revamped and honed their courses in the intervening time: fifteen syllabi have been redone, and five are new additions.

The process of selecting course materials for inclusion in this collection was governed by certain requirements. A syllabus needed either to cover in an exemplary manner a traditional area or time period within the purview of medieval history, or it had to suggest new means of organizing or presenting the history of the Middle Ages. Some of the most intriguing outlines received were, however, for courses which can not properly be called medieval since the chronological scope exceeds the traditional limits of 500 to 1500; others which also seemed to be of real interest are not truly within the discipline of history. Nevertheless, since the intent of this collection is to stimulate pedagogic creativity, a few courses have been included which do not fit exactly within the framework of medieval chronology or within the discipline of history but which may serve to pique the interest of other medievalists. Some of the courses included may seem at first glance to be relatively traditional but offer something innovative in interesting assignments, class organization, exam formats, reading lists, or out-of-class activities. Some which are team-taught and/or interdisciplinary suggest provocative possibilities for presenting what may be standard fare. Indeed, one medievalist who reviewed the proposed syllabi before they went to press commented that she felt as if she were at an appealing smorgasborg: one could take a little from this dish and a good dollop from that, and then a spoonful from several other platters to end up with an unusual and satisfying meal which would be uniquely her own. Just so, students and scholars may consult these outlines for topics, specific reading suggestions, and any other teaching technique or experiment which takes their fancy.

Many scholars were generous enough to submit syllabi for consideration so that it was possible to put together a fairly good representative range of courses. Indeed, one of the happy surprises was to discover how innovative instructors in medieval history can be; in fact, the only limits seem to be set by constraints of time and energy. On the other hand, the course outlines collected did not cover all fields; there was a tremendous duplication for some areas and a dearth of offerings in others. Thus, although I was wading around in syllabi dealing with women's history and crime, I was unable to come up with one syllabus in medieval urban history. Also, sadly, many courses could not be used because they are too condensed to be comprehensible to the outsider; rely heavily on collections of documents made by the instructor but unavailable outside the classroom; or primarily use foreign language titles or books which are out-of-print and not contained in any but the largest university libraries.

The organization of this collection is admittedly arbitrary and relies on my own reading of each instructor's intent; therefore the categorization of each course reflects my judgment and not necessarily that of the instructor. Also, of course, many courses can logically and appropriately fit into more than one niche. Thus, for example, Professor Ann Matter's course on Christian Thought could be included under Ecclesiastic History, but I have chosen to put it under Intellectual History as the thrust of the course seems to be to immerse the student in the work of great medieval thinkers who happen to have been mostly churchmen. Equally, it has been my choice to include in this volume courses intended for graduate as well as undergraduate students on the assumption that an instructor can amend a syllabus to the appropriate level of a class, and that advanced undergraduates are often working on the same material as first-year graduate students. Highly specialized graduate seminars were not amenable to the purposes of this collection since they generally rely on individual meetings with the instructor and foreign-language reading lists. Further, I have chosen more than one syllabus for a subject when the duplication offered a useful comparison of differing methods and approaches.

It has been a pleasure to have had contact with so many exciting and creative teachers all over the country and gratifying that so many responded generously to contribute their materials. My thanks go to all who shared syllabi and my regret that only a small percentage could actually be printed.

This collection of syllabi is offered to the graduate student in medieval history who is examining options in preparation for future employment; to the new teacher, who happily installed in a brand new academic job finds himself/herself facing the daunting prospect of creating a clutch of courses with little time to spare; to the established academic who is intrigued by the possibility of experimenting with the team-teaching approach, new methods, or new subject matter; and to all inveterate collectors of syllabi in medieval studies.

Penelope D. Johnson
New York University

CLASSICAL AND CHRISTIAN WORLDS
Carole Straw
Mount Holyoke College

This course will examine the continuities and contrasts in
classical and Christian traditions. We will pursue what
Clifford Geertz has called a "thick description" of culture,
noting how ideas, social patterns, political institutions, and
economic conditions interlock to form a distinct society. We
will focus on three major problems: 1.) What does it mean to
be human? Can we detect an increasing recognition of the
complexity of man's and woman's personality and psychology in
the sources? Is there what one historian has termed " a
development of conscience"? 2.) What is mankind's
relationship to the gods (or God)? How does the definition of
a god reflect human characteristics and human needs? What does
this relationship between mankind and god tell us about
mankind's control of the environment? 3.) How are the
political, social and economic patterns of a culture somehow an
expression of a complete thought world, rather than simply the
product of sheer necessity? In other words, to what extent is
history determined by external events, or created by
personalities and ideas interacting with an environment?

This course will emphasize teaching the student how to
interpret primary sources and how to write an analytical essay
We shall discuss guidelines for writing a paper in history at a
later date.

Books to be purchased:

Aeschylus, The Oresteian Trilogy(Penguin)
Augustine, The City of God(Image)
Augustine, The Confessions(Image)
Barrow, R. W., The Romans(Penguin)
Chadwick, Henry, The Early Church(Penguin)
Finley, M. I., ed., The Portable Greek Historians(Penguin)
Grant, M. ed., Cicero: Selected Works(Penguin)
Hadas, M. ed., The Stoic Philosophy of Seneca(Norton)
Jowett, B. tr., The Works of Plato(Modern Library)
Kitto, H. D. F., The Greeks(Penguin)
Plutarch, The Fall of the Roman Republic(Penguin)
Paolucci, H., The Political Writings of St. Augustine(Gateway)

Rieu, ed., <u>Homer: The Odyssey</u> (Bantom)
St. Pachomius, <u>Rule</u> (Eastern Orthodox Press)
Staniforth, ed., <u>Early Christian Writings</u>(Penguin)
Tacitus, <u>The Annals</u>(Penguin)
Waddell, Helen, <u>The Desert Fathers</u>(Ann Arbor)
Ward, B., <u>The Wisdom of the Desert Fathers</u> (Fairacres)

Requirements:

1. Preparation for and participation in class discussion.
2. Completion of short quizzes in class.
3. Midterm of five to seven pages due March 20. Late papers
are penalized 1/2 grade per day. The midterm may be rewritten
within one week of its return to the student.
4. A final paper will be due May 11. Late papers are
penalized 1/2 grade per day.

Class Meetings:

1. Introduction

2. Kitto, pp.7-64.

3. Homer, <u>The Odyssey,</u> bks. 1-5.
    Kitto, pp. 169-205.

4. Homer, <u>The Odyssey</u>, bks. 6-11.

5. Herodotus, in <u>The Portable Greek Historians,</u> pp. 81-157.
    Kitto, pp. 64-109.

6. Herodotus, pp. 157-215.
    SHORT QUIZ

7. Plutarch, <u>Solon</u>
    Selections of Solon's poems
    (begin next assignment of Kitto)

8. Kitto, pp. 109-69
    Aeschylus, <u>The Agamemnon,</u> in <u>The Oresteia Trilogy</u>, pp.
41-100.

9. Aeschylus, <u>The Choephori</u> and <u>The Eumenides,</u> in <u>The
Oresteia Trilogy</u>, pp. 103-182.

10. Sophocles, <u>Oedipus the King</u> and <u>Antigone,</u> in <u>The Complete
    Plays of Sophocles</u>, 77-114, and 117-147.

11. Euripides, <u>Electra</u>
    SHORT QUIZ

2

12. Plato, _Phaedo_, in _The Works of Plato_, pp. 109-189.

13. Plato, Selections from the _Republic_, in _The Works of Plato_ pp. 397-478

14. Midterm paper due.
    Thucydides, Pericles' "Funeral Oration" in _The Portable Greek Historians,_ pp. 265-273.
    Plutarch, _Pericles_, in _The Rise and Fall of Athens_ pp. 165-206.

15. HOLIDAYS (begin Barrows)

16. Plutarch, _Cicero_, in _The Fall of the Roman Republic_, pp. 311-361.
    Cicero, selections from "On Duties" pp. 186-212.

17. Cicero, _On Old Age_, in _Selected Works,_ pp. 213-46.
    Barrow, _The Romans_, pp. 9-78
    SHORT QUIZ

18. Tacitus, _The Annals,_ pp. 29-40; 88-101; 126-52.
    Barrows, pp. 79-111.

19. Seneca, _On Providence_ and _On Tranquility_, in _The Stoic Philosophhy of Seneca_, pp. 27-45,75-106.

20. St. Paul, I Corinthians

21. Chadwick, _The Early Christian Church,_ pp. 23-32, 54-73.
    Clement of Rome, _Epistle_, in _Early Christian Writing_, pp. 42-54.
    Ignatius of Antioch, pp. 119-130, in _ECW_
    SHORT QUIZ

22. Waddell, _The Desert Fathers_, pp. 60-126.
    St. Pachomius, _Rule_

23. Waddell, _The Desert Fathers_ pp. 126-201.

24. Augustine, _The Confessions,_ bk. 1-5

25. Augustine, _The Confessions_, bks. 6-10

26. Augustine, _The City of God_, pp. 39-118.

27. Augustine, _Political Writings_, pp. 153-83, 211-219.

28. Final paper due.

THE EARLY MIDDLE AGES

TEXTS: N. F. Cantor, Medieval History: The Life and Death of a
        Civilization.   (Second Edition.)
The Pirenne Thesis: Analysis, Criticism, and Revision,
        edited by A. F. Havighurst.   (latest edition)
F. L. Ganshof, Feudalism.   (Harper Torchbooks)
Einhard and Notker, Two Lives of Charlemagne, trans. L.
        Thorpe. (Penguin)
The Vinland Sagas: The Norse Discovery of America,
        translated by Magnus Magnusson and Hermann Palsson.
        (Penguin)

N.B. IN ACCORDANCE WITH UNIVERSITY POLICY, THE TAPING OF LECTURES IS NOT
PERMITTED. Exceptions will be made only for physically handicapped students
having the instructor's written permission.

      There follows a schedule of lectures, discussions, and readings.
With the exception of the texts listed above, all of the books will be found
in the Reserve Room in Sinclair Library. The large paperback by Cantor will
serve as the basic text throughout the course and it also covers the subject
matter of History 434, The High Middle Ages, which will be offered in the
spring semester. A class period has been set aside for discussion of each of
the smaller paperbacks. It is expected that each member of the class,
including auditors, will read each one before the assigned date and will
participate in the discussion.

      You are expected to pursue a research project throughout the greater
part of the semester, dealing with a topic or problem of your choice (which
must, however, have the instructor's approval). Submission of your topic (14
September, on a form which will be furnished) ipso facto will constitute
affirmation of the fact that you have checked out the library holdings to
determine the feasibility of the project and that the requisite primary
sources, monographic literature and periodical material all are available in
languages in which you are competent. A first draft of the paper, as nearly
as possible in final form and complete with scholarly apparatus, is to be
submitted for comment and criticism by 26 October. The final version,
impeccable in style, form, and content, and representing so far as possible a
significant original contribution to the sum total of human knowledge, will be
turned in on or before 7 December.

      I will gladly furnish advice and a reasonable degree of assistance,
both with the paper and with the course. My office is Sakamaki A-408. See me
MWF 7:00 - 7:20; 9:50 - 10:20 or by appointment.

Mon. 27 Aug.   ORIENTATION.
           N. F. Cantor, Medieval History, pp. 1-13.

Wed. 29 Aug.   The Crisis of the Roman World.
                 Cantor, pp. 14-30.
                 F. Lot, The End of the Ancient World and the Beginnings
                 of the Middle Ages. [This need not all be read at
                 once but try to read it sometime before the hour exam
                 on 19 Oct.]

Fri. 31 Aug.   The Crisis of the Roman World, II (and slides).

Mon. 3 Sept.   HOLIDAY.   (Labor Day)

Wed. 5 Sept.   The Rise of Christianity and the Early Church.
                 Cantor, pp. 31-57.
                 Documents of the Early Church, ed. H. S. Bettenson
                     (1947), pp. 3-22, 49-73, 88-104, 108-110.

Fri. 7 Sept.   Doctrinal Problems.

Mon. 10 Sept.   The Christological Controversy.

Wed. 12 Sept.   Christian Organization.

Fri. 14 Sept.   The Triumph of Christianity.   [TERM PAPER TOPICS DUE.]
                 Cantor, pp. 59-101.
                 Documents of the Christian Church, ed. H. S Bettenson,
                     pp. 22-33, 111-116.
                 A Source Book of Mediaeval History, ed. F. A. Ogg, pp.
                     78-83, 90-96.

Mon. 17 Sept.   Early Monasticism.

Wed. 19 Sept.   Germanic Society, I.
                 Cantor, pp. 105-116.
                 W. Schlesinger, "Lord and Follower in Germanic
                     Institutional History," in Lordship and Community in
                     Medieval Europe: Selected Readings, ed. F. L.
                     Cheyette, pp. 64-99.
                 Source Book ..., ed. Ogg, pp. 19-31.

Fri. 21 Sept.   Germanic Society, II.

Mon. 24 Sept.   The Barbarian Migrations, I.
                 Cantor, pp. 116-121.
                 Lot, pp. 187-200.
                 Source Book ..., ed. Ogg, pp. 32-46.

Wed. 26 Sept.   The Barbarian Migrations, II.

Fri. 28 Sept.   The Huns and the Coming of the Franks.

Mon. 1 Oct.   The Barbarian Kingdoms, I.
                 Cantor, pp. 121-136.
                 Lot, pp. 201-254, 276-284.

Wed. 3 Oct.   The Barbarian Kingdoms, II.

Fri. 5 Oct.   The Byzantine Reconquest.
                    Cantor, pp. 137-146.
                    Lot, pp. 255-275.

Mon. 8 Oct.   HOLIDAY   (Discoverers' Day - see the topics listed for the
                          final week of the course.)

Wed. 10 Oct.   The Byzantine Empire.

Fri. 12 Oct.   The Origins and Expansion of Islam.
                    Cantor, pp. 146-160.
                    Source Book ..., ed, Ogg, pp. 97-104.

Mon. 15 Oct.   Islamic Culture to the Tenth Century.

Wed. 17 Oct.   The Catholic Church, the Papacy, and the Lombards.
                    Cantor, pp. 161-175.
                    Lot, pp. 284-309.

Fri. 19 Oct.   HOUR EXAM!

Mon. 22 Oct.   The Early History of Anglo-Saxon England and Celtic Ireland.
                    Cantor, pp. 179-189.

Wed. 24 Oct.   The Frankish Kingdom, I.
                    Lot, pp. 310-337.
                    Source Book ..., ed. Ogg, pp. 47-67. [The Salic Law is
                       also printed in Select Historical Documents of the
                       Middle Ages, ed. E. F. Henderson, pp. 176-189.]

Fri. 26 Oct.   The Frankish Kingdom, II.   [FIRST DRAFT DUE]

Mon. 29 Oct.   DISCUSSION OF THE PIRENNE THESIS.
                    The Pirenne Thesis: Analysis, Criticism, and Revision,
                       ed. A. F. Havighurst.   (Heath)

Wed. 31 Oct.   Byzantine Missions in Southeastern Europe.

Fri. 2 Nov.   The Rise of the Carolingians.
                    Cantor, pp. 189-197.
                    Lot, pp. 337-407.
                    The Fourth Book of the Chronicle of Fredegar With Its
                       Continuations, trans J. M. Wallace-Hadrill, pp. 1-121.
                       (Having read this, you might also take a look at W.
                       Goffart, "The Fredegar Problem Reconsidered,"
                       Speculum, XXXVIII (1963), 206-241.

Mon. 5 Nov.   The Frankish Church and the Celtic Saints.

Wed. 7 Nov.   The Anglo-Saxon Mission to the Germans and Saint Boniface.

Fri. 9 Nov.   Saint Boniface and the Frankish Church.

Mon. 12 Dec.   HOLIDAY (Veterans' Day)

Wed. 14. Nov.   Charlemagne as King: Italy and Germany.
                Source Book ..., ed. Ogg, pp. 108-129.

Fri. 16 Nov.   DISCUSSION OF CHARLEMAGNE'S LIVES.
                Einhard and Notker, Two Lives of Charlemagne,
                    trans. L. Thorpe. (Penguin)

Mon. 19 Nov.   DISCUSSION OF CHARLEMAGNE'S IMPERIAL CORONATION.
                The Coronation of Charlemagne: What Did It Signify?
                    ed. R. Sullivan. [To be distributed in class.]
                Cantor, pp. 197-201.
                Source Book ..., ed. Ogg, pp. 130-134.

Wed. 21 Nov.   The Carolingian Renaissance.

Fri. 23 Nov.   HOLIDAY. [Post-holiday?]

Mon. 26 Nov.   The Significance of the Carolingian Empire (including slides)
                Source Book ..., ed. Ogg, pp. 123-148.

Wed. 28 Nov.   The Decline of the Carolingian Empire: The End of Unity.
                Cantor, pp. 203-214.
                Source Book ..., ed. Ogg, pp. 149-156.
                Select Historical Documents ..., ed. Henderson, pp. 206f.

Fri. 30 Nov.   Early Medieval Society and Technology.

Mon. 3 Dec.   DISCUSSION OF FEUDALISM AND ITS ORIGINS.
                Cantor, pp. 214-223.
                F. L. Ganshof, Feudalism.
                Lordship and Community in Medieval Europe: Selected
                    Readings, ed. F. L. Cheyette, pp. 12-61.
                Source Book ..., ed. Ogg, pp. 203-223.

Wed. 5 Dec.   Medieval Scandinavia and the Viking Age.
                Source Book ..., ed. Ogg, pp. 157-176.

Fri. 7 Dec.   Later Anglo-Saxon England.   [DEADLINE FOR TERM PAPERS!]

Mon. 10 Dec.   Medieval Scandinavian Expansion to the West: Medieval
                America.

Wed. 12 Dec.   DISCUSSION OF THE SOURCES ON THE VINLAND VOYAGES.
                The Vinland Sagas: The Norse Discovery of America,
                    translated by Magnus Magnusson and Hermann Palsson.
                    (Penguin)

Fri. 14 Dec.   Two Mysteries: Alleged Mooring Holes and the Newport
                    Tower.   (SLIDES)

            FINAL EXAMINATION: Monday, 17 December 1984, 7:30 - 9:30.
                                5 a

ORIENTATION.

C. H. Dawson, The Making of Europe.
A. R. Lewis, Emerging Medieval Europe, A.D. 400-1000.
R. S. Hoyt, Life and Thought in the Early Middle Ages.
H. Moss, The Birth of the Middle Ages, 395-814.
M. Grant, The Birth of Western Civilization.
E. K. Rand, Founders of the Middle Ages.
P. R. L. Brown, The World of Late Antiquity, A.D. 150-750.
M. L. W. Laistner, The Intellectual Heritage of the Early Middle Ages:
      Selected Essays.
R. Latouche, Caesar to Charlemagne: The Beginnings of France.   Trans. by
      J. Nicholson.
Early Medieval Society, ed. S. L. Thrupp.
C. Davies, The Emergence of Western Society.
L. Genicot, Contours of the Middle Ages.
A. Leighton, Transportation and Communication in Early Medieval Europe, A.D.
      500-1100.
H. O. Taylor, "Placing the Middle Ages," Speculum, 9 (1936), 437-455.
T. E. Mommsen, "Petrarch's Conception of the Dark Ages," ibid., 17 (1942),
      227-242.
P. Schaeffer, "The Emergence of the Concept "Medieval" in Central European
      Humanism," Sixteenth Century Journal, 7 (Oct. 1976), 21-30.
A. Dopsch, "Vom Altertum zum Mittelalter: Das Kontinuitätsproblem" Archiv für
      Kulturgeschichte, 16 (1926), 159-182.
H. Aubin, "Die Frage nach der Scheide zwischen Altertum und Mittelalter,"
      Historische Zeitschrift, 172 (1951), 245-263.
P. E. Hübinger, "Spätantike und frühen Mittelalter," Deutsche Vierteljahr-
      schrift für Literaturwissenschaft und Geistesgeschichte, 26 (1952), 1-48.
C. van der Kieft, "De periodisierung van de geschiedenis der middeleeuwen,"
      Tijdschrift voor geschiedenis, 81 (1968), 433-444.
F. Altheim, Literatur und Gesellschaft im ausgehenden Altertum.
J. Fischer, Oriens, Occidens, Europa: Begriff und Gedanke 'Europa' in der
      später Antike und in frühen Mittelalter.
H. Dannenbauer, Die Entstehung Europas.   (2 vols.)

THE CRISIS OF THE ROMAN WORLD.

F. Lot, The End of the Ancient World and the Beginnings of the Middle Ages,
      pp. 1-186.
E. Gibbon, The History of the Decline and Fall of the Roman Empire.
The Transformation of the Roman World: Gibbon's Problem After Two Centuries,
      ed. L. White, Jr.
D. P. Jordan, Gibbon and His Roman Empire.
M. J. Rostovstev, The Social and Economic History of the Roman Empire.
T. Frank, An Economic History of Ancient Rome.   (6 vols.)
M. Grant, The Climax of Rome: The Final Achievements of the Ancient World,
      A.D. 161-337.

T. D. Barnes, The New Empire of Diocletian and Constantine.
C. Bailey, The Legacy of Rome.
S. Dill, Roman Society in the Last Century of the Western Empire.
S. Mazzarino, The End of the Ancient World.
R. M. Hayward, The Myth of Rome's Fall.
W. C. Green, The Achievement of Rome.
A. E. R. Boak, Manpower Shortage and the Fall of the Roman Empire in the West.
R. MacMullen, Enemies of the Roman Order: Treason, Unrest and Alienation in
   the Empire.
A. Alföldi, A Conflict of Ideas in the Late Roman Empire: The Clash Between
   the Senate and Valentinian I.
R. Bianchi-Bandinelli, Rome, the Late Empire: Roman Art, A.D. 200-400.
W. Kaegi, Byzantium and the Decline of Rome.
J. H. Waldron, "Lead Poisoning in the Ancient World," Medical History, 17
   (1973), 391-399.
W. Goffart, "Zosimus, The First Historian of Rome's Fall," American Historical
   Review, 76 (1971), 412-441.
J. J. Saunders, "The Debate on the Fall of Rome," History, 68 (1963), No.
   162, 1-17.
G. Alföldy, "The Crisis of the Third Century as Seen by Contemporaries,"
   Greek, Roman and Byzantine Studies, 15 (1974), 89-111.
J. F. Gilliam, "The Plague Under Marcus Aurelius," American Journal of
   Philology, 82 (1961), 225-251.
S. McNally, "Diocletian's Palace: Split in the Middle Ages," Archaeology, 28
   (Oct. 1975), 248-259.
J. W. Rich, "The Supposed Roman Manpower Shortage of the Later Second Century
   B.C.," Historia, 32 (no. 3, 1983), 287-331.
W. N. Bayless, "The Treaty With the Huns of 443," American Journal of
   Philology, 97 (no. 2, 1976), 176-179.
A. R. Birley, "The Third Century Crisis in the Roman Empire," Bulletin of the
   John Rylands University Library, 58 (no. 2, 1976), 253-281.
W. Esslin, "Der Kaiser in der Spätantike," Hist. Zeit., 177 (1954), 449-
   468.
M. A. Wes, "Geschiedenis en late oudheid: Van Rostovtzeff tot Jones," Tijd-
   schrift voor geschiedenis, 82 (1969), 453-468.
E. Mayer, Römischer Staat und Staatsgedanke.

THE RISE OF CHRISTIANITY AND THE EARLY CHURCH,
INCLUDING THE DOCTRINAL CONTROVERSIES.

H. Chadwick, The Early Church.
A. von Harnack, The Mission and Expansion of Christianity in the First Three
   Centuries.
A. C. Flick, The Rise of the Medieval Church.
J. F. Bethune-Baker, The Christian Religion: Its Origin and Progress.
F. Cumont, The Oriental Religions in Roman Paganism.
M. Gough, The Early Christians.
A. C. McGiffert, A History of Christian Thought.
R. M Grant, Gnosticism and Early Christianity.
T. D. Barnes, Tertullian: A Historical and Literary Study.
M. L. W. Laistner, Christianity and Pagan Culture in the Later Roman Empire.

E. R. Dodds, Pagan and Christian in an Age of Anxiety: Some Aspects of
    Religious Experience from Marcus Aurelius to Constantine.
W. H. C. Frend, Martyrdom and Persecution in the Early Church.
P. Brown, "Approaches to the Religious Crisis of the Third Century," English
    Historical Review, 83 (1968), 542-558. [Review Article on the above
    books by Dodds and Frend.]
A. D. Nock, Conversion.
J. Guitton, Great Heresies and Church Councils.
K. Sarkissian, The Council of Chalcedon and the Armenian Church.
G. L. Keyes, Christian Faith and the Interpretation of History.
C. H. Dawson, Religion and the Rise of Western Culture.
W. H. C. Frend, The Rise of the Monophysite Movement: Chapters in the History
    of the Church in the Fifth and Sixth Centuries.
R. M. Ogilvie, The Romans and Their Gods in the Age of Augustus.
The Catacombs and the Colosseum: The Roman Empire as the Setting of Primitive
    Christianity, ed. S. Benko and J. J. O'Rourke.
D. L. Holland, "The Creeds of Nicea [sic!] and Constantinople Reexamined,"
    Church History, 38 (1969), 248-261.
A. Vööbus, "The Origin of the Monophysite Church in Syria and Mesopotamia,"
    ibid., 42 (1973), 17-26.
F. D. Gilliard, "The Apostolicity of Gallic Churches," Harvard Theological
    Review, 86 (Jan. 1975), 17-33.
E. A. Judge, "The Social Identity of the First Christians: A Question of
    Method in Religious History," Journal of Religious History, 11 (Dec.
    1980), 201-17.
J. Mahé, "Les anathématismes de saint Cyrille d'Alexandrie et les évêques
    orientaux du patriarchat d'Antioche," Revue d'histoire ecclésiastique, 7
    (1906), 505-542.
G. Rasneur, "L'Homoiousianisme dans ses rapports avec l'orthodoxie," ibid., 4
    (1903), 411-431.
The Orations of St. Athanasius Against the Pagans.
Documents Illustrating Papal Authority, A.D. 96-454, ed. E. Giles.
J. Marichez, "Le pasteur d'Hermas: Un nouveau manuscrit de l'ancienne version
    latine," Rev. d'hist. eccl., 6 (1905), 281-288.

THE TRIUMPH OF CHRISTIANITY.

R. M. Grant, The Sword and the Cross.
R. M. Grant, Augustus to Constantine: The Thrust of the Christian Movement
    Into the Roman World.
A. H. M. Jones, Constantine and the Conversion of Europe.
J. Burckhardt, The Age of Constantine the Great.
K. F. Morrison, Rome and the City of God.
K. F. Morrison, Tradition and Authority in the Western Church, 300-1140.
B. J. Kidd, The Roman Primacy to A.D. 461.
T. J. Gregory, Vox Populi: Popular Opinion and Violence in the Religious
    Controversies of the Fifth Century A.D.
R. MacMullen, Constantine.
P. R. L. Brown, Augustine of Hippo: A Biography.
G. W. Bowersock, Julian the Apostate.

P. Brown, The Cult of the Saints: Its Rise and Function in Latin Christianity.
L. W. Barnard, "Church-State Relations, A.D. 313-337," Journal of Church and
    State, 25 (no. 2, 1982), 337-355.
G. W. Bowersock, "The Emperor Julian on His Predecessors," Yale Classical
    Studies, 27 (1982), 159-172.
C. E. Braaten, "Modern Interpretations of Nestorius," Church History, 32
    (1963), 251-267.
G. T. Armstrong, "Imperial Church Building and Church-State Relations, A.D.
    313-363," ibid., 36 (1967), 3-17.
J. Plescia, "On the Persecutions of Christians in the Roman Empire," Latomus,
    30 (1971), 12 -132.
G. Fowden, "The Pagan Holy Man in Late Antique Society," Journal of Hellenic
    Studies, 102 (1982), 33-59.
A. C. Pegis, "The Mind of St. Augustine," Mediaeval Studies, VI (1944), 1-61.
A. S. McGrade, "Two Fifth-Century Conceptions of Papal Primacy," Studies in
    Medieval And Renaissance History, 7 (1970), 1-45.
W. Ullmann, "The Constitutional Significance of Constantine the Great's
    Settlement," Journal of Ecclesiastical History, 27 (Jan. 1976), 1-16.
A. Yarbrough, "Christianization in the Fourth Century: The Example of Roman
    Women," Church History, 45 (June 1976), 149-165.
H. Dörries, Constantine the Great.
H. Dörries, Constantine and Religious Liberty.
R. Browning, The Emperor Julian.
C. Callewaert, "Les premiers chretiens furent-ils persécutés par édits
    généraux ou par mesures de police? Observations sur la theorie de Mommsen
    principalement d'apres les écrits de Tertullien," Rev. d'hist. eccl., 2
    (1901), 771-797; III (1902), 5-15, 324-348, 601-614.
J. M. A. Salles-Dabadie, Les conciles oecumeniques dans l'histoire.
Julianus Apostata, The Works of the Emperor Julian. (3 vols.) "Against the
    Galileans" is in Vol. III, 313-427.
J. Bidez, La vie de l'empereur Julien.
H, Kraft, Kaiser Konstantins religiöse Entwicklung.
H. von Schubert, Geschichte der christlichen Kirche im Frühmittelalter.

EARLY MONASTICISM.

D. Knowles, Christian Monasticism.
L. C. Daly, Benedictine Monasticism.
H. C. Lea, The History of Sacerdotal Celibacy in the Christian Church.
G. Constable, Monastic Tithes From Their Origin to the Twelfth Century.
J. Décarreaux, Monks and Civilization: From the Barbarian Invasions to the
    Reign of Charlemagne.
C. A. Frazee, "The Origins of Clerical Celibacy in the Western Church," Church
    History, 41 (1972), 149-167.
C. H. Lawrence, "St. Benedict and His Rule," History, 67 (June 1982), 185-194.
M. Heimbucher, Die Orden und Kongregationen der katholischen Kirche.
H. E. Feine, Kirchliche Rechtsgeschichte: Die katholische Kirche.
F. Prinz, Frühes Mönchtum in Frankreich.
L. Ueding, Geschichte der Klostergründungen der frühen Merowingerzeit.

PRIMITIVE GERMANIC SOCIETY.

W. Schlesinger, "Lord and Follower in Germanic Institutional History," in
    Lordship and Community in Medieval Europe: Selected Readings, ed. F. L.
    Cheyette, pp. 64-99.
E. A. Thompson, The Early Germans.
M. Todd, The Northern Barbarians, 100 B.C. - A.D. 300.
M. Todd, Everyday Life of the Barbarians: Goths, Franks and Vandals.
F. L. Borchardt, German Antiquity in Renaissance Myth.
O. Brogan, "Trade Between the Roman Empire and the Free Germans," Journal of
    Roman Studies, 26 (1935), 195-222.
D. A. Bullough, "Early Medieval Social Groupings: The Terminology of Kinship,"
    Past and Present, No. 45 (Nov. 1969), pp. 3-18.
A. Helbok, "Volk und Staat der Germanen," Hist. Zeit., 154 (1936), 229-240.
A. H. Price, "Early Place Names Ending in -heim as Warrior Club Settlements
    and the Role of Soc in the Germanic Administration of Justice," Central
    European History, 14 (Sept. 1981), 187-199.
E. Schwarz, Germanische Stammeskunde.
K. F. Stroheker, Germanentum und Spätantike.
F. Behn, Altgermanische Kultur: Ein Bilderatlas.
A. Riese, Das rheinische Germanien in der antiken Literatur.
H. Kirchner, Das germanische Altertum in der deutschen Geschichtsschreibung des
    achtzehnten Jahrhunderts.
A. K. G. Kristensen, Tacitus' germanische Gefolgschaft.
G. Kossinna, Altgermanische Kulturhöhe.
M. Lintzel, Ausgewählte Schriften, I, 1-54, 235-445.
G. Waitz, Deutsche Verfassungsgeschichte, I.
J. de Vries, De germaansche oudheid.
K. F. H. de Kroon, "Caesar over het grondbezit bij der Germanen," Tijdschrift
    voor geschiedenis, 35 (1920), 270-278.

THE BARBARIAN MIGRATIONS.

J. B. Bury, The Invasion of Europe by the Barbarians.
T. Hodgkin, Italy and Her Invaders.   (8 vols.)
E. A. Thompson, The Visigoths in the Time of Ulfila.
E. A. Thompson, "The Date of the Conversion of the Visigoths," Journal of
    Ecclesistical History, 7 (1956), 1-11.
G. B. Ladner, "On Roman Attitudes Toward Barbarians in Late Antiquity," Viator,
    7 (1976), 1-26.
A. H. Price. "Differentiated Germanic Social Structures," Vierteljahrschrift
    für Sozial- und Wirtschaftsgeschichte, 55 (1969), 433-448. [Use with
    caution.]
B. S. Bachrach, "The Alans in Gaul," Traditio, 23 (1967), 476-489.
B. Croke, "Arbogast and the Death of Valentinian II," Historia, 25 (no. 2,
    1976), 235-244.
E. Demougeot, "L'invasion des Cimbres-Teutons-Ambrons et les Romains,"
    Latomus, 37 (no. 4, 1978), 910-938.
K. Schäferdiek, "Wulfila. Vom Bischof von Gotien zum Gotenbischof,"
    Zeitschrift für Kirchengeschichte, 90 (no. 2-3, 1979), 107-46; 253-92.

P. Stockmeier, "Bemerkungen zur Christianisierung der Goten im 4.
   Jahrhundert," Zeitschrift für Kirchengeschichte, 92 (no. 2-3, 1981),
   315-24.
M. Springer, "Haben die Germanen das weströmische Reich erobert?" Klio, 64
   (no. 1, 1982), 179-87.
L. Mussat, The Germanic Invasions.
F. Lot, Les invasions germaniques: La pénétration mutuelle du monde barbare et
   du monde Romain.
L. Halphen, Les barbares: Les grandes invasions aux conquêtes Turques du XIe
   siècle.
R. Guichard, Essai sur l'histoire du peuple burgonde, de Bornholm (Burgundar-
   holm) vers la Bourgogne et les Bourguignons.
F. Behn, Römertum und Völkerwanderung.   [Excellent plates]
A. Graf Schenk von Stauffenberg, Das Imperium und die Völkerwanderung.
H. Wolfram, Geschichte der Goten: Von den Anfängen bis zur Mitte des sechsten
   Jahrhunderts. Entwurf einer historischen Ethnographie.
R. Hachmann, Die Goten und Skandinavien.
E. Sander, "Die Germanisierung des römischen Heeres," Hist. Zeit., 160 (1939),
   1-34.
The Gothic History of Jordanes in English Version.
N. Wagner, Getica: Untersuchungen zum Leben des Jordanes und zur frühen
   Geschichte der Goten.

THE BARBARIAN KINGDOMS.

F. Lot, The End of the Ancient World and the Beginnings of the Middle Ages,
   pp. 187-296.
J. M. Wallace-Hadrill, The Barbarian West.
J. D. Randers-Pehrson, Barbarians and Romans: The Birth Struggle of Europe,
   A.D. 400-700.
W. Goffart, Barbarians and Romans, A.D. 418-584: The Techniques of
   Accommodation.
E. A. Thompson, Romans and Barbarians: The Decline of the Western Empire.
E. A. Thompson, The Goths in Spain.
P. D. King, Law and Society in the Visigothic Kingdom.
A. K. Ziegler, Church and State in Visigothic Spain.
E. James, Visigothic Spain.
B. S. Bachrach, A History of the Alans in the West.
C. M. Aherne, "Late Visigothic Bishops: Their Schools and the Transmission of
   Culture," Traditio, 22 (1966), 435-444.
H. Wolfram, "The Shaping of the Early Medieval Kingdoms," Viator, 1 (1970),
   1-20.
P. M. Bassett, "The Use of History in the Chronicon of Isidore of Seville,"
   History & Theory, 15 (no. 3, 1976), 278-292.
B. MacBain, "Odovacar the Hun?" Classical Philology, 78 (no. 4, 1983), 323-27.
B. S. Bachrach, "A Reassessment of Visigothic Jewish Policy, 589-711,"
   American Historical Review, 78 (1973), 11-34.
W. G. Sinningen, "Administrative Shifts of Competence under Theodoric,"
   Traditio, 21 (1965), 456-467.
G. B. Ladner, "On Roman Attitudes Toward Barbarians in Late Antiquity,"
   Viator, 7 (1976), 1-26.

J. Moorhead, "The Laurentian Schism: East and West in the Roman Church,"
     Church History, 47 (June 1978), 125-36.
E. A. Thompson, "Barbarian Invaders and Roman Collaborators," Florilegium, 2
     (1980), 71-88.
E. Maass, "Zum Germanenbild des Salvianus von Massilia," Altertum, 30 (no. 1,
     1984), 54-56.
M. Lintzel, Der historische Kern der Siegfriedsage.
F. S. Lear, Treason in Roman and Germanic Law: Collected Papers.
Salvian, The Writings of Salvian, the Presbyter, trans. J. F. O'Sullivan.
Orosius, Seven Books Against the Pagans.
Procopius, History of the Wars.
The Burgundian Code: Book of Constitutions or Law of Gundobad: Additional
     Enactments, trans. K. F. Drew.
Isodorus, Isidore of Seville's History of the Kings of the Goths, trans. G.
     Donini.
J. Fontaine, Isidore de Seville et la culture classique dans l'Espagne
     wisigothique.   (2 vols.)

THE HUNS AND THEIR IMPACT.

R. N. Webb, Attila, King of the Huns.
C. D. Gordon, The Age of Attila.
M. Brion, Attila, The Scourge of God.
H. Homeyer, Attila.
O. J. Maenchen-Helfen, The World of the Huns: Studies in Their History and
     Culture, ed. by Max Knight.
F. Altheim, Geschichte der Hunnen.   (5 vols.)
F. Altheim, Attila und die Hunnen.
L. Hambis, Attila et les Huns.
R. P. Lindner, "Nomadism, Horses and Huns," Past & Present, 94 (Aug. 1981),
     3-19.
E. Demougeot, "Bedeutet das Jahr 476 das Ende des Römischen Reiches im
     Okzident?" Klio, 60 (no. 2, 1978), 371-381.
L. Hambis, "Le Problème des Huns," Revue historique, 220 (1958), 249-270.

THE BYZANTINE RECONQUEST OF THE WEST.

J. W. Barker, Justinian and the Later Roman Empire.
P. N. Ure, Justinian and His Age.
G. Downey, Constantinople in the Age of Justinian.
R. Browning, Justinian and Theodora.
W. E. Kaegi, Jr., "Arianism and the Byzantine Army in Africa," Traditio, 21
     (1965), 23-53.
R. A. Marcus, "The Imperial Administration and the Church in Byzantine Africa,"
     Church History, 36 (1967), 18-23.
Procopius, History of the Wars.
Procopius, Secret History.

THE BYZANTINE EMPIRE.

Byzantium: An Introduction, ed. P. Whitting.
D. Obolensky, The Byzantine Commonwealth: Eastern Europe, 500-1453.
N. H. Baynes, The Byzantine Empire.
C. Diehl, Byzantium: Greatness and Decline.
S. Runciman, Byzantine Civilization.
A. A. Vasiliev, History of the Byzantine Empire, 324-1453.
G. Ostrogorsky, History of the Byzantine Empire.
N. H. Baynes, Byzantine Studies and Other Essays.
R. Jenkins, Byzantium: The Imperial Centuries.
D. A. Miller, The Byzantine Tradition.
D. A. Miller, Imperial Constantinople.   (Use with caution.)
H. W. Haussig, A History of Byzantine Civilization.
P. Arnott, The Byzantines and Their World.
B. C. P. Tsangadas, The Fortifications and Defense of Constantinople.
D. J. Constantelos, Byzantine Philanthropy and Social Welfare.
M. F. Hendy, Coinage and Money in the Byzantine Empire, 1081-1261.
D. J. Geanakopolos, Byzantine East and Latin West: Two Worlds of Christendom
   in Middle Ages and Renaissance.
D. J. Geanakopolos, Interaction of the 'Sibling' Byzantine and Western Cultures
   in the Middle Ages and Italian Renaissance.
K. G. Holum, Theodosian Empresses: Women and Imperial Dominion in Late
   Antiquity.
Hohlfelder, Robert L., (ed.), City, Town, and Countryside in the Early
   Byzantine Era.
J. Meyendorff, Byzantine Theology: Historical Trends and Doctrinal Themes.
A. Stratos, Byzantium in the Seventh Century.
R. Browning, Byzantium and Bulgaria: A Comparative Study Across the Early
   Medieval Frontier.
W. E. H. Lecky, History of European Morals From Augustus to Charlemagne.
C. Head, Justinian II of Byzantium.
A. Cameron, Circus Factions: Blues and Greens at Rome and Byzantium.
H. Kähler, Hagia Sophia.
A. S. Atiya, A History of Eastern Christianity.
G. Constable, People and Power in Byzantium.
W. E. Kaegi, Jr., Army, Society and Religion in Byzantium. [20 studies in
   English and Italian by a leading authority in the field.]
W. E. Kaegi, Jr., "Initial Byzantine Reactions to the Arab Conquest," Church
   History, 38 (1969), 139-149.
G. B. Ladner, "Origin and Significance of the Byzantine Iconoclastic Contro-
   versy," Mediaeval Studies, 2 (1940), 127-149.
P. Brown, "A Dark-Age Crisis: Aspects of the Iconoclastic Controversy,"
   English Historical Review, 88 (1973), 1-34.
P. J. Alexander, "The Strength of Empire and Capital as Seen Through Byzantine
   Eyes," Speculum, 37 (1962), 339-357.
W. T. Treadgold, "The Revival of Byzantine Learning and the Revival of the
   Byzantine State," American Historical Review, 84 (1979), 1245-1266.
D. J. Geanakopolos, "Church and State in the Byzantine Empire: A Reconsider-
   ation of the Problem of Caesaropapism," Church History, 34 (1965),
   381-403.

P. Lemerele, "Invasions et migrations dans les Balkans depuis la fin de
   l'époque Romaine jusqu'au VIIIe siècle," Rev. hist., 211 (1954),
   265-308.
L. Bréhier, "Les empereurs byzantins dans leur vie privée," ibid., 188/189
   (1940), 193-217.
C. Diehl, Justinien et la civilisation Byzantine au VIe siècle.
E. E. Lipsic, Byzanz und die Slawen.
Social and Political Thought in Byzantium from Justinian I to the Last Palaeologus: Passages From Byzantine Writers and Documents, ed. E. Barker.

                    THE ORIGINS AND EXPANSION OF ISLAM.

J. J. Saunders, A History of Medieval Islam.
P. K. Hitti, History of the Arabs.
   Andrae, Mohammed: The Man and His Faith.
R. W. Bulliet, The Camel and the Wheel.
F. McG. Donner, The Early Islamic Conquests.
P. Crone and M. Cook, Hagarism: The Making of the Islamic World.
W. Muir, Annals of the Early Caliphate From the Death of Mahomet to the Omeyyad
   and Abbaside Dynasties ...
The Cambridge History of Islam, ed. P. M. Holt et al.
E. A. Belyeav, Arabs, Islam and the Caliphate in the Early Middle Ages.
   [Example of Soviet scholarship in the field.]
A. R. Lewis, Naval Power and Trade in the Mediterranean, A.D. 500-1100.
H. A. R. Gibb, "Pre-Islamic Monotheism in Arabia," Harvard Theological Review,
   55 (1962), 269-280.
C. J. Speel, "The Disappearance of Christianity from North Africa in the Wake
   of the Rise of Islam," Church History, 29 (1960), 379-397.
M. S. G. Hodgson, The Venture of Islam: Conscience and History in a World
   Civilization.   (3 vols.)
W. M. Watt, A History of Islamic Spain.
S. M. Imamuddin, Some Aspects of the Socio-Economic and Cultural History of
   Muslim Spain.
K. de Planhol, Les fondements géographiques de l'histoire de l'Islam.
H. Ahrweiler, Byzance et la mer: La Maritime de guerre, la politique et les
   institutions maritimes de Byzance aux VIIe-XVe siècles.
R. P. A. Dozy, Histoire des Musselmans de l'Espagne.   (3 vols.)
M. Hamedullah, Le Prophete de l'Islam.
C. Sanchez Albornoz y Menduina, Estudios sobre las instituciones medievales
   Espanolas.
H. Ahrweiler, "L'Asie Mineure et les invasions arabes (VIIe-IXe siècles),"
   Rev. hist., 227 (1962), 1-32.
E. Eichhoff, Seekrieg und Seepolitik zwischen Islam und Abendland.
F. Altheim, Der Araber in der alten Welt.
O. Pretzl, "Muhammed als geschichtliche Persönlichkeit," Hist. Zeit., 161
   (1940), 157-176.
R. Paret, "Das islamische Weltreich," ibid., 187 (1959), 521-539.
R. Konetzke, "Islam und christliches Spanien im Mittelalter," ibid., 184
   (1957), 573-591.

ISLAMIC CULTURE TO THE TENTH CENTURY.

G. E. von Grunebaum, Classical Islam: A History, 600-1258.
G. E. von Grunebaum, Medieval Islam: A Study in Cultural Orientation.
A. J. Mensinck, The Muslim Creed: Its Genesis and Historical Development.
N. Daniel, The Arabs and Medieval Europe.
W. M. Watt, The Influence of Islam on Medieval Europe.
W. M. Watt, Islamic Philosophy and Theology.
F. E. Peters, Aristotle and the Arabs: The Aristotelian Tradition in Islam.
S. H. Nasr, Science and Civilization in Islam.
M. Z. Siddiqi, Studies in Arabic and Persian Medical Literature.
A. L. Udovitch, Partnership and Profit in Medieval Islam.
G. Quadri, La Philosophie arabe dans l'Europe médiévale, des origines à
   Averroès.
H. Laoust, Les schismes dans l'Islam: Introduction à une étude de la religion
   musulmane.
M. Steinschneider, Die arabischen Übersetzungen aus den Griechischen.
M. Eisler, Vorlesungen über die jüdischen Philosophen des Mittelalters.
G. Vadja, Introduction à la pensée juive du Moyen Age.
G. E. von Grunebaum, "Eastern Jewry under Islam," Viator, 2 (1971), 365-372.
G. Leiser, "Medical Education in Islamic Lands from the Seventh to the
   Fourteenth Century," Journal of the History of Medicine, 38 (Jan. 1983),
   48-75.
B. Hughes, "The Medieval Latin Translations of al-Khwarizmi's al jabr, "
   Manuscripta, 26 (Mar. 1982), 31-37.
M. Lombard, The Golden Age of Islam.

THE EARLY HISTORY OF CELTIC IRELAND AND ANGLO-SAXON ENGLAND.

P. Hunter Blair, Roman Britain and Early England, 55 B.C. - A.D. 871.
D. P. Kirby, The Making of Early England.
T. K. Derry and M. G. Blakeway, The Making of Early and Medieval Britain.
V. I. Evison, The Fifth-Century Invasions South of the Thames.
H. M. Porter, The Saxon Conquest of Somerset and Devon.
L. Alcock, Arthur's Britain: History and Archaeology, A.D. 367-643.
J. Morris, The Age of Arthur: A History of the British Isles From 350 to 650.
E. G. Bowen, Saints, Seaways and Settlements in the Celtic Lands.
J. M. Wallace-Hadrill, Early Germanic Kingship in England and on the Continent.
W. A. Chaney, The Cult of Kingship in Anglo-Saxon England: The Transition From
   Paganism to Christianity.
D. A. White, Litus Saxonum: The British Saxon Shore in Scholarship and
   History.
J. E. A. Jolliffe, Pre-Feudal England: The Jutes.
P. J. Helm, Alfred the Great.
P. Hunter Blair, The World of Bede.
R. Arnold, A Social History of England, 55 B.C. to A.D. 1215.
J. A. Duke, The Columban Church.
S. J. Crawford, Anglo-Saxon Influences on Western Christendom.
W. Levison, England and the Continent in the Eighth Century.
D. Whitelock, From Bede to Alfred. [thirteen studies by a great authority.]

Anglo-Saxon Saints and Heroes, ed. C. Albertson.
R. R. Bolgar, The Classical Heritage and Its Beneficiaries.
Dark-Age Britain: Studies Presented to E. T. Leeds, ed. by D. B. Harden.
Angles, Saxons and Jutes: Essays Presented to J. N. L. Myres, ed. V. Evison.
M. and L. de Paor, Early Christian Ireland.
A. R. Burn, 'Procopius and the Island of Ghosts," English Historical Review,
      70 (1955), 258-261.
J. Janzén, "The Viking Colonizatioon of England in the Light of Place-Names,"
      Names, 20 (1972), 1-25.
R. A. Marcus, "The Chronology of the Gregorian Mission to England," Journal of
      Ecclesiastical History, 14 (1963), 16-30.
C. J. Arnold, "Early Anglo-Saxon Settlement Patterns in Southern England,"
      Journal of Historical Geography, 3 (Oct. 1977), 309-16.
T. W. T. Tatton-Brown, "Camelon, Arthur's O'on and the Main Supply Base for
      the Antonine Wall," Britannia, 11 (1980), 340-343.
E. A. Thompson, "Gildas and the History of Britain," Britannia, 10 (1979),
      203-226.
K. Hughes, Early Christian Ireland: Introduction to the Sources.

                        THE FRANKISH KINGDOM.

J. M. Wallace-Hadrill, The Long-Haired Kings and Other Studies of Frankish
      History.
S. Dill, Roman Society in Gaul in the Merovingian Age.
B. S. Bachrach, Merovingian Military Organization, 481-751. [Use with caution]
B. S. Bachrach, "Procopius, Agathias and the Frankish Military," Speculum, 45
      (1970), 435-441.
R. P. C. Hanson, "The Church in Fifth-Century Gaul: Evidence from Sidonius
      Apollinaris," Journal of Ecclesiastical History, 21 (1970), 1-10.
F. D. Gilliard, "The Senators of Sixth-Century Gaul," Speculum, 54 (1979),
      685-697.
F. Lotter, "Methodisches zur Gewinning historischer Erkentnisse aus
      hagiographischen Quellen," Historische Zeitschrift, 229 (Oct. 1979),
      298-356.
E. H. Walter, "Hagiographisches in Gregors Frankengeschichte," Archiv für
      Kulturgeschichte, 48 (1966), 291-310.
D. Claude, "Zur Fragen frühfränkischer Verfassungsgeschichte." Zeitschrift der
      Savigny-Stiftung für Rechtsgeschichte, Germanistische Abteilung, 83
      (1966), 273-280.
H. Löwe, "Von Theoderich dem Großen zu Karl dem Großen: Das Werden des Abend-
      landes im Geschichtsbild des frühen Mittelalters," Deutsches Archiv, 9
      (1951/1952), 353-401.
R. Sprandel, "Struktur und Geschichte des merovingischen Adels," Hist. Zeit.,
      193 (1961), 33-71.
U. Nonn, "Erminethrud - eine vornehme neustrische Dame um 700," Historisches
      Jahrbuch, 102 (no. 1, 1982), 135-43.
J. M. van Winter, "Homines Franci: edelen of koningsvrijen?" Tijdschrift voor
      geschiedenis, 83 (1970), 346-350.
J. de Geyter, "Romeinse rechtsterminologie in de Merovingische tijd. Cessio:
      receptie of nieuw begrip?" Tijdschrift voor rechtsgeschiedenis (Revue
      d'histoire du droit), 40 (1972), 207-226.

                              16

E. Salin, La civilisation mérovingienne d'après les sépultures, les textes et le laboratoire. (4 vols.)
A. Bergengruen, Adel und Herrschaft in Merowingerreich.
W. Schultze, Die fränkischen Gaugrafschaften: Rheinbaierns, Rheinhessens, Starkenburgs und des Königreichs Württemberg.
M. Lintzel, Ausgewählte Schriften, I.
N. D. Fustel de Coulanges, Histoire des institutions politiques de l'ancienne France. (6 vols.)

THE PIRENNE THESIS AND EARLY MEDIEVAL ECONOMIC HISTORY.

The Pirenne Thesis: Analysis, Criticism, and Revision, ed. A. F. Havighurst. Third Edition. (Heath)
H. Pirenne, Mohammed and Charlemagne.
D. C. Dennett, Jr., "Pirenne and Muhammed," Speculum, 23 (1948), 165-190.
E. Perroy, "Encore Mahomet et Charlemagne," Rev. hist., 212 (1954), 232-238.
H. Pirenne, Medieval Cities: Their Origin and the Revival of Trade.
K. F. Morrison, "Numismtics and Carolingian Trade: A Critique of the Evidence," Speculum, 38 (1963), 403-432.
W. C. Bark, Origins of the Medieval World.
A. Dopsch, The Economic and Social Foundations of European Civilization.
R. Hodges and D. Whitehouse, Mohammed, Charlemagne, and the Origins of Europe: Archaeology and the Pirenne Thesis.
R. Latouche, The Birth of Western Economy: Economic Aspects of the Dark Ages.
A. R. Lewis, Naval Power and Trade in the Mediterranean.
A. R. Lewis, The Northern Seas: Shipping and Commerce in Northern Europe, A.D. 300-1100.
P. Grierson, "Commerce in the Dark Ages: A Critique of the Evidence," Transactions of the Royal Historical Society, Fifth Series, 9 (1959), 123-140.
W. H. C. Frend, "North Africa and Europe in the Early Middle Ages," ibid., Fifth Series, 5 (1955), 61-80.
D. Jellema. "Frisian Trade in the Dark Ages," Speculum, 30 (1955), 15-36.
G. C. Dunning, "Trade Relations Between England and the Continent in the Late Anglo-Saxon Period," Dark-Age Britain: Studies Presented to E. T. Leeds, ed. D. B. Harden, pp. 218-233.
R. Buchner, "Der Beginn des Mittelalters in westlicher Sicht," Deutsches Archiv, 3 (1939), 236-242.
H. Laurent, "Aspects économiques dans la Gaule franque: Marchands de palais et marchands d'abbayes," Rev. hist., 183 (1938), 281-297.
J. B. Akkerman, "De vroeg-middeleeuwse emporia," Tijdschrift voor rechtsgeschiedenis (Revue d'histoire du droit), 35 (1967), 230-283.

BYZANTINE RELIGIOUS MISSIONS IN SOUTHEASTERN EUROPE.

A. P. Vlasto, The Entry of the Slavs into Christendom: Introduction to the Medieval History of the Slavs.
F. Dvornik, Byzantine Missions Among the Slavs: Saints Constantine-Cyril and Methodius.
D. Obolensky, Byzantium and the Slavs: Collected Studies.
D. M. Dunlop, The History of the Jewish Khazars.
I. Boba, "The Episcopacy of St. Methodius," Slavic Review, 24 (1967), 85-93.

THE LOMBARDS AND THE PAPACY.

T. Hodgkin, Italy and Her Invaders.   (8 vols.)
F. H. Dudden, Gregory the Great.
P. Llewellyn, Rome in the Dark Ages.
J. Richards, Consul of God: The Life and Times of Gregory the Great.
R. Krautheimer, Rome: Profile of a City, 312-1308.
P. Llewellyn, "Papal-Lombard Relations During the Pontificate of Pope Paul I:
    The Attainment of Equilibrium of Power in Italy, 756-767," Catholic
    Historical Review, 55 (1969), 358-376.
H. von Schubert, Geschichte der christlichen Kirche im Frühmittelalter: Ein
    Handbuch.
J. Haller, Das Papssttum: Idee und Wirklichkeit.   (5 vols.)
W. Schönfeld, Das Rechtsbewußtsein der Langobarden auf Grund ihres Edikts.
M. Vaes, "La papauté et l'église franque à l'époque de Grégoire le Grand (590-
    604)," Rev. d'hist. eccl., 6 (1905), 537-556.

THE RISE OF THE CAROLINGIANS.

The Fourth Book of the Chronicle of Fredegar With Its Continuations, trans.
    J. M. Wallace-Hadrill, pp. 1-121.
W. Goffart, "The Fredegar Problem Reconsidered," Speculum, 38 (1963),
    206-241.
E. Peters, The Shadow King: Rex Inutilis im Medieval Law and Literature, 751-
    1327.
A. R. Lewis, "The Dukes in the Regnum Francorum: A.D. 550-751," Speculum, 51
    (1976), 381-401.
B. S. Bachrach, "Military Organization in Aquitaine Under the Early
    Carolingians," ibid., 49 (1974), 1-33.
W. Affeldt, "Königserhebung Pippins und Unlösbarkeit des Eides im Liber de
    unitate ecclesiae conservanda," Deutsches Archiv, 25 (1969), 313-346.
W. Affeldt, "Aspekte der Königserhebung Pippins in der Historiographie des 19.
    Jahrhunderts," Archiv für Kulturgeschichte, 59 (1977), 144-189.
R. Holtzmann, "Zum Strator- und Marshalldienst," Hist. Zeit., 145 (1931),
    301-350.
Lex Salica: 100 Titel-Text, ed. K. A. Eckhardt.
J. M. Potter, "The Development and Significance of the Salic Law of the
    French," Eng. Hist. Rev., 52 (1937), 235-253.
J. H. Roy and J. Deviosse, La bataille de Poitiers, Octobre 733.

THE CAROLINGIANS AND ITALY.

W. Ullmann, The Growth of Papal Government in the Middle Ages.
P. Partner, The Lands of St. Peter: The Papal State in the Middle Ages and the
    Early Renaissance.
P. J. Geary, Furta Sacra: Thefts of Relics in the Central Middle Ages.
D. H. Miller, "The Roman Revolution of the Eighth Century: A Study of the
    Ideological Background of the Papal Separation from Byzantium and Alliance
    with the Franks," Mediaeval Studies, 36 (1974), 79-133.

J. T. Hallenbeck, "The Election of Pope Hadrian I," Church History, 37 (1968), 261-270.
D. S. Sefton, "Pope Hadrian I and the Fall of the Kingdom of the Lombards," Catholic Historical Review, 65 (Apr. 1979), 206-220.
P. Henry, "What Was the Iconoclastic Controversy About?" Church History, 45 (March 1976), 16-31.
L. Halphen, "La papauté et le complot lombard de 771," Rev. hist., 182 (1938), 238-244.
A. Angenendt, "Das geistliche Bündnis der Päpste mit den Karolingern (754-796)," Historisches Jahrbuch, 100 (1980), 1-94.
H. Fuhrmann, "Konstantinische Schenkung und abendländisches Kaisertum: Ein Beitrag zur Überlieferungsgeschichte des Constitutum Constantini," Deutsches Archiv, 22 (1966), 63-178.
H. Fuhrmann, "Konstantinische Schenkung und Silvesterlegende in neuer Sicht," ibid., 15 (1959), 523-540.
A. Hauck, Kirchengeschichte Deutschlands, I.
M. Lintzel, Ausgewählte Schriften, I.

THE IRISH AND ANGLO-SAXON MISSIONS, ST. BONIFACE, AND THE FRANKISH CHURCH.

E. S. Duckett, The Wandering Saints of the Early Middle Ages.
K. Hughes, Early Christian Ireland: Introduction to the Sources.
W. Levison, England and the Continent in the Eighth Century.
S. J. Crawford, Anglo-Saxon Influence on Western Christendom.
G. W. Greenaway, Saint Boniface: Three Biographical Studies for the Twelfth Centenary Festival.
M. Herren, "Classical and Secular Learning among the Irish before the Carolingian Renaissance," Florilegium, 3 (1981), 118-57.
J. B. Russell, "Saint Boniface and the Eccentrics," Church History, 33 (1964), 235-247.
R. E. Sullivan, "The Papacy and Missionary Activity in the Early Middle Ages," Mediaeval Studies, 17 (1955), 46-106.
H. Mann, The Lives of the Popes in the Early Middle Ages, II.
A. Hauck, Kirchengeschichte Deutschlands, I.
C. Rodenberg, Pippin, Karlman und Papst Stephan II.
E. E. Stengel, "Zur Frühgeschichte der Reichsabtei Fulda: Zugleich ein Literaturbericht," Deutsches Archiv, 9 (1951-1952), 513-534.
The Letters of Saint Boniface, trans. E. Emerton.

CHARLEMAGNE AS KING AND THE CONQUEST OF SAXONY.

R. Winston, Charlemagne: From the Hammer to the Cross.
P. Munz, Life in the Age of Charlemagne.
F. L. Ganshof, The Carolingians and the Frankish Monarchy: Studies in Carolingian History.
B. Schlod, Charlemagne in Spain: The Cultural Legacy of Roncesvalles.
F. L. Ganshof, "Charlemagne," Speculum, 24 (1949), 520-528.
D. A. Bullough, "Europae Pater: Charlemagne and His Achievement in the Light of Recent Scholarship," Eng. Hist. Rev., 85 (1970), 59-105. [Review article.]
E. Fry, "Roncesvalles," ibid., 20 (1905), 22-32.

J. Horrent, "La bataille des Pyrénées de 778," Le Moyen Age, 78 (1972), 197-227.
L. Halphen, Etudes critiques sur l'histoire de Charlemagne.
P. E. Schramm, "Karl der Große," Hist. Zeit., 198 (1964), 306-345.
E. Rundnagel, "Der Mythos vom Herzog Widukind," ibid., 155 (1936-37), 475-505.
E. Rundnagel, "Der Tag von Verden," ibid., 157 (1937), 457-490.
H. Löwe, "Die Irminsul und die Religion der Sachsen," Deutsches Archiv, 5 (1940-1942), 1-22.
P. Lehmann, Das literarische Bild Karls des Großen.
H. Hoffmann, Karl der Große im Bilde der Geschichtsschreibung des frühen Mittelalters.
H. Hühlner, Die Sachsenkriege Karls des Großen in der Geschichtsschreibung der Karolinger- und Ottonenzeit.
M. Lintzel, Ausgewählte Schriften, I, 95-231.
Einhard, The Life of Charlemagne.
Two Lives of Charlemagne, trans. L. G. M. Thorpe.
Carolingian Chronicles: Royal Frankish Annals and Nithard's Histories, trans. B. W. Scholz and B. Rogers.

THE IMPERIAL CORONATION OF CHARLEMAGNE.

The Coronation of Charlemagne: What Did It Signify? ed. R. E. Sullivan (Heath)
F. L. Ganshof, The Imperial Coronation of Charlemagne: Theories and Facts.
  [This interpretation should be compared with that of W. Ullmann in The Growth of Papal Government in the Middle Ages. Both are excerpted in the Sullivan pamphlet above.]
R. Folz, The Concept of Empire in Western Europe From the Fifth to the Fourteenth Centuries.
P. Munz, The Origin of the Carolingian Empire.
N. Downs, "The Role of the Papacy in the Coronation of Charlemagne," Studies in Medieval Culture, 3 (1970), 7-22.
H. Adelson and R. Baker, "The Oath of Purgation of Pope Leo III in 800," Traditio, 8 (1952), 35-80.
L. Wallach, "The Genuine and the Forged Oath of Pope Leo III," ibid., 11 (1955), 37-63.
L. Wallach, "The Roman Synod of December 800 and the Alleged Trial of Leo III," Harvard Theological Review, 49 (1956), 123-142.
L. Halphen, Charlemagne et l'empire Carolingien.
Zum Kaisertum Karls des Großen: Beiträge und Aufsätze, ed. G. Wolf.
  [A valuable collection of articles in German.]
P. E. Schramm, Kaiser, Rom und Renovatio.
P. E. Schramm, "Die Anerkennung Karls des Großen als Kaiser: Ein Kapitel aus der Geschichte der mittelalterlichen Staatssymbolik,"Hist. Zeit., 179 (1951), 449-515.
C. Brühl, "Fränkischer Krönungsbrauch und das Problem der 'Festkronungen'," ibid., 194 (1962), 265-326.
H. Löwe, "Von den Grenzen des Kaisergedankens in der Karolingerzeit," Deutsches Archiv, 14 (1958), 345-374.
W. Ohnsorge, "Zur Frage der griechischen Abstammung des Papstes Leo III.," ibid., 23 (1967), 188-190.
K. J. Benz, "Cum ab oratio surgeret: Überlegungen zur Kaiserkrönung Karls des Großen," ibid., 31 (1975), 337-369.

THE CAROLINGIAN RENAISSANCE.

R. R. Bolgar, The Classical Heritage and Its Beneficiaries.

P. Riché, Education and Culture in the Barbarian West, Sixth Through Eighth Centuries.

W. Ullmann, The Carolingian Renaissance and the Idea of Kingship.

K. F. Morrison, The Two Kingdoms: Ecclesiology in Carolingian Political Thought.

E. S. Duckett, Alcuin, Friend of Charlemagne.

L. Wallach, Alcuin and Charlemagne: Studies in Carolingian History and Literature.

C. J. B. Gaskoin, Alcuin: His Life and Work.

J. Marenbon, From the Circle of Alcuin to the School of Auxerre: Logic, Theology and Philosophy in the Early Middle Ages.

R. McKitterick, The Frankish Church and the Carolingian Reforms, 789-895.

J. Hubert, J. Porcher, W. F. Volbach, The Carolingian Renaissance.
[Magnificent illustrations and excellent text.]

J. Hubert, Carolingian Art.

G. W. Trompf, "The Carolingian Renaissance," Journal of the History of Ideas, 34 (1973), 1-26.

R. J. Gariépy, "Lupus of Ferrières: Carolingian Scribe and Text Critic," Mediaeval Studies, 30 (1968), 90-105.

P. R. McKeon, "Archbishop Ebbo of Reims (816-835): A Study in the Carolingian Empire and the Church," Church History, 43 (1974), 437-447.

J.-L. Biget, "Hincmar de Reims, un archevêque dans son siècle," [r. art.] Moyen Age, 87 (no. 2, 1981), 263-78.

C. I. Hammer, Jr., "Country Churches, Clerical Inventories and the Carolingian Renaissance in Bavaria," Church History, 49 (1980), 5-17.

F. L. Ganshof, "Charlemagne et l'usage de l'écrit en matière administrative," Moyen Age, 57 (1951), 1-25.

F. C. Scheibe, "Alcuin und die Briefe Karls des Großen." Deutsches Archiv, 15 (1959), 181-193.

A. A. Haußling, "Alcuin und die Gottesdienst der Hofkapelle," ibid., 25 (1969), 223-229.

O. Herding, "Zum Problem des karolingischen "Humanismus" mit besonderer Rücksicht auf Walahfried Strabo," Studium Generale, 1 1948), 389-397.

H. Löwe, "Geschichtsschreibung der ausgehenden Karolingerzeit," Deutsches Archiv, 23 (1967), 1-30.

F. Thürlemann, "Die Bedeutung der Aachener Theoderich-Statue für Karl den Großen (801) und bei Walahfrid Strabo (829): Materialien zu einer Semiotik visueller Objekte im frühen Mittelalter," Archiv für Kulturgeschichte, 59 (1977), 25-65.

E. Patzelt, Die karolingische Renaissance.

M. Rissel, Rezeption antiker und patristischer Wissenschaft bei Hrabanus Maurus: Studien zur karolingischen Geistesgeschichte.

"The Letters of Einhard," trans. by Henry Preble. Papers of the American Society of Church History, Second Series, 1 (1913), 107-158.

THE SIGNIFICANCE OF THE CAROLINGIAN EMPIRE.

F. L. Ganshof, "The Impact of Charlemagne on the Institutions of the Frankish Realm," Speculum, 40 (1965), 47-62.

R. Fichtenau, The Carolingian Empire.

J. Boussard, The Civilization of Charlemagne.

S. Wemple, Women in Frankish Society: Marriage and the Cloister, 500 to 900.

H. H. Anton, "Zum politischen Konzept karolingischer Synoden und zur karolingischen Brüdergemeinschaft," Historisches Jahrbuch, 99 (1979), 55-132.

C. Brühl, Fodrum, Gistum, Servitium Regis: Studien zu den wirtschaftlichen Grundlagen des Königtums in Frankreich und in den fränkischen Nachfolgestaaten Deutschland, Frankreich und Italian vom 6. bis zur Mitte des 14. Jahrhunderts.

R. Faulhaber, Der Reichseinheitgedanke in der Literatur der Karolingerzeit bis zum Vertrag von Verdun.

W. Metz, Das karolingische Reichsgut.

THE DECLINE OF THE CAROLINGIAN EMPIRE: THE END OF UNITY.

F. L. Ganshof, The Carolingians and the Frankish Monarchy: Studies in Carolingian History.

E. L. Dümmler, Geschichte des ostfränkischen Reiches.   (3 vols.)

G. Tellenbach, Die Entstehung des deutschen Reiches: Von der Entwicklung des fränkischen und deutschen Staates im neunten und zehnten Jahrhundert.

Die Entstehung des deutschen Reiches (Deutschland um 900): Ausgewählte Aufsätze aus den Jahren 1928-1954, ed. H. Kämpf.

P. F. Kehr, Die Kanzlei Arnulfs.

R. Sprandel, "Grundherrlicher Adel, rechtsständische Freiheit und Königszins," Deutsches Archiv, 19 (1963), 1-29.

J. Hashagen, "Spätkarolingische Staats- und Soziallehren," Deutsche Vierteljahrsschrift für Literaturwissenschaft und Geistesgeschichte, 17 (1939), 301-311.

P. Classen, "Die Verträge von Verdun und von Coulaines 843 als politisches Grundlagen des westfränkischen Reiches," Hist. Zeit., 196 (1963), 1-35.

P. Kehr, "Aus den letzten Tagen Karls III.," Deutsches Archiv, 1 (1937), 138-146.

W. A. Eckhardt, "Das Protokoll von Ravenna 877 über die Kaiserkrönung Karls des Kahlen," ibid., 23 (1967), 295-311.

C. Carozzi, "Le dernier des Carolingiens:: De l'histoire au mythe," Moyen Age, 82 (no. 3-4, 1976), 453-476.

J. Boussard, "Les destinées de la Neustrie du IXe au XIe siècle," Cahiers de civilisation médiévale, 11 (1968), 15-28.

E. Lesne, "La dîme des biens ecclésiastiques aux IXe et Xe siècles," Rev. d'hist. eccl., 13 (1912), 477-503, 659-673; XIV (1913), 97-112, 489-509.

Notker, Notkers des Deutschen Werke nach dem Handschriften neu herausgegeben.

H. F. Haefele, "Studien zu Notkers Gesta Karoli," Deutsches Archiv, 15 (1959), 258-392.

Son of Charlemagne, trans. A. Cabaniss.

M. Buchner, "Entstehungszeit und Verfasser der "Vita Karoli" des 'Astronomen'," Historisches Jahrbuch, 60 (1940), 14-45.

EARLY MEDIEVAL SOCIETY AND TECHNOLOGY.

L. White, Jr., Medieval Technology and Social Change.
C. Stephenson, "The Problem of the Common Man in Early Medieval Europe,"
   American Historical Review, 51 (1946), 419-439.
G. Duby, Rural Economy and Country Life in the Medieval West.
G. Duby, The Early Growth of the European Economy: Warriors and Peasants From
   the Seventh to the Twelfth Century.
R. Hodges, Dark Age Economics: The Origins of Towns and Trade, A.D. 600-1000.
G. E. Fussell, "Ploughs and Ploughing before 1800," Agricultural History, 40
   (1966), 177-186.
J. Langdon, "The Economics of Horses and Oxen in Medieval England,"
   Agricultural History Review, 30 (1982), 31-40.
D. Herlihy, "The Agrarian Revolution in Southern France and Italy, 801-1150,"
   Speculum, 33 (1958), 23-41.
D. Herlihy, "Land, Family and Women in Continental Europe, 701-1200," Traditio,
   18 (1962), 89-120.
W. Horn, "Water Power and the Plan of St. Gall," Journal of Medieval History,
   1 (1975), 219-257.
A. R. H. Baker, "Observations on the Open Fields: The Present Position of
   Studies in British Field Systems," Journal of Historical Geography, 5
   (July 1979), 315-323.
N. D. Fustel de Coulanges, The Origin of Property in Land.
P. Boissonade, Life and Work in Medieval Europe.
K. D. White, Roman Farming.
K. Bosl, Die Gesellschaft in der Geschichte des Mittelalters.
F. Lütge, Geschichte der deutschen Agrarverfassung vom frühen Mittelalter bis
   zum 19. Jahrhundert.
F. Lütge, Studien zur Sozial- und Wirtschaftsgeschichte: Gesammelte Abhand-
   lungen.
G. Grosch, Markgenossenschaft und Grossgrundherrschaft im früheren Mittelalter.
K. S. Bader, Studien zur Rechtsgeschichte des mittelalterlichen Dorfes. (2 v.)

FEUDALISM.

F. L. Ganshof, Feudalism.
Lordship and Community in Medieval Europe: Selected Readings, ed. F. L.
   Cheyette. pp. 12-61.
C. Stephenson, Medieval Feudalism. [Rather elementary but a good introduction
   to Ganshof.]
C. Stephenson, "The Origin and Significance of Feudalism," Am. Hist. Rev., 46
   (1941), 788-812.
E. A. R. Brown, "The Tyranny of a Construct: Feudalism and Historians of
   Medieval Europe," ibid., 89 (1974), 1063-1088.
M. Bloch, Feudal Society.
J. R. Strayer, Feudalism.
B. S. Bachrach, "Charles Martel, Mounted Shock Combat, the Stirrup, and
   Feudalism," Studies in Medieval and Renaissance History, 7 (1970), 49-75.
B. S. Bachrach, "Early Medieval Fortifications in the 'West' of France: A
   Revised Technical Vocabulary," Technology and Culture, 16 ()ct. 1975),
   531-569.

M. A. Littauer, "Early Stirrups," Antiquity, 55 (July 1981), 99-105.
D. R. Kelley, "De origine feudorum: The Beginnings of an Historical Problem,"
    Speculum, 39 (1964), 207-228.
F. Behrends, "Kingship and Feudalism According to Fulbert of Chartres,"
    Mediaeval Studies, 25 (1963), 93-99.
G. Clark, "The Battle of Maldon: A Heroic Poem," Speculum, 43 (1968), 52-
    71. [For the probable location see G. R. Petty, Jr., and Susan Petty,
    "Geology and The Battle of Maldon," ibid., 51 (1976), 435-446.
C. E. Perrin, "La société féodale a propos d'un ouvrage récent," Rev. hist.,
    194 (1944), 23-41, 114-131. [Deals with Bloch's Feudal Society.]
A. Bondroit, ""Les 'precariae verbo regis' avant le concile de Leptinnes
    (a. 743)," Rev. d.'hist. eccl., 1 (1900), 41-60, 249-266, 430-447.
M. Heinzelmann, "La noblesse du Haut Moyen Age (VIIIe-XIe siècles): quelques
    problèms à propos d'ouvrages récents," Moyen Age, 83 (no. 1, 1977),
    131-44.
J. LeGoff, "Les trois fonctions indo-européennes, l'historien et l'Europe
    féodale," Annales: économies, sociétes, civilisations, 34 (Nov.-Dec.,
    1979), 1187-1215.
P. E. Guilhiermoz, Essai sur l'origine de la noblesse en France au Moyen Age.
H. Mitteis, Lehnrecht und Staatsgewalt im Mittelalter.
W. Kienast, "Lehnrecht und Staatsgewalt im Mittelalter: Studien zu dem
    Mitteis'chen Werk," Hist. Zeit., 158 (1938), 3-51.

MEDIEVAL SCANDINAVIA AND THE VIKING AGE.

J. Bronsted, The Vikings.
G. Jones, A History of the Vikings.
E. Oxenstierna, The Norsemen.
E. Oxenstierna, The World of the Norsemen.
P. H. Sawyer, Kings and Vikings: Scandinavia and Europe AD 700-1100.
D. M. Wilson, The Vikings and Their Origins.
W. A. Craigie, The Religion of Ancient Scandinavia.
E. O. Turville-Petrie, Myth and Religion of the North.
H. R. Davidson, Gods and Myths of Northern Europe.
H. R. Davidson, Pagan Scandinavia.
E. C. Polemé, Old Norse Literature and Mythology: A Symposium.
T. M. Andersson, The Icelandic Family Saga: An Analytical Reading.
G. Dumézil, Gods of the Ancient Northmen.
M. W. Williams, Social Scandinavia in the Viking Age.
P. H. Sawyer, The Age of the Vikings.
A. Olrik, Viking Civilization.
P. G. Foote and D. M. Wilson, The Viking Achievement: A Survey of the Society
    and Culture of Early Medieval Scandinavia.
T. Sjovold, The Oseberg Find and the Other Viking Ship Finds.
S. L. Cohen, Viking Fortresses of the Trelleborg Type.
S. Blöndal, The Varangians of Byzantium.
I. Boba, Nomads, Northmen and Slavs: Eastern Europe in the Ninth Century.
R. W. Ungar, "The Archaeology of Boats: Ships of the Vikings," Archaeology,
    35 (May-June 1982), 20-27.
B. McCreesh, "How Pagan Are the Icelandic Family Sagas?" Journal of English
and Germanic Philology, 79 (Jan. 1980), 58-66.

C. Blindheim, "Commerce and Trade in Viking Age Norway: Exchange of Products or Organized Transactions?" <u>Norwegian Archaeological Review</u>, 15 (no. 1-2, 1982), 8-18.

A. E. Christensen, "Viking Age Ships and Shipbuilding," <u>Norwegian Archaeological Review</u>, 15 (no. 1-2, 1982), 19-28.

S. A. Sussman, "Far From the Saxon Shores (A Tentative History of the Anglo-Varangian Guard of the Byzantine Emperors)," <u>Connecticut Review</u>, 3, 1 (1969), 69-82.

L. Musset, <u>Les invasions: Le seconde assaut contre l'Europe chrétienne VIIe-XIe siècles.</u>

O. A. Johnsen, "Le commerce et la navigation en Norvège au moyen âge," <u>Rev. hist.</u>, 178 (1936), 385-410.

J. S. Worm-Müller, "Histoire de la navigation norvégienne," <u>ibid.</u>, 179 (1937), 251ff.

L. Bril, "Les premiers temps du christianisme en Suède: Etude critique des sources litteraires hambourgeoises," <u>Rev. d'hist. eccl.</u>, 12 (1911), 17-37, 231-241, 652-669.

K. Randsborg, "Les activités internationales des Vikings: raids ou commerce?" <u>Annales: économies, sociétés, civilisations</u>, 36 (Sept-Oct. 1981), 862-68.

A. Stender-Petersen, "Die vier Etappen der russisch-varängischen Beziehungen," <u>Jahrbücher für Geschichte Osteuropas, Neue Folge</u>, 2 (1954), 137-157.

A. Poppe, <u>Das Reich der Rus im 10. und 11. Jahrhundert: Wandel der Ideenwelt</u>," <u>Jahrbuch für Geschichte Osteuropas</u>, 28 (1980), 334-354.

G. Schramm, "Die erste Generation der altrussischen Fürstendynastie: Philologische Argumente für die Historizität von Rjurik und seinen Brüdern," <u>Jahrbuch für Geschichte Osteuropas</u>, 28 (1980), 321-333.

G. Schramm, "Die Herkunft des Namens Rus': Die Kritik des Forschungsstandes," <u>Forschungen zur osteuropäischen Geschichte</u>, 30 (1982), 7-49.

W. Seegrün, <u>Das Papsttum und Skandinavien bis zur Vollendung der nordischen Kirchenorganisation (1164).</u>

Snorri Sturlusson, <u>Heimskringla.</u>

LATER ANGLO-SAXON ENGLAND.

F. W. Maitland, <u>Domesday Book and Beyond: Three Essays in the Early History of England.</u>

F. Stenton, <u>Anglo-Saxon England.</u>

J. Godfrey, <u>The Church in Anglo-Saxon England.</u>

F. Barlow, <u>The English Church, 1000-1066: A Constitutional History.</u>

C. W. Hollister, <u>Anglo-Saxon Military Institutions on the Eve of the Norman Conquest.</u>

F. Barlow, <u>Edward the Confessor.</u>

H. R. Loyn, "The King and the Structure of Society in Late Anglo-Saxon England," <u>History</u>, 42 (1957), No. 145, 87-100.

H. R. Loyn, "Gesiths and Thegns in Anglo-Saxon England From the Seventh to the Tenth Century," <u>Eng. Hist. Rev.</u>, 70 (1955), 529-549.

N. Banton, "Monastic Reform and the Unification of Tenth-Century England," <u>Studies in Church History</u>, 18 (1982), 71-85.

MEDIEVAL SCANDINAVIAN EXPANSION TO THE WEST: MEDIEVAL AMERICA.

The Vinland Sagas, trans. by Magnus Magnusson and Hermann Palsson.
Magnus Magnusson, Viking Expansion Westwards.
Barthi Guthmundsson, The Origin of the Icelanders.
K. Gjerset, History of Iceland.
V. Stefansson, Iceland: The First American Republic.
W. Craigie, The Icelandic Saga.
K. Liestol, The Origin of the Icelandic Family Sagas.
T. M. Anderson, The Problem of Icelandic Saga Origins.
T. M. Anderson, The Icelandic Family Saga.
H. M. Ingstad, Land Under the Pole Star.
F. Durand, "Les Vikings et l'Amerique," Etudes Germaniques, 16 (1961), 382-
    384. [Review article on Ingstad's book.]
V. Stefansson, Greenland.
F. Gad, The History of Greenland, I.
P. Norlund, Viking Settlers in Greenland and Their Descendants During Five
    Hundred Years.
F. Nansen, In Northern Mists.   (2 vols.)
C. O. Sauer, Northern Mists.
H. M. Jansen, A Critical Account of the Written and Archaeological Souorces'
    Evidence Concerning the Norse Settlements in Greenland. (Meddelelser om
    Gronland, 182). [Caution - he is excessively skeptical where the
    literary evidence is concerned.]
A number of valuable archaeological articles dealing with the medieval Green-
    land settlements will be found in Meddelelser om Gronland (in English).
    See especially Vols. 76, 88, 89.
The Finding of Wineland the Good: The History of the Icelandic Discovery of
    America, trans. A. M. Reeves. [The Vinland sagas in facsimile, with
    translations.]
J. Fischer, The Discoveries of the Norsemen in America, With Special Relation
    to Their Early Cartographic Representation.
R. A. Skelton et al., The Vinland Map and the Tartar Relation.
Proceedings of the Vinland Map Conference, ed. W. E. Washburn.
M. Thordarsson, The Vinland Voyages.
W. Hovgaard, The Voyages of the Norsemen to America.
W. Gathorne-Hardy, The Norse Discoverers of America.
E. I. Haugen, Voyages to Vinland.
H. R. Holand, A Pre-Columbian Crusade to America.
E. Reman, The Norse Discoveries and Explorations in America.
J. K. Tornöe, Early American History: Norsemen Before Columbus.
T. J. Oleson, Early Voyages and Northern Approaches, 1000-1632.
S. E. Morrison, The European Discovery of America: The Northern Voyages,
    A.D. 500-1600.
T. C. Blegen, The Kensington Rune Stone.
H. M. Ingstad, Westward to Vinland: The Discovery of Pre-Columbian House-Sites
    in North America.
A. S. Ingstad, Discovery of a Norse Settlement in America.
E. Wahlgren, "Some Further Remarks on Vinland," Scandinavian Studies, 40
    (1968), 26-35.
A. L. Binns, "Sun Navigation in the Viking Age, and the Canterbury Portable
    Sundial," Acta Archaeologica, 42 (1971), 23-34.

History 3003x
Early Middle Ages

Professor Suzanne Wemple
Fall 1985

This course outline provides the general subjects to be considered and
the reading assignments for each topic. In addition to class lectures there
will be discussions on the assigned readings. Works in the reading list are
on reserve at Barnard College Library. Most are available in the relatively
cheap editions noted in parenthesis after the title.

A final examination and a term paper of 8-10 pages will be required.
Some possible topics are listed at the end of the outline. Students are
encouraged to choose in consultation with the instructor other topics.

Suggestions for chronological outlines and maps: Colin McEvedy, The
Penguin Atlas of Medieval History, or Hoyt, Europe in the Middle Ages. The
latter will be available on library reserve.

1. On Medieval Studies:
   W.C., Bark, Origins of the Medieval World (Stanford Press), pp. 1-66

2. The Late Roman Regulatory State:
   C. Dawson, The Making of Europe (New American Library), 1-41
   M. Rostovtzeff, Rome (Oxford Galaxy), 266-321

3. Christianity: Growth and Victory:
   Henry Chadwick, The Early Church (Penguin, 1967), 9-73, 116-132, 237-246
   Dawson, pp. 42-57

4. The Patristic Tradition and Augustine:
   Augustine, Confessions, Books I,II,VII,VIII
   _____, City of God, Books XIV, XIX
   Chadwick, pp. 90-118, 133-151, 213-236
   H.A. Deane, Political and Social Ideas of St Augustine (Columbia U. Press)
   Th, E. Mommsen, "St Augustine and the Christian Idea of Progress"
      (Bobbs-Merrill Reprint, E-154, from Journal of the History of Ideas,
      Vol, XII, June 1951)

5. The Classical Tradition and Christianity:
   M.L.W. Laistner, Thought and Letters in Western Europe (Cornell) chapters 2-5
   Dawson, pp. 58-72

6. Monasticism and the Survival of Classical Culture:
   Chadwick, pp. 174-183
   Dawson, pp. 169-186

   Pierre Riché, "The Survival of Culture," in Literature of the Western World,
      II (London, Aldus Book, 1973). Xerox on reserve.
   Jean Leclercq, The Love of Learning and the Desire for God, pp. 19-48.
      (Fordham U. Press)

7. The Barbarian World:
    Dawson, pp. 73-99
    Tacitus, On Britain and Germany, ed. H. Mattingly (Penguin)
    Gregory of Tours, History of the Franks, trans. by Brehaut (Norton),
        Books 9-10, pp. 127-148
    Wallace-Hadrill, The Barbarian West (Harper Torch), pp. 1-90
    Georges Duby, The Early Growth of European Economy (Cornell), pp. 1-76

8. Byzantium:
    Dawson, pp. 103-117

9. Islam:
    Dawson, pp. 127-136

10. The Frankish Kingdom:
    Einhard, The Life of Charlemagne (Ann Arbor Paper)
    Duby, pp. 77-111
    Fichtenau, Heinrich, The Carolingian Empire (Univ. of Toronto Press
        Reprint), pp, 1-188
    Wallace-Hadrill, pp. 90-146

11. Renewed Invasions and European Society in the Feudal Era: Nov. 16, 18
    Dawson, pp. 202-217
    Marc Bloch, Feudal Society (Phoenix Books), Vol. I, pp. 1-102, 123-181,
        190-230, 241-270
    The Song of Roland, trans. P. Terry (Indianapolis)

12. The Economic Expansion of Western Europe:
    G. Duby, pp. 112-180

13. The German Empire:
    Dawson, pp. 218-238
    K.J. Leyser, Rule and Conflict in an Early Medieval Society (Arnold, 1979)
        9-43, 75-108
    C. Tellenbach, Church, State and Society in Early Medieval Society
        (Humanities), pp. 1-88

14. Ecclesiastical Revolution:
    Tellenbach, pp. 89-169

15. Early Medieval Art:
    Recommended: R. Hinks, Carolingian Art (Ann Arbor)

16. Conclusions:
    Bark, pp. 67-112

Possible Source Studies:

1. On the basis of Cassiodorus' <u>An Introduction to Divine and Human Readings</u>, ed. L.W. Jones, evaluate the contribution of monasticism to Western culture. (Suggested secondary source: H.B. Workman, <u>The Evolution of the Monastic Ideal</u> (Beacon Press).

2. Analyze the class structure of Germanic society either on the basis of the <u>Burgundian Code</u>, or the <u>Lombard Laws</u> (both are available in paperback from the University of Pennsylvania Press, translated by Katherine Fischer Drew).

3. Similar medieval source studies (the letters of Boniface, Gerbert, Gregory VII, the works of Orosius and Salvian, handbooks of penance, code of law, early medieval plays, etc.) are available in English translation in the <u>Columbia Records of Civilization Series</u>. Students are urged to look at these when choosing a topic. Ferrar and Evans, <u>English Translations from Medieval Sources</u>, will be available on library reserve. Students should consult this for additional early medieval sources available in English translation.

Europe in the Early Middle Ages

I. Medieval Origins

*H. Marrou, A History of Education in Antiquity, Part III, Chs. 4-7
*H. Pirenne, Mohammed and Charlemagne, 9-62, 75-96, 140-144,
236-264, 284-85
*W. Bark, Origins of the Medieval World, 1-40

II. Germanic Kingdoms

*Tacitus, On Britain and Germany, pp. on Germany.
D. Knowles, Great Historical Enterprises, 65-97
M. Todd, The Northern Barbarians, 19-42, 159-180, 209-212
Early Medieval Kingship, ed., P. Sawyer & Woods, 1-28
P. D. King, Law and Society in the Visigothic Kingdom, 23-51
B. Lyon, A Constitutional and Legal History of Medieval England,
3-82
W. A. Chaney, The Cult of Kingship in Anglo-Saxon England, 1-42;
247-59

III. The Church

*G. Barraclough, The Medieval Papacy, 7-37
J. Richards, Consul of God, 1-50, 228-266
Pope Gregory I, Dialogues, "Life of St. Benedict"
RB1980 The Rule of St. Benedict, 3-102, 157-181
P. Brown, The Cult of Saints, Preface, 1-22, 86-105

IV. Early Medieval Culture

*E. Curtius, European Literature and the Latin Middle Ages, chs. 4-5
*M. Laistner, Thought and Letters in Western Europe, 104-129
*J. Leclercq, The Love of Learning and the Desire for God, Pref.,
11-115
Medieval Studies, ed., James Powell, pp. 1-53
H. Delehaye, The Legends of the Saints, 1-59 or 1-40 depending on
edition.

V. Carolingian Empire

**P. Riché, Daily Life in the World of Charlemagne
*G. Barraclough, The Medieval Papacy, 39-61
**F. Ganshof, Feudalism, to p. 65

VI. Feudalism

**F. Ganshof, Feudalism, 65 to end
E. Brown, "The Tyranny of a Construct: Feudalism and Historians
of Medieval Europe," American Historical Review, V. 79, pp. 1063-88
**D. Herlihy, The History of Feudalism, 1-6, 66-97, 114-121, 131-177,
233-236

VII. Economic Factors

Cambridge Economic History, I, ch. VI by Marc Bloch
**G. Duby, The Early Growth of the European Economy
*L. White, Medieval Technology and Social Change, 39-69

History 237S (cont.)

VIII. Medieval Empire and Papacy

      *G. Barraclough, Medieval Papacy, 63-101
    **B. Tierney, The Crisis of Church and State, 1-95
      W. Ullman, The Growth of Papal Government in the Middle Ages,
         262-307
      B. Rosenwein, Rhinoceros Bound: Cluny in the Tenth Century,
         pp. xvii-29, 101-112
      G. Barraclough, History in a Changing World, 105-130
      F. Heer, The Holy Roman Empire, 22-64
      J. S. Robinson, Authority and Resistance in the Investiture
         Contest, vii, 1-49.

**Paperback to be purchased.
*On reserve, but available also in paperback.

History 434   W. A. Ernest
Spring Semester   1985

THE HIGH MIDDLE AGES

TEXTS: N. F. Cantor, Medieval History: The Life and Death of a
         Civilization   (Second Edition, 1969)
       The Crisis of Church and State, 1050-1300, ed. B. Tierney
         (Prentice-Hall, 1964)
       The Investiture Controversy: Issues, Ideals, and Results,
         ed. K. F. Morrison (Krieger, 1976)
       The Twelfth-Century Renaissance, ed. C. R. Young (Krieger)
       J. Gimpel, The Medieval Machine: The Industrial Revolution of the
         Middle Ages   (Penguin, 1976)

There follows a proposed schedule of lectures and readings. With the
exception of the texts listed above, all of the books will be found in the
Reserve Room in Sinclair Library. If you desire bibliographical suggestions
for further reading, you have only to ask!

You are expected to pursue a research project throughout the greater part
of the semester, dealing with a topic or problem of your choice (which must,
however, have the instructor's approval). Submission of your topic (8
February, on a form which will be provided) ipso facto will con-stitute
affirmation of the fact that you have checked out the library holdings to
determine the feasibility of the project and that the requisite primary
sources, monographic literature and periodical material all are available in
languages in which you are competent. A first draft of the paper, as nearly
as possible in final form and complete with scholarly apparatus, is to be
submitted for comment and criticism by 15 March. The final version,
impeccable in style, form, and content, and representing so far as possible a
significant original contribution to the sum total of human knowledge, will be
turned in on or before 3 May.

I will gladly furnish advice and a reasonable degree of assistance, both
with the paper and with the course. My office is Sakamaki Hall A408.
          See me MWF 7:00 - 7:20; 9:50 - 10:30 or by appointment.

PROPOSED SCHEDULE OF LECTURES AND DISCUSSIONS.

Mon. 21 Jan.   Orientation.

Wed. 23 Jan.   France: The Capetians to Philip Augustus.

    J.-F. Lemarignier, "Political and Monastic Structures in
       France at the End of the Tenth and the Beginning of
       the Eleventh Century," Lordship and Community in Medieval Europe:
       Selected Readings, ed. F. L. Cheyette, pp. 100-127.

Fri. 25 Jan.   The German Kingdom to 962.

    N. F. Cantor, Medieval History, pp. 227-240.
    Sources for the History of Medieval Europe from the mid-eighth to the
       mid-thirteenth century, ed. Brian Pullan, pp. 113-117.
    A Source Book for Mediaeval History, ed. O. J. Thatcher and E. H.
       McNeal (1907), pp. 69-77.
    G. Barraclough, The Origins of Modern Germany, pp. 1-53.
    T. Mayer, "The Historical Foundations of the German Constitution,"
       in Mediaeval Germany, 911-1250, ed. G.Barraclough, II, 1-33.
    B. Schmeidler, "Franconia's Place in the Structure of
       Mediaeval Germany," ibid., II, 71-93.

Mon. 28 Jan.   The Ottonian Empire.

    Barraclough, Origins, pp. 53-71.
    Sources ..., ed. B. Pullan, pp. 117-127.
    Source Book ..., ed. Thatcher , pp. 78-79; 114-121.
    "Liber de rebus gestis Ottonis," in The Works of Liudprand of
       Cremona, trans. F. A. Wright, pp. 213-232.
    The Rise of the First Reich: Germany in the Tenth
       Century, ed. B. H. Hill, Jr.

Wed. 30 Jan.   The Greater Norman Conquest.

Fri. 1 Feb.   Monasticism and Church Reform.

    Cantor, Medieval History, pp. 240-243.
    The Crisis of Church and State, 1050-1300, ed. B.
       Tierney, pp. 24-32.
    A Source Book of Mediaeval History, ed. F. A. Ogg, pp. 245-249.
    Select Historical Documents of the Middle Ages, ed. E. F.
       Henderson, pp. 267-314; 329-333.
    [N.B. These three source books involve some duplication.]
    H. Hirsch, "The Constitutional History of the Reformed
       Monasteries During the Investiture Contest," Mediaeval Germany, ed.
       G. Barraclough, II, 131-173.
    U. Stutz, "The Proprietary Church as an Element of Mediaeval
       Germanic Ecclesiastical Law," ibid. II, 35-70.
    J. W. Thompson, Feudal Germany, I, 3-67.

Mon. 4 Feb.   The Salians and the Church.

    Cantor, Medieval History, pp. 243-245.
    Source Book ..., ed. Thatcher, pp. 121-124.
    Barraclough, Origins, pp. 72-98.
        Thompson, Feudal Germany, I, 68-124.

Wed. 6 Feb..   Eastern and Western Europe Compared.

    Cantor, Medieval History, pp. 247-270.

Fri. 8 Feb.   The Reformed Papacy.   TERM PAPER TOPICS DUE.

    Sources ..., ed. Pullan, pp. 53-56, 58-63, 130-135.
    Source Book ..., ed. Thatcher, pp. 124-131.
    Select Historical Documents ..., ed. Henderson, pp. 336-337;
      361-365.
    D. B. Zema, "The Houses of Tuscany and of Pierleone in the Crisis
      of Rome in the Eleventh Century," Traditio,II, (1944), 155-175.
      [N. B. This article is printed (without documentation) in the
      Morrison pamphlet scheduled for discussion on Friday, 15 Feb.]

Mon. 11 Feb.   The Investiture Contest, I.

    Cantor, Medieval History, pp. 271-304.
    Crisis ..., ed. Tierney, pp. 33-95.
    Sources ..., ed. Pullan, pp. 135-159.
    Source Book ..., ed. Ogg, pp. 261-281.
    Source Book ..., ed. Thatcher, pp. 132-166.
    Select Historical Documents ..., ed. Henderson, pp.
      365-409.
      [Again some duplication!]
    Barraclough, Origins, pp. 101-164.
    P. Joachimsen, "The Investiture Contest and the German
    Constitution," Mediaeval Germany, ed. Barraclough, II, 95-129.

Wed. 13 Feb.   The Investiture Contest, II.

Fri. 15 Feb.   DISCUSSION OF THE INVESTITURE CONTEST.

    The Investiture Controversy: Issues, Ideals, and Results,
      ed. K. F. Morrison. (Krieger, 1976)

Mon. 18 Feb.   HOLIDAY: PRESIDENTS' DAY.

Wed. 20 Feb.   Normandy, the Norman Conquest, and Norman England.

    Cantor, Medieval History, pp. 305-316.
    Source Book ..., ed. Ogg, pp. 233-244.

Fri. 22 Feb.   SLIDES.

Mon. 25 Feb.   The Background of the Crusading Movement.

    Cantor, Medieval History, pp. 317-326.
    Source Book ..., ed. Thatcher, pp. 142-146.

Wed. 27 Feb.   The First Crusade.

    Sources ..., ed. Pullan, pp. 56-58.
    Source Book ..., ed. Ogg, pp. 282-296.

Fri. 1 Mar.   The Later Crusades.

    Cantor, Medieval History, pp. 326-331.
    Select Historical Documents ..., ed. Henderson, pp.
       333-336; 337-344.
    J. Prawer, "The Nobility and the Feudal Regime in the
       Latin Kingdom of Jerusalem," Lordship and Community in
       Medieval Europe: Selected Readings, ed. F. L Cheyette
       pp. 156-179.
    J. Prawer, "Estates, Communities and the Constitution of
       the Latin Kingdom," ibid., pp. 376-403.

Mon. 4 Mar.   Kingship and Law in the Middle Ages.

    Cantor, Medieval History, pp. 335-349; 421-433.
    K. Bosl, "Ruler and Ruled in the German Empire from the
       Tenth to the Twelfth Century," Lordship and Community
       in Medieval Europe: Selected Readings, ed. F. L.
       Cheyette, pp. 357-375.

Wed. 6 Mar.   Church and State in the Twelfth Century.
    Crisis ..., ed. Tierney, pp. 97-126.
    Sources ..., ed. Pullan, pp. 168-190.
    Select ... Documents, ed. Henderson, pp. 410-430.
    Source Book ..., ed. Thatcher, pp. 166-202.
    Barraclough, Origins, pp. 167-218.

Fri. 8 Mar.   HOUR EXAM!

Mon. 11 Mar.   The Concept of Empire.

   G. Barraclough, The Mediaeval Empire: Idea and Reality.

Wed. 13 Mar.   Feudalism and Its Divergent Tendencies.
   Cantor, Medieval History, pp. 214-223.
   Sources ..., ed. Pullan, pp. 235-243.
   Source Book ..., ed. Ogg, pp. 203-232.
   Lordship and Community in Medieval Europe: Selected
      Readings, ed. F. L. Cheyette, pp. 12-61; 128-136; 198-
      209; 217-221.
   If you have not already read F.-L. Ganshof, Feudalism,
      for some other course, I recommend it strongly.

Fri. 15 Mar. The Hohenstaufen and Feudalism in the Empire. FIRST DRAFT DUE!

   Source Book ..., ed. Thatcher, pp. 202-206.
   Sources ..., ed. Pullan, pp. 160-167.
   O. Freiherr von Dungern, "Constitutional Reorganization
      and Reform under the Hohenstaufen," Mediaeval Germany,
      ed. Barraclough, II, 203-233.
      H. Mitteis, "Feudalism and the German Constitution,"
      ibid., II, 235-279.

Mon. 18 Mar.   Angevin England to Magna Carta.

   Source Book ..., ed. Ogg, pp. 297-310.
   Select ... Documents, ed. Henderson, pp. 430-431.

Wed. 20 Mar.   SLIDES!

Fri. 22 Mar.   The Renaissance of the Twelfth Century.

   The Twelfth-Century Renaissance, ed. C. R. Young.
   Cantor, Medieval History, pp. 349-400.

  25 Mar. - 29 Mar. SPRING RECESS. READ BOOKS! WRITE PAPERS! HAVE FUN!

Mon. 1 Apr.   Trade and Commerce in the High Middle Ages.

Wed. 3 Apr.   Municipal Origins and Urban Society.

    Source Book ..., ed. Ogg, pp. 325-330.
    J. Dhondt, "Medieval Solidarities: Flemish Society in Transition,
        1127-1128," Lordship and Community in Medieval Europe: Selected
        Readings, ed. F. L. Cheyette, pp. 268-290.
    [The first chapter of C. Stephenson, Borough and Town, provides a
        useful survey of the older theories on the much-debated subject of
        medieval town origins.]

Fri. 5 Apr.   HOLIDAY: GOOD FRIDAY.

Mon. 8 Apr.   Serfdom, the Markgenossenschaft Theory, and Land
                      Reclamation..

    C. Stephenson, "The Problem of the Common Man in Early Medieval
        Europe," American Historical Review, LI (1946), 419-439. [Will be
        distributed in class.]
    B. Lyon, "Medieval Real Estate Developments and Freedom," Am. Hist.
        Rev., LXIII (1957), 47-61. [Will be distributed in class.]
    Source book ..., ed. Ogg, pp. 330-333.
    Thompson, Feudal Germany, II, 545-579.
    T. Mayer, "The State of the Dukes of Zähringen," Mediaeval Germany, ed.
        Barraclough, II, 175-202.
    H. Cam, "The Community of the Vill," Lordship and Community ..., ed.
        Cheyette, pp. 256-267.

Wed. 10 Apr.   The Wendish Crusade and the Northeastern German Frontier.

    Barraclough, Origins, pp. 249-281.
    Thompson, Feudal Germany, II, 387-528.

Fri. 12 Apr.   New Trends in Monasticism.

    Cantor, Medieval History, pp. 400-412, 455-459.
    Sources ..., ed. Pullan, pp. 77-90.
    Source Book ..., ed. Ogg, pp. 250-260; 360-379.
    Select ... Documents ..., ed. Henderson, pp. 344-349.

Mon. 15 Apr.   Medieval Heresy and the Inquisition.

    Cantor, Medieval History, pp. 412-420.
    Sources ..., ed. Pullan, pp. 90-98.

Wed. 17 Apr.   The French National Monarchy.
    Cantor, Medieval History, pp. 435-443.
    Sources ..., ed. Pullan, pp. 244-268.

Fri. 19 Apr.   The Papacy and the Secular State in the Thirteenth Century.

    Cantor, Medieval History, pp. 447-455.
    Crisis ..., ed. Tierney, pp. 127-157.
    Sources ..., ed. Pullan, pp. 191-206.
    Source Book ..., ed. Thatcher, pp. 208-226.
    Source Book ..., ed. Ogg, pp. 381-388.
    Select ... Documents ..., ed. Henderson, pp. 432-437.

Mon. 22 Apr.   Medieval England after Magna Carta

Wed. 24 Apr.   Reclamation and Emancipation in Thirteenth-Century Germany

Fri. 26 Apr.   Slides on Reclamation and Emancipation.

Mon. 29 Apr.   Medieval Technology and Science.

Wed. 1 May   DISCUSSION OF MEDIEVAL TECHNOLOGY, INDUSTRY AND SCIENCE.

    J. Gimpel, The Medieval Machine: The Industrial
              Revolution of the Middle Ages. (Penguin, 1976)

Fri. 3 May   Medieval Higher Education.   DEADLINE FOR TERM PAPERS!

    Cantor, Medieval History, pp. 461-473.
    Source Book ..., ed. Ogg, pp. 339-359.

Mon. 6 May   New Trends in Politics.

    Cantor, <u>Medieval History</u>, pp. 473-499.
    <u>Sources ...</u>, ed. Pullan, pp. 269-275.
    J. R. Strayer, <u>On the Medieval Origins of the Modern
        State.</u>
    <u>Select ... Documents</u>, ed. Henderson, pp. 437-439.
    <u>Crisis ...</u>, ed. Tierney, pp. 159-210.
    A. Marongiu, "The Theory of Democracy and Consent in the Fourteenth
        Century," <u>Lordship and Community ...</u>, ed. Cheyette, pp. 404-421.
    H. Baron, "Cicero and the Roman Civic Spirit in the Middle Ages and
        the Early Renaissance." <u>ibid.</u>, pp. 291-314.
    A. Brackmann, "The Beginnings of the National State in Mediaeval
        Germany and the Norman Monarchies," <u>Mediaeval Germany</u>, ed.
        Barraclough, II, 281-299.

Wed. 8 May   Slides.

Fri. 10 May   The Later Middle Ages: "Waning" and Legacy.

    Cantor, <u>Medieval History</u>, pp. 503-547.

FINAL EXAMINATION: Friday, 17 May 1985, 7:30 - 9:30.

INTRODUCTION AND ORIENTATION

F. C. Robinson, "Medieval, the Middle Ages," Speculum, 59 (Oct. 1984), 745-756.
Medieval Studies: An Introduction, ed. J. M. Powell.
R. W. Southern, The Making of the Middle Ages.
F. Heer, The Medieval World: Europe 1100-1350.
J. H. Mundy, Europe in the High Middle Ages.
Perspectives in Medieval History, ed. K. F. Drew and F. S. Lear.
B. D. Lyon, The Middle Ages in Recent Historical Thought.
R. S. Lopez, "Still Another Renaissance?" American Historical Review, 57
    (1951), 1-21.
B. C. Keeney, "A Dead Horse Flogged Again," Speculum, 30 (1955), 606-611.
T. Goldstein, "Medieval Civilization from the World-Historical View," Cahiers
    d'histoire mondiale, 6 (1960-61), 503-516.
L. White, Jr., "The Legacy of the Middle Ages in the American Wild West,"
    Speculum, 40 (1965), 191-202. See also the objections of O. Ulph, "The
    Legacy of the American Wild West in Medieval Scholarship," American West,
    3 (1966), 50ff.
E. King, England, 1175-1425.
G. Barraclough, The Origins of Modern Germany.
F. H. Bäuml, Medieval Civilization in Germany.
B. H. Hill, Medieval Monarchy in Action: The German Empire from Henry I to
    Henry IV.
E. S. Duckett, Death and Life in the Tenth Century.
M. Seidlmayer, Currents of Mediaeval Thought With Special Reference to Germany.
G. F. Jones, Honor in German Literature.
H. Daniel-Rops, Cathedral and Crusade.
W. Anderson, Castles of Europe: From Charlemagne to the Renaissance.
F. L. Ganshof, The Middle Ages: A History of International Relations.
J. R. Strayer, Medieval Statecraft and the Perspectives of History: Essays.
    With a Foreword by Gaines Post.
J. Le Goff, La Civilisation de l'occident médiéval.
G. Cohen, La grande clarté du moyen age.
H. Focillon, L'an mil.
J. Le Goff, Das Hochmittelalter.
W. von der Steinen, Der Kosmos des Mittelalters.
W. Lammers, Geschichtsdenken und Geschichtsbild im Mittelalter.
H. R. Guggisberg, Das europäische Mittelalter im amerikanischen Geschichts-
    denken des 19. und frühen 20. Jahrhunderts.

FRANCE: THE CAPETIANS TO PHILIP AUGUSTUS.

R. Fawtier, The Capetian Kings of France.
C. E. Petit-Dutaillis, The Feudal Monarchy in France and England.
M. Bloch, The Royal Touch, Sacred Monarchy, and Scrofula in England and France.
F. Funck-Brentano, The Middle Ages.

J. Evans, Life in Medieval France.
A. R. Lewis, The Development of Southern French and Catalan Society, 718-1050.
T. Evergates, Feudal Society in the Bailliage of Troyes Under the Counts of
    Champagne, 1142-1284.
S. Painter, The Scourge of the Clergy: Peter of Dreux, Duke of Brittany.
C. T. Wood, "Regnum Francie: A Problem in Capetian Administrative Usage,"
    Traditio, 23 (1967), 117-147.
F. Barlow, "The King's Evil," English Historical Review, 95 (1980), 3-27.
J. F. Benton, "The Revenue of Louis VII," Speculum, 42 (1967), 84-91.
J. Flach, "La royauté et l'église en France, du IXe au XIe siècle,"
    Revue d'histoire ecclésiastique, 4 (1903), 432-447.
Ehlers, Joachim, "Elemente mittelalterlicher Nationsbildung in Frankreich
    (10.-13. Jahrhundert)," Historische Zeitschrift, 231 (1980), 565-587.
W. Kienast, "Der Wirkungsbereich des französischen Königtums von Odo bis Ludwig
    VI. (888-1137) in Südfrankreich," Hist. Zeit., 209 (1969), 529-565.
P. E. Schramm, Der König von Frankreich: Das Wesen der Monarchie vom 9. bis
    zum 16. Jahrhundert. (2. v.)
W. Kienast, Deutschland und Frankreich in der Kaiserzeit.
W. Kienast, Der Herzogstitel in Frankreich und Deutschland.
J.-F. Lemarignier, Le gouvernement royal aux premiers temps Capétiens, (987-
    1108).
J. Duby, "Le gouvernement royal aux premiers temps capétiens," Le Moyen Age,
    72 (1966), 531-544.
Histoire des institutions françaises au moyen âge, ed. F. Lot and R. Fawtier.

THE GERMAN KINGDOM TO 962.

K. J. Leyser, Rule and Conflict in an Early Medieval Society: Ottonian Saxony.
K. J. Leyser, "The German Aristocracy from the Ninth to the Early Twelfth
    Century: A Historical and Cultural Sketch," Past and Present, 41 (1968),
    25-53.
K. J Leyser, "Henry I and the Beginnings of the Saxon Empire," English
    Historical Review, 83 (1968), 1-32.
K. J. Leyser, "The Battle at the Lech, 955: A Study in Tenth-Century Warfare,"
    History, 50 (1965), 1-25.
K. J. Leyser, "Ottonian Government," English Historical Review, 96 (1981),
    721-753.
H. L. Adelson, "The Holy Lance and the Hereditary German Monarchy," The Art
    Bulletin, 48 (1966), 177-192.
T. Reuter, "The 'Imperial Church System' of the Ottonian and Salian
    Rulers: A Reconsideration," Journal of Ecclesiastical History, 33 (July
    1982), 347-74.
C. S. Jaeger, "The Courtier Bishop in Vitae from the Tenth to the Twelfth
    Century," Speculum, 58 (no. 2, 1983), 291-325.
A. Alföldi, "Hasta - Summa Imperii: The Spear as Embodiment of Sovereignty in
    Rome," American Journal of Archaeology, 63 (1959), 1-27.
G. Tellenbach, Die Entstehung des deutschen Reiches.
R. Holtzmann, Geschichte der sächsischen Kaiserzeit, pp. 5-174.
M. Lintzel, Ausgewählte Schriften, II, 73-119, 222-275, 583-612.
R. Lüttich, Ungarnzüge in Europa im 10. Jahrhundert.
S. de Vajay, Der Eintritt des ungarischen Stämmebundes in die europäische
    Geschichte.

H. Büttner, Heinrichs I. Südwest- und Westpolitik.
G. Läwen, Stammesherzog und Stammesherzogtum: Beiträge zur Frage ihrer
   rechtlichen Bedeutung im 10.-12. Jahrhundert.
Die Entstehung des deutschen Reiches (Deutschland um 900): Ausgewählte Auf-
   sätze aus dem Jahren 1928-1954, mit einem Vorwort von Hellmut Kämpf.
W. von Giesebrecht, Geschichte der deutschen Kaiserzeit, I, 206-447.
Königswahl und Thronfolge in ottonisch-frühdeutscher Zeit, ed. E. Hlawitschka.
F. M. Fischer, Politiker um Otto den Großen.
H.-J. Freytag, Die Herrschaft der Billunger in Sachsen.
G. Waitz, Deutsche Verfassungsgeschichte. 8 vols. [Old but useful!]
W. Kienast, Der Herzogstitel in Frankreich und Deutschland.
H. Zielinski, "Zur Aachener Königserhebung von 936," Deutsches Archiv, 38
   (1972), 210-222.
C. Erdmann, "Die Burgenordnung Heinrichs I.," ibid., 6 (1943), 59-101.
C. Erdmann, "Das Grab Heinrichs I.," ibid., 4 (1940-41). 76-97.

THE OTTONIAN EMPIRE.

The Rise of the First Reich: Germany in the Tenth Century, ed. B. H. Hill, Jr.
F. J. Tschan, Bernward of Hildesheim. (3 vols.)
J. B. Morrall, "Otto III: An Imperial Ideal," History Today, 9 (1959).
   812-822.
A. Czajkowski, "The Congress of Gniezno in the Year 1000," Speculum, 24
   (1949), 339-356.
A. D. Frankforter, "Hroswitha of Gandersheim and the Destiny of Woman,"
   Historian, 41 (Feb. 1979), 295-314.
A. Hauck, Kirchengeschichte Deutschlands, III, 3-338.
E. Hlawitschka, Franken, Alemannen, Bayern und Burgunder in Oberitalien, 774-
   962.
Festschrift zur Jahrtausendfeier der Kaiserkrönung Ottos des Großen. (3 vols.)
G. A. Bezzola, Das ottonischen Kaisertum in der französischen Geschichts-
   schreibung des 10. und beginnenden 11. Jahrhunderts.
E. Winter, Russland und das Papsttum, I, 19-44.
M. Uhlirz, Die Krone des heiligen Stephan, des ersten Königs von Ungarn.
F. Koch, Wurde Kaiser Karl sitzend begraben?
K. und M. Uhlirz, Jahrbücher des deutschen Reiches Unter Otto II. und Otto
   III, vol. II.
D. Claude, Geschichte des Erzbistums Magdeburg bis in das 12. Jahrhundert, I.
H. Beumann, "Das Kaisertum Ottos des Großen," Hist. Zeit., 195 (1962), 529-
   573.
H. Keller, "Das Kaisertum Ottos des Großen im Verständnis seiner Zeit.,
   Deutsches Archiv, 20 (1964), 325-388.
D. Jank, "Die Darstellung Ottos des Großen in der spätmittelalterlichen
   Historiographie," Archiv für Kulturgeschichte, 61 (no. 1, 1979), 69-101.
Z. Wojciechowski, "La 'Renovatio imperii' sous Otton III et la Pologne," Revue
   historique, 201 (1949) 30-44.
K. Hampe, "Kaiser Otto III. und Rom," Hist. Zeit., 160 (1929), 513-533.
M. Uhlirz, "Kaiser Otto III. und das Papsttum," ibid., 171 (1940), 258-268.
R. Holtzmann, Geschichte der sächsischen Kaiserzeit, pp. 327-382.
Giesebrecht, op. cit., I, 718-743.   [A view now rejected!]
Sylvester II, The Letters of Gerbert, trans. H. P. Lattin.

THE GREATER NORMAN CONQUEST

J. J. C. Norwich, The Normans in the South, 1016-1130.
J. J. C. Norwich, The Kingdom in the Sun, 1130-1194.
        N. B. Both the titles above are good scholarly popularizations.
E. Curtis, Roger of Sicily and the Normans in Lower Italy, 1016-1154.
O. Demus, The Mosaics of Norman Sicily.
A History of the Crusades, ed. K. M. Setton, I & II.
E. Joranson, "The Inception of the Career of the Normans in Italy - Legend and
    History," Speculum, 23 (1948), 353-396.
A. Brackmann, "The Beginnings of the National State in Mediaeval Germany and
    the Norman Monarchies," Mediaeval Germany, 911-1250, ed. G. Barraclough,
    II, 281-299.
J. H. Pryor, "Transportation of Horses by Sea during the Era of the Crusades:
    Eighth Century to 1285 A.D.," Mariner's Mirror, 68 (1982), 9-27, 103-125.
M. E. Martin, "An Adriatic Hastings: Normans from Italy Invaded the Byzantine
    Empire, Robert Guiscard Sought the Imperial Crown," History Today, 27 Apr.
    1977), 219-225.
D. Abulafia, "The Reputation of a Norman King in Angevin Naples," Journal of
    Medieval History, 5 (June 1979), 135-47.
E. Jamison, "The Sicilian Norman Kingdom in the Mind of Anglo-Norman
    Contemporaries," Proceedings of the British Academy, 24 (1938), 237-85.
A. Marongiu, "A Model State in the Middle Ages: The Norman and Swabian
    Kingdom of Sicily," Comparative Studies in Society and History, 6
    (1963-64), 307-20. See also the "Comment" by J. R. Strayer, ibid., pp.
    321-24.
H. Wieruszowski, "Roger II of Sicily, Rex-Tyrannus in Twelfth-Century
    Political Thought," Speculum, 38 (1963), 46-78.
L.-R. Ménager, "L'institution monarchique dans les Etats normands d'Italie.
    Contribution à l'étude du pouvoir royal dans les principautés
    occidentales, aux XIe - XIIe siècles," Cahiers de civilisation médiévale,
    2 (1959), 303-31, 445-68.
A. Varvaro, "Les Normands en Sicile aux XIe et XIIe siècles: Présence
    effective dans l'île des hommes d'origine normande ou gallo romaine,"
    ibid., 23 (1980), 199-213.
A. Brackmann, "Die Wandlung der Staatsanschauungen im Zeitalter Friedrichs I,"
    Historische Zeitschrift, 145 (1932), 1-18.
E. Caspar, Roger II. (1101-1154) und die Gründung der normannisch-sicilischen
    Monarchie.

MONASTICISM AND CHURCH REFORM.

H. Hirsch, "The Constitutional History of the Reformed Monasteries During the
    Investiture Contest," Mediaeval Germany, 911-1250: Essays by German
    Historians, ed. and trans. G. Barraclough, II, 131-173.
U. Stutz, "The Proprietary Church as an Element of Mediaeval Germanic
    Ecclesiastical Law," ibid., II, 35-70.
J. W. Thompson, Feudal Germany, I, 3-67.
H. C. Lea, The History of Sacerdotal Celibacy in the Christian Church.
J. Bugge, Virginitas: An Essay in the History of a Medieval Ideal.
G. Constable, Religious Life and Thought (11th.-12th. Centuries).
G. Constable, Monastic Tithes From Their Origins to the Twelfth Century.

F. L. Ganshof, "La dîme monastique, du IXe à la fin du XIIe siècle,"
   Cahiers de civilisation médiévale, 11 (1968), 413-420. [Review article on
   Constable's book.]
J. Evans, Monastic Life at Cluny, 910-1157.
H. E. J. Cowdrey, The Clunics and the Gregorian Reform.
C. G. Coulton, Five Centuries of Religion. [Use with caution!]
K. J. Conant, "Mediaeval Academy Excavations at Cluny, X," Speculum, 45
   (1970), 1-39.
K. J. Conant, "Cluny Studies, 1968-1975," ibid., 50 (1975), 383-388, 16 plates.
C. B. Bouchard, "Laymen and Church Reform around the Year 1000: The
   Case of Otto-William, Count of Burgundy," Journal of Medieval History, 5
   (March 1979), 1-10.
B. R. Kemp, "Monastic Possession of Parish Churches in England in the Twelfth
   Century," Journal of Ecclesiastical History, 31 (Apr. 1980), 133-160.
K. Hallinger, "Zur geistigen Welt der Anfänge Klunys," Deutsches Archiv, 10
   (1954), 417-445.
J. Wollasch, "Muri und St. Blasien: Perspektiven schwäbischen Mönchtums in der
   Reform," ibid., 17 (1961), 420-446.
H. E. Feine, "Klosterreformen im 10. und 11. Jahrhundert und ihr Einfluß auf
   die Reichenau und St. Gallen," Aus Verfassungs- und Landesgeschichte:
   Festschrift ... T. Mayer, II, 77-91.
H. E. Feine, "Das Eigenkirchenwesen als Gesamterscheinung," Kirchliche Rechts-
   geschichte: Das katholische Kirche. 4. Aufl., pp. 160-182.
E. Sackur, Die Cluniacensur in ihrer kirchlichen und allgemein-geschichtlichen
   Wirksamkeit bis zur Mitte des elften Jahrhunderts. (2 vols.)
E. E. H. Stengel, Die Immunität in Deutschland bis zum Ende des 11. Jahr-
   hunderts.
A. Schulte, Der Adel und die deutsche Kirche im Mittelalter: Studien zur
   Sozial-, Rechts- und Kirchengeschichte.
T. Mayer, Fürsten und Staat: Studien zur Verfassungsgeschichte des deutschen
   Mittelalter
E. Landers, Die deutschen Klöster vom Ausgang Karls des Grossen bis zum Wormser
   Konkordat und ihre Verhältnis zu den Reformen.

THE SALIANS AND THE CHURCH.

K. Hampe, Germany Under the Salian and Hohenstaufen Emperors, pp. 47-59.
Cambridge Medieval History, III.
R. L. Poole, "Benedict IX and Gregory VI." Proceedings of the British Academy,
   8 (1917-1918), 199-235.
E. N. Johnson, "Adalbert of Hamburg-Bremen: A Politician of the Eleventh
   Century," Speculum, 9 (1934), 147-179.
P. Fournier, "Le Décret de Burchard de Worms: Ses caractères, son influence,"
   Rev. d'hist. eccl., 12 (1911), 451-473, 670-701.
T. Schieffer, "Heinrich II. und Konrad II. Die Umprägung des Geschichtsbildes
   durch die Kirchenreform des 11. Jahrhunderts," Deutsches Archiv, 8
   (1950-51), 384-437.
W. Kölmel, "Die kaiserlichen Herrschaft im Gebiet von Ravenna (Exarchat und
   Pentapolis) vor dem Investiturstreit (10./11. Jahrhundert)," Historisches
   Jahrbuch, 88 (1968), 257-299.
H. L. Mikoletzky, Kaiser Heinrich II. und die Kirche.

E. Müller, Das Itinerar Kaiser Heinrichs III. (1039 bis 1056) mit besonderer
    Berücksichtigung seiner Urkunden.
M. Lintzel, Die Beschlusse der deutschen Hoftage von 911 bis 1056.
K. Bosl, Die Reichsministerialität der Salier und Staufer. (2 vols.)
G. B. Ladner, Theologie und Politik vor dem Investiturstreit: Abendmahlstreit,
    Kirchenreform, Cluni - und Heinrich III.
Giesebrecht, op. cit., III, 3-230.
Adam of Bremen, History of the Archbishops of Hamburg-Bremen, trans. F. J.
    Tschan.

EASTERN AND WESTERN EUROPE COMPARED.

G. Ostrogorsky, History of the Byzantine State.
A. A. Vasiliev, History of the Byzantine Empire, 324-1453.
J. M. Hussey, Church And Learning in the Byzantine Empire, 867-1185.
C. Diehl, Byzantium: Greatness and Decline.
D. M. Nicol, The Last Centuries of Byzantium, 1261-1453. (1972)
D. M. Nicol, Church and Society in the Last Centuries of Byzantium: The
    Birkbeck Lectures, 1977.   (1979)
D. T. Rice, Constantinople from Byzantium to Istanbul.
H. Ahrweiler, Byzance et la mer: La marine de guerre, la politique et les
    institutions maritimes de Byzance aux VIIe-XVe siècles.
P. K. Hitti, History of the Arabs.
J. J. Saunders, A History of Medieval Islam.
G. E. von Grunebaum, Medieval Islam.
W. M. Watt, The Influence of Islam on Medieval Europe.
R. W. Bulliet, The Camel and the Wheel.
F. Oakley, The Medieval Experience: Foundations of Western Cultural
    Singularity.
F. Heer, The Mediaeval World.

THE REFORMED PAPACY.

W. Ullmann, The Growth of Papal Government in the Middle Ages.
H. Mann, The Lives of the Popes in the Middle Ages, VI.
H. E. J. Cowdrey, The Cluniacs and the Gregorian Reform.
S. Runciman, The Eastern Schism: A Study of the Papacy and the Eastern
    Churches During the XIth. and XIIth. Centuries.
F. Dvornik, Byzantium and the Roman Primacy.
G. Barraclough, The Medieval Papacy.
P. Partner, The Lands of St. Peter: The Papal State in the Middle Ages and the
    Early Renaissance.
A. L. Barstow, Married Priests and the Reforming Papacy: The Eleventh-Century
    Debates.
D. M. Nicol, "Byzantium and the Papacy in the Eleventh Century," Journal of
    Ecclesiastical History, 13 (1962), 1-20.
P. Charanis, "On the Question of the Hellenization of Sicily and Southern Italy
    During the Middle Ages," American Historical Review, 52 (1946), 74-86.
J. J. Ryan, "Cardinal Humbert De s. Romana ecclesia: Relics of Roman-Byzantine
    Relations 1053-1054," Mediaeval Studies, 20 (1958), 206-238.

H. E. J. Cowdrey, "The Peace and the Truce of God in the Eleventh Century,"
   Past and Present, 46 (1970), 42-67.
R. I. Moore, "Family, Community and Cult on the Eve of the Gregorian Reform"
   Transactions of the Royal Historical Society, 30 (1980), 49-69.
J. Sydow, "Untersuchungen zur kurialen Verwaltungsgeschichte im Zeitalter des
   Reformpapsttums," Deutsches Archiv, 11 (1954-55), 18-73.
H. Grundmann, "Eine neue Interpretation des Papstwahldekrets von 1059," ibid.,
   25 (1969), 234-236.
P. Herde, "Das Papsttum und die griechische Kirche in Süditalien vom 11. bis
   zum 13. Jahrhundert," ibid., 26 (1970), 1-46.
P. E. Schramm, Kaiser, Rom und Renovatio: Studien zur Geschichte des römischen
   Erneuerungsgedankens vom Ende des karolingischen Reiches bis zum
   Investiturstreit.
P. E. Schramm, Kaiser, Könige und Päpste: Gesammelte Aufsätze zur Geschichte
   des Mittelalters. (4 vols.)
H. Pahncke, Geschichte der Bischöfe Italiens deutscher Nation von 951-1264.
F. A. Gregorovius, Geschichte der Stadt Rom im Mittelalter.
A. Hauck, Kirchengeschichte Deutschlands, III, 391-752.
S. Borsari, Il Monachesimo bizantino nella Sicilia e nell' Italia meridionale
   prenormanne.

THE INVESTITURE CONTEST.

P. Joachimsen, "The Investiture Contest and the German Constitution," Mediaeval
   Germany, ed. Barraclough, II, 95-129.
Z. N. Brooke, "Lay Investiture and its Relation to the Conflict of Empire and
   Papacy," Proceedings of the British Academy, 25 (1939), 217-247.
S. B. Hicks, "The Investiture Controversy of the Middle Ages, 1075-1122:
   Agreement and Disagreement Among Historians," Journal of Church and State,
   15 (1973), 5-20.
K. F. Morrison, "Canossa: A Revision," Traditio, 18 (1962), 121-148.
R. Nineham, "The So-Called Anonymous of York," Journal of Ecclesiastical
   History, 14 (1963), 31-45.
G. A. Loud, "Abbot Desiderius of Monte Cassino and the Gregorian Papacy,"
   Journal of Ecclesiastical History, 30 (1979), 305-322.
R. E. Reynolds, "Liturgical Scholarship at the Time of the Investiture
   Controversy: Past Research and Future Opportunities," Harvard Theological
   Review, 71 (Jan.-Apr. 1978), 109-124.
I. S. Robinson, "Pope Gregory VII, the Princes and the 'Pactum'
   1077-1080," English Historical Review, 94 (1979), 721-756.
I. S. Robinson, "Periculosus homo: Pope Gregory VII and Episcopal
   Authority," Viator, 9 (1978), 103-131.
W. Ullmann, "Von Canossa nach Pavia: Zum Strukturwandel der
   Herrschaftsgrundlagen im salischen und staufischen Zeitalter,"
   Historisches Jahrbuch, 93 (no. 2, 1973), 265-300.
S. N. Vaughn, "St. Anselm and the English Investiture Controversy
   Reconsidered," Journal of Medieval History, 6 (Mar. 1980), 484-504.
J. T. Gilchrist, "Canon Law Aspects of the Eleventh Century Gregorian Reform
   Program," ibid., 13 (1962), 21-38.
S. A. Chodorow, "Magister Gratian and the Problem of 'Regnum' and "Sacer-
   dotium'," Traditio, 26 (1970), 364-381.

S. A. Chodorow, "Ecclesiastical Politics and the Ending of the Investiture
    Contest: The Papal Election of 1119 and the Negotiations of Mouzon,"
    Speculum, 46 (1971), 613-640.
G. Tellenbach, Church, State, and Christian Society at the Time of the
    Investiture Contest.
W. Ullmann, The Growth of Papal Government in the Middle Ages.
Cambridge Medieval History, V, cc. ii, iii.
T. F. Tout, The Empire and the Papacy.
N. Hunt, Cluny Under St. Hugh, 1049-1109.
K. F. Morrison, Tradition and Authority in the Western Church, 300-1140.
T. Schieffer, "Cluny et la querelle des investitures," Rev. hist., 225
    (1961), 47-72.
Canossa als Wende: Ausgewählte Aufsätze zur neueren Forschung, ed. H. Kämpf.
    [A valuable collection of important German articles on the subject.]
F. Baethgen, "Zur Tribur-Frage," Deutsches Archiv, 4 (1940-41), 394-411.
H. Naumann, "Die Schenkung des Gutes Schleuchsee an St. Blasien: Ein Beitrag
    zur Geschichte des Investiturstreites," ibid., XXIII (1967), 359-404.
H. Hoffmann, "Ivo von Chartres und die Lösung des Investiturproblems," ibid.,
    15 (1959), 393-440.
K. Mirbt, Die Publizistik im Zeitalter Gregors VII.
A. Scharnagel, Der Begriff der Investitur im den Quellen und der Literatur des
    Investiturstreites.
G. Koch, Manegold von Lautenbach und die Lehre von der Volkssouveränitat unter
    Heinrich IV.
W. Hartmann, "Manegold von Lautenbach und die Anfänge der Frühscholastik,"
    Deutsches Archiv, 17 (1970), 47-149.
H. Mordek, "Proprie auctoritates apostolice sedis: Ein zweiter Dictatus Papae
    Gregors VII.?" ibid., 28 (1972), 105-132.
R. Kottje, "Zur Bedeutung der Bischofsstädte für Heinrich IV,"
    Historisches Jahrbuch, 97-98 (1978), 131-57.
R. Schieffer, "Gregor VII. - Ein Versuch über die historische Größe,"
    Historisches Jahrbuch, 97-98 (1978), 87-107.
A. Overmann, Gräfin Mathilde von Tuscien.
O. H. Kost, Heinrich V.: Gestalt und Verhängnis des letzten salischen Kaisers.
W. Seegrün, Das Papsttum und Skandinavien, bis zur Vollendung der nordischen
    Kirchenorganisation (1164).
J. Haller, Das Papsttum: Idee und Wirklichkeit, II.
A. Hauck, Kirchengeschichte Deutschlands, III, 753-923.

Sources on the Investiture Contest.

The Correspondence of Pope Gregory VII: Selected Letters From the Registrum,
    trans. E. Emerton.
The Epistolae Vagantes of Pope Gregory VII, ed. and trans. by H. E. J. Cowdrey.
A. Murray, "Pope Gregory VII and his Letters," Traditio, 22 (1966), 149-202.
U.-R. Blumenthal, "Canossa and Royal Ideology in 1077: Two Unknown
    Manuscripts of 'De penitentia regis Salomonis'," Manuscripta, 32 (1978),
    91-96.
I. S. Robinson, "The Dissemination of the Letters of Pope Gregory VII During
    the Investiture Contest," Journal of Ecclesiastical History, 34 (Apr.
    1983), 175-193.

Imperial Lives and Letters of the Eleventh Century, trans. T. E. Mommsen and
    K. F. Morrison.
Die Briefe Kaiser Heinrichs IV., trans. K. Langosch.
Die Texte des normannischen Anonymous, ed. K. Pellens.
The Letters of Peter the Venerable, ed. G. Constable.
Monumenta Germaniae historica: Libelli de Lite Imperatorum et Pontificum
    saeculis XI et XII conscripti. (3 vols.)
An excellent survey of the period and of the older printed source editions is
    Jahrbücher des deutschen Reiches Unter Heinrich IV. und Heinrich V., by
    G. Meyer von Knonau. (7 vols.)

NORMANDY, THE NORMAN CONQUEST, AND NORMAN ENGLAND.

R. A. Brown, The Normans and the Norman Conquest.
S. Körner, The Battle of Hastings, England, and Europe, 1035-1066.
D. C. Dougles, William the Conqueror.
F. M. Stenton, The Bayeux Tapestry. (2nd. ed.)
D. C. Douglas, The Norman Achievement.
D. Bates, Normandy before 1066.
R. A. Brown, Origins of English Feudalism.
R. H. C. Davis, The Normans and Their Myth.
D. F. Renn, Norman Castles in Britain.
C. W. Hollister, The Military Organization of Norman England.
V. H. Galbraith, The Making of Domesday Book.
R. W. Finn, The Domesday Inquest.
G. W. Keeton, The Norman Conquest and the Common Law.
N. F. Cantor, Church, Kingship and Lay Investiture in England, 1089-1135.
H. A. Cronne, The Reign of Stephen, 1135-1154: Anarchy in England.
M. Brett, The English Church Under Henry I.
F. M. Stenton, The First Century of English Feudalism, 1066-1166.
J. W. Alexander, Ranulf of Chester: A Relic of the Conquest.
D. C. Douglas, "The First Century of English Feudalism," Economic History
    Review, 9 (1939), 128-143.
C. W. Hollister, "1066: The 'Feudal Revolution'," American Historical Review,
    73 (1968), 708-723.
C. W. Hollister, "Normandy, France and the Anglo-Norman Regnum," Speculum, 51
    (1976), 202-242.
S. B. Hicks, "The Impact of William Clito upon the Continental
    Policies of Henry I of England," Viator, 10 (1979), 1-21.
F. Barlow, "William I's Relations with Cluny," Journal of Ecclesistical
    History, 32 (Apr. 1981), 131-141.
C. Morton, "Pope Alexander II and the Norman Conquest," Latomus, 34
    (Apr.-June 1975), 362-382.
K. Schnith, "Die Wende der englischen Geschichte im 11. Jahrhundert,"
    Historisches Jahrbuch, 86 (1966), 1-53.

THE BACKGROUND OF THE CRUSADING MOVEMENT.

C. Erdmann, The Origin of the Idea of Crusade.
R. W. Southern, Western Views of Islam in the Middle Ages.
D. C. Munro, "The Western Attitude Toward Islam During the Period of the
   Crusades," Speculum, 6 (1931), 329-343.
W. E. Kaegi, Jr., "The Contribution of Archery to the Turkish Conquest of
   Anatolia," ibid., 39 (1964), 96-108.
J. Streater, "The Battle of Manzikert," History Today, 17 (1967), 257-263.
E. O. Blake, "The Formation of the 'Crusade Idea'," Journal of Ecclesiastical
   History, 21 (1970), 11-31.
O. Springer, "Mediaeval Pilgrim Routes from Scandinavia to Rome," Mediaeval
   Studies, 12 (1950), 92-122.
E. Joranson, "The Problem of the Spurious Letter of Emperor Alexius to the
   Count of Flanders," American Historical Review, 55 (1949-50), 811-832.
T. A. T. Rice, The Seljuks in Asia Minor.
H. E. Mayer, The Crusades.
A History of the Crusades, ed. K. M. Setton, I.
S. Runciman, A History of the Crusades. (3 vols.)
D. R. Howard, Writers and Pilgrims: Medieval Pilgrimage Narratives and Their
   Posterity.
V. and H. Hall, The Great Pilgrimage of the Middle Ages: The Road to St. James
   of Compostella.
C. Courtois, "Grégoire VII et l'Afrique du Nord: Remarques sur les communautés
   chretiennes d'Afrique au XIe siècle," Rev. hist., 195 (1945), 97-122,
   193-226.
G. Constable, "Monachisme et pèlerinage au Moyen Age," Revue historique, 523
   (1977), 3-28.
W. Holtzmann, Beiträge zur Reichs- und Papstgeschichte des hohen Mittelalters,
   pp. 51-105.
A. Waas, Geschichte des Kreuzzüge. (2 vols.)
U. Schwerin, Die Aufrufe der Päpste zur Befreiung des Heiligen Landes von den
   Anfängen bis zum Ausgang Innocenz IV

THE FIRST CRUSADE.

A. C. Krey, "Urban's Crusade - Success or Failure?" American Historical
   Review, 53 (1948), 235-250.
L. A. M. Sumberg, "The 'Tafurs' and the First Crusade," Mediaeval Studies, 21
   (1959), 224-246.
H. E. J. Cowdrey, "Pope Urban's Preaching of the First Crusade," History, 55
   (1970), 177-188.
H. Dickerhof, "Über die Staatsgründung des ersten Kreuzzugs," Historisches
   Jahrbuch, 100 (1980), 95-130.
J. France, "The First Crusade and Islam," Muslim World, 57 (Oct. 1977),
   16.
J. France, "The Election and Title of Godfrey de Bouillon," Canadian Journal
   of History, 18 (Dec. 1983), 321-29.

B. Stemberger, "Zu den Judenverfolgungen in Deutschland zur Zeit der
    ersten beiden Kreuzzüge," Kairos, 20 (no. 1 & no 2, 1978), 53-72, 151-157.
R. Crozet, "Le voyage d'Urban II et ses négociations avec le clergé de France,"
    Rev. hist., 179 (1937), 271-310.
J. Riley-Smith, What Were The Crusades?
A. Becker, Papst Urban II (1088-1099).
The First Crusade: The Accounts of Eye-Witnesses and Participants, ed. A. C.
    Krey.
Fulcher of Chartres, A History of the Expedition to Jerusalem, 1095-1127,
    trans. F. R. Ryan.
(Setton, Runciman, Mayer and Waas as above.)

THE LATER CRUSADES.

J. Prawer, "The Nobility and the Feudal Regime in the Latin Kingdom of Jeru-
    salem," Lordship and Community in Medieval Europe: Selected Readings,
    ed. F. L. Cheyette, pp. 156-179.
J. Prawer, "Estates, Communities and the Constitution of the Latin Kingdom,"
    ibid., pp. 376-403.
D. C. Munro, The Kingdom of the Crusaders.
A. S. Atiya, Crusade, Commerce and Culture.
M. Purcell, Papal Crusading Policy, 1244-1291: The Chief Instruments of Papal
    Crusading Policy and Crusade to the Holy Land from the Final Loss of Jeru-
    salem to the Fall of Acre.
E. Joranson, "The Palestine Pilgrimage of Henry the Lion," Medieval and
    Historiographical Essays in Honor of James Westfall Thompson, ed. J. L.
    Cate and E. N. Anderson, pp. 146-225.
G. Constable, "The Second Crusade as Seen by Contemporaries," Traditio,
    9 (1953), 213-279.
C. M. Brand, "The Byzantines and Saladin, 1185-1192: Opponents of the Third
    Crusade," Speculum, 38 (1962), 167-181.
C. M. Brand, "A Byzantine Plan for the Fourth Crusade," ibid., 43 (1968),
    462-475.
R. Chazan, "Emperor Frederick I, the Third Crusade, and the Jews,"
    Viator, 8 (1977), 83-93.
P. W. Edbury, "John of Ibelin's Title to the County of Jaffa and Ascalon,"
    English Historical Review, 98 (Jan. 1983), 115-133.
A. J. Forey, "Constitutional Conflict and Change in the Hospital of St. John
    during the Twelfth and Thirteenth Centuries," Journal of Ecclesiastical
    History, 33 (Jan. 1982), 15-29.
A. J. Forey, "The Military Orders in the Crusading Proposals of the
    Late-Thirteenth and Early-Fourteenth Centuries," Traditio, 36 (1980),
    317-345.
M. E. Martin, "The Venetian-Seljuk Treaty of 1220," English Historical
    Review, 95 (1980), 321-330.
D. E. Queller & G. W. Day, "Some Arguments in Defense of of the
    Venetians on the Fourth Crusade," American Historical Review, 81 (Oct.
    1976), 717-737.
D. E. Queller & I. B. Katele, "Attitudes towards the Venetians in
    the Fourth Crusade: The Western Sources," International History Review, 4
    (Feb. 1982), 1-36.
D. E. Queller and S. J. Stratton, "A Century of Controversy on the Fourth
    Crusade," Studies in Medieval and Renaissance History, 6 (1969), 233-277.

D. E. Queller, T. K. Compton, and D. A. Campbell, "The Fourth Crusade: The
   Neglected Majority," Speculum, XLIX (1974), 441-465.
R. H. Schmandt, "The Fourth Crusade and the Just War Theory," Catholic
   Historical Review, 61 (1975), 191-221.
J. Riley-Smith, "The Assise sur la ligece and the Commune of Acre," Traditio,
   27 (1971), 179-204.
J. Hill, "From Rome to Jerusalem: An Icelandic Itinerary of the Mid-Twelfth
   Century," Harvard Theological Review, 76 (Apr. 1983), 175-203.
T. D. Matijasic, "Christian vs. Christian: The Fourth Crusade and the Sack of
   Zara," Journal of Historical Studies, 5 (no. 2, 1982), 1-19.
R. C. Smail, Crusading Warfare.
D. Seward, Monks of War: The Military Religious Orders.
A. Ben-Ami, Social Change in a Hostile Environment: The Crusaders' Kingdom of
   Jerusalem.
J. Prawer, The Crusaders' Kingdom: European Colonization in the Middle Ages.
D. E. Queller, The Fourth Crusade: The Conquest of Constantinople, 1201-1204.
E. D. S. Bradford, The Great Betrayal: Constantinople 1204.
J. A. Brundage, Medieval Canon Law and the Crusader.
J. A. Brundage, Richard Lion Heart.
J. Kritzeck, Peter the Venerable and Islam.
J. J. Saunders, Aspects of the Crusades.
R. L. Nicholson, Joscelyn III and the Fall of the Crusader States, 1134-1199.
J. Riley-Smith, The Feudal Nobility and the Kingdom of Jerusalem, 1174-1277.
J. Riley-Smith, The Knights of St. John in Jerusalem and Cyprus, c. 1050-1310.
C. M. Brand, Byzantium Confronts the West, 1180-1204.
A. E. Bakalopoulos, Origins of the Greek Nation: The Byzantine Period, 1204-
   1461.
B. Lewis, The Assassins: A Radical Sect in Islam.
T. S. R. Boase, Castles and Churches of the Crusading Kingdom.
W. Müller-Wiener, Castles of the Crusaders.
J. Hartmann, Die Persönlichkeit des Sultans Saladin im Urteil der abendländ-
   ischen Quellen.
H. Vriens, "De kwestie van den vierden kruistocht," Tijdschrift voor
   geschiedenis, 37 (1922), 50-82.
F. W. Wentzlaff-Eggebert, Kreuzzugsdichtung des Mittelalters.
E. Gerland, Geschichte des lateinischen Kaiserreichs von Konstantinopel.
R. Röricht, Beiträge zur Geschichte der Kreuzzüge.
F. Gabrieli, "Introduction aux historiens arabes des croisades," Cahiers de
   civilisation médiévale, 13 (1970), 221-228.
H. E. Mayer, "Das Pontificale von Tyrus und die Krönung der lateinischen Könige
   von Jerusalem: Zugleich ein Beitrag zur Forschung über Herrschaftszeichen
   und Staatssymbolik," Dumbarton Oaks Papers, 21 (1967), 141-232.
M. L. Bulst, "Zur Geschichte der Ritterorden und des Königreichs Jerusalem im
   13. Jahrhundert bis zur Schlacht bei La Forbie am 17. Okt. 1244," Deutsches
   Archiv, 22 (1966), 197-226.
E. Lavisse, Histoire de France, II, 2, pp. 227-250.
Willliam of Tyre, A History of Deeds Done Beyond the Sea, trans. E. A. Babcock
   and A. C. Krey.
R. C. Schwinges, "Kreuzzugsideologie und Toleranz im Denken Wilhelms von
   Tyrus," Saeculum, 25 (1974), 367-385.
Odo of Deuil, De Profectione Ludovici VII in orientem, ed. and trans. by V. G.
   Berry.

Ambroise, The Crusade of Richard Lion-Heart, trans. M. J. Hubert and J. L.
  LaMonte.
Arab Historians of the Crusades, ed. and trans. by F. Gabrieli.
Ibn al-Kalanisi, The Damascus Chronicle of the Crusades.
Ceux qui conquirent Constantinople, récits de la quatrième croisade, ed. N.
  Coulet.

KINGSHIP AND LAW IN THE MIDDLE AGES.

F. Kern, Kingship and Law in the Middle Ages.
P. E. Schramm, A History of the English Coronation.
H. G. Richardson, "The English Coronation Oath," Speculum, 24 (1949), 44-75.
S. J. T. Miller, "The Position of the King in Bracton and Beaumanoir," ibid.,
  31 (1956), 263-296.
E. Kantorowicz, The King's Two Bodies: A Study in Mediaeval Political Theology
E. Kantorowicz, Laudes Regiae: A Study in Liturgical Acclamations and
  Mediaeval Ruler Worship.
E. Peters, The Shadow King: Rex Inutilis in Medieval Law and Literature,
  751-1327.
S. Malarkey, "The 'Corones Tweyne': An Interpretation," Speculum, 38 (1963),
  473-478.
O. Gierke, Political Theories of the Middle Ages.
H. Mitteis, The State in the Middle Ages: A Comparative Constitutional History
  of Feudal Europe, trans. H. F. Orton.
A. J. and R. W. Carlyle, A History of Mediaeval Political Theory in the West.
  (6 vols.)
J. Gardelles, "Les palais dans l'Europe occidentale chrétienne du Xe au
  XIIe siècle," Cahiers de civilisation médiévale, 19 (Apr.-June 1976),
  115-134.
W. Ullmann, "Der Souveränitätsgedanke in den mittelalterlichen Krönungs-
  ordines," Festschrift Percy Ernst Schramm, I, 72-89.
W. Ullmann, "Schranken der Königsgewalt im Mittelalter," Historisches Jahrbuch,
  91 (1971), 1-21.
P. E. Schramm, "Die Geschichte des mittelalterlichen Herrschertums im Lichte
  der Herrschaftszeichen," Hist. Zeit., 178 (1954), 1-24.
H. Beumann, "Die Historiographie des Mittelalters als Quelle für die Ideen-
  geschichte des Königtums," ibid., 180 (1955), 449-488.
R. Buchner, "Der Titel rex Romanorum in deutschen Königsurkunden des 11.
  Jahrhunderts," Deutsches Archiv, 19 (1963), 327-338.
H. Hoffmann, "Die Unveräußlichkeit der Kronrechte im Mittelalter,"
  ibid., 20 (1964), 389-474.
S. Gagnér, Studien zur Ideengeschichte der Gesetzgebung.
R. Scheyhing, Eide, Amtsgewalt und Bannleihe: Eine Untersuchung zur Bannleihe
  im hohen und späten Mittelalter.
H. Mitteis, Die deutsche Königswahl: Ihre Rechtsgrundlagen bus zur Goldenen
  Bulle.
G. Theuerkauf, Lex, Speculum, Compendium Juris: Rechtsaufzeichnungen und
  Rechtsbewußtsein in Norddeutschland vom 8. bis zum 16. Jahrhundert.
Eike von Repgow, Sachsenspiegel.

CHURCH AND STATE IN THE TWELFTH CENTURY.

J. A. Yunck, "Economic Conservatism, Papal Finance and the Medieval Satires on Rome," Change in Medieval Society: Europe North of the Alps, ed. S. L. Thrupp, pp. 72-85.
M. W. Baldwin, Alexander III and the Twelfth Century.
R. Somerville, "The Council of Pisa, 1135: A Re-examination of the Evidence for the Canons," Speculum, 45 (1970), 98-114.
N. M. Haring, "Notes on the Council and Consistory of Rheims (1148)," Mediaeval Studies, 28 (1966), 39-59.
J. G. Rowe, "Hadrian IV, the Byzantine Empire, and the Latin Orient," Essays in Medieval History Presented to Bertie Wilkinson, ed. T. A. Sandquist and M. R. Powicke, pp. 3-16.
H. V. White, "Pontius of Cluny, the Curia Romana and the End of Gregorianism in Rome," Church History, 27 (1958), 195-219.
K. Hampe, Germany under the Salian and Hohenstaufen Emperors.
R. Folz, "La chancellerie de Frédéric Ier et la canonisation de Charlemagne," Le Moyen Age, 70 (1964), 13-31.
T. Mayer, "Papsttum und Kaisertum: Werden, Wesen und Auflösung einer Weltordnung," Hist. Zeit., 187 (1959), 1-53.
A. Brackmann, "Die Ursache der geistigen und politischen Wandlung Europas im 11. und 12. Jahrhundert," ibid., 149 (1934), 229-239.
H.-W. Klewitz, "Das Ende des Reformpapsttums," Deutsches Archiv, 3 (1939), 371-412.
F. J. Schmale, "Papsttum und Kurie zwischen Gregor VII. und Innocenz II.," Hist. Zeit., 193 (1961), 265-285.
W. Levison, "Die mittelalterliche Lehre von den beiden Schwerten," Deutsches Archiv, 9 (1951-52), 14-42.
H. Hoffmann, "Die beiden Schwerten im hohen Mittelalter," ibid., 20 (1064), 78-114.
G. Baaken, "Die Verhandlungen zwischen Kaiser Heinrich VI. und Papst Coelestin III. in den Jahren 1195-1197," ibid., 27 (1971), 457-513.
J. Goetz, "Kritische Beiträge zur Geschichte der Pataria," Archiv für Kulturgeschichte, 12 (1916), 17-55, 164-194.
M. Pacaut, Alexandre III: Etude sur la conception du pouvoir pontifical dans sa pensée et dans son ouvre.
P. Rassow, Honor Imperii: Die neue Politik Friedrich Barbarossas, 1152-1159.
A. Waas, Heinrich V.: Gestalt und Verhängnis des letzten salischen Kaisers.
F. Böhm, Das Bild Friedrich Barbarossas und seines Kaisertums in den ausländischen Quellen seiner Zeit.
I. Schnack, Richard von Cluny, seine Chronik und sein Kloster in den Anfängen der Kirchenspaltung von 1159.
I. Friedländer, Die päpstlichen Legaten in Deutschland und Italien am Ende des XII. Jahrhundert.
F. Hausmann, Reichskanzlei und Hofkapelle Unter Heinrich V. und Konrad III.
G. Duncken, Die politische Wirksamkeit der päpstlichen Legaten in der Zeit des Kampfes zwischen Kaisertum und Papsttum in Oberitalien unter Friedrich I.
H. Pahncke, Geschichte der Bischöfe Italiens deutscher Nations von 951-1254.
A. Hauck, Kirchengeschichte Deutschlands, IV, 3-324.
J. Haller, Das Papsttum: Idee und Wirklichkeit, III.
E. Orthbandt, Die Zeit der Staufer.

THE CONCEPT OF EMPIRE.

J. Bryce, The Holy Roman Empire.   [The classic but long out-dated introduction
   to the subject.]
R. Folz, The Concept of Empire in Western Europe From the Fifth to the
   Fourteenth Century.
G. Barraclough, The Mediaeval Empire: Idea and Reality.
F. Heer, The Holy Roman Empire.
W. Ullmann, "Reflections on the Mediaeval Empire," Transactions of the Royal
   Historical Society, Fifth Series, 14 (1964), 89-108.
J. A. Brundage, "Widukind of Corvey and the 'Non-Roman' Imperial Idea,"
   Mediaeval Studies, 22 (1960), 15-26.
M. Bloch, "The Empire and the Idea of Empire Under the Hohenstaufen," Land and
   Work in Mediaeval Europe, pp. 1-43.
R. Buchner, "Der Titel rex Romanorum in deutschen Königsurkunden des 11. Jahr-
   hunderts," Deutsches Archiv, 19 (1963), 327-338.
A. Diehl, "Heiliges römisches Reich deutscher Nation," Hist. Zeit., 156
   (1937), 457-484.
R. Holtzmann, "Der Weltherrschaftsgedanke des mittelalterlichen Kaisertums und
   die Souveränität der europäischen Staaten," ibid., 159 (1939), 251-264.
C. Erdmann, "Das ottonische Reich als imperium Romanum," Deutsches Archiv, 6
   (1943), 412-441.
E. E. Stengel, "Kaisertitel und Souveränitätsidee: Studien zur Vorgeschichte
   des modernen Staatsbegriffs," ibid., 3 (1939), 1-56.
F. Rörig, "Heinrich IV. und der 'Westherrschaftsanspruch' des mittelalterlichen
   Kaisertums," ibid., 7 (1944), 200-203.
E. E. Stengel, Abhandlungen und Untersuchungen zur Geschichte des Kaiser-
   gedankens im Mittelalter.
P. E. Schramm, Kaiser, Rom und Renovatio: Studien zur Geschichte des römischen
   Erneuerungsgedankens vom Ende des karolingischen Reiches bis zum
   Investiturstreit.
E. Nellmann, Die Reichsidee in deutschen Dichtung der Salier und frühen
   Stauferzeit.
W. Smidt, Deutsches Königtum und deutscher Staat des Hochmittelalters während
   und unter dem Einfluß der italischen Heerfahrten.
U. Allers, The Concept of Empire in German Romanticism and its Influence on the
   National Assembly at Frankfurt, 1848-1849.

FEUDALISM AND ITS DIVERGENT TENDENCIES.

Lordship and Community in Medieval Europe: Selected Readings, ed. F. L.
   Cheyette, pp. 12-61, 128-136, 198-209, 217-221.
F. L. Ganshof, Feudalism.
M. Bloch, Feudal Society.
S. Painter, Feudalism and Liberty.
H. Mitteis, The State in the Middle Ages: A Comparative Constitutional History
   of Feudal Europe, trans. by H. F. Orton.
B. D. Lyon, From Fief to Indenture: The Transition from Feudal to Non-Feudal
   Contract in Western Europe.
J. W. Thompson, Feudal Germany, pp. 232-337.

T. Evergates, Feudal Society in the Bailliage of Troyes Under the Counts of Champagne, 1152-1284.
E. A. R. Brown, "The Tyranny of a Construct: Feudalism and Historians of Medieval Europe," American Historical Review, 79 (1974), 1063-1088.
H. A. Cronne, "The Salisbury Oath," History, 19 (1934-35), 248-252.
K. B. McFarlane, "Bastard Feudalism," Bulletin of the Institure of Historical Research, 20 (1943-1945), 161-180.
B. S. Bachrach, "Enforcement of the Forma Fidelitatis: The Techniques Used by Fulk Nerra, Count of the Angevins (987-1040)," Speculum, 59 (Oct. 1984), 796-819.
H. Mitteis, Lehnrecht und Staatsgewalt.
W. Kienast, "Lehnrecht und Staatsgewalt im Mittelalter," Hist. Zeit., CLVIII (1938), 3-51.
R. Boutruche, Seigneurie et féodalité.
E. Perroy, La féodalité en France du Xe au XIIe siècle.
H. Spangenberg, Vom Lehnstaat zum Ständestaat.

THE HOHENSTAUFEN AND FEUDALISM.

O. Freiherr von Dungern, "Constitutional Reorganization and Reform under the Hohenstaufen," Mediaeval Germany, ed. G. Barraclough, II, 203-233.
H. Mitteis, "Feudalism and the German Constitution," ibid, II, 235-279.
P. Munz, Frederick Barbarossa: A Study in Medieval Politics.
P. Munz, "Frederick Barbarossa and Henry the Lion in 1176," Hist. Stud.: Australia and New Zealand, 12 (1965), 1-21.
M. Bloch, "A Problem in Comparative History: The Administrative Classes in France and in Germany," Land and Work in Mediaeval Europe, pp. 82-123.
K. Hampe, "Heinrichs des Löwen Sturz im politisch-historischer Beurteilung," Hist. Zeit., 109 (1912), 49-82.
F. Güterbock, Der Prozeß Heinrichs des Löwen.
E. E. Stengel, "Zum Prozeß Heinrichs des Löwen," Deutsches Archiv, 5 (1942), 493-510.
T. Mayer et al., Kaisertum und Herzogsgewalt im Zeitalter Friedrichs I.
R. Schmidt, "Heinrich der Löwe: Seine Stellung in der inneren und auswärtigen Politik Deutschlands," Hist. Zeit., 154 (1936), 241-284.
H. Meyer, "Bürgerfreiheit und Herrschergewalt unter Heinrich dem Löwen," ibid., 147 (1932), 277-319.
W. Ohnsorge, "Die Byzanzpolitik Friedrich Barbarossas und der 'Landesverrat' Heinrichs des Löwen," Deutsches Archiv, 6 (1943), 118-149.
K. F. Krieger, "Die königliche Lehngerichtsbarkeit im Zeitalter der Staufer," ibid., 26 (1971), 400-433.
J.-L. Kupper, "La politique des ducs de Zähringen entre la Moselle et la mer du Nord dans la seconde moitié du XIIe siècle," Moyen Age, 78 (1972), 427-466.
G. Baaken, "Recht und Macht in der Politik der Staufer," Hist. Zeit., 221 (1975), 553-570.
K. Bosl, Die Reichsministerialität der Salier und Staufer.   (2 vols.)
W. Goez, Der Leihezwang.
R. Hildebrand, Der sächsische 'Staat' Heinrichs des Löwen.
E. Gronen, Die Machtpolitik Heinrichs des Löwen und sein Gegensatz gegen das Kaisertum.

D. von Gladiss, Beiträge zur Geschichte der staufischen Reichsministerialität.
H. Büttner, Staufer und Zähringer im politischen Kräftespiel zwischen Bodensee
   und Genfersee während des 12. Jahrhunderts.
[Thompson and Mitteis as above.]

ANGEVIN ENGLAND TO MAGNA CARTA.

A. L. Poole, From Domesday Book to Magna Carta.
W. L. Warren, Henry II.
A. R. Kelly, Eleanor of Aquitaine and the Four Kings.
J. A. Brundage, Richard Lion Heart: A Biography.
J. T. Appleby, England Without Richard.
E. J. Kealey, Roger of Salisbury: Viceroy of England.
C. R. Young, Hubert Walter: Lord of Canterbury and Lord of England.
C. R. Cheney, Hubert Walter.
J. T. Appleby, John, King of England.
S. Painter, The Reign of King John.
Z. N. Brooke, The English Church and the Papacy from the Conquest to the Reign
   of John.
F. M. Powicke, Stephen Langton.
F. Thompson, Magna Carta: Its Role in the Making of the English Constitution,
   1300-1629.
S. E. Thorne et al., The Great Charter: Four Essays on Magna Carta and the
   History of Our Liberty.
W. F. Swindler, Magna Carta: Legend and Legacy.
J. W. Alexander, "The Becket Controversy in Recent Historiography," Journal of
   British Studies, 9 (1970), 1-26.
V. H. Galbraith, "Good Kings and Bad Kings in Medieval English History,"
   History, New Series, 30 (1945), 119-132.
C. W. Hollister, "King John and the Historians," Journal of British Studies,
   1 (1961), 1-19.
W. Ullmann, "Arthur's Homage to King John," English Historical Review, 94
   (Apr. 1979), 356-64.

THE TWELFTH CENTURY RENAISSANCE.

C. H. Haskins, The Renaissance of the Twelfth Century.
C. Morris, The Discovery of the Individual, 1050-1200.
R. W. Southern, Medieval Humanism and Other Studies.
H. Waddell, The Wandering Scholars: The Life and Art of the Lyric Poets of the
   Latin Middle Ages.
G. R. Evans, Anselm and a New Generation.
W. Ullmann, Medieval Foundations of Renaissance Humanism.
R. L. Benson, and G. Constable with C. D. Lanham (eds.) Renaissance and
   Renewal in the Twelfth Century. Papers presented at a conference marking
   the 50th anniversary of the publication of Charles Homer Haskins's
   Renaissance of the Twelfth Century and held in Cambridge, Mass., Nov.
   26-29, 1977.
U. T. Holmes, Jr., Daily Living in the Twelfth Century: Based on the
   Observations of Alexander Neckam in London and Paris.

Twelfth-century Europe and the Foundations of Modern Society, ed. M. Clagett,
   G. Post and R. Reynolds.
L. Genicot, "On the Evidence of the Growth of Population in the West from the
   Eleventh to the Thirteenth Century," Change in Medieval Society, ed. S.
   Thrupp, pp. 14-29.
H. Gibb, "The Influence of Islamic Culture on Medieval Europe," ibid., pp.
   155-167.
J. B. Ross, "A Study of Twelfth-Century Interest in the Antiquities of Rome,"
   Medieval and Historiographical Essays in Honor of James Westfall Thompson,
   ed. J. L. Cate and E. N. Anderson, pp. 302-321.
R. W. Southern, "The Place of England in the Twelfth-Century Renaissance,"
   History, 45 (1960), 201-216.
J. F. Benton, "The Court of Champagne as a Literary Center," Speculum, 36
   (1961), 551-591.
J. H. M. McCash, "Marie de Champagne and Eleanor of Aquitaine: A Relationship
   Reexamined," ibid., 54 (1979), 698-711.
C. W. Bynum, "Did the Twelfth Century Discover the Individual?"
   Journal of Ecclesiastical History, 31 (Jan. 1980), 1-17.
A. J. Denomy, "Concerning the Accessibility of Arabic Influences to the
   Earliest Provencal Troubadours," Mediaeval Studies, 15 (1953), 147-158.
A. J. Denomy, "An Inquiry into the Origins of Courtly Love," ibid., 6 (1944),
   175-260.
J. C. Moore, "'Courtly Love': A Problem of Terminology," Journal of the
   History of Ideas, 40 (Oct.-Dec. 1979), 621-32.
T. Stiefel, "The Heresy of Science: A Twelfth-Century Conceptual
   Revolution," Isis, 68 (Sept. 1977), 347-62.
R. Witt, "Medieval 'Ars Dictaminis' and the Beginnings of Humanism: A
   New Construction of the Problem," Renaissance Quarterly, 35 (Spring 1982),
   1-35.
R. M. Thomson, "England and the Twelfth-Century Renaissance," Past & Present,
   101 (Nov. 1983), 3-21.
L. T. Topsfield, Troubadours and Love.
J. Lindsay, The Troubadours and Their World of the Twelfth and Thirteenth
   Centuries.
J. W. Baldwin, Masters, Princes, and Merchants: The Social Views of Peter the
   Chanter and His Circle.   (2 Vols.)
M. Seidlmayer, Currents of Mediaeval Thought With Special Reference to Germany.
N. F. Partner, Serious Entertainments: The Writing of History in Twelfth-
   Century England.
B. Stock, The Implications of Literacy: Written Language and Models of
   Interpretation in the Eleventh and Twelfth Centuries.
C. W. Bynum, Docere Verbo et Exempla: An Aspect of Twelfth-Century
   Spirituality.
A. V. Murray, Abelard and St. Bernard: A Study in Twelfth-Century Modernism.
Wine, Women and Song: Medieval Latin Student Songs Now First Translated into
   English Verse, by J. A. Symonds.
A. Fourrier, L'Humanisme médiévale dans les littératures romanes du XIIe au
   XIVe siècles.
O. Cartellieri, Abt Suger von Saint-Denis, 1081-1151.
J. Flori, "La notion de Chevalerie dans les Chansons de Geste du XIIe
   siècle: Etude historique du vocabulaire," Moyen Age, 81 (no. 2, 1975),
   211-244.

P. Lehmann, "Die Vielgestalt des zwölften Jahrhunderts," Hist. Zeit., 178
    (1954), 225-250.
A. Borst, "Abälard und Bernhard,"ibid., 186 (1958), 497-526.
N. M. Häring, "Zur Geschichte der Schulen von Poitiers im 12. Jahrhundert,"
    Archiv für Kulturgeschichte, 47 (1965), 23-47.
F. von Bezold, Das Fortleben der antiken Götter im mittelalterlichen
    Humanismus.

TRADE AND COMMERCE IN THE MIDDLE AGES.

R.-H. Bautier, The Economic Development of Medieval Europe.
H. L. Adelson, Medieval Commerce.
A. R. Lewis, Naval Power and Trade in the Mediterranean,
A. R. Lewis, The Northern Seas.
P. Dollinger, The German Hansa.
J. A. Gade, The Norwegian Control of Norwegian Commerce During the Late Middle
    Ages.
M. K. James, Studies in the Medieval Wine Trade.
T. H. Lloyd, The English Wool Trade in the Middle Ages.
S. D. Goitein, A Mediterranean Society: The Jewish Communities of the Arab
    World as Portrayed in the Documents of the Cairo Geniza.   (2 vols.)
Essays in Economic History, ed. E. M. Carus-Wilson, Vol. I.
O. Cippola, "Currency Depreciation in Medieval Europe," Change in Medieval
    Society, ed. S. L. Thrupp, pp 227-236.
A. L. Udovich, "At the Origins of Western Commenda: Islam, Israel, Byzantium?"
    Speculum, 37 (1962), 198-207.
M. Bloch, "Natural Economy or Money Economy: A Pseudo-Dilemma," Land and Work
    in Medieval Europe, pp. 230-243.
M. Bloch, "The Problem of Gold in the Middle Ages," ibid., pp. 186-229.
J. F. McGovern, "The Rise of New Economic Attitudes - Economic Humanism,
    Economic Nationalism - During the Later Middle Ages and the Renaissance,
    A.D. 1200-1550," Traditio, 26 (1970), 217-253.
R. K. Barlow, "The Development of Business Techniques Used at the Fairs of
    Champagne From the End of the Twelfth Century to the Middle of the
    Thirteenth Century," Studies in Medieval and Renaissance History, 8
    (1971), 3-52.
A. R. Lewis, "Medieval Social and Economic History as Viewed by North
    American Medievalists," Journal of Economic History, 35 (Sept. 1975),
    630-634.
R. W. Unger, "Warships and Cargo Ships in Medieval Europe," Technology
    and Culture, 22 (Apr. 1981), 233-252.
M. Eckoldt, "Navigation on Small Rivers in Central Europe in Roman and
    Medieval Times," Int. J. Nautical Archaeol., 13 (Feb. 1984), 3-10.
W. von Stromer, "Nuremberg in the International Economics of the Middle Ages,"
    Business History Review, 44 (1970), 210-225.
G. S. Harrison, "The Hanseatic League in Historical Interpretation," Historian,
    33 (1971), 385-397.
U. Dirlmeier, Mittelalterliche Hoheitsträger im wirtschaftlichen Wettbewerb.
Cambridge Economic History of Europe, II, III.
A Source Book for Medieval Economic History, ed. R. C. Cave and H. H. Coulson.
Y. Renouard, "Le grand commerce des vins de Gascogne au moyen âge," Rev.
    hist, CCXXI (1959), 261-304.

MUNICIPAL ORIGINS AND URBAN SOCIETY.

C. Stephenson, Borough and Town. [The first chapter provides a useful survey of the older theories on the much-debated subject of medieval town origins.]

J. Tait, The Mediaeval English Borough: Studies on Its Origins and Constitutional History. [Shows that Stephenson's generalizations are not fully applicable to England.]

H. Pirenne, Medieval Cities.

H. Pirenne, Belgian Democracy: Its Early History.

The Medieval City, ed. H. A. Miskimin, D. Herlihy and A. Udovitch.

F. Rörig, The Medieval Town. [Use with caution.]

P. Strait, Cologne in the Twelfth Century.

D. M. Nicholas, "Medieval Urban Origins in Northern Continental Europe: State of Research and Some Tentative Conclusions," Studies in Medieval and Renaissance History, 6 (1969), 55-114.

F. Rörig, "Heinrich der Löwe und die Grundung Lübecks: Grundsätzliche Erörterung zur städtischen Ostsiedlung," Deutsches Archiv, 1 (1937), 408-456.

E. Coornaert, "Les ghildes médiévales," Rev. hist., 199 (1948), 22-55, 208-243.

C. Goehrke, "Die Anfänge des mittelalterlichen Städtewesens in eurasischer Perspektive," Saeculum, 31 (1980), 194-220, 221-239.

A. Luchaire, Les communes francaises à l'époque des Capétiens directs.

H. Planitz, Die deutsche Stadt im Mittelalter.

Die Stadt des Mittelalters, ed. C. Haase. (3 vols.)

W. Ebel, Der Bürgereid als Geltungsgrund und Gestaltungsprinzip des deutschen mittelalterlichen Stadtrechts.

J. Bärmann, Die Städtegründungen Heinrichs des Löwen und die Stadtverfassung des 12. Jahrhunderts.

R. Pernoud, Les villes marchandes aux XIVe et XVe siècles.

R. Sprandel, "Die Handwerker in den nordwestdeutschen Städten des Mittelalters," Hansische Geschichtsblätter, LXXXVI (1968), 37-62.

SERFDOM AND THE MARKGENOSSENSCHAFT THEORY.

C. Stephenson, "The Problem of the Common Man in Early Medieval Europe," American Historical Review, 51 (1946), 419-439.

N. D. Fustel de Coulanges, The Origin of Property in Land.

W. J. Bossenbrook, "Justus Möser's Approach to History," Medieval and Historiographical Essays in Honor of James Westfall Thompson, ed. Cate and Anderson, pp. 397-422.

Cambridge Economic History of Europe, I, esp. pp. 224-277.

M. Bloch, French Rural History.

E. Le Roy Ladurie, The Peasants of Languedoc.

W. O. Ault, Open-Field Farming in Medieval England: A Study of Village By-Laws.

C. J. Dahlmann, The Open Field System and Beyond: A Property Rights Analysis of an Economic Institution.

Z. Razi, "The Toronto School's Reconstitution of Medieval Peasant Society: A Critical View," Past and Present, 85 (1979), 141-157.

Z. Razi, "Family, Land, and the Village Community in Later Medieval
   England," Past & Present, 93 (Nov. 1981), 3-36.
H. Grundmann, "Freiheit als religiöses, politisches und persönliches Postulat
   im Mittelalter," Hist. Zeit., 233 (1957), 23-53.
G. Grosch, Markgenossenschaft und Grossgrundherrschaft im früheren Mittelalter.
F. Zimmermann, Die Weistümer und der Ausbau der Landeshoheit in der Kurpfalz.
S. Epperlein, Bauernbedrückung und Bauernwiderstand im hohen Mittelalter.
A. Dopsch, Die freien Marken in Deutschland: Beitrag zur Agrar- und
   Sozialgeschichte des Mittelalters.
A. Dopsch, Herrschaft und Bauer in der deutschen Kaiserzeit.
K. S. Bader, Studien zur Verfassungsgeschichte des mittelalterlichen Dorfes
   (3 vols.)
F. Lütge, Studien zur Sozial= und Wirtschaftsgeschichte: Gesammelte
   Abhandlungen.
G. von Below, Geschichte der deutschen Landwirtschaft des Mittelalters in ihren
   Grundzügen, ed. by F. Lütge.

LAND RECLAMATION AND PEASANT EMANCIPATION: THE LOW COUNTRIES.

B. Lyon, "Medieval Real Estate Developments and Freedom," American Historical
   Review, 63 (1957), 47-61.
S. J. Fockema Andreae, "Embanking and Drainage Authorities in the Netherlands
   During the Middle Ages," Speculum, 27 (1952), 158-167.
B. H. Slicher van Bath, The Agrarian History of Western Europe, 500-1850.
A. M. Lambert, The Making of the Dutch Landscape: A Historical Geography of
   the Netherlands.
H. Pirenne, Histoire de Belgique, I.
J. F. Niermeyer, "De vroegste berichten omtrent bedijking in Nederland,"
   Tijdschrift voor econmomische en sociale geografie, 49 (1958), 226-231.
G. H. Kurtz, "De oudste dijkbrieven voor de Lekdijkscolleges," Tijdschrift
   voor geschiedenis, 50 (1935), 276-292.
I. H. Gosses, "De vorming van het graafschap Holland," Verspreide Geschriften,
   ed. F. Gosses and J. F. Niermeyer, pp. 239-344.
C. A. van Kalveen, "Het polderdistrict Veluwe in de middeleeuwen," Bijdragen en
   Mededelingen van het Historisch Genootschap, 79 (1965), 219-334.
S. J. Fockema Andreae, Het Hoogheemraadschap van Rijnland: Zijn Recht en zijn
   Bestuur van den vroegsten Tijd tot 1857.
S. J. Fockema Andreae, Willem I, graaf van Holland, 1203-1222, en de Hollandse
   hoogheemraadschappen.
S. J. Fockema Andreae, Studiën over Waterschapsgeschiedenis. (7 vols.)
J. F. Niermeyer, Delft en Delftland: Hun Oorsprung en vroegste geschiedenis.
L. A. Warnkönig, Flandrische Staats- und Rechtsgeschichte bis zum Jahre 1305.
   (3 vols.)   [Valuable documentary appendices.]
H. Halbertsma, Terpen tussen Vlie en Eems.   (2 vols.)
I. H. Gosses, De rechterlijke organisatie van Zeeland in de middeleeuwen.
I. H. Gosses, Handboek tot de staatkundige geschiedenis der Nederlanden,
   I: De Middeleeuwen.
Das Rüstringer Recht, ed. W. J. Buma and W. Ebel.

RECLAMATION AND EMANCIPATION: GERMANY IN THE TWELFTH CENTURY.

T. Mayer, "The State of the Dukes of Zähringen,: Mediaeval Germany, 911-1250,
    ed. G. Barraclough, II, 175-202.
J. W. Thompson, Feudal Germany, II, 545-579.
W. Müller-Wille, "Die Hagenhufendörfer in Schaumburg-Lippe," Petermanns
    Geographische Mitteilungen, 90 (1944), 245-247.
T. Mayer, "Königtum und Gemeinfreiheit im frühen Mittelalter," Deutsches
    Archiv, 6 (1943), 329-362.
H. K. Schulze, "Rodungsfreiheit und Königsfreiheit: Zu Genese und Kritik
    neuerer verfassungsgeschichtlicher Theorien," Hist. Zeit., 219 (1974),
    529-550.
T. Mayer, Mittelalterliche Studien: Gesammelte Aufsätze.

THE WENDISH CRUSADE AND THE NORTHEASTERN GERMAN FRONTIER.

G. Barraclough, The Origins of Modern Germany, pp. 249-281.
J. W. Thompson, Feudal Germany, II, 387-528.
. Dvornik, The Slavs: Their Early History and Civilization, pp. 293-311.
F. Carsten, The Origins of Prussia.
E. Christiansen, The Northern Crusades: The Baltic and the Catholic Frontier,
    1100-1525.
W. Urban, The Prussian Crusade.
W. Urban, The Baltic Crusade.
D. Seward, "The Teutonic Knights," History Today, 20 (1970), 859-866.
K. Slaski, "North-Western Slavs in Baltic Sea Trade from the VIIIth to
    the XIIIth Century," Journal of European Economic History, 8 (Spring
    1979), 83-107.
R. Spence, "Pope Gregory IX and the Crusade in the Baltic," Catholic
    Historical Review, 69 (Jan. 1983), 1-19.
H. Schreiber, Teuton and Slav: The Struggle for Central Europe.
The Cambridge History of Poland from the Origins to Sobieski.
Cambridge Economic History of Europe, I, 361-397.
W. Urban, "The Organization of Defense of the Livonian Frontier in the
    Thirteenth Century," Speculum, 48 (1973), 525-532.
W. Schlesinger, "Die geschichtliche Stellung der mittelalterlichen deutschen
    Ostbewegung," Hist. Zeit., 183 (1957), 517-542.
R. Kötzschke and W. Ebert, Geschichte der ostdeutschen Kolonisation.
H. Conrad, Die mittelalterliche Besiedlung des deutschen Ostens und das
    deutsche Recht.
W. Schlesinger, Mitteldeutsche Beiträge zur deutschen Verfassungsgeschichte des
    Mittelalters.
R. Kötzschke, Deutsche und Slawen in mitteldeutschen Osten: Ausgewählte
    Aufsätze, ed. W. Schlesinger.
M. Bünding, Das Imperium Christianum und die deutschen Ostkriege vom zehnten
    bis zum zwölften Jahrhundert.
E. Caspar, Hermann von Salza und die Gründung des Deutschordenstaates in
    Preussen.
Heidenmission und Kreuzzugsgedanke im der deutschen Ostpolitik des Mittel-
    alters, ed. H. Beumann.
Die deutsche Ostsiedlung im Mittelalter, ed. K. H. Quirin.
Quellen zur Geschichte des deutschen Ordens, ed. W. Hubatsch.
Helmold of Bosau, Chronicle of the Slavs, trans. F. J. Tschan.

NEW TRENDS IN MONASTICISM.

B. K. Lackner, The Eleventh-Century Background of Citeaux.
W. Williams, Saint Bernard of Clairvaux.
Bernard of Clairvaux: Studies presented to Dom Jean Leclercq.
A. A. King, Citeaux and Her Elder Daughters.
L. J. Lekai, The Cistercians: Ideals and Reality.
N. F. Cantor, "The Crisis of Western Monasticism, 1050-1130," American
   Historical Review, 66 (1960), 47-67.
R. Roehl, "Plan and Reality in a Medieval Monastic Economy: The Cistercians,"
   Studies in Medieval and Renaissance History, 9 (1972), 83-113.
M. W. Bloomfield, "Joachim of Flora," Traditio, 13 (1957), 249-309.
B. McGinn, "The Abbot and the Doctors: Scholastic Reactions to the Radical
   Eschatology of Joachim of Fiore," Church History, 40 (1971), 30-47.
C. W. Bynum, "The Cistercian Conception of Community: An Aspect of
   Twelfth-Century Spirituality," Harvard Theological Review, 68 (July-Oct.
   1975), 273-86.
M. Reeves, The Influence of Prophecy in the Later Middle Ages: A Study in
   Joachimism.
D. C. West and S. Zimdars-Swartz, Joachim of Fiore: A Study in Spiritual
   Perception and History.
E. A. Armstrong, Saint Francis, Nature Mystic: The Derivation and Significance
   of the Nature Stories in the Franciscan Legend.
M. E. Almedingen, Francis of Assisi.
J. Moorman, A History of the Franciscan Order: From Its Origins to the
   Year 1517.
E. R. Daniel, The Franciscan Concept of Mission in the High Middle Ages.
M. D. Lambert, Franciscan Poverty: The Doctrine of the Absolute Poverty of
   Christ and the Apostles in the Franciscan Order, 1210-1323.
B. D. Hill, English Cistercian Monasteries and Their Patrons in the Twelfth
   Century.
W. Braunfels, Monasteries of Western Europe: The Architecture of the Orders.
M. Volke, "Zu einigen Aspekten der Wirtschaftspolitik deutscher
   Zisterzienserkloster während des 12. und 13. Jahrhunderts," Jahrbuch für
   Wirtschaftsgeschichte, 1979, II, 169-182.
I. W. Frank, "Die Spannung zwischen Ordensleben und wissenschaftlicher Arbeit
   im frühen Dominikanerorden," Archiv für Kulturgeschichte, 49 (1967),
   164-207.
Chartes et documents concernant l'abbaye de Cîteaux, 1098-1182, ed. J.Marilier.

MEDIEVAL HERESY AND THE INQUISITION.

M. Lambert, Medieval Heresy: Popular Movements from Bogomil to Hus.
H. C. Lea, The Inquisition of the Middle Ages.
A. S. Turberville, Mediaeval Heresy and the Inquisition.
S. Runciman, The Medieval Manichee.
J. Strayer, The Albigensian Crusade.
D. Obolensky, The Bogomils.
W. L. Wakefield, Heresy, Crusade, and Inquisition in Southern France, 1100-
   1250.
R. E. Lerner, The Heresy of the Free Spirit in the Later Middle Ages.

R. I. Moore, "The Origins of Medieval Heresy," History, New Series, 55 (1970),
     21-36.
C. N. L. Brooke, "Heresy and Religious Sentiment, 1000-1250," Bulletin of the
     Institute of Historical Research, 41 (1968), 115-131.
A. P. Evans, "Hunting Subversion in the Middle Ages," Speculum, 33 (1958),
     1-22.
D. Walther, "A Survey of Recent Research on the Albigensian Cathari," Church
     History, 34 (1965), 146-177.
R. Abels & E. Harrison, "The Participation of Women in Languedocian
     Catharism," Mediaeval Studies, 41 (1979), 215-251.
J. Russell, "Interpretations of the Origins of Medieval Heresy," Mediaeval
     Studies, 15 (1963), 26-53.
D. Berger, "Christian Heresy and Jewish Polemic in the Twelfth and
     Thirteenth Centuries," Harvard Theological Review, 68 (July-Oct. 1975),
     287-303.
N. J. Housley, "Politics and Heresy in Italy: Anti-Heretical Crusades,
     Orders and Confraternities, 1200-1500," Journal of Ecclesiastical History,
     33 (Apr. 1982), 193-208.
R. E. Lerner, "The Uses of Heterodoxy: The French Monarchy and Unbelief in the
     Thirteenth Century," French Historical Studies, 4 (1965), 198-202.
D. Radcliff-Umstead, "The Catharists and the Failure of Community,"
     Mediaevalia, 1 (no. 2, 1977), 63-87.
G. W. Davis, The Inquisition at Albi.
J. B. Russell, Witchcraft in the Middle Ages.
E. Le Roy Ladurie, Montaillou: The Promised Land of Error.
H. Grundmann, "Ketzerverhöre des Spätmittelalters als quellenkritische
     Problem," Deutsches Archiv, 21 (1965), 519-575.
L. Christiani, " La tolérance et l'intolérance de l'Eglise en matiere doctrinale
     depuis les premiers siècles jusqu'à nos jours," Cahiers d'histoire
     mondiale, 5 (1959-60), 71-93.
H. Taviani, "Le mariage dans l'hérésie de l'an mil," Annales, 32
     (Nov.-Dec. 1977), 1074-89.
C. Moeller, "Les buchers et les auto-da-fé de l'inquisition depuis le moyen
     âge," Rev. d'hist. eccl., XIV (1913), 720-751; XV (1914), 50-69.
J. Musy, "Mouvements populaires et hérésies au XIe siècle en France,"
     Rev. hist., 253 (1975), 33-76.
F. Sanjek, "Le rassemblement hérétique de Saint-Felix-de-Caraman (1167) et les
     églises cathares au XIIe siècle," ibid., 67 (1972), 767-799.
A. Pales-Gobilliard, "Le Catharisme dans le comté de Foix, des origines
     au début du XIVe siècle," Revue de l'histoire des religions, 189 (Apr.
     1976), 181-200.
A. Borst, "Neue Funde und Forschungen zur Geschichte der Katharer," Hist.
     Zeit., 174 (1952), 17-30.
P. Braun, "Die Bekämpfung der Ketzerei in Deutschland durch die Päpste bis zum
     Laterankonzil von 1215," Archiv für Kulturgeschichte, 9 (1911), 475-481.
M. Ligniéres, L'hérésie albigeois et la croisade.
J. J. I. Döllinger, Beiträge zur Sektengeschichte des Mittelalters.
L. Förg, Die Ketzerverfolgung in Deutschland unter Gregor IX.
A. Borst, Die Katharer.
Y. Dossat, Les crises de l'Inquisition toulousaine au XIIIe siècle.
Heresies of the High Middle Ages, trans. W. Wakefield and A. P. Evans.

Documents pour servir à l'histoire de l'Inquisition dans le Languedoc,
    ed. C. Dousais.
The Summa Contra Haereticos Ascribed to Praepositus of Cremona, ed. J. N.
    Garvin and J. A. Corbett.

THE FRENCH NATIONAL MONARCHY.

R. Fawtier, The Capetian Kings of France.
F. M. Powicke, The Loss of Normandy.
F. C. Pegues, The Lawyers of the Last Capetians.
C. T. Wood, The French Apanages and the Capetian Monarchy, 1224-1328.
T. N. Bisson, Assemblies and Representation in Languedoc in the Thirteenth
    Century.
M. W. Labarge, Saint Louis: The Life of Louis IX of France.
G. J. Campbell, "The Protest of Saint Louis," Traditio, 15 (1959), 405-418.
G. Post, "Two Notes on Nationalism in the Middle Ages," ibid., 9 (1953),
    281-320.
E. A. R. Brown, "Taxation and Morality in the Thirteenth and Fourteenth
    Centuries: Conscience and Political Power and the Kings of France,"
    French Historical Studies, 8 (1973), 1-28.
A. W. Lewis, "The Capetian Apanages and the Nature of the French
    Kingdom," Journal of Medieval History, 2 (June 1976), 119-134.
J. Madaule, The Albigensian Crusade.   [Use with caution!]
M. Bloch, La France sous des deniers Capétiens, 1223-1328.
Y. Renouard, "Essai sur le rôle de l'empire angevin dans la formation de la
    France et de la civilisation francaise aux XIIe et XIIIe siècles,"
    Rev. hist., 195 (1945), 289-304.
F. Kern, Die Anfänge der französischen Ausdehnungepolitik bis zum Jahre 1308.
Histoire des institutions francaises au moyen âge, ed. F. Lot and R. Fawtier.
J. de Joinville, The Life of Saint Louis.

THE PAPACY AND THE EMPIRE IN THE THIRTEENTH CENTURY.

Innocent III: Vicar of Christ or Lord of the World? ed. J. M. Powell   (Heath)
    [A useful survey of some divergent interpretations.]
J. A. Watt, The Theory of Papal Monarchy in the Thirteenth Century.
L. E. Elliott-Binns, Innocent III.
J. Clayton, Pope Innocent III and His Times.
W. Ullmann, Medieval Papalism: The Political Theories of the Medieval
    Canonists.
B. Tierney, Origins of Papal Infallibility, 1150-1350: A Study on the Concepts
    of Infallibility, Sovereignty, and Tradition in the Middle Ages.
P. Andrewes, Frederick II of Hohenstaufen.
T. C. van Cleve, The Emperor Frederick II of Hohenstaufen: Immutator Mundi.
E. Kantorowicz, Frederick the Second, 1194-1250.
D. Abulafia, "Kantorowicz and Frederick II," History, 62 (June 1977),
    193-210.
F. Geldner, Konradin, das Opfer eines großen Traumes: Größe, Schuld und Tragik
    der Hohenstaufen.

J. C. Moore, "Count Baldwin IX of Flanders, Philip Augustus, and the Papal
    Power," Speculum, 37 (1962), 79-89.
J. W. Baldwin, "The Intellectual Preparations for the Canon of 1215 Against
    Ordeals," ibid., 36 (1961), 613-636.
J. A. Watt, "The Constitutional Law of the College of Cardinals: Hostiensis to
    Johannes Andreae," Mediaeval Studies, 33 (1971), 127-157.
D. L. D'Avray, "A Letter of Innocent III and the Idea of Infallibility,"
    Catholic Historical Review, 66 (July 1980), 417-421.
S. Runciman, The Sicilian Vespers.
Cambridge Medieval History, VI.
H. Tillmann, "Zur Frage des Verhältnisses von Kirche und Staat in Lehre und
    Praxis Papst Innocenz III.," Deutsches Archiv, 9 (1951-52), 136-181.
A.-D. von den Brincken, "Die Mongolen im Weltbild der Lateiner um die Mitte des
    13. Jahrhunderts, unter besonderer Berücksichtigung des 'Speculum
    Historiale' des Vincenz von Beauvais," Archiv für Kulturgeschichte, 57
    (1975), 117-140.
H. Marc-Bonnet, "Le Saint Siege et Charles d'Anjou sous Innocent IV et
    Alexandre IV (1245-1261)," Rev. hist., 200 (1948), 38-65.
F. Kempf, Papsttum und Kaisertum bei Innocenz III.
W. Neumann, Die deutschen Königswahlen und die päpstlichen Machtanspruch
    während des Interregnums.
K. Hampe, Urban IV. und Manfred (1261-1264).
K. Ganzer, Papsttum und Bistumsbesetzung in der Zeit von Gregor IX. bis
    Bonifaz VIII.: Ein Beitrag zur Geschichte der päpstlichen Reservationen.
J. Haller, Das Papsttum: Idee und Wirklichkeit, IV, V.
A. Hauck, Kirchengeschichte Deutschlands, IV, 684-949; V, 3-582.
Stupor Mundi: Zur Geschichte Friedrichs II. von Hohenstaufen, ed. G. Wolf.
Kaiser Friedrich II. in Briefen und Berichten seiner Zeit, ed. and trans. by
    K. J. Heinisch.

RECLAMATION AND EMANCIPATION IN THIRTEENTH CENTURY GERMANY.

There is no good treatment of this subject in the library. The closest thing
is F. D. C. von Cronhelm, "Historisches Bericht von den alten und neueren
Rechten und Gerichte in Holstein," Corpus Constitutionum Regio-Holsaticarum,
IV, 56-74, which was written in the middle of the eighteenth century. See also
E. Finder, Die Vierlande: Beiträge zur Geschichte, Landes- und Volkskunde
Niedersachsens, although this should be used with some caution. Some of the
readings listed under the headings dealing with reclamation and emancipation
in the Low Countries and in North Germany are relevant here also.

MEDIEVAL TECHNOLOGY AND SCIENCE.

L. T. White, Jr., Medieval Technology and Social Change.
J. Gimpel, The Medieval Machine: The Industrial Revolution of the Middle Ages.
Science in the Middle Ages, ed. D. C. Lindberg.
C. H. Haskins, Studies in the History of Mediaeval Science.
A. C. Crombie, Medieval and Early Modern Science.   (2 vols.)
M. Clagett, The Science of Mechanics in the Middle Ages.
L. Thorndyke, A History of Magic and Experimental Science.   (6 vols.)

S. C. Easton, Roger Bacon and His Search for a Universal Science.
A. C. Crombie, Robert Grosseteste and the Origins of Experimental Science.
A. Maier, On the Threshhold of Exact Science: Selected Writings of Anneliese
    Maier on Late Medieval Natural Philosophy. Ed. and trans. Steven D.
    Sargent.
M. Bloch, "Mediaeval 'Inventions'," Land and Work in Mediaeval Europe, pp. 169-
    185.
L. T. White, Jr., "Technology and Invention in the Middle Ages," Speculum, 15
    (1940), 141-159.
L. T. White, Jr., "Natural Science and Naturalistic Art in the Middle Ages,"
    American Historical Review, 52 (1947), 421-435.
L. T. White, Jr., "Technology Assessment from the Stance of a Medieval
    Historian," ibid., 79 (1974), 1-13.
L. T. White, Jr., "The Study of Medieval Technology, 1924-1974: Personal
    Reflections," Technology and Culture, 16 (Oct. 1975), 519-530.
J. A. Weisheipl, "Classification of the Sciences in Mediaeval Thought,"
    Mediaeval Studies, 27 (1965), 54-90.
J. F O'Brien, "Some Medieval Anticipations of Inertia," New Scholasticism,
    44 (1970), 345-371.
D. C. Lindberg, "Lines of Influence in Thirteenth-Century Optics: Bacon,
    Witelo, and Pecham," Speculum, 46 (1971), 66-83.
P. Marshall, "Nicole Oresme on the Nature, Reflection and Speed of Light,"
    Isis, 72 (Sept, 1981), 357-74.
M. R. McVaugh, "Quantified Medical Theory and Practice at Fourteenth-Century
    Montpellier," Bulletin of the History of Medicine, 43 (1969), 397-413.
E. Rosen, "The Invention of Eyeglasses," Journal of the History of Medicine,
    9 (1956), 13-46.
V. Ilardi, "Eyeglasses and Concave Lenses in Fifteenth-Century Florence and
    Milan: New Documents," Renaissance Quarterly, 29 (1976), 341-360.
K. B. Bales, "Nicole Oresme and Medieval Social Science: The 14th Century
    Debunker of Astrology Wrote an Early Monetary Treatise," Am. J. Ec.
    Sociol., 42 (Jan. 1983), 101-12.
E. Grant, "Celestial Matter: A Medieval and Galilean Cosmological Problem,"
    Journal of Medieval and Renaissance Studies, 13 (Fall 1983), 157-86.
J. McEvoy, "The Chronology of Robert Grosseteste's Writings on Nature and
    Natural Philosophy," Speculum, 58 (no. 3, July 1983), 614-655.
R. Dales, The Scientific Achievement of the Middle Ages.
M. Clagett, Archimedes in the Middle Ages.
D. Pearsall and E. Salter, Landscapes and Seasons of the Medieval World.
C. Wilson, William Heytesbury: Medieval Logic and the Rise of Mathematical
    Physics.
V. L. Bullough and B. Bullough, The Care of the Sick: The Emergence of Modern
    Nursing.
B. Gille, "Les developpements technologiques en Europe de 1100 à 1400," Cahiers
    d'histoire mondiale, 3 (1956), 63-108.
A. Maier, Zwei Grundproblem der scholastischen Naturphilosophie: Das Problem
    der intensiven Grosse; die Impetustheorie.
W. Ganzenmüller, Die Alchemie im Mittelalter.
A Source Book in Medieval Science, ed. E. Grant.

MEDIEVAL HIGHER EDUCATION.

H. Rashdall, The Universities of Europe in the Middle Ages.   (3 vols.)
A. L. Gabriel, Garlandia: Studies in the History of the Medieval University.
C. H. Haskins, The Rise of Universities.
A. B. Cobban, The Medieval Universities: Their Development and Organization.
J. W. Thompson, The Literacy of the Laity in the Middle Ages.
N. Orme, Emglish Schools in the Middle Ages.
B. Smalley, The Becket Conflict and the Schools: A Study in Intellectuals in
    Politics.
G. Leff, Paris and Oxford Universities in the Thirteenth and Fourteenth
    Centuries.
V. L. Bullough, The Development of Medicine as a Profession: The Contribution
    of the Medieval University to Modern Medicine.
J. C. Russell, "The Early Schools of Oxford and Cambridge," The Historian, 5
    (1943), 61-76.
G. L. Haskins, "The University of Oxford and the 'Jus ubique docendi',"
    English Historical Review, 56 (1961), 281-292.
B. Bischoff, "The Study of Foreign Languages in the Middle Ages," Speculum,
    36 (1961), 209-224.
J. T. Muckle, "Greek Works Translated Directly Into Latin Before 1350,"
    Mediaeval Studies, 4 (1942), 33-42; V (1943), 102-114.
J. A. Weisheipl, "Curriculum of the Faculty of Arts at Oxford in the Early
    Fourteenth Century," ibid., 26 (1964), 143-185.
L. Thorndyke, "Elementary and Secondary Education in the Middle Ages,"
    Speculum, 15 (1940), 400-408.
P. R. McKeon, "The Status of the University of Paris as Parens Scientiarum:
    An Episode in the Development of Its Autonomy," ibid., 39 (1964), 651-
    675.
L. DeMaitre, "Theory and Practice in Medical Education at the University of
    Montpellier in the Thirteenth and Fourteenth Centuries," Journal of the
    History of Medicine and Allied Sciences, 30 (Apr. 1975), 103-123.
H. Stehkämper, "Über die geschichtliche Größe Alberts des Großen: Ein
    Versuch," Historisches Jahrbuch, 102 (no. 1, 1982), 72-93.
P. Classen, "Die hohen Schulen und die Gesellschaft im 12. Jahrhundert,"
    Archiv für Kulturgeschichte, 48 (1966), 155-180.
P. Classen, "Zur Geschichte der 'Akademischen Freiheit', vornehmlich im Mittel-
    alter," Hist. Zeit., 232 (1981), 529-553.
P. Delhaye, "L'Organisation scolaire aux XIIe siècle." Traditio, 5 (1947),
    211-268.
Les Universités du Languedoc au XIIIe siècle.
J. Koch, Artes Liberales von der antiken Bildung zur Wissenschaft des
    Mittelalters.
University Records and Life in the Middle Ages, ed. L. Thorndyke.
Statuta collegii sapientiae, ed. J. Kerer.

NEW TRENDS IN POLITICS.

A. Brackmann, "The Beginnings of the National State in Mediaeval Germany and the Norman Monarchies," Mediaeval Germany, ed. G. Barraclough, II, 281-299.
J. R. Strayer, On the Medieval Origins of the Modern State.
G. Post, Studies in Medieval Legal Thought: Public Law and the State, 1100-1322.
W. Ullmann, The Individual and Society in the Middle Ages.
J. R. Strayer, The Reign of Philip the Fair.
J. B. Henneman, Royal Taxation in Fourteenth-Century France: The Captivity and Ranson of John II, 1356-1370.
E. L. Cox, The Eagles of Savoy: The House of Savoy in Thirteenth-Century Europe.
Universities in Politics: Case Studies From the Late Middle Ages and Early Modern Period, ed. J. W. Baldwin and R. A. Goldthwaite.
W. E. Brynteson, "Roman Law and Legislation in the Middle Ages," Speculum, 41 (1966), 420-437.
E. Lewis, "King Above Law? 'Quod principi placuit' in Bracton," ibid., 39 (1964), 240-269.
W. Ullmann, "The Development of the Mediaeval Idea of Sovereignty," English Historical Review, 64 (1949), 1-33.
E. Kantorowicz, "Mysteries of State: An Absolutist Concept and Its Late Medieval Origins," Harvard Theological Review, 48 (1955), 65-91.
E. A. R. Brown, "The Ceremonial of Royal Succession in Capetian France: The Funeral of Philip V," Speculum, 55 (1980), 266-293.
B.-A. Procquet de Haut-Jussé, "Une idée politique de Louis IX: La sujéction éclipse la vassalité," Rev. hist., 226 (1961), 383-398.
H. Angermeier, Königtum und Landfriede im deutschen Spätmittelalter.
H. Aubin, Die Entstehung der Landeshoheit nach niederrheinischen Quellen.

THE LATER MIDDLE AGES: 'WANING' AND LEGACY.

J. Huizinga, The Waning of the Middle Ages.
The Waning Middle Ages: An Exhibition of French and Netherlandish Art From 1350 to 1500 Commemorating the Fiftieth Anniversary of the Publication of The Waning of the Middle Ages by Johan Huizinga: Catalog by J. L. Schrader.
D. Hay, Europe in the Fourteenth and Fifteenth Centuries.
B. Z. Kadar, Merchants in Crisis: Genoese and Venetian Men of Affairs and the Fourteenth-Century Depression.
M. Seidlmayer, Currents of Mediaeval Thought With Special Reference to Germany.
E. B. Bax, German Society at the Close of the Middle Ages.
M. Mollat, The Popular Revolutions of the Late Middle Ages.
F. Oakley, The Western Church in the Later Middle Ages.
S. Ozment, The Age of Reform, 1250-1550: An Intellectual and Religious History of Late Medieval and Reformation Europe.
R. S. Gottfried, Epidemic Disease in Fifteenth-Century Europe: The Medical Response and the Demographic Consequences.
M. W. Dols, The Black Death in the Middle East.
R. S. Gottfried, The Black Death: Natural and Human Disaster in Medieval Europe.

R. Kieckhefer, European Witch Trials: Their Foundatin in Popular and Learned
     Culture, 1300-1500.
K. Cohen, Metamorphosis of a Death Symbol: The Transi Tomb in the Late Middle
     Ages and the Renaissance.
B. Tuchman, A. Distant Mirror: The Calamitous Fourteenth Century.
     [This may be the most widely read book ever written on the fourteenth
     century but, for the reservations of a medievalist, see the review by C.
     T. Wood, Speculum, 54 (1979), 430-435.]
N. J. G. Pounds, "Overpopulation in France and the Low Countries in the Later
     Middle Ages," Journal of Social History, 3 (1970), 225-247.
A. R. Lewis, "The Closing of the Medieval Frontier, 1250-1350," Speculum,
     33 (1958), 475-483.
H. S. Lucas, "The Great European Famine of 1315, 1316 and 1317," ibid., 5
     (1930), 343-377.
A. R. Bridbury, "Before the Black Death," Economic History Review, 30 (1977),
     393-410.
W. J. Courtenay, "The Effect of the Black Death on English Higher Education,"
     ibid., 55 (1980), 696-714.
R. Gyug, "The Effects and Extent of the Black Death of 1348: New Evidence for
     Clerical Mortality in Barcelona," Mediaeval Studies, 45 (1983), 385-98.
N. J. Mayhew, "Numismatic Evidence and Falling Prices in the Fourteenth
     Century," Economic History Review, 27 (1974), 1-15.
P. P. A. Biller, "Birth-Control in the West in the Thirteenth and Early
     Fourteenth Centuries," Past & Present, 94 (Feb. 1982), 3-26.
E. Pilz, "Die Wirtschaftskrise des Spätmittelalters," Vierteljahrschrift für
     Sozial- und Wirtschaftsgeschichte, 52 (1965), 347-367.
J. van Klaveren, "Die wirtschaftliche Auswirkung des Schwarzen Todes," ibid.,
     54 (1967), 187-202.
A. Borst, "Das Erdbeben von 1348: Ein historischer Beitrag zur
     Katastrophenforschung,", Historische Zeitschrift, 233 (1981), 529-569.
N. Bulst, "Der Schwarze Tod. Demographische, wirtschafts- und
     kulturgeschichtliche Aspekte der Pestkatastrophe von 1347-1352: Bilanz
     der neueren Forschung," Saeculum, 30 (no. 1, 1979), 45-67.
H. Rosenfeld, "Der Totentanz als europäischen Phänomen," Archiv für Kultur-
     geschichtre, 48 (1966), 54-83.
La danse macabre de 1485, pref. de P. Vaillant.
Villages désertés et histoire économique, XIe - XVIIIe siècle.

Europe in the High Middle Ages

I. Feudal Monarchy

N. Cantor, "The Interpretation of Medieval History" in V. Mudroch and
   G. Couse, Essays on the Reconstruction of Medieval History, 1-17
*R. Fawtier, The Capetian Kings of France, 1-26, 60-88 (ch. 4), 96-136
   (ch. 6)
P. Munz, Frederick Barbarossa, 3-43, 315-360
**B. Tierney, The Crisis of Church and State, 91-115
*D. C. Douglas, William the Conqueror, 181-210, 265-288, 367-376
*W. L. Warren, Henry II, 317-361, 399, 447-517
W. W. Kibler, Eleanor of Aquitaine, 9-24, 35-52
Leopold Genicot, "Recent Research on the Medieval Nobility," in the
   Medieval Nobility, ed. T. Reuter, 17-29

II. Economic Revival (11th and 12th centuries)

Robert Lopez, The Commercial Revolution of the Middle Ages, 85-167
Peasants, Knights, and Heretics, ed., R. Hilton, 10-56
R. H. Hilton, A Medieval Society, 88-166
A. Baker and R. Butlin, Studies of Field Systems in the British Isles,
   24-40, 619-656
E. Ennen, The Medieval Town, 1-16, 63-93

III. Cultural Revival (11th and 12th centuries)

**C. Young, The Twelfth Century Renaissance
*R. W. Southern, Medieval Humanism, 29-60, 86-104
C. Morris, The Discovery of the Individual, 1-19, 48-95, 158-167
H. Rashdall, The Universities, I, 271-343
A. B. Cobham, The Medieval Universities, 3-74, 196-217
M. T. Clanchy, From Memory to Written Record, 1-28, 149-201, 258-265

IV. The Medieval Church at Its Height

J. Powell, Innocent III
**B. Tierney, The Crisis of Church and State, 110-210
J. Leuschner, Germany in the Late Middle Ages, 25-41
D. Knowles, The Monastic Order in England, 448-471, 679-693
J. Moorman, A History of the Franciscan Order, 3-45, 188-204, 278-294
R. Finucane, Miracles and Pilgrims, 9-14, 113-126
H. C. Lea, The Inquisition of the Middle Ages, I, 399-476
W. Wakefield, Heresy, Crusade and Inquisition in Southern France 1100-1251,
   17-80, 237-257
**E. LeRoy Ladurie, Montaillou

V. Medieval Synthesis of Thought and Learning

**D. Knowles, The Evolution of Medieval Thought, 221-288
A. Maurer, "Medieval Philosophy and Its Historians" in V. Mudroch and G.
   Couse, Essays on the Reconstruction of Medieval History
T. Van Cleve, The Emperor Frederick II, 283-318, 531-540
*O. Von Simson, The Gothic Cathedral, 3-39, 50-58, 227-231
*E. Panofsky, Gothic Architecture and Scholasticism, all 88 pp.
P. Frankl, Gothic Architecture, 1-14, 217-242

VI. Representative Institutions

    A. Marongiu, Medieval Parliaments, 9-76, 95-127
    B. Lyon, A Constitutional and Legal History of England, 408-430, 535-561
    G. O. Sayles, The King's Parliament of England, 3-47, 70-93, 133-136

VII. End of Middle Ages

    *The Fontana Economic History of Europe, I, 25-68
    J. Hatcher, Plague, Population, and the English Economy, 1-73
    G. Fourquin, The Anatomy of Popular Rebellion, xi-xiv, 129-163
    B. Hanawalt, "The Female Felon in Fourteenth Century England," in Women
       in Medieval Society, ed. S. Stuard, 125-138
    **D. Knowles, The Evolution of Medieval Thought, 291-340
    *A. Kors & E. Peters, Witchcraft in Europe, 105-189
    G. Leff, The Dissolution of the Medieval Outlook, 1-31, 90-102, 118-147
    J. Leuschner, Germany in the Late Middle Ages, xiii-xxxii, 149-178

**To be purchased for this course.
*On reserve, but available also in paperback.

THE LATE MIDDLE AGES:
1250-1453
G57.1114

Penelope D. Johnson
New York Universit

Sept. 18   Introduction

Sept. 25   Edward Cheyney, The Dawn of a New Era 1250-1453.(Harper
            Torch). If unavailable, read Hay instead.
            Denys Hay, Europe in the Fourteenth and Fifteenth
            Centuries.(Longman).
            *W. K. Ferguson, Europe in Transition (1962).
            *J. Heers, L'occident aux XIV et XV siêcles (1972).

SOCIAL AND ECONOMIC ENVIRONMENT

Oct. 2   Harry Miskiman, The Economy of Early Renaissance Europe
          (Cambridge)
          C. M. Cipolla, "Currency Depreciation in Medieval Europe,"
          EHR (1962), 413-21.
          M. Postan, "The Rise of a Money Economy," EHR 14 (1944), 123-
          134.
          *C. M. Cipolla, "Economic Depression of the Renaissance,"
          EHR 16 (1964), 370-524.
          *E. Perroy, "Social Mobility Among the French Noblesse in
          the Later Middle Ages," Past and Present 21 (1962), 23-58.

Oct. 9   Sylvia Thrupp, The Merchant Class of Medieval London
          (Michigan).
          First short paper (no more than 6pp.) due in class:
Using Thrupp's material, test a major contention about the late Middle
Ages put forth by Cheyney or Hay.
          *A. R. Myers, London in the Age of Chaucer. (1972).
          *Eileen Power, The Wool Trade in English Medieval I istory
          (1941).
          *Fritz Rorig, The Medieval Town (1967).
          *Edith Ennen, The Medieval Town, tr. N. Fryde (1979).

OUTSIDERS: DUALISTS AND FOLLOWERS OF ISLAM

Oct. 16   Steven Runciman, The Medieval Manichee (reissued 1982)
           R. W. Southern, Western Views of Islam in the Middle Ages
           (1962).
           *Steven Runciman, A History of the Crusades vol. 3.
           *Arno Borst, Die Katharer (1953), tr. in Fr. (1978).
           *N. Daniel, Islam and the West: The Making of an Image (1960)
           GUEST LECTURER: Sir Steven Runciman

            *Asterix denotes suggested further readings.

Oct. 23   Philip Ziegler, <u>The Black Death</u> (Harper Row).
          H. S. Lucas, "The Great European Famine of 1315, 1316,
            1317," <u>Speculum</u> (1930), 343-377.
          David Herlihy, "Population, Plague and Social Change in
            Rural Pistoia 1201-1430," <u>EHR</u> (1965).
          *William Bowsky, "The Impact of the Black Death upon Siennese
            Government and Society," <u>Speculum</u> (1964), 1-34.
          *J. M. W. Bean, "Plague, Population and Economic Decline,"
            <u>EHR</u> 15 (1962), 423-437.

Oct. 30   Jean Froissart, <u>The Chronicles</u> (Penguin) pp. 9-259, &
            421-471.
          *G. Cuttino, "Historical Revision of the Causes of the One
            Hundred-Years War," <u>Speculum</u> (1956), 463-77.
          *Edouard Perroy, <u>The Hundred Years War</u> (1965).
          *Robert Fawtier, <u>La crise d'une société durant la guerre de
            Cent Ans</u> (1947).
     Rewritten first paper due in class.

--Nov. 6   Holiday--

Nov. 13   J. Huizinga, <u>The Waning of the Middle Ages</u>
            (Doubleday).

ECCLESIASTICAL AND INTELLECTUAL DEVELOPMENTS

Nov. 20   read <u>one</u> of the following:
          ON RESERVE AT BOBST:
            G. Mollat, <u>The Popes at Avignon</u> (1949).
            Walter Ullmann, <u>The Origins of the Great Schism</u> (1948).
            A. C. Flick, <u>The Decline of the Medieval Church</u> 2 vols.
              (1930).
            E. F. Jacob, <u>Essays in the Conciliar Epoch</u> 2nd ed. (1953).
          NOT ON RESERVE:
            A. J. Black, <u>Monarchy and Community: Political Ideas in the
              Later Conciliar Controversy</u> (1970).
            B. Guillemain, <u>La cour pontificale d' Avignon 1309-1376</u>
              (1962).
            V. Martin, <u>Les origines du Gallicanisme</u> (1939).
     Second paper due in class. (No more than 6 pages.) Write a concise
   critical review of the book you have read for this week.

Nov. 27   Aquinas, <u>The Pocket Aquinas</u> (WSP).
          Etienne Gilson, <u>Reason and Revelation in the Middle Ages</u>
            (Scribner).
          Gordon Leff, "Changing Patterns of Thought in the Earlier
            Fourteenth Century," <u>Bulletin of the John Rylands Library</u> 43
            (1961), 354-372.

*Gordon Leff, Paris and Oxford Universities in the Thirteenth and Fourteenth Centuries (Krieger).
*H. Oberman, The Harvest of Medieval Theology (1963).
*Jacques LeGoff, Les intellectuels au moyen âge (1957).
*David Knowles, The Evolution of Medieval Thought (1962).
*P. Vignaux, Le nominalisme au XIVe siècle (1948).

OUTSIDE OF ECCLESIASTICAL AND POLITICAL CONTROLS:

Dec. 4   Julian of Norwich, Revelations of Divine Love (Penguin).
Meister Eckhart, Sermons (xeroxed section.)
*David Knowles, The English Mystical Tradition (1966)
*J. N. Clark, The Great German Mystics (1949).
*Gordon Leff, Heresy in the Later Middle Ages 2 vols. (1967).
*K. W. McFarlane, John Wycliffe and the Beginnings of English Nonconformity (1952).
*Richard Kieckhefer, Repression of Heresy in Medieval Germany, (1979).
Rewritten second paper due in class.

Dec. 11   Norman Cohn, Europe's Inner Demons (NAL).
Dennis Devlin, "Feminine Lay Piety in the High Middle Ages The Beguines," in Distant Echoes: Medieval Religious Women vol. i, ed. John Nichols and Shank.
*Richard Kieckhefer, European Witch Trials: Their Foundations in Popular and Learned Culture 1300-1500 (1976).
*Ernest McDonnell, The Beguines and Beghards in Medieval Culture (1969).
*Dayton Philips, Beguines in Medieval Strasbourg (1941).

Dec. 18   William Langland, Piers Ploughman (Penguin)
De Vericour, "The Jacquerie," Transactions of the Royal Historical Society 1 (1875), 187-203.
*G. G. Coulton, "The Peasants' Revolt," in Great Events in History, ed. G. R. Stirling-Taylor (1934), 197-274.
*Charles Oman, The Great Revolt of 1381 reissued (1969).
*Barbara Hanawalt, Crime and Conflict in English Communities 1300-1348 (1979).

LATE MEDIEVAL CREATIVE GENIUS:

Jan. 8   Either read Dante, The Inferno or Chaucer, The Canterbury Tales.
Be prepared to write an essay in class in response to a question which I will pose about the late Middle Ages. This question will draw on all the material read for this class, and will use the reading of Dante or Chaucer as a focus.

REQUIREMENTS:
Attendance at and participation in class.
Two short written exercises.
One in-class written exercise.

74

Reading Lists to Agument Lectures
Late Middle Ages

GENERAL:

Léepold Genicot, Le XIIIe siècle européen (Paris: 1968)
Jacques Heers, L'occident aux XIVe et XVe siècles: Aspects économiques et sociaux (Paris: 1966).
Both are Nouvelle Clio: l'histoire et ses problèmes
Both have excellent, extensive, multi-language bibliographies.

THE LOW COUNTRIES:

Craeybeckx, "Economic History in Belgium and the Netherlands, 1939-1948" The Journal of Economic History 10 (1950), 261-72.
Jean Gilissen, "Les villes en Belgique: Histoire des institutions administratives et judiciaires des villes belges," Recueils Jean Bodin 6 (1954), 531-604.
Léopold Genicot, L'économie rurale Namuroise au bas moyen-âge vol 2 Les hommes-La noblesse (1960).
Henri Pirenne, Early Democracies in the Low Countries tr. 1963.

USURY AND THE JEWS:

Benjamin Nelson, TheIdea of Ususry: From Tribal Brotherhood to Universal Otherhood sec. ed. 1969
S. W. Baron, A Social and Religious History of the Jews vol. 3 to 12 (1957-67).
Richard Emery, The Jews of Perpignan in the Thirteenth Century: An Economic Study (1959)

ITALIAN TRADERS AND ADVENTURERS:

The Travels of Marco Polo
Robert Lopez, "Marjorcan and Genoese on the North Sea Route in the XIIIth Century," Revue Belge de Philologie et d'histoire (1951)
Y. Renouard, Les hommes d'affaires italiens au moyen âge (1950)
A. Sapori, The Italian Merchant in the Middle Ages tr. 1970.

Oct. 23   A VISUALIZATION OF THE LATE MIDDLE AGES

Oct. 30   JOAN OF ARC
    Marina Warner, Joan of Arc: The Image of Female Heroism (1982)
    Etienne Delaruelle, "La spiritualité de Jeanne d'Arc" Bulletin de litterature ecclésiastique 65 (1964).
    Anne Barstow, Joan of Arc: Heretic, Mystic and Shamen (1984).
    Jeanne d'Arc: une époque, un rayonnement (Paris:1982).
    John Keegan, "Agincourt," chap. 2 The Face of Battle (1977).

Nov. 13   CHIVALRY
    Léon Gauthier, La chevalerie (1884)
    Sidney Painter French Chivalry (1957
                        . William Marshall: Kight-Errant, Baron, and Regnet of England (1933).
    Maurice Keen, Chivalry (1984)

Nov. 27   LATE MEDIEVAL THEOLOGY
    Jaroslav Pelikan, The Growth of Medieval Theology (600-1300) vol. 3 of The Christian Tradition (1978).
    André Forest and F. van Steenberghen, M. de Gandillac, Le mouvement doctrinal du XI au XIVe siècle (1951).
    Gordon Leff, Medieval Thought from Saint Augustine to Ockham (1958).

Dec. 4   WOMEN MYSTICS OF THE LATE MIDDLE AGES
    Evelyn Underhill, Mysticism (1955).
    Elmer O'Brien, Varieties of Mystic Experience: An anthology and interpretation of the key writing of the major mystics (1964).
    Caroline Bynum, Jesus as Mother: Studies in the Spirituality of the High Middle Ages (1982).
    Clarissa Atkinson, Mystic and Pilgrim: The Book and the World of Margery Kempe (1983).

Dec. 11   LATE MEDIEVAL DISSENT
    R. I. Moore, The Origins of European Dissent (1977).
    Gordon Leff, Heresy in the Later Middle Ages: the Relation of Heterodoxy to Dissent ca. 1250-1450 (1967).
    Walter Wakefield, and Austin Evans, Heresies of the High Middle Ages (1969).

Dec. 18   LATE MEDIEVAL REVOLT
    F. Vercauteren, Les luttes sociales à Liège (XIIIe-XIVe siècles (1946.
    E. Searle and R. Burghart, "The Defense of England and the Peasants' Revolt," Viator 3 (1972).
    Barbara Hanawalt, "Fur Collar Crime: The Pattern of Crime Among the Fourteenth-Century English Nobility," Journal of Social History 8 (1975).
    P. Wolff, "The 1391 Pogrom in Spain, Social Crisis or Not?" Past and Present 50 (1971).

THE LATER MIDDLE AGES

History 104B
Spring 1983
Dr. Bouchard

Constance Bouchard
U. of California
San Diego

This course covers the history of medieval Europe from the beginning
of the twelfth century to the fifteenth century. It includes the
political, institutional, ecclesiastical, social, and economic history
of the period. The principal focus will be France and England, but
other western nations will also be covered.

Requirements for the course, aside from doing all the reading and
attending all the classes, are a midterm, a paper, a final examination,
and participation in class discussions.

Required Texts (at the bookstore, except for the Waley book)

Georges Duby, The Chivalrous Society
Jean Gimpel, The Medieval Machine
Denys Hay, Europe in the Fourteenth and Fifteenth Centuries
R. W. Southern, Western Society and the Church in the Middle Ages
David Knowles, Christian Monasticism
Daniel Waley, Italian City Republics (this book on reserve only)
Froissart, Chronicles

Recommended Text (at the bookstore and at Central Library reserve)

Robert Hoyt and Stanley Chodorow, Europe in the Middle Ages
        (note that there is one required reading from this text)

PART ONE
THE HIGH MIDDLE AGES

Week 1 (April 4-8). (no class Friday)
Introduction. England in the Twelfth Century.
Read: Duby, pp. 1-14; Hay, pp. 1-25; Gimpel, pp. vii-xi, 1-58,
        Hoyt and Chodorow (recommended), pp. 329-354.

Week 2 (April 11-15) (regular Friday classes from now on)
England and France in the twelfth and thirteenth centuries.
Read: Gimpel, pp. 59-113; Hoyt and Chodorow (required), pp. 474-
        485, 490-508.

Week 3 (April 18-22)
Germany and the popes.
Read: Southern, pp. 15-44, 100-133, 188-213; Hoyt and Chodorow
        (recommended), pp. 354-364, 432-447, 461-474, 486-490.

Week 4 (April 25-29)
Monasticism. The friars. Heresy.
Read: Southern, pp. 214-299; Knowles, pp. 83-123; Hoyt and
        Chodorow (recommended), pp. 365-388, 447-459).

Week 5 (May 2-6)
Universities and learning. Architecture. Society.
Read: Duby, pp. 94-122, 134-157, 171-185; Southern, pp. 300-318;
Hoyt and Chodorow (recommended), pp. 390-431, 514-528.

Week 6 (May 9-13)
Economic changes. The growth of Cities.
Read: Waley, pp. 9-109; Gimpel, pp. 171-198; Hoyt and Chodorow
(recommended), pp. 530-538.
MIDTERM

PART TWO
THE LATE MIDDLE AGES

Week 7 (May 16-20)
Economy and the plague. Italian cities.
Read: Waley, pp. 164-239; Hay, pp. 26-44; Duby, pp. 186-215; Gimpel,
pp. 199-252; Hoyt and Chodorow (recommended), pp. 612-620, 632-6

Week 8 (May 23-27)
France and the popes. Avignon. The Templars.
Read: Hay, pp. 45-125, 266-298; Hoyt and Chodorow (recommended),
pp. 595-604.

Week 9 (May 30-June 3)
England in the Late Middle Ages. Parliament.
Read: Hay, pp. 126-162; Froissart, pp. 9-23, 37-96; Hoyt and
Chodorow (recommended), pp. 508-513, 573-594, 620-631.

Week 10 (June 6-June 10)
Hundred Years War. End of the Middle Ages. Conclusions.
Read: Hay, pp. 163-186; Knowles, pp. 135-141; Froissart, pp. 201-230,
392-401, 421-471; Hoyt and Chodorow (recommended), pp. 604-610.

erm Paper

The paper is due at the end of the eighth week of the quarter
May 27). A one-week extension (until June 3) is hereby granted to
nyone who needs extra time. No further extensions will be granted
xcept for medical emergency.

The paper should be based on an analysis of primary sources
one or more), that is, works written by medieval men during the
iddle Ages (obviously, you will read them in translation, rather
han the original Latin). I shall suggest possible topics during
he quarter. A list of "sources" available in English translation
s given at the end of each chapter of the Hoyt-Chodorow textbook;
his is another place to find suitable topics. In choosing a topic,
ou should choose the <u>source</u> first and then base the actual questions
ou plan to explore on what the source might be able to answer. I
trongly urge you to consult me on paper topics.

After you have chosen your source(s) and read them, you should
hoose some method of analysis--that is, rather than just summarizing
hat the medieval author said, <u>analyze</u> what he says, why, how, in
hat manner. Ask yourself questions like (for example), Does he say
hat bishops were very powerful during his period and yet show in his
wn examples that bishops were always being pushed around? Do these
wo authors (if you are using two) have the same or different ideas
n what a king should be? etc. It may be easier to come up with a
pecific question if you are using two sources, because then you can
ompare them, but one can also write an excellent paper analyzing
ne source.

In your analysis, try not to rely too much on secondary sources
i.e., modern authors). I want <u>your</u> ideas, not someone else's ideas
ehashed. In fact, it is possible to write a good paper without reading
ny secondary sources. Many however may prefer to read some modern
uthors to set the context and the like. It might also be interesting
o have a page or so at the end where you compare your conclusions with
hose of modern authors. Don't feel you have to agree with them; if
ou disagree, and can prove it with quotes from the primary source,
hen you have made an original contribution to historical thought.

Overall the paper should run between 5 and 15 pages, plus footnotes
nd bibliography. Needless to say, it should be typed double-spaced
n one side of standard paper, be written grammatically and be free
f spelling errors (have someone else proofread if your spelling is
ad). Use a dictionary!! (This will tell you how words are spelled
nd keep you from using words incorrectly.) Don't feel compelled to
rite in a "high-fallutin" style. I strongly suggest writing a first
raft; I shall be happy to discuss it with you.

THE BYZANTINE EMPIRE
John Meyendorff
Fordham University

Requirements:
1. regular participation in class discussions.
2. two short papers (maximum 5 pages) on topics related to both class work and readings.
3. a longer paper on a topic agreed on with the instructor.
4. a final exam covering the work of the semester.

1. The Empire. The New Capital. The Roman State and the Christian Religion.

2. The Christian Church: doctrinal disputes and schisms. Byzantine Orthodoxy.
    Reading completed of: Ostrogorsky, 27-68 or
    Vasiliev 1, 43-128; Brand, 5-7.

3. Emperor Justinian and the Reconquest.
    Ostrogorsky, 68-86, or Vasiliev, 129-192.
    Barker, Justinian and the Later Empire

4. Emperor Heraclius and the Persians.
    Ostrogorsky, 92-109; Vasiliev, 193-233.
    Barker, Justinian

5. The Rise of Islam.
    Ostrogorsky, 110-146; Vasiliev, same as above.
    Brand, 135-180.

6. Iconoclasm in Byzantium: a crisis of civilization.
    Ostrogorsky, 147-209; Vasiliev, 234-299.

7. Charlemagne and Byzantium. The cultural and political separation between East and West.

8. The Conversion of the Slavs. Patriarch Plotius.
    Ostrogrosky, 210-269; Vasiliev, 301-351.

9. The Macedonian Dynasty: economic reforms and military conquests.
    Ostrogorsky, 270-320; Vasiliev, same as above.

10. The Schism between Rome and Byzantium. Crusades begin.
    Ostrogorsky, 320-375; Vasiliev, 351-412.

11. The Commenian Dynasty. The Fourth Crusade.
    Ostrogrosky, 374-417; Vasiliev, 412-505.

12. The Palaeologan Dynasty. Union negociations.
     Ostrogorsky, 418-533; Vasiliev, 506-629.

13. The Council of Florence. The Fall.
     Ostrogorsky, 533-572; Vasiliev, 629-722.

14. Byzantine Civilization. Art, architecture, literature.

REQUIRED READING:

Brand, Ch., Icon and Minaret: Sources of Byzantine and Islamic Civilization
Ostrogorsky, G., History of the Byzantine State, rev. ed., 1969.
Barker, J. W., Justinian and the Later Roman Empire,
Vasiliev, A. A., History of the Byzantine Empire, Vols. I & II.

RECOMMENDED READING:
Jones, A. H. M., The Later Roman Empire, 284-602: A Social, Economic and Administrative Survey, 1964.
Meyendorff, J., Byzantine Theology, 1979.
The Cambridge Medieval History, vol. IV. "The Byzantine Empire" Part 1 & 2. ed. Hussey, 1967.
Nicol, D. M., The Last Centuries of Byzantium, 1972.
Dvornik, F., The Photian Schism: History and Legend, 1948.
Runciman, S., The Eastern Schism: A Study of the Papacy and the Eastern Churches during the XI and XII Centuries, 1955.
Gill, J., The Council of Florence, 1959.
Meyendorff, J., St. Gregory Palamas and Orthodox Spirituality, 1975.

TRANSLATED SOURCES:
Barker, E., Social and Political Thought in Byzantium from Justinian I to the Last Palaeologus, 1957.
Psellus, M., Fourteen Byzantine Rulers: tr. Sewter, 1966.
Procopius, The Secret History
Comena, Anna, The Alexiad, tr. Sewter, 1969.
Porplyrogenitus, Constantine, De Administrando Imperio, tr. Moravczik and Jenkins.

James Alexander
University of Georgia

HISTORY 445F/645F

NORMAN AND EARLY ANGEVIN ENGLAND, 1066-1307

J. W. Alexander
   Office, 542-2053
   Home,   549-3504

required texts for this course are:

Lyon, Constitutional and Legal History of Medieval England
Stephenson, Marcham, Sources of English Constitutional History I

The Normans and England
Lyon, 3-121, 127-138, 200-217

David Douglas, et. al., English Historical Documents, vol. 2
(1042-1189), pp. 107-203, 204-14, 279-89. Undergraduates are
to read enough of the Anglo-Saxon Chronicle to get the flavour
of it; graduate students are to read it in its entirety. This
book is hereafter cited EHD.
Carl Stephenson and Frederic Marcham, Sources of English
   Constitutional History, pp. 33-46, 58-69, 61. This book
   is hereafter cited S-M.

Henry I and Stephen of Blois, 1100-1154
Lyon, 121-127, 138-200
S-M, 46-58, 59-70

R. W. Southern, "The Place of Henry I in English History," in
   Southern, Medieval Humanism and Other Studies (graduate
   students may wish to own this), or in Proceedings of the
   British Academy, 48 (1962), 127-70.
EHD, 290-313.

I. Crown and Pallium, 1066-1189
    Lyon, 200-217, 300-305

    EHD, 673-678, 702-776
    David Knowles, "Archbishop Thomas Becket," Proceedings of the
       British Academy, 35 (1949), 1-31 (undergraduate only)
    David Knowles, The Episcopal Colleagues of Thomas Becket (entire)

"Perhaps the Greatest English King:" Henry II, 1154-1189
Lyon, 217-234, 279-300

S-M, 71-96
EHD, 322-392
Charles Young, Hubert Walter

'I. Lionheart and Softsword, 1189-1216
    Lyon, 234-279, 305-329
    Sidney Painter, William Marshal

    Harry Rothwell, English Historical Documents, III (hereafter
        EHD), 51-63, 307-332.
    S-M, 96-126

    Asinus coronatus: Henry III, 1216-1272
    Lyon, 329-345, 351-408

    EHD, 63-153, 197-209, 332-350, 351-354, 355-357, 359-60,
        361-367, 370-392, 751-55, 806-23, 899-918.
    S-M, 127-153

    Bertie Wilkinson, Constitutional History of Medieval England,
        1. 110-116, 126-130, 163-186; vol. 3, 170-185, 222-232,
            251-263, 297-305.

    "The English Justinian": Edward I, 1272-1307
    Lyon, 345-350, 408-475
    Haskins, The Growth of English Representative Government (entire)

    EHD, 209-265, 396-410, 414-427, 428-66, 482-87, 496-502
    S-M, 153-189

    Wilkinson, Const. Hist. 1. 211-232; 3. 305-321, 390-98.
    C. H. Lawrence, The English Church and the Papacy, 117-161.

            ADDITIONAL READING FOR HISTORY 645F

    R. W. Southern, "Ranulf Flambard," in his Medieval Humanism or
        in Transactions of the Royal Historical Society, ser. 4, v.
        16 (1933, 95-128.)
    David Douglas, William the Conqueror
    EHD, 232-278; 851-905, 916-919

    H. G. Richardson and G. O. Sayles, The Governance of Medieval
        England 22-135

    R. H. C. Davis, King Stephen (entire)

    EHD, 400-407, 422-428, 434-437, 459-62, 572-75, 928-932

EHD, 609-649

David Knowles, Thomas Becket (entire)

J. W. Alexander, "The Becket Dispute," Journal of British Studies,
    May, 1970, 1-26
Richardson and Sayles, Governance, 285-320

EHD, 407-421, 437-8, 462-82, 906-916, 937-944
Jacques Boussard, Le Gouvernement d'Henri II Plantagenet, 81-158

VI.   Charles Duggan, "From the Conquest to the Reign of John," in
    The English Church and the Papacy, ed. C. H. Lawrence, 63-116.
F. M. Powicke, The Loss of Normandy, 79-169, 280-309
Sidney Painter, "Norwich's Three Geoffreys" Speculum, 28 (1953),
    808-813

R. F. Treharne, "The Knights in the Period of Reform and Rebellion,"
    Bulletin of the Institute of Historical Research 21 (1946-8),
    1-12

NORMAN AND EARLY ANGEVIN ENGLAND,
1066-1307

Graduate students should familiarize themselves with the following
documentary and narrative collections, which are the basic source materials
for English medieval history. Undergraduate students should at least be
aware of their existence.

I) Sources

The indispensable set of chronicles is Great Britain, Rerum Brittanicarum
Medii Aevi Scriptores. Commonly known as the Rolls Series, the works
herein vary widely in standards of editing. A detailed list of the contents
of these 99 is in Mullins, Texts and Calendars (below). Nelson's (now
Oxford) Medieval Texts is a relatively new series, still publishing;
it consists of critical Latin texts with facing English translations.
As with the Rolls Series, editors vary, but the series holds to a uniformly
high standard. It includes Glanvill, the histories of Ordericus Vitalis,
the best edition of the Dialogue on the Exchequer, John of Salisbury's
Letters, and other works.

For Church history, valuable material is in both series cited above,
and in the publications of local record societies (again, refer to Mullins
for these). As well, there is William Dugdale's Monasticon Anglicanum,
8 volumes of charter and other evidence relating to the monastic order in
England. Wilkins' Concilia is being superseded by a projected collection
of conciliar and other ecclesiastical documents of the medieval English
Church, of which the first part (actually, vol. II) has appeared: F. M.
Powicke and C. R. Cheney, Councils and Synods, 1205-1313. Papal acta
concerning England can be found in Migne, Patrologia latina, supplemented
by Walther Holtzmann, Papsturkunden in England, and by C. R. and Mary G.
Cheney, the Letters of Pope Innocent III Concerning England and Wales.
Relevant material is also in the superbly-edited series, Corpus christianorum,
series latina (e. g., the works of the Venerable Bede).

The public records are principally found in two great series. The old
Record Commission published records invaluable for the reigns of John
and early Henry III, including the Charter Rolls for John, the letters
patent and close, miscellaneous exchequer documents, Norman Rolls, etc.
Also in this series are Domesday Book (which is translated, county by
county, in the first volume of the Victoria County History of England),
the Hundred Rolls, Placita de quo warranto, the Valor ecclesiasticus,
Statutes of the Realm, etc. The Texts and Calendars of the Public Record
Office picked up the Record Commission's work in the later nineteenth
century, and in some instances (e. g., the Book of Fees) superseded it.
The PRO publications include texts and calendars of exchequer and chancery
enrollments (letters close, patent; charter rolls; ancient correspondence;
diplomatic documents; liberate and fine rolls, etc.), calendars of foreign
archives as they relate to England (from the papacy, Venice, etc.), feudal
inquisitions (the Books of Fees; Feudal Aids), and many miscellaneous
materials (such as the Register of the Black Prince, the Inquisitions post
mortem, etc.). They are listed in Mullins.

The publications of the Selden Society are indispensable for the study of medieval English law and social history. They include commentaries (Bracton, Azo, "Fleta," etc.), year books (but those for Edward I, which are in the Rolls Series), selected cases from the central courts and from those of justices in eyre, cases and commentaries in forest law and feudal courts, borough charters, and several important studies (such as van Caenegem's Royal Writs in England from the Conquest to Glanvill). All are well-edited, some superbly so, by such scholars as G. O. Sayles, Plucknett, Lady Stenton, Maitland, and Thorne.

The royal charters and writs of the Norman period are calendared, and in some cases printed in full, in Regesta regum anglo-normannorum, ed. H. W. C. Davis (1: 1066-1100), Charles Johnson and H. A. Cronne (II: 1100-1135), and H. A. Cronne and R. H. C. Davis (III and IV: 1135-1154). Only the charters of Henry II which pertain to continental affairs have been collected for this reign: Léopold Delisle, Receuil des actes d'Henri II (4 vols.). Eyton published an inadequate Itinerary of King Henry II, which calendars some charters. Lionel Landon's Itinerary of Richard I (Pipe Roll Society) is a model of its type, and calendars or prints most of Lionheart's charters. The itinerary of King John is not a calendar: it is printed at the beginning of Sir Thomas Duffus Hardy's edition of the Patent Rolls of John. There is neither calendar nor itinerary for Henry III, but H. Gough's Itinerary of Edward I is once again in print; it is not very good, as may be seen by comparing it with J. B. Trabut-Cussac's itinerary of Edward in France, 1286-1289 (Bulletin of the Institute of Historical Research, XXV [1952], 160-203). The lack of calendars for the charters and writs of the Angevin kings is somewhat compensated for by the generally excellent indices in the Record Commission and PRO Texts and Calendars.

The Record Commission published the first extant Pipe Rolls (for 31 Henry I and 2, 3, and 4 Henry II) and that for 1 Richard I. The others are still in process of publication by the Pipe Roll Society, commencing with that of 5 Henry II and at present writing extending to 3 Henry III; the pipe and chancellor's rolls of 14 Henry III are also in the PRS publications, as are some miscellaneous materials (rolls of the king's court for Henry II and Richard I, the Rotuli de dominabus of 1185, Feet of Fines for Henry II and Richard I, the Worcester Cartulary, Interdict Documents, etc.) There are also pipe roll extracts relating to various counties in the publications of local record societies (see Mullins).

Many well-edited texts and records are available in the local record and historical societies of Great Britain. For a comprehensive guide to the local as well as the national historical society publications, consult E. L. C. Mullins, Texts and Calendars.

Several continental collections are essential for English medieval history:

> Dom M. Bouquet, et al., <u>Receuil</u> <u>des</u> <u>historiens</u> <u>des</u> <u>Gaules</u> <u>et</u> <u>de</u> <u>la</u>
>   <u>France</u> (24 vols.)
> Publications of the <u>Société</u> <u>de</u> <u>l'histoire</u> <u>de</u> <u>France</u>
> A. Teulet, <u>Layettes</u> <u>de</u> <u>trésor</u> <u>des</u> <u>chartes</u>
> The registers of the French kings often have material pertinent to
>   English medieval history; for a partial guide, <u>v</u>. Robert
>   Fawtier, <u>The</u> <u>Capetian</u> <u>Kings</u> <u>of</u> <u>France</u>, c. i., to whose
>   apparatus add the second through fourth volumes of the <u>Recueil</u>
>   <u>des</u> <u>actes</u> <u>de</u> <u>Phillippe-Auguste</u>

French provincial and municipal historical societies have published
many works indispensable for medieval English history; unfortunately,
no guide comparable to that of Mullins for England exists. The most
important collections for this course are the publications of the
Société des antiquaires de Normandie. For the period beginning in
1154, the publications of societies lying within lands formerly
possessed by the Angevin kings -- Anjou, Brittany, Gascony, etc. --
are relevant as well.

The great German set, the <u>Monumenta</u> <u>Germaniae</u> <u>historica</u>, contains a
great deal of material pertinent to English history in the middle
ages.

II. Research Aids

A. Bibliographies

> Edgar B. Graves, <u>A</u> <u>Bibliography</u> <u>of</u> English History <u>to</u> <u>1485</u>.
> The volumes of the Oxford History of England for the medieval
> period contain valuable bibliographical essays, and list
> bibliographical guides as well.
>
> > F. M. Stenton, <u>Anglo-Saxon</u> <u>England</u>
> > A. L. Poole, <u>From</u> <u>Domesday</u> <u>Book</u> <u>to</u> <u>Magna</u> <u>Carta</u>
> > F. M. Powicke, <u>The</u> <u>Thirteenth</u> <u>Century</u>
> > May McKisack, <u>The</u> <u>Fourteenth</u> <u>Century</u>
> > E. F. Jacob, <u>The</u> <u>Fifteenth</u> <u>Century</u>
>
> The Conference on British Studies has commenced a bibliographical
> series: M. Altschul, <u>Anglo-Norman</u> <u>England</u>, <u>1066-1154</u>, and Bertie
> Wilkinson, <u>The</u> <u>High</u> <u>Middle</u> <u>Ages</u> <u>in</u> <u>England</u>, <u>1154-1307</u>. See also
> <u>English</u> <u>Historical</u> <u>Documents</u>, general ed. David Douglas, vols. 1-3.
>
> For the publications of all national, government, ecclesiastical and
> local record and historical societies, a virtually-complete guide is
> E. L. C. Mullins, <u>Texts</u> <u>and</u> <u>Calendars</u>.

Since any bibliographical guide is out of date before it sees print, the student should supplement the material in the guides above by book reviews and publication lists in The English Historical Review, the Bulletin of the Institute of Historical Research, the American Historical Review, Speculum, Revue historique, Historische Zeitschrift, the Revue d'histoire ecclésiastique, etc.

Although both incomplete and outdated, Farrar and Evans, English Translations from Medieval Sources is satisfactory for works published before 1945; supplemented by Mary Anne Ferguson, Bibliography of English Translations from Medieval Sources, 1948-1968. The most important translating work now being done in serial publications is in Medieval Texts and in the Columbia University Records of Civilization. Important documents illustrating the development of English constitutional history after 1216 may be found in Bertie Wilkinson, Constitutional History of Medieval England (3 vols.); unlike those in Stubbs' Select Charters, they are printed in translation. Most of the Selden Society volumes also contain translations of the texts which they contain.

B. Handbooks, Manuals, Dictionaries.

V. H. Galbraith, Introduction to the Use of the Public Records

The Royal Historical Society published invaluable research tools; they include:

  Mullins, Texts and Calendars
  F. M. Powicke and E. N. Fryde, Handbook of British Chronology, which includes the regnal years of kings, terms of office of British officers of state, archiepiscopal and episcopal pontifical terms of office, years of incumbancy of the higher nobility, and a great deal of miscellaneous information.
  C. R. Cheney, Handbook of Dates, which is essential for dating documents. The series, "Helps for Students of History"

Charles Trice Martin, The Record Interpreter. Primarily for the research scholar, this little vade mecum is a dictionary of abbreviations (Latin and French), coupled with a glossary of Latin place-names for the British Isles. For the latter, see also Chevin, Dictionnaire des noms latins de lieux and the third (index) volume of the Book of Fees. For help in placing sites in the proper county, see E. Ekwall, Concise Dictionary of English Place-Names. The student in this course will have little need to have a knowledge of paleography or of diplomatics; anyone wishing a bibliography of this field may have the syllabus for my seminar in these disciplines on request.

I. Sanders, English Baronies, is a handbook of origins and descents.
G. E. C. [okayne], Complete Peerage, lists biographical and feudal
information under the names of lordships. The Dictionary of National
Biography gives concise sketches of important medieval English
figures. See also Joseph Strayer (ed.), Dictionary of the Middle Ages.

The Revised Medieval Latin Word-List (ed. Latham) is, despite some
flaws, the best medieval Latin dictionary for English sources. It
should be supplemented with the best one-volume Latin dictionary, which
is that of Lewis and Short (Oxford).

England in the Later Middle Ages, 1307-1485

312 LeConte Hall   James Alexander
Home phone: 549-3504   University of Georgia

These are the textbooks required for this course; all are in paperback:

Bertie Wilkinson, The Later Middle Ages in England
W.A. Pantin, The English Church in the XIV Century
Jack Lander, Conflict and Stability in Fifteenth-century England
H.S. Bennett, The Pastons and their England
Boris Ford, Medieval Literature

Following is a week-by-week reading list. The additional readings
headed 645G for each week pertain to the graduate students only.

I. Edward II, 1307-27

    Wilkinson, Later MA, 1-132
    Carl Stephenson and Frederic Marcham, Sources of English
       Constitutional History, 190-205
    Bertie Wilkinson, Constitutional History of Medieval England,
       2.112-76

    645: Margaret Hastings, 'High History or Hack History: England in
       the Later Middle Ages,' Speculum 36 (April, 1961), 225-253

II. Edward III, 1327-77

    Wilkinson, 132-157
    Stephenson/Marcham, 205-232
    Wilkinson. Const. Hist. 2.176-227

    645: Alec Myers, English Historical Documents, IV: 1327-1485,
       35-122, 403, 420-23, 439-49; 482-3, 497-502, 512-15, 533-43.
       W.A. Morris, et al., The English Government at Work, 1327-1337,
       1.394-467, 3.105-41, 467

III. Richard II, 1377-99

    Wilkinson, 157-184
    Stephenson/Marcham, 232-49
    Gervase Mathew, The Court of Richard II
    Wilkinson, Const. Hist. 2.227-329, 3.322-76

    645: Myers, 122-178, 403-14, 449-53, 483-85, 502-3; R.H. Hilton,
       Bond Men Made Free.

IV. England in the Fourteenth Century

    Pantin, English Church in the XIV Century
    Geoffrey Chaucer, Canterbury Tales,

Sir Gawain and the Green Knight (entire)
Langland, Vision of Piers the Ploughman, Prologue and all of part one
Ford, Medieval Literature

645: Myers, 653-65, 785-6, 811-28, 837-50, 878-887, 984-1005,
    1115-17, 1137-43, 1179-94

V. The Reigns of Henry IV and Henry V. 1399-1422

Wilkinson, 234-257
Stephenson/Marcham, 249-65, 273-76

645: Myers, 178-213, 414-15, 453-63, 485-87, 543-47
    Bertie Wilkinson, Constitutional History of Enland in the
    Fifteenth Century, Chapter 1

VI. Henry VI, 1422-61

Wilkinson, 237-286
Bennett, The Pastons and Their England
Stephenson/Marcham, 265-71, 276-77

645: Myers, 231-88, 423-36, 463-73, 487-89, 503-7, 515-25, 547-57;
    Wilkinson, Fifteenth Century, chapter 2.

VII. The Yorkist Kings, 1461-85

Wilkinson, 286-305
Lander, Conflict and Stability
Stephenson-Marcham, 272-73, 277-78

Paul Murray Kendall, Richard III, 465-514
Thomas More, History of Richard III
Wilkinson, Fifteenth Century, Chapter 3

645: Myers, 288-351, 514-20, 436-39, 473-82, 489-97, 507-12,
    525-33, 557-60
W.H. Dunham and C.T. Wood, "The Right to Rule England," AHR 81[4]
    (Oct. 1976), pp. 738-761

VIII. England in the Fifteenth Century

Wilkinson, 184-234
W.S. Furnivall, The Babees' Book, pp. 1-9, 31-47, 122-141, 174-5

645: Myers, 655-98, 730-31, 733-35, 828, 837, 850-78, 887-907,
    1005-17, 1117-37, 1143-53, 1194-1208

IX. English Society in the Fifteenth Century

Wilkinson, 305-397
Stephenson/Marcham, 279-96
K.B. MacFarlane, 'Bastard Feudalism,' Bulletin of the Institute of
Historical Research, 20 (1943-45)
F.R.H. duBoulay, An Age of Ambition

History 445G/645G

ENGLAND IN THE LATER MIDDLE AGES, 1307-1485

1) Bibliographical Tools

There is little point in here listing the essential works in this field; the standard bibliographies for late medieval England are full guides to both primary and secondary materials. They are included in:

D.J. Guth, Late Medieval England, 1377-1485.
Edgar B. Graves, A Bibliography of English History to 1485.
Margaret Hastings, "High History or Hack History," Speculum, 1961, 225-53.
E.F. Jacob, The Fifteenth Century.
May McKisack, The Fourteenth Century.
Alec Myers, English Historical Documents, IV.
R.C. Van Caenegem, Guide to the Sources of Medieval History.
Bertie Wilkinson, Constitutional History of Medieval England (3 vols)
_____, Constitutional History of England in the Fifteenth Century.

There are both gains and losses in printed sources when later medieval England is compared with the Norman and early Angevin periods. We have no pipe rolls in print, the Patrologia latina ends in the early thirteenth century, and none of the royal acts are calendared as in the Regesta regum Anglo-Normannorum. The gains are considerable, however: there are more, and fuller, public records (for an analytical guide, see Mullins, Texts and Calendars), such as the charter, patent, close, fine, and liberate rolls. Inquisitions post mortem are fuller than those of the reign of Henry III. Legal records are more abundant—the Selden Society publishes many later medieval legal and judicial records. For military inquests, see Feudal Aids (6 vols.) and The Book of Fees (3 vols.: both PRO).

French history continues to be influential upon that of England in this period. The more important collections are:

the publications of the Société de l'histoire de France, and of the various provincial and local record and historical societies.
Documents inédits sur l'histoire de France.
A. Teulet, Layettes de trésor des chartes.
Bibliotheque de l'École des Chartes.
The great Bouquet Recueil does not extend forward in time into our period.

2) Research Aids

For a splendid bibliographical index to all publications of the British government, national, ecclesiastical, and local record and historical societies, see the splendid work Texts and Calendars, by E.L.C. Mullins. It is to be supplemented, for works published after 1958, by the bibliographical apparatus of the English Historical Review and of the Billetin of the Institute for Historical Research. For government publications, see the (periodically revised) Sectional List

#17 (for publications of theRoyal Commission on Historical Manuscripts) and Sectional List #24 (British National Archives).

Although both incomplete and outdated, Farrar and Evans, <u>English Translations from Medieval Sources</u> is satisfactory for works published before 1945. Mary Anne Ferguson, <u>Bibliography of English Translations From Medieval Sources, 1944-1968</u>. (For works published since 1968, see the bibliographical information in <u>Speculum</u>). The most important translating work now being done in serial publications are in the Oxford Medieval Texts and in the Columbia University Records of Civilization.

A convenient collection of constitutional documents in the original languages in Chrimes and Brown, <u>Select Documents Of English Constitutional Histroy, 1307-1485</u>, a successor in time to Stubbs' <u>Select Charters</u>, which ends in 1307.

Handbooks, Manuals, Dictionaries.

V.H. Galbraith, <u>Introduction to the Use of Publick Records</u>

<u>Guide to the Contents of the Public Record Office</u>, I.

TheRoyal Historical Society published invaluable research tools; they include:

> Mullins, <u>Texts and Calendars</u>, I (1958), II (1983).
> F.M. Powicke and E.B. Fryde, <u>Handbook of British Chronology</u>, which includes the regnal years of kings, terms of office of British officers of state, archiepiscopal and episcopal terms of office, years of incumbency of the higher nobility, and a great deal of miscellaneous information.

C.R. Cheney, <u>Handbook of Dates</u>, which is essential for dating documents. The series, "Helps for Students of History."

M Pacaut, <u>Guide de l'étudiant en histoire médievale</u>

Pierre Chaplais, <u>English Royal Documents, 1199-1461</u>

Charles Trice Martin, <u>The Record Interpreter</u>. Primarily for the research scholar, this little <u>vade mecum</u> is a dictionary of abbreviations (Latin and French), coupled with a glossary of Latin place names for the British Isles. For the latter, see also Chevin, <u>Dictionnaire des noms latins de lieux</u> and the third (index) volume of the <u>Book of Fees</u>. For help in placing sites in the proper county, see E. Ekwall, <u>Concise Dictionary of English Place-Names</u>. The studentin this course will have littel need to have a deep knowledge of paleography or of deplomatics; anyone wishing a bibliography of this field may have the syllabus for my seminar in these disciplines on request.

I. Sanders, <u>English Baronies</u>, is a handbook of origins and descents. G.E.C. (okayne)., <u>Complete Peerage</u>, lists biographical and feudal information under the names of lordships. <u>The Dictionary of National Biography</u> gives concise sketches of important medieval English figures.

The Rivised Medieval Latin Word-List (ed. Latham) is, despite some
flaws, the best medieval Latin dictionary for ENglish sources. It
should be supplemented with the best one-volume Latin dictionary, which
is that of Lewis and Short (Oxford).

3) Supplementary bibliographical recommendations.

    Following are some important books which have appeared since the
publication of the bibliographical aids listed above, or which I wish
particularly to recommend:

S. Armitage-Smith, John of Gaunt
J. M. W. Bean, The Decline of English Feudalism, 1215-1540
S. B. Chrimes, Fifteenth-Century England
_____, Lancastrians, Yorkists, and Henry VII
_____, Introduction to the Administrative History of Medieval
            England
J. Conway Davies, The Baronial Oppositiont to Edward II
M. T. Clanchy, From Memory to Written Record
F. R. H. du Boulay, An Age of Ambition
_____, The Lordship of Canterbury
W. H. Dunham, Lord Hastings' Indentured Retainers
John Ferguson, English Diplomacy, 1422-1461
Kenneth Fowler, The King's Lieutenant: Henry de Grosmont
Kenneth Fowler, The Age of Plantagenet and Valois
E. B. Fryde and Edward Miller, Historical Studies of the English
                               Parliament
N. Fryde, The Tyranny and Fall of Richard II
A. Goodman, The Loyal Conspiracy: The Lords Appellant
_____, The Wars of the Roses
Ralph A. Griffiths, The Reign of King Henry VI
A. Hanham, Richard III and His Early Historians, 1483-1535
G. L. Harriss, King Parliament, and Public Finanace in Medieval England
              to 1369
H. J. Hewitt, The Organization of War under Edward III
R. H. Hilton, Bond Men Made Free
_____, The Decline of Serfdom in Medieval England
George Holmes, The Good Parliament
Harold Hutchison, King Henry V: A Biography
E. F. Jacob, Henry V and the Invasion of France
R. H. Jones, The Royal Policy of Richard II
C. L. Kingsford, Prejudice and Promise in XV Century England
J. L. Kirby, Henry IV of England
David Knowles, The Religious Orders in England, 2 and 3
Jack Lander, Conflict and Stability in Fifteenth-Century England
_____, Crown and Nobility, 1450-1509
_____, Government and Community in England, 1450-1509
C. H. Lawrence, The English Church and the Papacy in the Middle Ages
Gervase Matthew, The Court of Richard II
K. B. McFarlane, John Wycliffe and English Nonconformity
_____, Lancastrian Kings and Lollard Knights
_____, The Nobility of Later Medieval ENgland
W. A. Morris et al., The English Government at Work, 1327-1336
Colin Morris, Medieval England
G. R. Owst., Literature and Pulpit in Medieval England

W. A. Pantin, The English Church in the XIV Century
J. R. S. Phillips, Aymer de Valence, Early of Pembroke
T. F. T. Plucknett, A Concise History of the Common Law
Michael Powicke, Military Obligation in Medieval England
Michael Prestwich, The Three Edwards
Joel Rosenthal, The Purchase of Paradise
              , Nobles and the Noble Life, 1295-1500
C. D. Ross, Edward IV: Richard III.
G. O. Sayles, The King's Parliament of England
R. W. Somerville, History of the Duchy of Lancaster
A. L. Storey, The End of the House of Lancaster
T. F.Tout, The Place of Edward II in English History
R. Tuck, Richard II and the English Nobility
J. Vale, Edward III and Chivalry
M. Vale, War and Chivalry

MEDIEVAL ENGLAND, 1042-1485
Donald Sutherland
University of Iowa

The period as a whole is one of violent ups and downs for the English: the Norman conquest, the growth and then the failure of the economy, wars with all neighbors but especially with the French and repeated civil war. Through all the turmoil there appears a strange steadiness. The royal government continually became stronger, parliament was created and gained a regular place in government, and personal freedom increased. The experiences and the accomplishments of its Middle Ages left England, around 1500, as a nation that would be a guide to much of the world in the centuries that followed, in law and government, science and industry, learning and belief.

The course will consist mainly (as a course should) in reading. A little of the reading will be in short articles but most will be in five books each of which we will read whole. The books by Frank Barlow and Bertie Wilkinson will be our "textbooks," providing between them a narrative of the four and a half centuries that we are covering. For a special look at the English economy we will use J.L. Bolton's book, for a provocative examination of the earliest growth of parliament the book by George O. Sayles, and finally for a study of the church in one concentrated period the work of William Pantin. Everyone who takes the course had better buy all these books.

Frank Barlow, The Feudal Kingdom of England, 1042-1216, 3rd ed., 1971.

B. Wilkinson, The Later Middle Ages in England, 1216-1485, 1969.

J.L. Bolton, The Medieval English Economy, 1150-1500, 1980.

G.O. Sayles, The King's Parliament of England, 1974.

W.A. Pantin, The English Church in the Fourteenth Century, 1955.

As a back up, there will be a copy of each of these books on reserve for you in the library. Also on reserve will be copies of each of the short articles that are included in the reading of the course, as mentioned below.

Begin the course in its first month, from January 17 to February 16, by reading Frank Barlow's book and then, when you have finished the book, these two articles that reflect in different ways on the times of which the book tells:

James Campbell, "Observations on English Government from the Tenth to the Twelfth Century," *Transactions of the Royal Historical Society*, 5th series, vol 25 (1975), pp. 39-54.

Richard W. Southern, "England's First Entry into Europe," *Medieval Humanism and Other Studies* (1970), pp. 135-57.

After that, from February 17, take up Wilkinson's book and read his chapters 1-6, which cover the years from 1216-1399. As an illustration of the difficulties in maintaining law and order that plagued England during the latter part of this period, also read this article:

E. L. G. Stones, "The Folvilles of Ashby-Folville, Leicestershire, and their Associates in Crime," *Transactions of the Royal Historical Society*, 5th series, vol. 7 (1957), pp. 117-136.

Complete all this reading by March 3. We will use one of the class-hours just after, on March 4 or March 7, for a mid-term examination covering all the material of the course so far.

The course will turn then to some special reading on the economy, parliament, and the church, in that order. From March 4 and before the beginning of the spring vacation on March 19, read Bolton's *Medieval English Economy*, chapters 1-7. In the week after the spring vacation, March 28 to April 3, read Sayles' *King's Parliament of England*. And then in the two weeks following read Pantin's *English Church in the Fourteenth Century*, completing it by April 17.

Finally, read about the fifteenth century. Begin by finishing Wilkinson's book, with chapters 7-11 and the Epilogue. Have this done by April 27. From the story of these times, the horrid mystery of who murdered the young King Edward V and his brother, in 1483 or soon after, remains fascinating. No better detective work had been done with the case than by Paul Murray Kendall, *Richard III*, (1956), Appendix I, "Who Murdered the Princes?", pp. 465-95. Read this appendix, Then in what remains of the semester complete Bolton's *Medieval English Economy*, with chapters 8-10.

During the semester we will use the class-meetings to discuss these readings, as you take them up according to this schedule, and to discuss more generally the developments in English life of which the readings tell.

All of our writers assume that their readers are acquainted with English geography and with the chronology of the reigns of the kings. Most of the writers are in fact English, and refer to Shropshire and Yorkshire as readily as an American writing about America would refer to California and Virginia, to Edward I and Edward III as readily as an American historian would speak of the presidencies of Lincoln and Wilson. To enable you to keep up with them, learn the counties of England and the reigns of the kings from 1042-1485. If you do not, you will be miserable all semester. It is painful to have to read without being able to understand.

The mid-term examination, and the final examination, will each begin with a short-answer section that will call upon you to identify specifically, and date, each of a a dozen or so items, names of men and women, events, institutions. That part will be for one-third of the grade of the examination. For the other two-thirds of the grade, each of the examinations will call for an essay (or in the case of the final examination, perhaps two essays) on a topic or topics that you choose from several that will be announced in advance. So that you can be more confident of writing these examination-essays well, I will call upon everyone to write a practice essay of five pages or so on an assigned topic, once in the first half the semester and once in the second half. These will be graded and commented upon and returned to you well before the mid-term and the final.

In determining grades for the semester, the final examination will be the controlling factor. Often the grade of the final examination will be the grade for the semester. But to calculate the semester grade the grade of the final examination will be averaged in with any grades previously earned for either of the two practice essays or for the mid-term examination, if those earlier grades will help to raise the semester grade. Any of the earlier grades that would tend to lower the semester grade, below the level of the final examination, will be ignored. In averaging in what is to be averaged in according to this rule, a practice essay will count as a factor of 1, the mid-term as a factor of 2, and the final examination as a factor of 4.

FRANCE, from the Stone Age to Joan of Arc.

Jeremy duQuesnay Adams, Southern Methodist University.

This syllabus consists of a sequence of topics which can
be presented on several levels and in several pedagogic directions,
depending on which sequence of readings is used to give synchronic
dimension to its diachronic narrative continuity.

At present this course is offered as History 4372, a lecture course with higher expectations than a 3000-level medieval
European survey course (for example) and more modest goals than a
5000-level seminar. However, it could easily function as an undergraduate seminar using readings-track A or B, or as a graduate (or
advanced honors undergraduate) seminar with track C supplementing
track A. Track B is a sequence of readings designed to appeal to
students interested in French language or civilization; it should
be combined with several of the track A readings for coherence and
depth.

In any of these metamorphoses, the basic course structure
suggests a pair of complementary intersecting cones, the vertex
of each resting at the
center of the other's
base (see sketch). Cone
D represents the course's
commitment to diachronic
report, cone S its concern
for synchronic analysis.

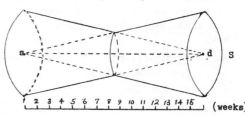

The course's attempt at narrative coverage is widest, both spati-
ally and temporally, in week #1 (Geography and the Paleolithic Era);
subsequent sections narrow until in week #15 Jeanne d'Arc becomes
the central phenomenon (though far from the sole individual) treated.
Conversely, the discrete units of data considered in week #1 can
receive only cursory attention; in week #15 Jeanne d'Arc becomes
the object of detailed and leisurely analysis. Parity between these
two pedagogic principles should be attained as the Franks settle
into the region which thereafter comes to bear their name.

The term France, transcendentally significant to Jeanne,
is of course blatantly anachronistic when applied to the Kultur-

gebiet of Magdalenian and Aurignacian cave-painters. Critique of
the notion of the hexagone géographique, still dear to the contemporary French schoolbook, provides an illuminating point de départ
and orientation point for the semester's discourse. Among the orga-
nizational motifs maintained throughout is a dual regional focus:
on the Paris Basin (broadly defined) and on one other region of
what eventually becomes France. The evolution of the city of Paris
a persistent motif, is set against the perspective of urban development elsewhere (Marseille, Tours, Reims, Bruges, etc.).

    In its present format, the model week-unit consists of a
Monday lecture, a discursive exposition-cum-slides or other visual
material on Wednesday, and a Friday discussion of one clearly fo-
cussed reading assignment, ideally in a translated primary source
available in paperback edition. Textbook continuity is envisioned
(and required) only for the weeks dedicated to Capetian France, the
course's pedagogic center of gravity.

    The readings assigned as track A are essential to the course
in any of its adaptations, and constitute the required maximum of
the 4000-level lecture format. Track B is designed to appeal to
those interested in French civilization, whether classical or avant-
garde in style, and able to read some French. Track C is designed
to provide selective supplements for advanced students with a taste
for historiographic variety as well as an initiation into continental intellectual traditions. Both tracks offer useful and varied
orientation to the instructor attempting only track A. The Larousse
Histoire de la France under the general direction of Georges Duby
can serve multiple duty; it is a wonderfully convenient réunion of
several current French schools.

    Some salient examples of the supplementary-track approach:
In weeks #3-4 one can track the development of French attitudes tow
the issue of Gallic identity, from the post-Prussian nostalgia of
the early medievalist Lot to Latouche's judicious Common-Market-era
revision to the synthesis attempted twenty years later (1984) by
Harmand, an historian of both Roman and Celtic antiquity; all this
in track C. In the previous week, track B has provided a model
nouvelle-histoire assessment. In weeks #7-9, we encounter the
quintessentially British school of Wallace-Hadrill; in week #13,

attempting assessment of the motives of Philip the Fair, we sample
in brief statements the range of an American school. In the final
week (inspired by Charles T. Wood's Dartmouth seminar on Joan of
Arc), and perhaps also in a term paper, the student following track
C can observe the extraordinary range of significance the Maid has
embodied. For Michelet, she was the precursor of the liberating
tradition of French democracy; for the twentieth-century positivist
Perroy, little more than an annoyingly inflated peripheral episode;
the current feminists Pernoud and Warner go further than Michelet.
Alternatively, the student can explore remorseful revisions across
the Channel just after World War I: Shaw's complex presentation of
Joan as an innocent herald of modern nationalism; Murray's insis-
tence that she was indeed a witch, a category of victim close to
the hearts of Michelet and the feminists). Either option could
fruitfully supplement track B's 60-year sequence of French literary
celebrations of la Pucelle.

History 4372 normally requires one term paper, normally based
the readings assigned. Some typical topics: "Pacification: Caesar according to himself and Louis VI according to Suger"; "Urban sedition in the Gaul of Gregory of Tours and the Flanders of Galbert of
Bruges"; "The communal uprising of Laon, according to Guibert of
Nogent and Suger of Saint-Denis"; "The proper comportment of queens,
according to Gregory of Tours and Jean de Joinville"; "The king's
role in society, as perceived by Jean de Joinville and Jeanne d'Arc".
For other typical topics, see weeks #9 and 15.

J.Adams: Hst.4372

Syllabus of topics and assigned readings, required (Track A) and
recommended in various circumstances (Track B and C)

Week 1 :
Geography and the Paleolithic Era. (The mythic hexagone; presentation of Lower Paleolithic sites at and near Fontainebleau and of
the Upper Paleolithic art - and supposed supporting society - of
the Dordogne.)
Reading: A: André Leroi-Gourhan, "The Evolution of Paleolithic
Art," in C. C. Lamberg-Karlovsky, Hunters, Farmers,
and Civilizations: Old World Archeology (Scientific
American-Freeman, 1979), pp. 36-47.

B: Jacqueline Beaujeu-Garnier, in Histoire de la France, genl. ed.
Georges Duby (Paris: Larousse, 1970), ch. I, "Le pays."

C: P.-R. Giot, intr.; and J.-L. Monnier, pt. I, ch. iv, Préhistoire
de la Bretagne (Rennes: Ouest-France, 1979).

Week 2 :
'Neolithicization' and the Bronze Age. (Cultural definitions; relation (?) of metallurgy and megalith erection; the Seine-Oise-
Marne Culture and the megalithic cult-centers of Brittany, esp.
the Carnac-Locmariaquer-Gavrinnis complex. The modern imagination.)
A: Glyn Daniel, The Megalith-Builders of Western Europe (Penguin
pb, 1958-62), chs. 1, 5, 7.

B: Denise de Sonneville-Bordes, in Duby, Histoire de la France (hereafter,
HF), ch. II, "La préhistoire."

C: Georges Briard, L'age du bronze en Europe barbare: des mégalithes
aux Celtes (Paris: Hespérides, 1976), chs. 4, 5 (pp. 133-47, 165-7),
épilogue.
- J. L'Helgouach'h, pt. II, ch. i; P.-R. Giot, pt. III, Préhistoire de
la Bretagne.
- Eleanor Clark, The Oysters of Locmariaquer (Chicago Phoenix pb, 1964,'7

Week 3 :
"Nos Ancêtres les Gaulois": The Iron Age and the Celts. (La Tène he-
gemony and the first encounter with Greek culture. The Parisii
and Massilia.)
A: G. Bertier de Sauvigny & David Pinkney, History of France,
tr. J. Friguglietti (Forum pb, 1983), intr., ch. 1 (1-10).

B: René Joffroy, in Duby HF, ch. III, "La Gaule avant la conquête romaine.

C: Ferdinand Lot, La Gaule, rev. Paul-Marie Duval (Verviers: Fayard, Mara-
bout, 1967), pt. I, bk. I.

Week 4 :
Caesar. (Division and conquest. The fate of the Haedui; alternatives
- the Remi (alliance) or the Veneti (genocide)).
A: C. Julius Caesar, The Conquest of Gaul, tr. S.A. Handford
(Penguin pb, 1983).

B: cf. C, infra.

C: Robert Latouche, Gaulois et Francs: de Vercingétorix à Charlemagne
(Paris: Arthaud, 1965), ch. I.

- F. Lot, La Gaule, pt. I, bk. II.
- Jacques Harmand, Vercingétorix (Fayard, 1984).

Week 5 :
Gallia Romana. ('Civilization': Lutetia Parisiorum and Durocortorum
  Remorum; civitates et viae; the bases of diocesan and departmental
  organization.)
>   A: Bertier de Sauvigny-Pinkney, ch. 1 (pp. 10-13).
>
>   B: René Joffroy, in Duby HF, ch. IV, "Les gallo-romains."
>
>   C: R. Latouche, Gaulois et Francs, chs. II, III.
>   - F. Lot, La Gaule,
>   - Histoire de la France urbaine, genl. ed. Georges Duby: vol. I, La ville
>   antique, pt. I ("Le réseau urbain"), pt. III ("Les villes de la paix
>   romaine").

Week 6 :
Gallia Christiana. (The world of Martin of Tours.)
>   A: Sulpicius Severus, The Life of Martin, Bishop of Tours, tr.
>   F. R. Hoare in The Western Fathers (Harper Torchbook pb).
>   - Gregory of Tours, History of the Franks, tr. L. Thorpe (Pen-
>   guin pb, 1976), bk. I (prol., chs. 1, 28-48).
>
>   B: R. Latouche, Gaulois et Francs, ch. IV.
>
>   C: Luce Pietri, La ville de Tours, du IVe au VIe siècle: naissance d'une
>   cité chrétienne (Rome: Ecole Française de Rome, 1983).
>   - G. Duby, ed. Histoire de la France urbaine, vol. I, pt. IV ("Vetera et
>   nova"), pp. 423-49, 456-60, 479-93.
>   - P.-M. Duval, Résumé du Paris antique (Paris: Hermann, 1972).

Week 7 :
The Franks. (The external challenge becomes the new internal ingredi-
  ent; 'barbarism' and 'civilization'; the requirements of assimila-
  tion -according to whom?; Clovis, the master blender.)
>   A: Gregory of Tours, History, bk. II (and Thorpe's intr.).
>
>   B: Lucien Musset, in Duby HF, ch. V, "Les migrations barbares, IVe-Ve siècle:
>
>   C: R. Latouche, Gaulois et Francs, ch. V.
>   - J. M. Wallace-Hadrill, The Long-Haired Kings and Other Studies in Frank-
>   ish History (Toronto: MART pb, 1982), chs. I ("Frankish Gaul"), III ("The
>   Work of Gregory of Tours in the Light of Modern Research"), VII, i & ii
>   ("Reges criniti" and "Pugnator egregius").

Week 8 :
The Merovingians, 451-751. (A dynasty and its domains; the dynamics
  of decadence; the place of women.)
>   A: Gregory of Tours, History: bk. IV, chs. 1, 4, 11, 19, 26-28,
>   35-6, 49; bk. V; bk. VI, chs. 10, 27, 29, 32, 45-6; bk. VII,
>   chs. 4-5, 12-13, 15, 19-20, 24, 42, 47; bk. VIII, chs. 15-16
>   28-29, 33, 40; bk. IX, chs. 2, 9, 18-19, 30, 34, 39-43;
>   bk. X, chs. 5, 9, 15-17, 20, 27, 30-31. (Students choose
>   themes to follow: cities, queens and other women, male vil-
>   lains, model bishops, relations with the Bretons.)
>
>   B: Bertier de Sauvigny-Pinkney, ch. 2.
>   - Pierre Riché, in Duby HF, ch. VI, "Les temps mérovingiens."
>
>   C: Latouche, Gaulois et Francs, chs. VI, VII.
>   - Suzanne Wemple, Women in Frankish Society, 600-900 (Philadelphia: U. Penn-
>   sylvania Press, 1983).
>   - J.M. Wallace-Hadrill, Long-Haired Kings, chs. VI ("The Bloodfeud of the
>   Franks"), VII, iii-v ("Gregory's kings," "Fredegar's kings," "The
>   rois fainéants").

Week 9 :
Carolingians (687-987). (Less about Charlemagne than about his forbears
and West-Frankish successors – especially Charles the Bald – and the
society which produced that dynasty. Its efforts to reshape that society in turn; grandeur and decline despite the family's commitment
to reform. This week the student experiences a shift in the ratio
of density between lecture and reading. The assigned and suggested
readings are especially heavy in order to provide material for term
papers attempting synthetic research rather than comparative text
analyses.)

> A: either Nithard, History of the Sons of Louis the Pious in Bern-
> hard Scholz, Carolingian Chronicles (Ann Arbor pb, 1972)
> (for political-psychological narrative according to the
> Old History),
> or Pierre Riché, Daily Life in the Age of Charlemagne, tr. J. A.
> McNamara (U. Pennsylvania pb, 1978), esp. chs. 1, 3, 7-20,
> 23-26 (for the concerns of the New History).

> B: Bertier de Sauvigny-Pinkney, ch. 3.
> – Adriaan Verhulst, in Duby HF, ch. VII, "La construction carolingienne."
> – R. Latouche, Gaulois et Francs, ch. VIII.

> C: Einhard and Notker the Stammerer, Two Lives of Charlemagne, tr. L. Thorpe
> (Penguin pb), + the rest of Scholz' Carolingian Chronicles.
> – J.M. Wallace-Hadrill, "A Carolingian Renaissance Prince: The Emperor
> Charles the Bald," in Proceedings of the British Academy (London, 1978),
> pp. 155-84.
> – Wallace-Hadrill, "History in the Mind of Archbishop Hincmar," in The Writing
> of History, edd. R.H.C. Davis & J.M. Wallace-Hadrill (Oxford U. Press,
> 1981), pp. 43-70.
> – Rosamond McKitterick, "The Carolingians and the See of Reims," in Ideal and
> Reality in Frankish and Anglo-Saxon Society, edd. F. Wormald & R. Collins
> (Oxford U. Press, 1984), pp. 228-49.

Week 10 :
The Capetians, 987-1180. (Another new dynasty, with its variant style
well adapted to its environment. Did it have a 'policy'?)

> A: Elizabeth Hallam, Capetian France, 987-1328 (Longman pb, 1980),
> chs. 1-3.
> – Suger, Life of Louis the Fat, tr. J. Adams (forthcoming U. Penn-
> sylvania Press pb; now in typescript), sel. chs.

> B: Bertier de Sauvigny-Pinkney, ch. 4.
> – Georges Duby, in Duby HF, ch. IX, "Les féodaux."

> C: Robert Fawtier, The Capetian Kings of France, tr. L. Butler & R.J. Adam
> (New York: St. Martin's pb, 1962), chs. 1-3, 7.
> – Georges Duby, The Three Orders: Feudal Society Imagined, tr. A. Goldham-
> mer (Chicago U. Press, 1980): "Revelation;" "Eclipse," ii.

Week 11 :
Capetian France, from Louis the Fat to Philip Augustus. (Cultural attitudes in a time of expanding horizons.)

> A: Hallam, Capetian France, ch. 4.
> – John Benton, Self and Society in Medieval France: The Memoirs
> of Guibert of Nogent (Toronto: MART pb, 1984).

> B: R. Fawtier, Capetian Kings, ch. 12.
> – André Joris, in Duby HF, ch. X, "L'essor du XIIe siecle, 1075-1180."

> C: Erwin Panofsky, Abbot Suger on the Abbey Church of St.-Denis and Its Art
> Treasures, 2 ed. (Princeton pb, 1977).

apetian France: Urban Explosion and Social Change. (Bruges and Paris.)

A: Galbert of Bruges, The Murder of Charles the Good, Count of
   Flanders, tr. & intr. J.B. Ross (Toronto: 1 ART pb, 1982).

B: Bertier de Sauvigny-Pinkney, ch. 5.
- Jacques Rossiaud, in Duby HF, ch.XI, "La synthèse capétienne."

C: R. Fawtier, Capetian Kings, ch. 11.
- Jacques Le Goff, in Histoire de la France urbaine, vol. II: La ville médiévale, pt. II ("L'apogée de la France urbaine médiévale, 1150-1330").

ae Capetian Ideal and Its Abuse, 1226-1328. (The sainteté of Louis IX
   and the hybris of his grandson, Philip the Fair; France - and Paris -
   at the center of Europe.)

A: Hallam, Capetian France, chs. 5-6.
- Jean de Joinville, Life of St. Louis, in M.R.B. Shaw (tr.),
  Chronicles of the Crusades (Penguin pb).

B: R. Fawtier, Capetian Kings, chs. 4, 5, 10.
- Elisabeth Carpentier, in Duby HF, ch. XII, "Le grand royaume, 1270-1348."

C: Charles T. Wood, Philip the Fair and Boniface VIII (Holt-Rinehart-Winston
   European Problem Studies: 2 ed., 1971).
- Joseph Strayer, "Philip the Fair - a 'Constitutional' King," in Medieval
  Statecraft and the Perspectives of History (Princeton U. Press, 1971),195-21:
- Elizabeth A.R. Brown, "Philip IV the Fair, of France," Encyclopedia Britan-
  nica, 15th ed. (1983): Macropaedia vol. 14, pp. 223-25.

ae Valois, 1328-1498. (Decline and disaster on all fronts.)

A: Hallam, Capetian France, ch. 7.

B: Bertier de Sauvigny-Pinkney, chs. 6, 7.
- Noël Coulet, in Duby HF, ch. XIII, "Le malheur des temps, 1348-1440."
- Michel Mollat, " "   " ch. XIV, "La reconstruction, 1440-1515."

C: Edouard Perroy, The Hundred Years War(1945), tr. W. Wells (New York: Capricorn, 1965), esp. pts. I-IV, VI, VIII(1-3), IX(2, 4).
- Jacques Rossiaud, in Histoire de la France urbaine, vol. II, pt. III ("Crises
  et consolidations, 1330-1530"), pp. 408-553.

anne d'Arc. (Recovery, real and symbolic; the militant miracle.)

A: The Trial of Joan of Arc, tr. W.F. Scott (Westport, Conn.: Associ-
   ated Booksellers).

B: Maurice Boutet de Monvel, Joan of Arc (1895), tr. Albert Guérard (Ann Arbor pb
- Paul Claudel, Jeanne d'Arc au Bûcher (w. A. Honegger: 1938).   1957
- Jean Anouilh, L'alouette (1953): The Lark, tr. Christopher Fry (1955).

C: 1) Jules Michelet, Joan of Arc (1843), tr. (Ann Arbor pb, 1957).
      E. Perroy, Hundred Years War, VIII(1).
      Régine Pernoud, Joan of Arc, By Herself and Her Witnesses (New York: Stein
        & Day pb, 1969).
      Marina Warner, Joan of Arc, The Image of Female Heroism (New York: Random
        House pb, 1982).
   2) George Bernard Shaw, Saint Joan (1923).
      Margaret A. Murray, The Witch-Cult in Western Europe (1923; Oxford UP pb,
        1962), appendix IV.

CAPETIAN AND EARLY VALOIS FRANCE, 987-1498
History 445P/645P

James Alexand
University of Georg

Required "textbooks," all in paperback:

    Robert Fawtier, The Capetian Kings of France
    Elizabeth Hallam, Capetian France, 987-1328
    J. H. Huizinga, The Waning of the Middle Ages
    Emmanuel le Roy Ladurie, Montaillou: The Promised Land of Error
    Sidney Painter, French Chivalry
    J. R. Strayer, On the Medieval Origins of the Modern State

A spaced line separates readings on reserve from those to be owned by
the student; * indicates a reading selection on reserve which is also
available in paperback, for purchase if you wish to own it. Additiona
assignments may be made in class for the graduate students. Assignmen
should be read before the week to which they pertain. Cambridge
Medieval History is listed as optional reading.

WEEK   ASSIGNMENT

1   Feudal France in the Eleventh Century: The Early Capetians, 987-11

        Hallam, 1-108
        Painter, French Chivalry
        Fawtier, Capetian Kings

        Cambridge Medieval History (hereafter cited as CMH), III,
            99-133: Louis Halpehn, "France in the Eleventh Century.
        S. Everett Gleason, An Ecclesiastical Barony of the Middle
            Ages: The Bishopric of Bayeux, 1066-1204 (entire)
        Frederic Cheyette, Lordship and Community in Medieval Europe,
            198-210, 100-128, 137-155

        Graduate students should read as well J. F. Lemarignier, Le
            Gouvernement royal aux premiers temps capetiens, 987-110
            first and last chapters, and acquaint themselves with W.
            H. Newman, Le Domaine royal sous les premiers capetiens.

2   Louis VI and Louis VII, 1108-1180

        Hallam, 108-203
        Fawtier, Capetian Kings, 19-24, 137-143, 156-226

        CMH, V, 592-604: Halpehn, "Louis VI and Louis VII"

Philip Augustus and Louis VII , 1180-1226

Fawtier, Capetian Kings, 24-27, 143-151

Luchaire, Social France in the Age of Philip Augustus
CMH, VI, 285-330: F. M. Powicke, "The Reigns of Philip Augustus
and Louis VIII"
T. Evergates, Feudal Society in the Bailliage of Troyes, 1-15,
136-154

Additional reading for first 3 weeks:
*Odo of Deuill, De profectione Ludovivi VII in orientem
(entire)
*Galbert of Bruges, The Murder of Charles the Good
(entire)

St Louis and Philip III, 1226-1285

Hallam, 204-272
Fawtier, Capetian Kings, 27-34, 41-109, 151-228

CMH, VI, 331-361: Ch. Petit-Dutaillis, "St. Louis"
Sidney Painter, The Scourge of the Clergy
Jean de Joinville, Life of St Louis (variously titled)
Eudes Rigaud, The Register of Eudes of Rouen, XV-XXXVI and any
1 year of the register

6 The Last Capetians: Philip "The Fair" through Charles IV, 1285-1328

Hallam, 273-end
Fawtier, Capetian Kings, 34-41, 227-230
le Roy Ladurie, Montaillou

CMH, VII, 305-339: Hilda Johnstone, "The Last Capetians"
*Wood, Philip the Fair and Boniface VIII

The Hundred Years' War

Froissart, Chronicles, 1.28-65, 114-151, 174-202; 2.1-31,
53-104
CMH, VII, 340-392: A. Couville, "France: The Hundred Years'
War"
G. P. Cuttino, "The Causes of the Hundred Years' War," Speculum
XXXI (1956), 463-472

Henneman, French Monarchy, 123-136
Huizinga, The Waning of the Middle Ages
Strayer, On the Medieval Origins of the Modern State

P. S. Lewis, Later Medieval France (and through week 9)
Geoffrey de la Tour Landry, The Book of the Knight of the
    Tower, chapters 6, 14, 15, 16-18, 20-22, 35, 36, 103, 111
    119, 120, page 29 (lines 36ff.), p. 43 (lines 29ff.), pag
    73 (lines 10ff.), pp. 115-119, 122-33, 135-6.

9-10 France at the Close of the Middle Ages

Henneman, French Monarchy, 136-end

CMH, VII, 232-305:   J. Calmette, "The Reign of Charles VII" a
    "Louis XI"
P. S. Lewis, The Recovery of France in the Fifteenth Century,
    185-216, 242-265, 294-end
E. Perroy, "Feudalism or Principalities in Fifteenth-Century
    France," Bulletin of the Institute of Historical Research
    XX (1943-45), 181-85
Philippe de Commynes, Memoirs 1.93-146, 297-368; 2.371-435
Cheyette, Lordship and Community, 240-255
Shirley, A Parisian Journal
Vaughan, Valois Burgundy

Students should familiarize themselves with the following source
collections, indispendable for the scholarly study of medieval French
history.

The two great "national" narrative and chronicle series are:

Dom M. Bouquet, et. al., Recueil des historiens des Gaules et
    de la France.

Société de l'histoire de France: Publications

Government records and collections of charters:

NB: The acta of many medieval French kings are available, edited
according to reign; some are still incomplete (e.g., the Recueil d
actes de Philippe-Auguste has reached only vol. IV).   Most are in
the first series below.

Chartes et deplomes, publiés par les soins de L'Acadmie des
    Inscriptions et Belles-Lettres
Congregation of St. Maur (eds), Galla christina
Dom de Laurier, et al. (eds), Ordonnances des rois de France la
    troisième race
M. Isambert, et. al. (eds), Recueil generale des anciennes lois
    françaises

A. Teulet (ed), <u>Layettes du Trésor des Chartes</u>
<u>Collections des documents inédits sur l'histoire de France</u>
    (which includes, e.g. <u>Les Olim</u>)
<u>The Bibliothéque de l'école des Chartes</u> publishes records and
    documents as well as articles. Great Britain's Record
    Commission and Public Record Office have published much
    material pertininet to medieval French history; see E. L.
    C. Mullins, <u>Texts and Calendars</u>, for details of
    publication and contents.

Many excellent editions are among the publications of local French
cord and historical societies; they hold to an almost uniformly high
andard of excellence. Unfortunately, there is no French equivalent to
llins' <u>Texts and Calendars</u>, an exhaustive analytical index of all
tional and local historical society publications in England. A.
anklin's <u>Les sources de l'histoire de France</u> is a century old, and
tthast's <u>Bibliotheca hsitorica medii aevi</u>, 70 (a new edition is in
eparation); these are the only comprehensive guides to the French
storical source collections (but see below, A). Frere's <u>Bibliographie</u>
rmande pertains to Normandy only.

Among more general series, the following are particularly valuable
r the history of medieval France:

The Rolls series (Chronicles and Memorials of Great Britain and
    Ireland During the Middle Ages)
J. Mansi, <u>Sacrorum Conciliorum nova et amplissima collectio</u>
Publications in the <u>Monumenta Germaniae historica</u>, especially the
    Scriptores and Leges
J.P. Migne, <u>Patrologiae latinae cursus completus</u>
<u>Recueil des historiens des Croisades</u>
<u>Corpus Christianorum, Series Latina</u>

<u>Bibliographies</u>

Since there is no single modern bibliography of medieval French
history, the following must serve as a substitute:

R. C. van Caenegem, <u>Gruide to the Sources of Medieval History</u>
C.V.J. Chevalier, <u>Repertoire des sources historiques de Moyen Age</u>
<u>Collection des inventaires -- sommaires des Archives départmental</u>
    antérieures a 1790
L. H. Cottineau, <u>Répertoire topobibliographique des abbayes et</u>
    prieurés
Fawtier, <u>Capetian Kings,</u> esp C. I.
Franklin and Potthast, <u>supra.</u>
G. Gayet, Sources de l'histoire des intstitutions et de droit
    francais
Louis Halphen, <u>Initiation aux études d'histoire du Moyen Age</u>
L. J. Koenigswarter, <u>Sources et monuments de droit français</u>
    anteérieures au 15e siécle
R. Lasteyrie and A. Vidier, <u>Bibliographie générale des travaux</u>
    <u>historiques et archéologiques publiés par les sociétés</u>
    <u>savants de la France</u> (11 vols., 1898-1950)

J. F. Lemarignier, <u>La France médiévale</u>, pp. 386-402
Gabriel Lepointe and Andre Vandenbossche, <u>Elements de bibliographi</u>
    <u>sur l'histoire des institutions et des faits sociaux, 987-187</u>
<u>Les Annales (Economies, Sociétés, Civilisations)</u> and continuations
A.L.Molinier, <u>Les sources de l'histoire de France de origines aux</u>
    <u>guerres d'Italie</u>
Marcel Pacaut, <u>Guide de l'étudiant en histoire médiévale</u>
L. J. Paetow, <u>A Guide to the Study of Medieval History</u> (Rev. Gray
    C. Boyce)
Ch. Petit-Dutaillis, <u>The Feudal Monarchy in France and England</u>,
    301-409
H. Stein, <u>Bibliographie générale des cartulaires françaises relati</u>
    <u>a l'histoire de France</u>
American Historical Society, <u>Guide to Historical Literature</u>

Manuscript collections are frequently described in published French
library catalogues.

For current bibliography, see the reviews and lists in such journals a
    <u>Speculum, English Historical Review</u>, <u>Annals</u>, <u>American Historical</u>
    <u>Review</u>, <u>Revue historique</u>, <u>Historische Zeitschrift</u>, <u>History</u>, <u>Clio:</u>
    <u>Introduction aux Etudes historiques</u>, and other historical
    periodicals. <u>Revue d'histoire ecclésiastique</u>, (thrice
    annually),<u>Bibliographie annuele de l'histoire de France.</u> Theodore
    Besterman, <u>World Bibliography of Bibliographies</u>, Library of
    Congress, Reference Division, <u>Current National Bibliographies</u>

Local history: V. Carriere, <u>Introduction aux études d'histoire</u>
    <u>ecclésiastiqu locale</u>

B. Dictionaries, manuals, etc.

    Chevin, <u>Dictionnaire des noms latins de lieux</u>
    G. Kitson Clark, <u>Guide for Research Students</u>, pp. 40ff, for MS
        collections
    A. de Bourard, <u>Manuel de diplomatique française et pontificale</u>
     (2 volumes of text, three of plates)
    Dom Cottineau, <u>Repertoire topo-bibliographique des abbayes et</u>
        <u>prieures</u>
    A.J.K. Esdaile, <u>A Student's Manual of Bibliography</u> (ed. 3)
    Farrar and Evans, <u>English Translations from Medieval Sources</u>
        although incomplete, remains the only work of its kind,
        supplemented by Mary Anne Ferguson, <u>Bibliography of English</u>
        <u>Translations from Medieval Sources, 1948-1968</u>
    A. Giry, <u>Manuel de diplomatique</u>
    A. Longonon, <u>Atlase historique de la France</u>
    C.T. Martin, <u>The Record Interpreter</u>
    M. Prou, <u>Manuel de Paléographie latine et française du VI au XVII</u>
        <u>siècle</u>
    G. Tessier, <u>Diplomatique royal française</u>
    <u>The Revised Medieval Latin Word-List</u> should be supplemented by the
        best one-volume Latin dictionary, which is that of Lewis and
        Short

. Fundamental Studies

   Most will be found listed in the required readings for this course,
or in the bibliographies above. An attempt will be made in the lectures
to acquaint students with current historical writing in the field, with
the nature of the sources, and with the more interesting and important
controversies pertinent to the history of France in the middle ages.
The following works are recent enough to have eluded most
bibliographies.

   John W. Baldwin, Masters, Princes and Merchants
   A. Becker, Studien zum Investiturproblem in Frankreich
   Thomas Bisson, Assemblies and Representation in Languedoc in the
      Thirteenth Century
   Marc Bloch, La France sous les derniers capetiens
   Georges Duby, The Chivalrous Society
   Georges Duby, La société aux XIe et XIIe siècles dans la région
      mâconnaise
   Theodore Evergates, Feudal Society in the Baillage of Troyes
   Kenneth Fowler, The Hundred Years War
   M. Hallam, Capetian France, 987-1328
   John Bell Henneman, Royal taxation in XIV France
   Wm. C. Jordan, Louis IX and the Challenge of the Crusade
   F. Lavisse (ed.), Histoire de France, vols 2 and 3
   J.F. Lemarignier, La France médiévale: Institutions et société
   Lemarignier, cited for week 1
   E. Lesne, Histoire de la propriété ecclesiastique en France (5
      vols.; much broader than its title would indicate)
   Andrew W. Lewis, Royal succession in Capetian France
   Archibald Lewis, The Development of Southern France and Catalan
      Society, 718-1750
   P.S. Lewis, Later Medieval France
   F. Lot and R. Fawtier, Histoire des institutions françaises au moyen
      age
   Bryce Lyon and A.E. Verhulst, Medieval Finance
   J. Russel Major, Representative Institution in Renaissance France,
      1421-1559
   Fliche et Martin, Histoire de l'Eglise
   Pacaut, cited for week 2
   Frank Pegues, The Lawyers of the Last Capetians
   E. Perroy, The Hundred Years Was
   Joseph Strayer, Medieval Statecraft and the Perspectives of History
   Joseph Strayer, The Administration of Normandy Under St. Louis
   J. R. Strayer, The Reign of Philip IV
   M.G.A. Vale, Charles VII
   M.G.A. Vale, War and Chilvary
   Richard Vaughan, Philip the Bold: John the Fearless; Philip the
      Good; Charles the Rash
   Charles T. Wood, The French Apanages and the Capetian Monarchy
      1224-1328
   Gérardd Sivéry, Saint Louis et son siècle
   Jean Richard, St Louis
   And see the titles recommended throughout this syllabus for the
      attention of graduate students.

   I have not attempted to list the substantial number of exceedingly
fine studies of French provinces in the middle ages; many may be found
in the apparatus to the Lot and Fawtier set cited above.

HISTORY OF MEDIEVAL GERMANY TO 1546.

TEXTS: G. Barraclough, The Origins of Modern Germany. (Capricorn)
Einhard and Notker, Two Lives of Charlemagne, trans. L. Thorpe.
(Penguin)
The Investiture Controversy: Issues, Ideals, and Results,
ed. K. F. Morrison. (Krieger)
The Reformation: Basic Interpretations, ed. L. Spitz. Second edition.
(D. C. Heath)

N.B. IN ACCORDANCE WITH UNIVERSITY POLICY, THE TAPING OF LECTURES IS NOT
PERMITTED! Exceptions will be made only for physically handicapped students
having the instructor's written permission.

Barraclough's Origins will serve as the basic text throughout the greater part
of the course, although not during the earlier period. Additional reading is
listed in the following syllabus, but please do not panic! You are not
expected to read all of this material or even the greater part of it. Each
item you are asked specifically to read is marked with an asterisk (*) and,
with the exception of the texts listed above, will be found in the Reserve Room
in Sinclair Library. Discussion periods have been scheduled for the Einhard,
Morrison and Spitz pamphlets, and some other topics may be handled on a
discussion or semi-discussion basis.

You are expected to pursue a research project throughout the greater part of
the semester, dealing with a topic or problem of your choice, which must,
however, fall within the time and subject areas of the course and have the
instructor's approval. Submission of your topic (17 September, on a form
which will be furnished) ipso facto will constitute affirmation of the fact
that you have checked out the library holdings and that the requisite primary
sources, monographic literature, and periodical material all are available in
languages in which you are competent. A first draft of the paper, as nearly
as possible in final form and complete with scholarly apparatus, will be
submitted for comment and criticism by 19 October. The final version,
impeccable in style, form, and content, and representing so far as possible a
significant original contribution to the sum total of human knowledge, will be
turned in on or before 12 December.

I will gladly furnish advice and a reasonable degree of assistance, both with
the paper and with the course. My office is Sakamaki Hall A-408. See me MWF
7:00 - 7:20; 9:50 - 10:30 or by appointment.

PROPOSED SCHEDULE OF LECTURES AND DISCUSSIONS.

Mon. 27 Aug.   The Geography of Germany and Primitive Germanic Society.

   *A Source Book of Mediaeval History, ed. F. A. Ogg, pp. 19-31.

R. E. Dickinson, The Regions of Germany.
C. T. Smith, An Historical Geography of Western Europe Before 1800.
E. A. Thompson, The Early Germans.
R. E. Oakeshott, The Archaeology of Weapons. (Provocative discussion of the Indo-Europeans.)
M. Todd, Everyday Life of the Barbarians: Goths, Franks and Vandals.
W. Schlesinger, "Lord and Follower in Germanic Institutional History," Lordship and Community in Medieval Europe: Selected Readings, ed. F. L. Cheyette (1968), pp. 64-99.
F. S. Lear, "The Idea of Fidelity in Germanic Customary Law," Treason in Roman and Germanic Law: Collected Papers (1965), pp. 73-107.

Wed. 29 Aug.   Ibid.

Fri. 31 Aug.   The Germanic Tribes and the Roman Empire.

*Source Book ..., ed. Ogg, pp. 32-46.
P. L. MacKendrick, Romans on the Rhine: Archaeology in Germany.
R. MacMullen, Enemies of the Roman Order: Treason, Unrest and Alienation in the Roman Empire.
F. Lot, The End of the Ancient World and the Beginnings of the Middle Ages.
The Transformation of the Roman World: Gibbon's Problem after Two Centuries, ed. L. White, Jr.
M. Rostovtsev, The Social and Economic History of the Roman Empire.
J. B. Bury, The Invasion of Italy by the Barbarians.
T. Hodgkin, Italy and Her Invaders.   (8 vols.)

Mon. 3 Sept.   HOLIDAY (Labor Day)

Wed. 5 Sept.   The Merovingian Kingdom.

*Source Book ..., ed. Ogg, pp. 47-67. [A fuller version of the Salic Law appears in Select Historical Documents of the Middle Ages, ed. E. F. Henderson, pp. 176-189.]
J. M. Wallace-Hadrill, The Long-Haired Kings and Other Studies of Frankish History.
S. Dill, Roman Society in Gaul in the Merovingian Age.
B. S. Bachrach, Merovingian Military Organization, 481-751. [Use with caution.]
B. S. Bachrach, "Procopius, Agathias and the Frankish Military," Speculum, XLV (1970), 435-441.
A. R. Lewis, "The Dukes in the Regnum Francorum, A.D. 550-751," ibid., (1976), 381-410.
R. P. C. Hanson, "The Church in Fifth-Century Gaul: Evidence from Sidonius Apollinaris," Journal of Ecclesiastical History, XXI (1970), 1-10.
Gregory of Tours, History of the Franks.

Fri. 7 Sept.   The Rise of the Carolingians.

   *Select Historical Documents of the Middle Ages, ed. E. F.
      Henderson, pp. 319-329.
   *A Source Book for Mediaeval History, ed. O. J. Thatcher and
      E. H. McNeal, pp. 37-38, 101-105.
   The Fourth Book of the Chronicle of Fredegar With Its
      Continuations, trans. J. M. Wallace-Hadrill, pp. 1-121.
   W. Goffart, "The Fredegar Problem Reconsidered," Speculum,
      XXXVIII (1963), 206-241.

Mon. 10 Sept.   The Conversion of Germany and the Reform of the Frankish Church.

   W. Levison, England and the Continent in the Eighth Century.
   S. J. Crawford, Anglo-Saxon Influence on Western Christendom.
   G. W. Greenaway, Saint Boniface: Three Biographical Studies
      for the Twelfth Centenary Festival.
   J. B. Russell, "Saint Boniface and the Eccentrics," Church
      History, XXXIII (1964), 235-247.
   D. H. Miller, "The Roman Revolution of the Eighth Century: A
      Study of the Ideological BAckground of the Papal Separation
      from Byzantium and Alliance With the Franks," Mediaeval
      Studies, XXXVI (1974), 79-133.
   R. E. Sullivan, "The Papacy and Missionary Activity in the Early
      Middle Ages," ibid., XVII (1955), 46-106.
   The Letters of Saint Boniface, trans. E. Emerton.

Wed. 12. Sept.   Charlemagne as King and the Conquest of Saxony.

   *Source Book..., ed. Ogg, pp. 108-148.
   R. Winston, Charlemagne: From the Hammer to the Cross.
   P. Munz, Life in the Age of Charlemagne.
   F.-L. Ganshof, "Charlemagne," Speculum, XXIV (1949), 520-528.
   D. A. Bullough, "Europae Pater: Charlemagne and his Achievement in
      the Light of Recent Scholarship," English Historical
      Review, LXXXV (1970), 59-105. [Review article.]
   M. Lintzel, Ausgewählte Schriften, I.

Fri. 14 Sept.   DISCUSSION of the Lives of Charlemagne and the Imperial
                 Coronation.

   *Einhard and Notker, Two Lives of Charlemagne, trans. B. Thorpe
   *The Coronation of Charlemagne: What Did It Signify? ed. R. E.
      Sullivan. [Will be distributed in class.]
   F.-L. Ganshof, The Imperial Coronation of Charlemagne:
      Theories and Facts. This interpretation should be compared
      with that of W. Ullmann, The Growth of Papal Government in
      the Middle Ages.
   R. Folz, The Concept of Empire in Western Europe From the
      Fifth to the Fourteenth Century.
   P. Munz, The Origin of the Carolingian Empire.
   N. Downs, "The Role of the Papacy in the Coronation of Charle-
      magne," Studies in Medieval Culture, III (1970), 7-22.

Zum Kaisertum Karls des Großen: Beiträge und Aufsätze, ed. G. Wolf.
[A collection of important articles in German.]
W. Ullmann, The Growth of Papal Government in the Middle Ages,
pp. 1-118.

Mon. 17 Sept.   Carolingian Institutions.   [TERM PAPER TOPICS DUE]

*Select Historical Documents ..., ed. Henderson, pp. 189-201, or the
same in Source Book ..., ed. Ogg, pp. 134-144.
F.-L. Ganshof, "The Impact of Charlemagne on the Institutions of the
Frankish Realm," Speculum, XL (1965), 47-62.
F. N. Estey, "The Meaning of placitum and mallum in the
Capitularies," ibid., XXII (1947), 433-439.
F. N. Estey, "The scabini and the Local Courts," ibid., XXVI
(1951), 119-129.
J. T. Rosenthal, "The Public Assembly in the Time of Louis the
Pious," Traditio, XX (1964), 25-40.
F.-L. Ganshof, "Benefice and Vassalage in the Age of Charlemagne,"
Cambridge Historical Journal, VI (1939), 149-175.
P. R. McKeon, "Archbishop Ebbo of Reims (816-835): A Study in
the Carolingian Empire and the Church," Church History,
XLIII (1974), 437-447.
J. W. Thompson, The Dissolution of the Carolingian Fisc in the
Ninth Century.

Wed. 19 Sept.   The Carolingian Renaissance.

*Source Book ..., ed. Ogg, pp. 144-148.
*Source Book ..., ed. Thatcher and McNeal, pp. 55-57.
R. R. Bolgar, The Classical Heritage and Its Beneficiaries.
W. Ullmann, The Carolingian Renaissance and the Idea of
Kingship.
K. F. Morrison, The Two Kingdoms: Ecclesiology in Carolingian
Political Thought.
E. S. Duckett, Alcuin, Friend of Charlemagne.
F. W. Buckler, Harun al Rashid and Charles the Great.
L Wollach, Alcuin and Charlemagne: Studies in Carolingian History
and Literature.
J. Huber, J. Porcher, W. F. Volbach, The Carolingian Renaissance.
[Emphasizes art. Magnificent illustrations; excellent text.]
G. W. Trompf, "The Carolingian Renaissance," Journal of the History
of Ideas, XXXIV (1973). 1-26.
R. J. Gariepy, "Lupus of Ferrières: Carolingian Scribe and Text
Critic," Mediaeval Studies, XXX (1968), 90-105.
R. Kottje, "Hrabanus Maurus - 'Praeceptor Germaniae'?" Deutsches
Archiv, XXXI (1975), 534-545.
"The Letters of Einhard," trans. by H. Preble, Papers of the
American Society of Church History, Second Series, I (1913),
107-158.

Fri. 21 Sept.   Slides on the Carolingian Empire.

Mon. 24 Sept.   The Later Carolingian Empire and the East Frankish Kingdom.

    *Source Book ..., ed. Ogg, pp. 149-176.
    *Select Historical Documents ..., ed. Henderson, pp. 201-207.
    *Source Book ..., ed. Thatcher and McNeal, pp. 59-69.
    H. Fichtenau, The Carolingian Empire.
    F.-L. Ganshof, The Carolingians and the Frankish Monarchy:
       Studies in Carolingian History.
    P. R. McKeon, Hincmar of Laon and Carolingian Politics.
    E. Dümmler, Geschichte des ostfränkischen Reiches.   (3 vols.)
    Carolingian Chronicles: Royal Frankish Annals and Nithard's
       Histories, trans. B. W. Scholz and B. Rogers.
    Son of Charlemagne, trans. A. Cabaniss.

Wed. 26 Sept.   The Formation of the German Kingdom.

    *G. Barraclough, The Origins of Modern Germany, pp. 1-23.
    *T. Mayer, "The Historical Foundations of the German Constitution,"
       Mediaeval Germany, 911-1250: Essays by German Historians,
       trans. by Geoffrey Barraclough, II, 1-33.
    *B. Schmeidler, "Franconia's Place in the Structure of Mediaeval
       Germany," ibid., II, 71-93.
    K. Bosl, "Ruler and Ruled in the German Empire from the Tenth to the
       Twelfth Century," Lordship and Community in Medieval Europe:
       Selected Readings, ed. F. L. Cheyette, pp. 268-290.
    K. Leyser, "The German Aristocracy from the Ninth to the Early Twelfth
       Century: A Historical and Cultural Sketch," Past and Present,
       XLI (1968), 25-53.
    G. Läwen, Stammesherzog und Stammesherzogtum: Beiträge zur Frage
       ihrer rechtlichen Bedeutung im 10.-12. Jahrhundert.

Fri. 28 Sept.   The Saxon Dynasty: Henry I and Otto I.

    *Barraclough, Origins of Modern Germany, pp. 24-53.
    B. H. Hill, Jr., Medieval Monarchy in Action: The German Empire From
       Henry I to Henry IV, pp. 7-42, 111-163.
    K. Leyser, Rule and Conflict in an Early Medieval Society: Ottonian
       Saxony.
    K. Leyser, "Henry I and the Beginnings of the Saxon Empire," English
       Historical Review, LXXXIII (1968), 1-32.
    H. L. Adelson, "The Holy Lance and the Hereditary German Monarchy,"
       The Art Bulletin, XLVIII (1966), 177-192.
    A. Alföldi, "Hasta - Summa Imperii. The Spear as Embodiment of Sover-
       eignty in Rome," American Journal of Archaeology, LXIII (1959),
       1-27.
    K. Leyser, "The Battle at the Lech, 955: A Study in Tenth-Century
       Warfare," History, L (1965), 1-25.
    C. Erdmann, "Das Grab Heinrichs I.," Deutsches Archiv, IV (1940-41),
       76-97.

Mon. 1 Oct.   The Ottonian Empire.

*Barraclough, Origins of Modern Germany, pp. 53-71.
B. H. Hill, Jr., The Rise of the First Reich: Germany in the Tenth
   Century.
J. N. Sunderland, "The Mission to Constantinople in 968 and Liudprand
   of Cremona," Traditio, XXXI (1975), 55-81.
W. Holtzmann, Geschichte der sächsischen Kaiserzeit, pp 175-249.
A. Hauck, Kirchengeschichte Deutschlands, III, 3-338.
D. Claude, Geschichte des Erzbistums Magdeburg bis in das 12.Jahrhund-
   ert, I: Die Geschichte der Erzbischöfe bis auf Ruotger (1124).
H. Beumann, "Das Kaisertum Ottos des Großen," Historische Zeitschrift,
   CXCV (1962), 529-573.

Wed. 3 Oct.   Otto II and Otto III: Renovatio Imperii.

Hill, Medieval Monarchy in Action, pp. 43-60, 163-183.
J. B. Morrall, "Otto III: An Imperial Ideal," History Today, IX
   (1959), 812-822.
A. F. Czajkowski, "The Congress of Gniezno in the Year 1000,"
   Speculum, XXIV (1949), 339-356.
F. J. Tschan, Bernward of Hildesheim.   (3 vols.)
Z. Wojciechowski, "La 'Renovatio Imperii' sous Otton III et la
   Pologne," Revue historique, CCI (1949), 30-44.
K. Hampe, "Kaiser Otto III. und Rom," Hist. Zeit., CLX (1929),
   513-533.
M. Uhlirz, "Kaiser Otto III. und das Papsttum," ibid., CLXXI (1940),
   258-268.
K. and M. Uhlirz, Jahrbücher des deutschen Reiches Unter Otto II. und
   Otto III.   Vol. II.
F. Koch, Wurde Kaiser Karl sitzend begraben?
P. E. Schramm, "Die 'Heilige Lanze,' Reliquie und Herrschaftszeichen
   des Reiches und ihre Replik in Krakau: Ein Überblick über die
   Geschichte der Königslanze," Herrschaftszeichen und Staats-
   symbolik, II, 493-537.
Sylvester II (Pope), The Letters of Gerbert, trans. H. Lattin.

Fri. 5 Oct.   Henry II and Conrad II: Domestic and Ecclesiastical Adjustments

*Barraclough, Origins of Modern Germany, pp. 72-98.
Hill, Medieval Monarchy in Action, pp. 61-84, 183-208.
K. Hampe, Germany Under the Salian and Hohenstaufen Emperors, trans.
   R. Bennett (1973), pp. 33-46.
H. J. Lang, "The Fall of the Monarchy of Mieszko II, Lambert,"
   Speculum, XLIX (1974), 623-639.
T. Schieffer, "Heinrich II. und Konrad II. Die Umprägung des
   Geschichtsbildes durch die Kirchenreform des 11. Jahrhunderts,"
   Deutsches Archiv, VIII (1950-51), 384-437.
H. L. Mikoletzky, Kaiser Heinrich II. und die Kirche.

Mon. 8 Oct.   HOLIDAY (Discoverers' Day)

Wed. 10 Oct.   HOUR EXAM.

Fri. 12 Oct.   Monasticism and Church Reform.

    *"The Foundation Charter of Cluny." in Source Book ..., ed. Ogg,
        pp. 245-249, or in Select Historical Documents ..., ed.
        Henderson, pp. 329-333.
    *H. Hirsch, "The Constitutional History of the Reformed Monasteries
        During the Investiture Contest," Mediaeval Germany, 911-1250,
        ed. G. Barraclough, II, 131-173.
    *U. Stutz, "The Proprietary Church as an Element of Mediaeval Germanic
        Ecclesiastical Law," ibid., II, 35-70.
    *J. W. Thompson, Feudal Germany, I, 3-67.
    H. C. Lea, The History of Sacerdotal Celibacy in the Christian Church.
    G. Constable, Monastic Tithes From Their Origins to the Twelfth
        Century.
    J. Evans, Monastic Life at Cluny, 910-1157.
    H. E. J. Cowdrey, The Cluniacs and the Gregorian Reform.
    K. J. Conant, "Mediaeval Academy Excavations at Cluny, X," Speculum,
        XLV (1970), 1-39.

Mon. 15 Oct.   The Salians and the Church: Henry III.

    *Barraclough, Origins of Modern Germany, pp. 72-98. [Assigned above.]
    *Thompson, Feudal Germany, I, 68-124.
    Hill, Medieval Monarchy in Action, pp. 85-98, 209-214.
    Hampe, Germany Under the Salian and Hohenstaufen Emperors, pp. 47-59.
    R. L. Poole, "Benedict IX and Gregory VI," Proceedings of the British
        Academy, VIII (1917-1918), 199-235.
    D. B. Zema, "The Houses of Tuscany and Pierleone in the Crises of Rome
        in the Eleventh Century," Traditio, II (1944), 155-175. [This
        article is printed in the Morrison pamphlet which will be read
        prior to the discussion scheduled for Friday, 21 Oct.]
    E. N. Johnson, "Adalbert of Hamburg-Bremen: A Politician of the
        Eleventh Century," Speculum, IX (1934), 147-179.
    H. H. Anton, "Bonifaz von Canossa, Markgraf von Tuszien, und die
        Italienpolitik der frühen Salier," Historische Zeitschrift,
        CCXIV (1972), 529-556.
    Adam of Bremen, History of the Archbishops of Hamburg-Bremen, trans.
        F. J. Tschan.

Wed. 17 Oct.   Henry IV: Minority and Saxon Wars.

    *Thompson, Feudal Germany, I, 185-216.
    *Select Historical Documents ... ed. Henderson, pp. 361-365.
    Hill, Medieval Monarchy in Action, pp. 99-106, 214-241.
    Hampe, Germany Under the Salian and Hohenstaufen Emperors, pp. 60-79.
    G. Meyer von Knonau, Jahrbücher des deutschen Reiches Unter Heinrich
        IV. und Heinrich V.   Vols. I-II.

Fri. 19 Oct.   The Investiture Contest, I.   [FIRST DRAFT DUE.]

    *Barraclough, Origins of Modern Germany, pp. 101-127.
    *Source Book ..., ed. Ogg, pp. 261-281.

*Select Historical Documents ..., ed. Henderson, pp. 365-409. See also
    Select Historical Documents ..., ed. Thatcher and McNeal, pp.
    132-166.
*P. Joachimsen, "The Investiture Contest and the German Constitution,"
    Mediaeval Germany, 911-1250, ed. G. Barraclough, II, 95-129.
*J. W. Thompson, Feudal Germany, I, 125-166, 217-265.
Z. N. Brooke, "Lay Investiture and Its Relation to the Conflict of
    Empire and Papacy," Proceedings of the Britich Academy, XXV
    (1939), 217-247.
K. F. Morrison, "Canossa: A Revision," Traditio, XVIII (1962),
    121-148.
J. T. Gilchrist, "Canon Law Aspects of the Eleventh Century Gregorian
    Reform Program," Journal of Ecclesiastical History, XIII (1962),
    21-38.
S. A. Chodorow, "Magister Gratian and the Problem of 'Regnum' and
    'Sacerdotium'," Traditio, XXVI (1970), 364-381.
G. H. Williams, The Norman Anonymous of 1100 A.D.
R. Nineham, "The So-Called Anonymous of York," Journal of Ecclesiast-
    ical History, XIV (1963), 31-45.
G. Tellenbach, Church, State, and Christian Society at the Time of the
    Investiture Contest.
N. Hunt, Cluny Under Saint Hugh, 1049-1109.
K. F. Morrison, Tradition and Authority in the Western Church,
    300-1400.
Hampe, Germany Under the Salian and Hohenstaufen Emperors, pp. 80-107.
P. Segl, "Zum Itinerar Abt Hugos I. von Cluny (1049-1109)," Deutsches
    Archiv, XXIX (1973), 206-219.
G. Koch, Manegold von Lautenbach und die Lehre von der Volks-
    souveränität unter Heinrich IV.
A. Overmann, Gräfin Mathilde von Tuscien.

The Correspondence of Pope Gregory VII: Selected Letters from the
    Registrum, trans. E. Emerton.
The Epistolae Vagantes of Pope Gregory VII, trans. H. E. J. Cowdrey.
A. Murray, "Pope Gregory VII and His Letters," Traditio, XXII (1966),
    149-202.
Imperial Lives and Letters of the Eleventh Century, trans. T. E.
    Mommsen and K. F. Morrison.

Mon. 22 Oct.   The Investiture Contest, II.

Wed. 24 Oct.   DISCUSSION of The Investiture Controversy: Issues, Ideals,
                  and Results, ed. K. F. Morrison. (Krieger, 1976.).

Fri. 26 Oct.   Henry V and the End of the Investiture Contest.

*Barraclough, Origins of Modern Germany, pp. 127-153.
Hampe, Germany Under the ... Emperors, pp. 108-122.
S. A. Chodorow, "Ecclesistical Politics and the Ending of the
    Investiture Contest: The Papal Election of 1119 and the
    Negotiations of Mouzon," Speculum, XLVI (1971), 613-640.
A. Waas, Heinrich V.
G. Meyer von Knonau, Jahrbücher des deutschen Reiches Unter Heinrich
    IV. und Heinrich V. Vols. VI-VII.

Mon. 29 Oct.   The Northeast German Frontier to the Summons of 1108.

    *J. W. Thompson, Feudal Germany, II, 387-528.
    M. Bünding, Das Imperium Christianum und die deutschen Ostkriege vom
       zehnten bis zum zwölften Jahrhundert.
    Heidenmission und Kreuzzugsgedanke in der deutschen Ostpolitik des
       Mittelalters, ed. H. Beumann.
    Adam of Bremen, History of the Archbishops of Hamburg-Bremen, trans.
       F. J. Tschan.

Wed. 31 Oct.   Lothar and Conrad III: Decline of the Empire.

    *Barraclough, Origins of Modern Germany, pp. 153-164.
    Hampe, Germany Under the ... Emperors, pp. 123-153.

Fri. 2 Nov.   An Age of Recovery: Frederick Barbarossa.

    *Barraclough, Origins of Modern Germany, pp. 167-186.
    *Source Book ..., ed. Ogg, pp. 398-402.
    *Select Historical Documents ..., ed. Henderson, pp. 410-430.
    *Select Historical Documents ..., ed. Thatcher and McNeal, pp. 176-191.
    Hampe, Germany Under the ... Emperors, pp. 153-219.
    P. Munz, Frederick Barbarossa: A Study in Medieval Politics.
    M. Pacaut, Frederick Barbarossa.
    M. Baldwin, Alexander III and the Twelfth Century.

Mon. 5 Nov.   Social and Economic Developments.

    B. H. Slicher van Bath, The Agrarian History of Western Europe,
       A.D. 500-1850.
    G. Duby, Rural Economy and Country Life in the Medieval West.
    L. White, Jr., Medieval Technology and Social Change.
    J. D. Lewis, The Genossenschaft-Theory of Otto von Gierke: A Study in
       Political Thought. (University of Wisconsin Studies in the
       Political Sciences and History, No. 25.)
    G. Kisch, The Jews in Medieval Germany: A Study of Their Legal and
       Social Status.
    I. A. Agus, The Heroic Age of Franco-German Jewry: The Jews of
       Germany and France of the Tenth and Eleventh Centuries.
    R. S. Lopez, "Still Another Renaissance?". American Historical
       Review, LVII (1951), 1-21.
    R. G. Witt, "The Landlord and the Economic Revival of the Middle
       Ages," American Historical Review, LXXVI (1971), 965-988.
    D. M. Nicholas, "Medieval Urban Origins in Northern Continental
       Europe: State of Research and Some Tentative Conclusions,"
       Studies in Medieval and Renaissance History, VI (1969), 55-114.
    L. White, Jr., "The Life of the Silent Majority," Life and Thought in
       the Early Middle Ages, ed. R. S. Hoyt, pp. 85-100.
    The Ruodlieb: The First Medieval Epic of Chivalry from Twelfth-
       Century Germany, trans. G. B. Ford, Jr.

Wed. 7 Nov.   The Mightiest Vassal: Henry the Lion.

R. Hildebrand, Der sächsischen 'Staat' Heinrichs des Löwen.
E. Gronen, Die Machtpolitik Heinrichs des Löwen und sein Gegensatz
   gegen das Kaisertum.
J. Bärmann, Die Städtegründungen Heinrichs des Löwen und die
   Stadtverfassung des 12. Jahrhunderts.

Fri. 9 Nov.   Germany to the Twelfth Century.   SLIDES!

Mon. 12 Nov.   HOLIDAY! (Veterans' Day)

Wed. 14 Nov.   The Feudalization of Germany and Barbarossa's Grand Design.

*Barraclough, Origins of Modern Germany, pp. 186-192.
*Select Historical Documents ..., ed. Henderson, pp. 211-218.
*H. Mitteis, "Feudalism and the German Constitution," Mediaeval
   Germany, 911-1250, ed. G. Barraclough, II, 235-279.
*O. Freiherr von Dungern, "Constitutional Reorganization and Reform
   Under the Hohenstaufen," ibid., II, 203-233.
*A. Brackmann, "The Beginnings of the National State in Germany and the
   Norman Monarchies," ibid., II, 281-299.
 M. Bloch, "A Problem in Comparative History: The Administrative
   Classes in France and in Germany," Land and Work in Mediaeval
   Europe (1966), pp. 82-123.
 K. F. Morrison, "Otto of Freising's Quest for the Hermeneutic Circle,"
   Speculum, LV (1980), 207-236.
 W. Ohnsorge, "Die Byzanzpolitik Friedrich Barbarossas und der 'Landes-
   verrat' Heinrichs des Löwen," Deutsches Archiv, VI (1943),
   118-149.
 K. Hampe, "Heinrichs des Löwen Sturz in politisch-historischer
   Beurteilung," Hist. Zeit., CIX (1912), 49-82.
 E. Otto, "Von der Abschliessung des Ritterstandes," ibid., CLXII
   (1940), 19-39.
 F. Güterbock, Der Prozeß Heinrichs des Löwen: Kritische
   Untersuchungen.
 W. Goez, Der Leihezwang: Eine Untersuchung zur Geschichte des
   deutschen Lehnrechts.
 H. Mitteis, Lehnrecht und Staatsgewalt: Untersuchungen zur mittel-
   alterlichen Verfassungsgeschichte.
 W. Biereye, "Die Kämpfe gegen Heinrich den Löwen in den Jahren 1177
   bis 1181," Forschungen und Versuche zur Geschichte und der
   Neuzeit: Festschrift Dietrich Schäfer (1915), pp. 149-196.
 K. Bosl, Die Reichsministerialität der Salier und Staufer. (2 vols.)

Fri. 16 Nov.   Land Reclamation and Peasant Emancipation: The First Phase.

    *J. W. Thompson, Feudal Germany, II, 545-579.
    *Source Book ..., ed. Ogg, pp. 330-333.
    *T. Mayer, "The State of the Dukes of Zähringen," Mediaeval Germany,
       911-1250, ed. G. Barraclough, II, 175-202.
    A. Dopsch, Die freien Marken in Deutschland: Beitrag zur Agrar- und
       Sozialgeschichte des Mittelalters.
    J. F. Niermeier, "De vroegste berichten omtrent bedijking in
       Nederland," Tijdschrift voor economische en sociale geografie,
       IL (1958), 226-231.

Mon. 19 Nov.   The Concept of Empire.

    J. Bryce, The Holy Roman Empire. [The classic but long outdated
       introduction to the subject which, please note, was written
       originally as an undergraduate honors thesis!]
    G. Barraclough, The Mediaeval Empire: Idea and Reality.
    R. Folz, The Concept of Empire in Western Europe From the Fifth to
       the Fourteenth Century.
    F. Heer, The Holy Roman Empire.
    W. Ullmann, "Reflections on the Mediaeval Empire," Transactions of the
       Royal Historical Society, Fifth Series, XIV (1964), 89-108.
    J. Brundage, "Widukind of Corvey and the 'Non-Roman' Imperial Idea,"
       Mediaeval Studies, XXII (1960), 15-26.
    M. Bloch, "The Empire and the Idea of Empire Under the Hohenstaufen,"
       Land and Work in Mediaeval Europe (1966), pp. 1-43.
    A. Diehl, "Heiliges römisches Reich deutscher Nation," Hist. Zeit.,
       CLVI (1937), 457-484.
    C. Erdmann, ""Das ottonische Reich als Imperium Romanum," Deutsches
       Archiv, VI (1943), 412-441.
    P. E. Schramm, Kaiser, Rom und Renovatio: Studien zur Geschichte des
       römischen Erneuerungsgedankens vom Ende des Karolingischen
       Reiches bis zum Investiturstreit.
    E. E. Stengel, Abhandlungen und Untersuchungen zur Geschichte des
       Kaisergedankens im Mittelalter.
    H. Hostenkamp, Die mittelalterlichen Kaiserpolitik in der deutschen
       Historiographie seit von Sybel und Ficker.

Wed. 21 Nov.   The Diversion of Imperial Energies: Henry VI and Frederick II.

    *Barraclough, Origins of Modern Germany, pp. 193-246.
    *Source Book ..., ed. Ogg, pp. 402-409.
    Hampe, Germany Under the ... Hohenstaufen Emperors, pp. 220-306.
    J. Leuschner, Germany in the Late Middle Ages, pp. 1-64.
    T. van Cleve, The Emperor Frederick II of Hohenstaufen: Immutator
       Mundi
    P. Andrewes, Frederick II of Hohenstaufen.
    E. Kantorowicz, Frederick the Second, 1194-1250.
    W. Seegrün, "Kirche, Papst und Kaiser nach der Anschauungen Kaiser
       Friedrichs II.", Hist. Zeit., CCVII (1968), 4-41.
    H. Krabbo, Die Besetzung der deutschen Bistümer unter der Regierung
       Kaiser Friedrichs II. (1212-1250).

K. Frey, Die Schicksale des königlichen Gutes in Deutschland unter
den letzten Staufern seit König Philipp.
The Liber Augustalis or Constitutions of Melfi Promulgated by the
Emperor Frederick II for the Kingdom of Sicily in 1231, trans.
J. M. Powell.

Fri. 23 Nov.   HOLIDAY!

Mon. 26 Nov.   Land Reclamation and Peasant Emancipation.   The Second Phase.
                 [No adequate treatments of this topic have been published.]

Wed. 28 Nov.   Slides on Reclamation and Emancipation.

Fri. 30 Nov.   The Wendish Crusade and the Northeast German Frontier.

*Barraclough, Origins of Modern Germany, pp. 249-281.
*Thompson, Feudal Germany, II, 612-658.
D. Seward, "The Teutonic Knights," History Today, XX (1970), 859-866.
W. Urban, "The Organization of Defense of the Livonian Frontier in the
     Thirteenth Century," Speculum, XLVIII (1973), 525-532.
I. Sterns, "Crime and Punishment Among the Teutonic Knights," ibid.,
     LVII (1982), 84-111.
W. Urban, The Baltic Crusade.
H. Schreiber, Teuton and Slav: The Struggle for Central Europe.
Cambridge Economic History of Europe, I, 361-397.
K. H. Quirin, Die deutsche Ostsiedlung im Mittelalter.
R. Kötzschke & W. Ebert, Geschichte der ostdeutschen Kolonisation.
W. Schlesinger, Mitteldeutsche Beiträge zur deutschen Verfassungs-
     geschichte des Mittelalters.
Helmold of Bosau, Chronicle of the Slavs, trans. F. J. Tschan.

Mon. 3 Dec.   The Decline of the Empire to the Mid-Fourteenth Century.

*Barraclough, Origins of Modern Germany, pp. 282-319.
J. R. Strayer, "The Fourth and the Fourteenth Centuries," American
     Historical Review, LXXVII (1972), 1-14.
H. S. Offler, "Empire and Papacy: The Last Struggle," Transactions of
     the Royal Historical Society, Fifth Series, VI (1956), 21-47.
J. Leuschner, Germany in the Late Middle Ages, pp. 65-147.
N. Denholm-Young, Richard of Cornwall.
T. W. E. Roche, The King of Almayne.
R. Moeller, Ludwig der Bayer und die Kurie im Kampf um das Reich.
H. Wieruszowski, Vom Imperium zum nationalen Königtum.
A. Haauck, Kirchengeschichte Deutschlands, V.

Wed. 5 Dec.   Emperor Charles IV and the Art of the Possible.

J. Leuschner, Germany in the Late Middle Ages, pp. 149-178.
P. Moraw, "Kaiser Karl IV. im deutschen Spätmittelalter," Historische
     Zeitschrift, CCXXIX (1979), 1-24.
R. Schneider, "Karls IV. Auffassung vom Herrscheramt," ibid., CCXVI
     (1973), 122-150.
H. Stoob, "Kaiser Karl IV. und der Ostseeraum," Hansische Geschichts-
     blätter, LXXXVIII (1970), 163-214.

E. L. Petersen, "Studien zur goldenen Bulle von 1356," Deutsches
  Archiv, XXII (1966), 226-253.
The Golden Bull of 1356 is translated in Select Historical Documents
  ..., ed. Henderson, pp. 220-261.

Fri. 7 Dec.   Late Medieval Germany to the Reformation.

*Barraclough, Origins of Modern Germany, pp. 320-352.
*Select Historical Documents ..., ed. Henderson, pp. 262-266.
 J. W. Stieber, Pope Eugenius IV, the Council of Basel, and the Secular
   and Ecclesiastical Authorities in the Empire: The Conflict Over
   Supreme Authority and Power in the Church.
 H. J. Cohn, The Government of the Rhine Palatinate in the Fifteenth
   Century.
 P. Dollinger, The German Hansa
 L. W. Spitz, The Religious Renaissance of the German Humanists.
 E. Pitz, "Die Wirtschaftskrise des Spätmittelalters," Vierteljahr-
   schrift für Sozial- und Wirtschaftsgeschichte, LII (1965),
   347-367.
 J. Aschbach, Geschichte Kaiser Sigmunds. 4 vols.

Mon. 10 Dec.   SLIDES OF LATE MEDIEVAL GERMANY.

Wed. 12 Dec.   The Social and Religious Situation in the Late Medieval German
                Town: The Example of Würzburg.   [DEADLINE FOR TERM PAPERS!]

 P. Dollinger, The German Hansa.
 H. Planitz, Die deutsche Stadt im Mittelalter.
 Die Stadt des Mittelalters, ed. C. Haase. [An extremely valuable
   three-volume collection of previously published articles.]
 K. Trüdinger, Stadt und Kirche im spätmittelalterlichen Würzburg.

Fri. 14 Dec.   DISCUSSION OF THE REFORMATION IN GERMANY.

*The Reformation: Basic Interpretations, ed. L. W. Spitz. (2nd. ed.)
*Barraclough, Origins of Modern Germany, pp. 355-381.
 H. Holborn, A History of Modern Germany: The Reformation.
 H. Boehmer, Road to Reformation: Martin Luther to the Year 1521.
 R. H. Fife, The Revolt of Martin Luther.
 D. C. Steinmetz, Luther and Staupitz: An Essay in the Intellectual
   Origins of the Protestant Reformation.
 E. G. Schwiebert, Luther and His Times.
 P. Smith, Life and Letters of Martin Luther.
 H. Holborn, Ulrich von Hutten and the German Reformation.
 C. L. Manschreck, Melanchthon: The Quiet Reformer.
 K. Brandi, The Emperor Charles V.
 O. von Hapsburg, Charles V.
 Luther and the Dawn of the Modern Era, ed. H. A. Obermann.
 W. R. Hitchcock, The Background of the Knights' Revolt, 1522-1523.

FINAL EXAMINATION: Monday, 17 December 1984, 9:45 - 11:45.

THE VIKING AGE

Ruth Mazo Karras
University of Pennsylvania

History of the Viking kingdoms and their expansion overseas, and the development of Viking Age society and culture. A wide variety of source materials, including art, archeology, runes, sagas and other literature, and laws will be discussed, and special attention paid to problems of writing the history of a non-literate culture.

Week

1. Historical Sketch and Introduction to Source Problems

   Jones, A History of the Vikings, 1-140
   Sawyer, Kings and Vikings, 1-38

2. Mythological early history

   Saxo Grammaticus, History of the Danes, selections
   Snorri Sturlusson, Ynglinga Saga, selections

3. Religion

   Snorri Sturlusson, Prose Edda
   Poems of the Vikings, tr. Terry, selections

4. Expansion of Settlement: Iceland

   Jones, 269-311
   Landnamabok, selections
   Islendingabok, selections

5. Vikings in Britain and France, I: Early Contact and Raiding

   Sawyer, 65-97
   Jones, 145-240

6. Vikings in Britain and France, II: Settlement

   Sawyer, 98-112
   Egil's Saga

7. Vikings in the East

   Sawyer, 113-130
   Jones, 241-268
   King Harold's Saga

8. Kingship and the State

   Saxo, selections
   Heimskringla, selections
   Erik Lönnroth, "Genesis of the Scandinavian Kingdoms," in
        Lönnroth, The Scandinavians: Selected Historical Essays
        (Göteborg, 1977)

9. Viking Society, I: Legal Sources

   Sawyer, 39-64
   Niels Lund, "Viking Age Society in Denmark: Evidence and
        Theories," in Danish Medieval History: New Currents,
        ed. Niels Skyum-Nielsen and Niels Lund (Copenhagen, 1981)
   Law Codes, selections

10. Viking Society, II: Archeological Evidence

    Randsborg, The Viking Age in Denmark

11. Viking Society, III: Literary Sources

    Njal's Saga

12. Conversion and the Integration into Europe

    Jones, 315-415
    Sawyer, 131-147
    Aksel E. Christiansen, "Denmark between the Viking Age and the
         Time of the Valdemars," Medieval Scandinavia 1 (1968):
         28-50

13. In Summary: Uses and Abuses of the Viking Age

Spain in the Middle Ages
Professor Paul Freedman
Vanderbilt University

1.   Spain in Image and Reality

2.   Geography and Culture of Spanish Regions
      V. S. Pritchett, Spanish Temper (1976), 37-69
      140-152,201-234,245-260.
      Michele Rodde, and Michele Affergan, Spain Observed,tr.
      Stephen Hardman, (N.Y., 1973), (look at pictures).
      Maps

3.   The Course of Medieval Spanish History
      Henry Kamen, Concise History of Spain, (N.Y.,1973), 15-63.

4.   Visigothic and Islamic Spain
      Gabriel Jackson, The Making of Medieval Spain, (1972),
      9-51.

5.   The Reconquista
      El Cid (complete)

6.   Islamic Civilization
      W. Montgomery Watt, A History of Islamic Spain no. 4,
      Islamic Surveys (Edinburgh, 1965), (complete).

Vacation

7.   Christian Spain
      Jackson, 53-114.

8.   The Jews in Spain
      Y. Baer, The Jews in Christian Spain, introduction, Inner
      Life, Mysticism.
9.   The Late Middle Ages
      Jackson, 117-154.
         FIRST PAPER DUE

10.   Everyday Life
      Scholberg, 74-176.
11.   Problems in Spanish History
      tba

Subsequent meetings will include presentations of some of your
research. The second paper will be due April 20.

SPAIN IN THE MIDDLE AGES

History 115, Prof. Freedman

Research and Style Handbooks

The Elements of Style. By W. Strunk and E.P. White. (Ref. PE1408.S772 1979)
Historian's Handbook: A Key to the Study and Writing of History. By Wood Gray et
   (Ref. D13.G78 1964)
How to Study History. By Norman Cantor and Richard I. Schreider. (D16.2.C32)
Student's Guide for Writing College Papers. By Kate L. Turabian. (Ref. LB2309.T8

Atlases, Chronologies, Biographies

The Atlas of Medieval Man. (Ref. CB351.P55 1980)
Cambridge Medieval History. See maps. (Ref. D117.C3)
Chronology of the Medieval World, 800-1491. By R.L. Storey. (Ref. D118.S855 1973
The Timetable of History: A Horizontal Linkage of People & Events. By Bernard Gr
   (Ref. D11.G78)
Who's Who in the Middle Ages. By John Fines. (Ref. D115.F5 1970)

Encyclopedias

Encyclopedia of Islam. (Div. Ref. DS37.E523)
Encyclopedia Judaica. (Div. Ref. DS102.8.E496 v.1-1b)
New Catholic Encyclopedia. Edited by William J. McDonald. (Div. Ref. BX841.N44 1

Bibliographies, Indexes and Abstracts, Guides

Bibliographical Essays on Medieval Jewish Studies. (Div. Ref. Z6368.B53)
British Humanities Index. (Ref. AI3.B7 Index Stand 2)
C.R.I.S.: The Combined Retrospective Index Set to Journals in History, 1838-1974.
   (Ref. Z6205.C18 Index Stand 3)
Humanities Index. (Ref. AI3.H85 Index Stand 2)
Index of Articles on Jewish Medieval Studies. (Div. Ref. Z6366.J6)
An Index of Medieval Studies Published in Festschriften, 1865-1946. By Harry F.
   Williams. (Ref. Z6203.W5)
Index to Jewish Periodicals. (Div. Ref. Z6367.I38)
International Bibliography of Historical Sciences. (Ref. Z6205.I61)
   A selected list of historical publications, articles, and books. Section on
   Middle Ages (Historia de la edad media)--sub headings indicated at the beginnin
   the section, e.g. Judios. References are to citation numbers.
International Medieval Bibliography. (Ref. Z6203.I583)

Histories

he Agrarian Life of the Middle Ages. (HC240.C312 v.1)
ambridge Economic History of Europe. Vols 1-3. (HC240.C3)
he Cambridge History of Islam. (Div. Ref. DS35.6.C3 v.1-2)
he Cambridge Medieval History. (Ref. D117.C3 also Div. Ref. D117.C32 v.1-8)
 History of Medieval Spain. By Joseph F. O'Callaghan. (DP96.025)
 History of the Jews in Christian Spain. By Y. Baer. (Div. Judaica DS135.S7B343)
ewish Medieval and Renaissance Studies. (Div. Judaica BM180.J59)
he Jews in Spain: Their Social, Political and Cultural Life. (Div. Judaica
   DS135.S7N4 v.1-2)
pain in the Middle Ages. By Agnus MacKay. (DP99.M23 1977)
he Making of Medieval Spain. By Gabriel Jackson. (DP.J32 1972b)

Some Subject Headings in Card Catalog

hurch History--Middle Age 600-1500
hurch History--Spain
nquisition--Spain
slamic Empire--Civilization
slamic Empire--History
ews--History--70-1789
udaism--History--Medieval and Early Modern Period, 425-1789
ortugal--History--to 1385
pain--History--Arab Period, 711-1492

lease ask the Reference Librarians for help in finding and using these and other
ources of information in the library.

Some Possible Topics for the First
Research Paper

Visigothic institutions   *Thompson, The Goths in Spain

Arab-Christian Cultural Interaction   Anwar Chejne in Islam in
the Medieval West DS 36.855176

*Watt, Influences of Islam in Medieval
Europe DS 36.85 I8, no. 9
Millás Vallicrosa, "Arab and Hebrew
Contributions...," Journal of World History 6 (1961),
732-751 (on microfilm)
Amerigo Castro, The Structure of Spanish History
Glick & Sunyer, article in Comparative Studies in
Society & History 11 (1969), 136-154.

Almoravids and Almohads   R. Le Tourneau, The Almohad Movement in
North Africa
Norris, article in Journal of African
History DT 199L4 vol. 12 (1971), 255-2

The Arabs under Christian Rule   John Boswell, The King's Treasure
Robert I. Burns, Medieval Colonialism
Robert I. Burns, Islam under the Crusade

Arab Poetry   Nicholson, A Literary History of the Arabs 892.709
N62L1930
Arberry, Arabic Poetry 892.71008 A66a
Nykl, Hispano-Arab Poetry 892.710N99h
Gibb, Arabic Literature 892.709 G43ar1963

The Philosophy of Maimonides, or of Ibn Paqudah

Jewish Poetry: Zinberg, A History of Jewish Literature, vol. 1
PJ5008 Z5313
Ibn Gabirol, Judah Halevi, poems in translation
*A Jewish Prince in Moslem Spain PJ5050S3A28

Jewish Medicine *Joseph ben Meir Zabara, The Book of Delight

Anti-Semitism   Wolff, article in Past & Present 50 (1971), 4-18
McKay in Past & Present 55 (1972)
Kamen, The Inquisition (in Divinity Library)

The Origins of Portugal

Military and Social Organization of the Reconquest
*Lomax, The Reconquest
(R)McKay, Spain in the Middle Ages

Catalan Expansion   J. Lee Schneidman, Rise of the Aragonese-Catala
Empire

Formation of Asturias   ⋆Lomax, The Reconquest
O'Callaghan, A History of Medieval Spain

Paul Freedman
History 115
Spring 1981
Second Paper Topic Possibilities

The Jewish **Converso** and **Marrano** population and the Spanish Inquisition.

The Inquisition as a political institution

The expulsion of the Jews (1492)

The seaborne empire of Aragon–Catalonia (conquests of Sardinia, Sicily, Naples, Athens. . .)

Castilian enterprise before the discovery of America

Arabs under Christian rule (Mudejars)

The powers of the military orders of knights

The conquest and consolidation of Valencia

Romanesque (or Gothic) art and architecture in Spain

The "problem" of Spain (reasons for its differences from Northern Europe)

The civil wars of the 14th and fifteenth centuries, causes and results.

Origins of Spanish anti-Semitism and/or anti-Moorish sentiment.

Islamic-Christian Interaction and Exchanges of Technology

James Given
University of Califor
Irvine

HISTORY 1176

SOCIAL CONFLICT IN MEDIEVAL EUROPE

Feb. 4:   Introduction

Section I: Peasant Unrest

General Reading: *Georges Duby, Rural Economy and Country
Life in the Medieval West, 61-357
*Eric Wolf, Peasants, entire
Recommended for those with no knowledge of medieval histor
R.S. Hoyt and S. Chodorow, Europe in the Middle
Ages (3rd ed.), 181-650

Feb. 11: International Encyclopedia of the Social Sciences
(1968), s.v. Conflict, Vol. 3, pp. 226-241
A.R. Beals and B.J. Siegel, Divisiveness and
Social Conflict, 1-27
*E. Hobsbawm, Primitive Rebels, chs. 1-7
E. Terray, "Class and Class Conflict in the Abron
Kingdom of Gyaman," in Marxist Analyses and
Social Anthropology, ed. by Maurice Bloch,
85-133

Feb. 18: *R.H. Hilton, Bond Men Made Free, entire
R.B. Dobson, The Peasants' Revolt, 1-44

Feb. 25: Mich el Mollat and Philippe Wolff, Popular
Revolutions of the Late Middle Ages, entire

Mar. 4: Guy Fourquin, The Anatomy of Popular Rebellion
in the Middle Ages, entire

Mar. 11: *Norman Cohn, The Pursuit of the Millenium
(rev. ed.), 9-234, 281-286

Mar. 18: *Eric Wolf, Peasant Wars of the Twentieth Century,
Preface, Chs. 1-3, Conclusion

Section II: Heresy

General Reading: Malcolm Lambert, Medieval Heresy, 3-94,
151-216, 335-339
Recommended: R.W. Southern, Western Society and the Church
in the Middle Ages

Apr. 1: *R.I. Moore, The Origins of European Dissent, entir

Section II: Heresy (cont.)

Apr. 8: W. Wakefield, <u>Heresy, Crusade and Inquisition</u>
          <u>in Southern France</u>, entire
          Lambert, 95-150

Apr. 15: K.B. McFarlane, <u>John Wycliffe and the Beginnings</u>
          <u>of English Nonconformity</u>, entire
          Lambert, 217-334

Apr. 22: A.P. Evans, "Social Aspects of Medieval Heresy,"
          in <u>Persecution and Liberty: Essays in</u>
          <u>Honor of George Lincoln Burr</u>, 93-116
          J.B. Russell, "Interpretations of the Origins
          of Medieval Heresy," <u>Medieval Studies</u>, 25
          (1963), 25-53

Reading Period: *Norman Cohn, <u>Europe's Inner Demons</u>, entire

All titles have been placed on reserve in Lamont and Hilles,
except for the <u>International Encyclopedia of the Social Sciences</u>,
which is in the Widener Reference Room. Copies of many of the
assigned works may also be found in the History Department
Library in Robinson Hall. Those works marked with an asterisk (*)
have been ordered for the Coop.

Three papers, each 8-15 pages in length and each worth
one-third of the final grade, are required. There will be
no final examination. The topics for the three essays are as
follows:

Essay #1: Due April 1. Discuss what you believe to be
the principal causes of the major peasant uprisings of the
late middle ages.

Essay #2: Due April 29. Discuss whether or not heresy
can be considered as a form of social protest or resistance
in the middle ages.

Essay #3: Due May 12. Discuss whether or not Europe
in the period of the late twelfth through the early fifteenth
centuries had certain characteristic patterns of social conflict. Is it possible to speak of a specifically medieval
pattern of social conflict?

B350

Knights, Peasants and Bandits

Professor B. A. Hanawalt   Fall 1983
Indiana University, Bloomington

Books:

H.S. Bennett, Life on the English Manor (Cambridge University Press, Cambridge,197
Geoffrey Chaucer, The Canterbury Tales, tr. Nevill Coghill (Penguin Books, 1951)
Joseph and Frances Gies, Life in a Medieval Castle (Harper & Row, New York, 1974)
George Holmes, The Later Middle Ages, 1272-1485 (W.W. Norton, New York, 1962)

The course will explore the ways that ordinary people and some not so ordinary
people coped with the major historical events that occurred in England from the
Norman Conquest to the Tudor dynasty. We will look at what happened to the Anglo-
Saxon population during and after the Conquest, the life of the serfs and free
peasants and how this changed over the centuries, the growth of towns and the
bourgeoisie, and the rewards and problems of being a member of the nobility. In
trying to keep up with historical change, all classes of society resorted to
manipulation of the economy and the law. They also were not slow to use brute
force and crime to achieve their ends. They formed mutual aid societies and
relied heavily on family and neighbors as well. The course is a practical guide
on how to survive the middle ages.

Putting Together English Society:

The Component Parts

Sept.	2	Anglo-Saxons & Vikings	
	4	Norman Conquest	
	9	The Anglo-Norman Settlement: Doomesday Book	Gies, pp. 1-31

Knights, Kings, Saints, Sinners:

12th & 13th Centuries

	11	Knights, Barons and Feudalism	Gies, pp. 32-56, 166-185
	16	Government and Law	
	18	Castles and their Functions	Gies, pp. 57-74, 186-217
	23	Estates of the Nobility	Gies, pp. 147-165
	25	Love & Marriage among the Nobility	Chaucer, "Knight's Tale," "The Wife of Bath's Tale," Gies, pp. 75-108
	30	Amusements of Nobility	Gies, pp. 109-124
Oct.	2	Politics of Kings and Barons	Gies, pp. 206-224, Holmes, Ch. 6
	7	Crime and the Nobility	Holmes, Ch. 4
	9	Clergy: Secular and Regular	Holmes, Ch. 8, Chaucer, "The Prioress' Tale," "The Nun's Priest's Tale"

Oct. 14   Examination

Peasants and Manors

16	The Land and Labor	Bennett, pp. 1-26, 75-96
21	Villages and Housing	Bennett, pp. 36-73
23	Manors and their Social Organization	Bennett, pp. 127-192
29	Social Tensions in Villages and with the Lord	Bennett, pp. 193-221
30	Peasant Families	Bennett, pp. 223-274 Chaucer, "Miller's Tale," "Reeve's Tale"
Nov. 4	Feasts, Games, and Religion	Bennett, pp. 27-37, 319-336
6	Economic Trends and Urban Development	Bennett, pp. 257-317
11	Examination	

Social Change of the Later Middle Ages

13	The Black Death and the Golden Age of Bacteria	Holmes, Ch. 7
18	Peasant Prosperity and Peasant Revolt	Holmes, Ch. 9, 10
20	The New Class: Knights of the Shire and Gentry	Holmes, Ch. 11, 12
25	Family Life	Chaucer, "Clerk's Tale," "Merchant's Tale"
Dec. 2	Education and Its Rewards	
4	Urban Life & Consumer Economy	Chaucer, "Wife of Bath's Prologue," "Canon's Yeoman's Prologue"
9	Robin Hood and Other Scoundrels	
11	Examination	

Requirements: Three examinations. A paper may be substituted for one of first two examinations.

Wyclif and the Lollards: A Case Study in the Origins of Dissent

W. R. Jones
Department of History
University of New Hampshire

(Students should use the following bibliographical citations
as aids both for defining term paper topics and for the compilation of appropriate bibliographies.)

1. Both medieval and modern observers have remarked on the
relative absence of heresy in pre-Wycliffite England and
have adduced various explanations for this phenomenon:

Makower, Felix. The Constitutional History and Constitution
of the Church of England. London: 1895 (reprint 1960), p.
183.

Pollock, Sir Frederick, and Maitland, Frederic William. A
History of English Law before the Time of Edward I. 2d.
ed.; 2 vols.; Cambridge: reissue 1968, II, 544.

Stubbs, William. Report of the Commissioners aapointed to
inquire into the constitution and working of the ecclesiastical courts .... London: 1883, "Historical Appendix (2),
I,52.

Richardson, H. G. "Heresy and the Lay Power under Richard II,"
English Historical Review, LI (1936), 1-28.

Leff, Gordon. Heresy in the Later Middle Ages: the Relation
of Hereterodoxy to Dissent ca. 1250-1450. 2 vols.; New York
1967, II, 33.

Moore, R. I. The Origins of European Dissent. New York: 1977.

Lambert, Malcolm. Medieval Heresy: Popular Movements from
Bogomil to Hus. New York: 1977, p. 269, n. 164.

Le Goff, Jacques. Hérésies et sociétés dans l'Europe pré-
industrielle, 11⁻-18ᵉ siècles. Paris: 1968.

Maitland, Frederic. "The Deacon and the Jewess," Roman Canon
Law in the Church of England. London: 1898.

Brooke, C. N. L. "The Missionary at Home: the Church in the
Towns, 1000-1250," The Mission of the Church and the
Propagation of the Faith. ed. G. J. Cuming. Studies in
Church History, 6; Cambridge: 1970, p. 79.

Brooke, C. N. L. "Heresy and Religious Sentiment: 1000-1250,"
Medieval Church and Society: Collected Essays. London:
1971, pp. 139-61.

Nelson, Janet. "Society, Theodicy and the Origins of Heresy:
towards a Reassessment of the Medieval Evidence," Schism,
Heresy and Religious Protest, ed. Derek Baker, Studies in
Church History, 9. Cambridge: 1972, pp. 66ff.

Bolton, Brenda. "Tradition and Temerity: Papal Attitudes to
Deviants, 1159-1216,"Schism, Heresy, etc. ed. Baker, pp.
79-91.

Moore, R. I. "Heresy as Disease," The Concept of Heresy in
the Middle Ages (11th-13th C.). eds. W. Lourdaux and D.
Verhelst. Leuven and The Hague: 1976, pp. 1-11.

Wakefield, Walter and Evans, Austin P. Heresies of the High
Middle Ages. New York and London: 1969. pp. 245-6.

Russell, Jeffrey B. Dissent and Reform in the Early Middle
Ages. Berkeley and Los Angeles: 1965, pp. 224-7 and 309-10

(Some of the questions and issues which should be addressed
are how do the writers account for the religious orthodoxy
of pre-Wycliffite England; what was the role of geography,
political control, social conditions, and the absence or
presence of radical leadership. You might contrast societal
and political conditions in late medieval England, where there
was little heresy before Wyclif, with southern France and
northern Italy, where it abounded.)

John Wyclif as Heresiarch

a. General biographies are K. B. McFarlane, John Wycliffe
and the Beginnings of English Nonconformity. London: 1952;
and the older work by H. B. Workman, John Wyclif: A Study
of the English Medieval Church. 2 vols; Oxford: 1926.
Wyclif's early philosophical career is discussed by J. A.
Robson, Wyclif and the Oxford Schools, Cambridge: 1966; and
the general intellectual background in W. A. Pantin, The
English Church in the Fourteenth Century. Cambridge: 1955,
pp. 105-85. Consult David Knowles' The Religious Orders in
England. 3 vols. Cambridge, 1956-9 for the careers and
writings of some of his more important contemporaries.
For Wyclif as political activist and religious reformer,
see Michael Wilks, "Reformatio regni: Wyclif and Hus as Leaders
of Religious Protest Movements," Schism, Heresy, etc. ed. Baker,
pp. 109-30; William Farr, John Wyclif as Legal Reformer. Leiden:
1974; Gordon Leff, "John Wyclif: the Path to Dissent," Proceedings of the British Academy, 52 (1966); Edith Tatnall,
"John Wyclif and the Ecclesia Anglicana," Journal of Ecclesiastical History, XX (1969), 19-43. A good overview of the
church's reaction to Wyclif is provided by Joseph H. Dahmus,
The Prosecution of John Wyclyf, New Haven, 1952.
(Some questions to be considered are what were the sources
of Wyclif's theological radicalism; what were his connections
with the English royal family, especially John of Gaunt and
the Black Prince's household; what was the rationale of his
appeal to the crown and lay lords to reform English Christianity;
what was his role in sparking the Lollard movement.)

. Wyclif's Early Oxford Critics

Read the brief biographies of several of the more important
of Wyclif's academic opponents in Dictionary of National
Biography, eds. Leslie Stephen and Sidney Lee. 22 vols. London:
1959-65 (DNB); and Biographical Register of the University
of Oxford to AD 1500, ed. A. B. Emden. 3 vols; Oxford: 1957-9
(Emden). For the names of these early academic critics, see
the brief summaries in Workman, Wyclif, II, 119-48; McFarlane,
Wycliffe, 148.
        (Kenningham) Robson, Wyclif and Oxford Schools, 162ff;
    DNB, XI, 361-2; Maidstone, DNB, XII, 783-4, Emden, II,
    1204; A. Williams, "Protectorium Pauperis: A Defence of
    the Begging Friars by Richard of Maidstone, O. Carm. (d.
    1396)," Carmelus, V (1958), 132-80; (Patrington) DNB,
    XV, 492-3, Emden, III, 1435-6; (Netter) DNB, XIV, 231-4,
    Emden, II, 1343-4, Robson, Wyclif and Oxford Schools,
    233-40; (Wodeford) DNB, XXI, 867-8, Emden, III, 2081-2;

137

(Sutherey) Emden, III, 1734; (Wells) Emden, III, 210-11; (Alyngton)
Emden, I, 30-31; (Sharpe) Emden, III, 1680; (Strode) III, 1807-8;
(Binham) DNB, II, 518, Emden, I, 189; (Ashborne) Emden, I, 54;
(Waldby) Emden, III, 1958; and I discuss several of the anti-
Wyclif and anti-Lollard authors in my "Lollards and Images: the
Defense of Religious Art in Later Medieval England," Journal of
the History of Ideas, XXXIV (1973), 39ff. More extended discussions
of the careers and works of individual apologists for orthodoxy
against the Wycliffites may be found in the following: James Crompton,
"Fasciculi Zizaniorum, I, II," Journal of Ecclesiastical History,
XII (1961), 35-45, 155-66; W. A. Pantin, "Two Treatises of Uthred
of Boldon on the Monastic Life," Studies in Medieval History
Presented to Frederick Maurice Powicke, ed. R. W. Hunt, W. A. Pantin
and R. W. Southern (Oxford, 1948), 364-66; Anne Hudson, "The Debate
on Bible Translation, Oxford, 1401," English Historical Review, XC
(1975),9-10; W. A. Pantin, "The Defensorium of Adam Easton," English
Historical Review, LI (1936), 675-80; Michael Hurley, "Sciptura Sola:
Wyclif and His Critics," Traditio, XVI (1960), 275-352; P. Conrad
Walmsley, "Two Long Lost Works of William Wodeford and Robert of
Leicester," Archivum Franciscanum Historicum, XLVI (1953), 458-70;
Andrew G. Little, The Grey Friars in Oxford (Oxford, 1892), 246-9;
Joseph McNulty, "William of Rymington, Prior of Salley Abbey, Chan-
cellor of Oxford, 1372-2," Yorkshire Archaeological Journal, XXX
(1931), 231-47; W. A. Pantin, "A Benedictine Opponent of John Wyclif,"
English Historical Review, XLIII (1928), 73-7; E. F. Jacob, "Reginald
Pecock: Bishop of Chichester," Proceedings of the British Academy,
XXXVII (1952), 121-53; V. H. H. Green, Bishop Reginald Pecock: A
Study in Ecclesiastical History and Thought (Cambridge, 1945); J.
M. Russell-Smith, "Walter Hilton and a Tract in Defence of the
Veneration of Images," Dominican Studies, VII (1954), 180-214;
Eric Doyle, "William Wodeford's 'De dominio civili'clericorum'
against John Wiclif," Archivum Franciscanum Historicum, LXVI (1973),
49-109; Eric Doyle, "William Wodeford, O.F.M., and John Wyclif's
De Religione," Speculum, LII (1977), 329-36; Aubrey Gwynn, The Eng-
lish Austin Friars in the Time of Wyclif (London, 1948); Margaret
Deanley, The Lollard Bible and Other Medieval Biblical Versions.
(Cambridge, 1920);

You should acquaint yourselves (by glancing through the table of
contents and English marginalia) with the unofficial "history"
of Wycliffism in England and Bonhemia compiled by the London
Carmelites and partly published in the Rolls Series, Fasciculi
Zizaniorum Magistri Johannis Wyclif ... Ascribed to Thomas Netter
of Walden, ed. Walter W. Shirley, Rolls Series, 5, London, 1858.
For the authorship and significance of this unique work, see the
article of James Crompton cited above.

(Issues to be considered are: did Wycliffism change intent and
personality in its progress from Oxford classrooms to the English
countryside; what distinguished academic Wycliffism (heterodoxy)
from popular Lollardy (a mass religious movement); what was Wyclif's
connection with the growth of a revolutionary sect; what were the
political objectives (if any) of later Lollardy and how did these
differ from Wyclif's reformist goals; what did the critics of
Wycliffism perceive to be most disturbing or dangerous in his
teaching; how effective was persuasion, as contrasted with the use
of force, in defeating heresy?)

4. The Later Lollards and the Reformation "Connection"

See the general treatments of McFarlane, _Wycliffe_, pp. 107ff;
Workman, _Wyclif_, II, 325ff. The definitive work on the subject
is John A. F. Thomson, _The Later Lollards: 1414-1520_ (xford, 1965);
see also Claire Cross, _Church and People: 1450-1660: the Triumph
of the Laity in the English Church_ (Atlantic Highlands, 1976);
K. B. McFarlane, _Lancastrian Kings and Lollard Knights_ (Oxford, 1972),
on the Lollard gentry; M. E. Aaston, "Lollardy and Sedition, 1381-
1431," _Past & Present_, XVII (1960), 1-44, which has been reprinted
in _Peasants, Kinights and Heretics: Studies in Medieval English
Social History_, ed. R. H. Hilton (Cambridge, 1976), 273-318;
A. G. Dickens, _Lollards and Protestants in the Diocese of York:
1509-1558_ (Oxford, 1959); A. G. Dickens, _The English Reformation_
(New York, 1964), pp. 22-37. For the mythical Wyclif, see
V. Mudroch, _The Wyclyf Tradition_ (Athans, O., 1979).

For a fascinating glimpse of eccentric forms of religious opinion,
see Walter L. Wakefield, "Some Unorthodox Popular Ideas of the
Thirteenth Century," _Medievalia et Humanistica_, New Series, IV
(1973), 25-35, which discusses manifestations of popular folk
belief mentioned by Thomson and Dickens in their treatment of
later Lollardy.

There has recently been a revival of interest in Wycliffism,
mainly the work of the scholarship of Anne Hudson of Oxford
University, whose articles and books show how much more is
to be discovered about this tired, old subject. See her "A
Lollard Compilation and the Dissemination of Wycliffite Thought,"
Journal of Theological Studies, new series, XXIII (1972), 65-81;
"A Lollard Sermon-Cycle and Its Implications," Medium Aevum, XL
(1971), 142-56; and her edition of Lollard writings, _Selections
from English Wycliffite Writings_ (Cambridge, 1978). Dr. Hudson
is presently engaged in editing and publishing the Lollard sermons;
the first volume of her edition has recently appeared.

(Some matters for thought: what was the connection between later
Lollardy and political dissent; what was the social basis (if any)
of the Lollard movement (i.e., did the fact that many of the
Lollards were enaged in textile manufacturing and sale imply any
economic or vocational basis of the sect); what was the relation
(if any) of later Lollardy with early Protestantism (did the
Wycliffites, in any sense, pave the way for general reform)?)

STATE UNIVERSITY OF NEW YORK
at Stony Brook

DEPARTMENT OF HISTORY

HISTORY 451: Medieval Personalities   Spring 1982
Professor Helen Lemay

COURSE REQUIREMENTS:

1. A research paper, approximately 20 pages long, on a medieval per-
    sonality or group of individuals (e.g. the School of Chartres).
    This paper constitutes the only written requirement for this course,
    and will make up 75% of your final grade. It must include analysis
    of primary source material in translation, and an extensive biblio-
    graphy of secondary sources.

By Tuesday, March 2 you MUST have chosen your topic. You must come
into class with TWO copies of a short report giving the following
information:

        1. Your topic. (e.g., Joan of Arc and Medieval Mystics)
        2. Sources you have consulted that deal with this topic
            Author, Title, Publication Place, date, Stony Brook
            Library call no.
        3. Sources you plan to consult. (same format as above)

Please TYPE this report and turn it in ON TIME. One copy will be
given to the reference librarian who will prepare a presentation
for the class on how to do a good bibliography for this particular
assignment. Although you will receive hlep from me and from the
reference librarian, you are responsible for putting in the work
to develop a good bibliography. Please remember that the quality
of your bibliography will determine in large measure the quality
of your paper. If you do your research in general works on medieval
history, your paper will be general in nature and therefore not very
good; if you research a specific aspect of your topic, on the other
hand, you will have a good grasp of it. This means that your bibliography will include a good deal of periodical material published in
scholarly journals.

        The purpose of your research is not merely to collect information;
you must devote much of your effort to interpreting it. Your research
is supposed to have direction. You should be investigating the answer
to a question or testing a hypothesis that you have formulated during
your preliminary reading. This way your paper will have a THESIS and
will present, expound and prove the validity of your point of view on
your chosen subject. For example, you will not simple write a p ,er
on Joan of Arc that says she had visions which determined the course
of her military career. Your paper would discuss instead what was
significant about her hystical experiences: that they occurred to an

unlettered lay woman in a time when femal mystics were educated
members of the monastic orders, that they urged her to take on the
"masculine" military role rather than the "feminine" contemplative
one. You must not only do research, therefore; you must THINK about
what is important about the information you have uncovered.

I would like to see your paper at various stages, if this is
at all possible for you. Since the paper is due on Tuesday, May 4,
do not submit first drafts or partial first drafts on May 3. But
if you get the material to me in March and April (bibliographies,
outlines, a few pages, or an entire draft) I should be able to help
you in its preparation. Please feel free to consult with me often
about your paper. Many students have never conducted a research
project of this magnitude before, and have trouble determining how
to go about it. I consider this project to be one of the most important in your undergraduate career; it trains you in research, analysis
and writing skills that have wide application in your future careers
and in your life in general. If you can do a good job with a problem
pertaining to the middle ages, you have the ability to research topics
relating to business, politics, education, social issues, to name
only a few. This is one of the few truly small classes most of you
will have at Stony Brook, and it is the only really small course that
I teach. The time that I spend in HIS 316 on 200 people I can spend
with you this semester; do not hesitate to take advantage of this
help.

2. Oral reports and participation in class discussion. This will make
up the other 25% of your final grade.

In preparing and presenting oral reports, please keep the following considerations in mind:

First of all, consider yourself as a member of a community of
scholars, not as a student with an assignment to read 30 or 40 pages.
In a seminar, the purpose is to bring to the class what is relevant
to the subject under discussion, and to have the judgement to leave out
what is not. You should try to relate your material to the main topic
at hand (e.g. Peter Abelard and intellectual freedom in the Twelfth
Century) as well as to other topics covered in class (e.g. the role
of women in this scholastic milieu). Please present your material
in such a manner that other students feel free to interrupt you to
clarify or comment on a point you are making, and as a participant
in the seminar please make an effort to take part in class discussion.
This will be a very dull class if it consists of nothing more than
twenty or so "mini-lectures" a month.

If you discover that an article you have read covers almost the
same topic as the ne you are assigned, do not hesitate to present
your material in discussion with the student reporting--your assignment of a class presentation holds only if the material assigned

proves valuable to the class. I have not read all of the works I
have listed; many of them I have merely skimmed, and often the content
appears different after merely skimming them than it does after a
careful reading. Finally, most important of all, try to relate the
secondary material you have been assigned to the primary source reading
which will have been read by all class members. Do not just come to
class and tell us, for example, what Etienne Gilson said about
Abelard and Heloise's love affair. Relate what he said to your own
reading in the Letters and in the Historia Calamitatum and give your
own opinion whenever you have been able to form one.

Please make an effort to inform me in advance if you are unable
to attend class when you are scheduled to report. Telephone the
History Department and leave a message 246-6500 or else telephone
me in my office 246-6511 or at home 928-2312. Please do not telephone
after 8:30 P.M.

Please remember that you are going to have to share the books on
reserve with other members of the seminar. Do not race out of class,
take out the book, and keep it for a week, thereby preventing anyone
else from doing his or her assignment. Stick around for a few minutes
to make arrangements for everyone to have a turn.

Tuesday, February 2: INTRODUCTION

Tuesday, February 9: ABELARD, HELOISE AND LOVE

All students should read The Letters of Abelard and Heloise,
Penguin Paperback, in the bookstore.

Individual student assignments: Introduction to love in the
Twelfth Century

1. Superstar to give an oral report on the topic "Introduction
    to Love in the Twelfth Century" A superstar presents the
    information in the reading assignment in accordance with
    the directions on the syllabus above.

    John C. Moore, Love in Twelfth-Century France
    Chapter 3 - The monasteries, pp. 47-74
    Chapter 4 - The Courts, pp. 75-100
    Chapter 5 - The Towns, 101-130

2. Interrupter #1. An interrupter interrupts the superstar
    during his or her report with brilliant comments based upon
    the reading he or she has done.

    Colin Morris, The Discovery of the Individual, Chapter 5:
    The Self and Other Selves, pp. 96-120.

3. Interrupter #2. Christopher Brooke, The Twelfth-Century
    Renaissance

    Chapter 2: Heloise and Abelard, pp. 19-52

Individual student assignments: Heloise and Abelard

1. Three superstars are to give reports on Etienne Gilson,
    Heloise and Abelard, on reserve for the course. You will
    have to arrange to share this book.

    Superstar #1: Sources of Drama, pp. 1-10
                   Secrecy of Marriage, pp. 20-36
                   Between Two Separations, pp. 37-46
    Superstar #2: Ethics of Pure Love, pp. 47-65
                   Conversion of Abelard, 66-86
                   Mystery of Heloise, 87-104
    Superstar #3: End of Drama, pp. 105-123
                   Conclusion, pp. 124-144

2. Interrupter to read D. W. Robertson, Abelard and Heloise,
    on reserve

    Comedy of love, pp. 149-164
    Baroque Passion, pp. 165-179
    Saint of love, pp. 205-225

Individual student assignments: The Authenticity of the Correspondence

    1. Superstar

        Peter Dronke, Abelard and Heloise in Medieval Testimonies
        PA 8201 A9D7 o⁻   ,erve pp. 7-31

    2. Superstar

        John F. Benton, "fraud, Fiction and Borrowing in the Corres-
        pondence of Abelard and Heloise," in Pierre Abelard-Pierre
        le Venerable on reserve PA 8201 Z5 P5 pp. 469-512

    3. Interrupter

        Etienne Gilson, Heloise and Abelard, Authenticity of
        Correspondence pp. 145-166.

Individual student assignments: Heloise and the Position of Women

    1. Superstar

        Mary M. McLaughlin, "Peter Abelard and the dignity of
        Women: Twelfth-Century Feminism in Theory and Practice,"
        pp. 287-334 of Pierre Abelard-Pierre le Venerable

    2. Superstar

        Peter Von Moos, "Le silence d'Heloise et les ideologies
        modernes," pp. 425-468 of Pierre Abelard-Pierre le Venerable

Tuesday, February 16: ABELARD AND THE TWELFTH-CENTURY INDIVIDUAL

    1. Superstar. "The Search for the Self," Chapter 4 of
        Colin Morris, The Discovery of the Individual, pp. 64-95.

    2. Superstar. Gerard Verbeke, "Peter Abelard and the Concept
        of Subjectivity," in Peter Abelard: Proceedings of the
        International Congress, pp. 1-11 B765 A24 P47

    3. Superstar. Donald K. Frank, "Abelard as Imitator or Christ,"
        Viator I (1970) 107-113

    4. Superatar. J. J. N. McGurk, "Peter Abelard, knight errant
        of the medieval schools," History Today 24:9 (1974) 648-655.

    5. Superstar. Pierre Riche. "L'enfant dans la societe
        monastique au XIIe siecle," pp. 689-701 of Pierre Abelard-
        Pierre le Venerable

ABELARD AND TWELFTH-CENTURY INTELLECTUAL LIFE

1. ABELARD AND JUDAISM

    Superstar. Peter Abelard. A Dialogue of a Philosopher
    with a Jew and a Christian. Read introcution and as much
    as you can stand of the first part (Dialogue with a Jew).
    Is Abelard anti-Jewish? on reserve B765 A23 D613 1979

    Interrupter. Aryeh Grabois. "Un chapitre de tolerance
    intellectuelle dans la societe occidentale au XIIe siecle:
    Le dialogus de Pierre Abelard et le Kuzari d'Yehudan Halevi.
    pp. 641-654 of Pierre Abelard-Pierre le Venerable

2. ABELARD AND MONASTICISM

    Superstar. Thomas J. Renna. "Abelard vs. Bernard: An
    Event in Monastic History." Citeaux 27,3 (1976) 189-206

    Interrupter. David Luscombe. "Pierre Abelard et le monachisme,"
    pp 271-6 of Pierre Abelard-Pierre le Venerable.

3. ABELARD AND SCHOLASTICISM

    Superstar. D.E. Luscombe. The School of Peter Abelard:
    The Influence of Abelard's Thought in the Early Scholastic
    Period BX4705 A2 L8 Read whatever section you want (except
    chapter on condemnation of 1140 and give a report on it).

    Interrupter. John F. Benton, "Philology's Search for Abelard
    in the Metamorphosis Goliae Speculum 50, 2 (1975) 199-219

4. ABELARD AND MUSIC

    Superstar. Joseph Szoverffy, "A Conscious Artist in Medieval
    Hymnody: Introduction to Peter Abelard's Hymns" in Classica
    et Iberica: A Festschrift in Honor of the Rev. Joseph M.F.
    Marique, S.J. Worcester, Mass: Institute for Early Christian
    Iberian Studies, College of the Holy Cross, 1975. pp. 119-159.

    Interrupter. Michel Huglo. "Abelard, Poete et Musicien,"
    Cahiers de civilisation medievale 22 (1979) 349-361.

5. ABELARD AND ASTROLOGY

    M. T. d'Alverny. "Abelard et l'astrologie," pp. 611-630 of
    Pierre Abelard-Pierre le Venerable

HIS 451: MEDIEVAL PERSONALITIES

JOAN OF ARC

I. The Source Material
What sources do we have for the history of Joan of Arc? How reliable are they? What biases do historians bring to their interpretation of Joan's life?

Superstars to discuss these questions:

Superstar #1: Charles Lightbody, The Judgments of Joan, on reserve DC103 L67 19 pp 36-83.

Superstar #2: Charles Lightbody, Judgments. pp 85-117

Superstar #3: The First Biography of Joan of Arc on reserve DC 103 .06813 pp

Superstar #4: First Biography, pp 111-142.

Interrupters for this topic:

Interrupter #1: Regine Pernoud, Joan of Arc, on reserve DC103 P373 pp 5-54

Interrupter #2: Charles Roessler, Jeanne d'Arc: Heroine and Healer-- Documenta
Evidences DC 103 R64 on reserve read selections

II. Joan's Early Life

A. Life in France During Joan's Time

Superstar: Joan Evans, Life in Medieval France Chap 8 pp 135-145
DC 33.2 E8 1969. Not on reserve

Interrupter: Marcellin Defourneaux La Vie Quotidienne au temps de Jeanne
d'Arc Paris 1952 Not on reserve DC 33.2 D43
Read: Part I, Chap IX La vie et le sentiment religieux
Part 2, Chap 1, La guerre et l'aventure

B. Joan of Arc's life

Superstar: Edward Lucie-Smith, Joan of Arc pp 1-27

Interrupter: Michelet, Joan of Arc On reserve DC 103 M612 pp 3-26

III. Joan the Knight and the Political Situation

A. The Political Situation

Superstar: Regine Pernoud, Joan of Arc, pp 55-134

Interrupter #1: Marina Warner, Joan of Arc On reserve DC 103 W27 1981 pp

Interrupter #2: Edouard Perroy, The Hundred Years War Not on reserve
DC96 P413 1951 Part I: The Adversaries, Part VIII: The Fi
Recovery

Interrupter #3: Edw. Lucie-Smith, Joan of Arc pp 39-60

Interrupter #4: Desmond Seward, <u>The Hundred Years War</u> Not on reserve
DC 96 S48 1978 Chapters 1 and 2 and 9 or what interests you

B. Joan the Knight

Superstar: Marina Warner, <u>Joan of Arc</u>, pp 159-182

Interrupter: J. Huizinga, <u>The Waning of the Middle Ages</u>, Not on reserve
CB 353 H8 Chapter 4: The idea of chivalry

Joan of Arc and Virginity in the Middle Ages

Conditional Superstar: John Bugge, <u>Virginitas: An Essay in the History of the</u>
<u>Medieval Ideal</u>, The Hague, 1975. This book is not in
the Stony Brook library. Your being a superstar is conditional upon your finding this elsewhere.

Conditional Superstar #2: Deborah Fraioli, "The Literary Image of Joan of Arc:
Prior Influences," <u>Speculum</u>. This may not yet be
published in <u>Speculum</u>. It is not in any of the issues
in the stacks. Look in current periodicals and see if
you can find it.

Unconditional Superstar: Marina Warner, <u>Joan of Arc</u>, Chapter 1.

Unconditional Interrupter: Marina Warner, <u>Alone of All Her Sex: The Myth and the</u>
<u>Cult of the Virgin Mary</u> Chapters 3-5, pp 34-78

Joan and Medieval Saints, Prophets, Mystics

Superstar #1: Marina Warner, <u>Joan of Arc</u>, Chapter 4

Superstar #2: R. Jacquin, "Un precurseur de Jeanne d'Arc," <u>Revue des deux</u>
<u>mondes</u>, 15 May 1967, pp 222-226 xeroxed

Superstar #3: R. Lerner, <u>The Heresy of the Free Spirit in the Later Middle Ages</u>
BT 1358 L47 1972 Not on reserve. Chap 7: The Fifteenth Century
How would you relate Joan to the mysticism described in these
chapters?

Superstar #4: P. Franklin Chambers, <u>Juliana of Norwich</u>, NY: Harper, 1955. J78
1958a Not on reserve. Read pp 1-72 on her life. What was the
experience of another female medieval mystic? Was Joan different?
Was there common ground?

Interrupter #1: Julian of Norwich, <u>Showings</u>, New York: Paulist Press, 1978.
BV 4831 J8 1978 Not on reserve Preface 1-14 and Selection from
"Showings"

Interrupter #2: Jules Michelet, <u>Joan of Arc</u>, 44-122

Interrupter #3: Lina Eckenstein, <u>Women Under Monasticism</u>, Cambridge, 1896, a selection

Interrupter #4: E. Wagenknecht, "The Problem of the Voices" Chap 2 of <u>Joan of</u>
<u>Arc: An Anthology</u> DC 103 W 15 on reserve

Interrupter $5:   J. Huizinga, <u>Waning of the Middle Ages</u>, Chapter XI:Religious
                Thought Crystallizing into Images BV 4831 J82 1978 not on reserv

VI. JOAN AND THE ISSUE OF MEN'S CLOTHING

Superstar #1: Marina Warner, <u>Joan of Arc</u>, Chapter 7

Superstar #2: John Anson, "The Female Transvestite in Early Monasticism: The
               Origin and Development of a Motif," <u>Viator</u> 5 (1974), 1-32 xeroxed

Superstar #3: Vern Bullough, "Transvestites in the Middle Ages," <u>American Journa</u>
               of Sociology 79 (6), 1381-94.

VII. JOAN, MEDIEVAL HERESY, AND THE INQUISITION

Superstar #1: Marina Warner, <u>Joan of Arc</u>, Chapter 5, 6

Superstar #2: Henry C. Lea, <u>Inquisition of the Middle Ages</u> Chapter 3, The Inquisi
               torial Process, Chapter 4, Evidence BX 1711 L415 1969 not on reser

Superstar #3: Henry C. Lea, <u>Inquisition of the Middle Ages</u>, Chap 5 The Defence,
               Chapter 6, The Sentence, Chapter 7 The Stake

Superstar #4: <u>The Trial of Jeanne d'Arc</u> tr. W.P. Barrett DC105.6 T7 on reserve
               Read selections and give us your impression of the trial with examp

Interrupter #1: Ed. Lucie-Smith, <u>Joan of Arc</u>, pp 61-82

Interrupter #2: Edw. Lucie-Smith, <u>Joan of Arc</u>, pp 231-283.

VIII. JOAN IN HISTORY AND LITERATURE

I. Raknem, <u>Joan of Arc in History, Legend and Literature</u> DC 105.9 R33 on reserve

Superstar #1: pp 23-69 (goes to eighteenth century)

Superstar #2: pp 70-95 Joan of Arc in 18c literature

Superstar #3: pp 96-161 Joan of Arc in 19c Literature

Superstar #4: pp 167-255 Joan of Arc in 20c literature

> Interrupters for Superstar #4:

> Interrupter #1: G.B. Shaw, <u>Saint Joan: A Screenplay</u> on reserve PR 5363 S3

> Interrupter #2: S. Weintraub, <u>Saint Joan: Fifty Years After</u>. Read what
>   interests you. On reserve PR 5363 S33 W4

> Interrupter #3: Jean Anouilh, <u>The Lark</u> On reserve PQ 2601 N67 A692 1956a

> Interrupter #4: J. Huizinga, "Mr. Shaw's Saint Joan," in <u>Men and Ideas: Hist</u>
>   <u>The Middle Ages, the</u> Renaissance, tr. J. Holmes and H Van
>   Manche, London 1960 Not on reserve D7 H823

General interrupters:

General Interrupter #1: Charles Lightbody, <u>Judgments of Joan</u> pp 154-171

General Interrupter #2: Marina Warner, <u>Joan of Arc</u>, whatever you can stand of chapters 10, 11, 12, 13 (one or more of these)

General Interrupter #3: E. Wagenknecht, <u>Joan of Arc: An Anthology of History and Literature</u> Whatever interests you except Chap 2 which is already done

THE REHABILITATION

Superstar #1: Charles Lightbody, <u>Judgments of Joan</u>, pp 118-153

Interrupter #1: Regine Pernoud, <u>The Retrial of Joan of Arc</u>, Read first few chapters— as much as you can stand

Interrupter #2: Regine Pernoud, <u>Joan of Arc</u>, pp 135-179

Interrupter #3: Marina Warner, <u>Joan of Arc</u>, pp 185-197.

THE CHURCH AND THE FAMILY IN THE MIDDLE AGES
Professor JoAnn McNamara
Hunter College

Text: Edward Peters, Europe: The World of the Middle Ages
    A take-home midterm will be given on March 15.
A paper will be required from each student due on May 17. This
will consist of a full historiographical study of some problem
related to the subject matter of this course, and should be
about 15-20 pages in length. Instructions for the paper are
given on separate sheets.
    In addition to special collections and books given within
the syllabus, a start may be made in your research by
consulting relevant journals and bibliographical collections.
Some of the more important among these are:
    Francia
    International Medieval Bibliography
    Speculum: A Journal of Medieval Studies
    Medieval Studies
    The Journal of Interdisciplinary History
    Psycho-History formerly the History of Childhood Quarterly
    Annales: Economies, Sociétés, Civilisations

Part One: The Formation of the European social system.
    1. Introduction: the family in society.
    2. Christian attitudes to the family in antiquity
    3. The family in the Christian Empire
    4. The conversion of Europe.

BIBLIOGRAPHY: PRIMARY SOURCES:

The Ante-Nicene, Nicene and Post Nicene Fathers a collection of
    translations of the major Christian writers for the first
    through the fifth centuries. Other editions and
    translations are available separately.
Bede, Ecclesiastical History of the English People.
Codex Justinianus, ed. P. Krueger (Berlin, 1954). Some of the
    more important legal treatises of the classical period of
    Roman Law, notably Gaius, Paulus and Ulpian are available
    in separate editions. Similarly the Codex Theodosianis
    is separately available.
Gregory of Tours, History of the Franks

Hefele, C. H., _History of the Councils,_ includes most of the decisions of the early church councils. A complete record can be found in Mansi, G. D., _Sacrorum, conciliorum nova et amplissima collectio,_ as well as more specialized modern editions of conciliar decrees.

Liebermann, F., _Die Gesetze der Angelsachsen,_ (Halle, 1903-16) is the most complete work on early English Law but there are smaller English versions.

Other Barbarian laws can be found in the appropriate volumes of the _Monumenta Germaniae Historica_ as well as some individual English editions.

Migne, J-P., ed. _Patrologia cursus completus_ is the most complete collection available of early Christian and medieval writers up to the mid-12th century.

Mishnah, a collection of Jewish law contemporary with the classical Romans.

Monumenta de viduis, diaconissis, virginibus. . . ed. J. Mayer.

Tacitus, _Germania_

SECONDARY SOURCES:

Baron, S., _Religious and Social History of the Jews,_ vol. II

Bullough, D. V., "Early Medieval Social Groupings. . ."_Past and Present_ 45 (1969) 3-18.

Chanson, Paul, _Le Mariage Chrétien selon Saint Paul_

Corbett, Percy, _The Roman Law of Marriage_

Dauvillier, J., _Les Temps apostoliques_

Gaudemet, J., _L'Eglise dans l'Empire Romain_

Herlihy, David, "Land, Family and Women . . ." in _Women in the Middle Ages,_ ed. Susan Stuard

Jolowicz, Herbert, _Historical Introduction to the Study of Roman Law_

McNamara, JoAnn, "Sexual Eqality and the Cult of Virginity in Early Christian Thought," _Feminist Studies,_ 3 (1976).

Phillpotts, Bertha, _Kindred and Clan in the Middle Ages_

Volterra, Edoardo, _La Conception du mariage d'après les juristes romains._

Part Two: Imperial Europe

1. The Carolingian Empire: a rustic world
2. The Rise of the Seigneury: ties of blood and loyalty
3. Mother Church: in loco parentis

Bibliography:

Barthelemy, A., "Le Droit du Siegneur, Revue des Questions Historique, I, 1866,?5-
Beech, George T., A world Unto Itslef: Life in a Medieval Village
Beitscher, Jane, "As the twig is bent..." J. of Medieval History, 2:3 (1976), 181-
Bloch, M., The Feudal Society
Coleman, E., "Infanticide in the Early Middle Ages", in Women in Medieval Society
_____, "Some Medieval Marriage Characteristics," in The Family in History
Cornney, L, La regime de la "dos" aux époques mérovingiennes et carolingienne.
Darby, H.C., Domesday England.
Daudet, P., L'établissement de la compétence de l'église en matière de divorce...
Duby, G., The Early growth of the Eruopean Economy: Warrior and Peasant 7-12th c.
Fleury, J., Recherches Historiques sur les empechements de Parente...
Fossier, R., "Land, castle, money and family..." in Medieval Settlement:Continuity
Gaudemet, J., Les communauaés familiales, Paris, 1963.
Genicot, L, La noblesse au moyen age dans l'ancienne Francia, Annales, 17, 1962.
Howarth, W.D., Droit du Seigneur: fact or fantasy? J of European Studies, 1971, I,
Huggett, Frank E., The Land Question and Eruopean Society
MacFarlane, A. et al., Reconstructing Historical Communities
McLaughlin, Mary, "Survivors and Surrogates..." in de Mause, L., H story of Childh
McNamara, J., & Wemple, S., "Marriage and Divorce in the Frankish Kingdom"
_____ "Power of Women thru the Family," in Clio's Consciousness Raised
Noonan, J., Contraception
Riché, P., "Léenfant dans le haut moyen age," Annales de Demographie Historique,
Ritzer, K., Le mariage dans les eglises chretiennes du I-IX siecles.
Russell, J.C., Aspects demographiques des debuts de la feodalité, Annales, 20, 196
_____, British Medival Population,
Sarrier, G., De quelques recherches concernant le mariage contrat-sacrement...
Weinberger, S ephen, "Peasant households in Provence, 800-1100, Speculum, 48, 1973
Wheaton, R., "Family and Kinship in Western Europe". Jour. Interdisciplinary Hist
Whitelock, D., Anglo-Saxon Wills   1 '7
Wojnar, M.M., "Legal Relationship and Guardianship as Matrimonial Impediments"
_____ The Jurist, 30, 1970, 343-55; 456-98.
Young, Ernest, "The Anglo Saxon Family Law", Essays in Anglo Saxon Law

Part Three: The High Middle Ages: Papal Europe.

. The Victory of Canon Law
. Love and property
. City family and country family.

Bibliography:

Ault, Warren O., Manor Court and ParishRolls.
Abbott, E. (trans., The Fifteen Joys of Marriage
Beech, George, A Rural Society in Medieval France
Brooke, C.N.L., :Married men among the English Higher Clergy, 1066-1200" Cambridge
                                        Historical Journal, 12 (1956)
Contamine, P., ed., La nobless au Moyen Age
Dauvillier, J., Le mariage dans le droit canonique
Duby, G., "in northwestern France: Youth in 12th c..." in Cheyette, Lordship and
Esmein, A., Le mariage en Droit Canonique   Community
Flandrin, J-L., Familles, Parentes, Maison et Sexualité
Fossier, R., "La demographie medievale" Annales de demographie historique (1975)
Fourquin, G., Seigneurie et féodalité au Moyen Age, 1977.
Furnivall, F.J., Child Marriages, divorces & ratifications, Early Eng. Text.,
Gautier-Dalche, J., A Tolede a la fin du XIII siecle, in Econ. et Soc. du Moyen Age
Forster and Ranum, Family and Society
Goodich, M., "Childhood and Adolescence among 13th c. Saints, Hist. of Childhood Quart.
Hair, P., ed., Before the bawdy court.   vol. 1.
Hajdu, R., "Family and Feudal Ties..." Jour. Interdisciplinary History, 1977.
Hajnal, J., "European Marriage Patterns..." in Glass and Eversley, Populaion in History
Hallam, H.E., "Some 14th century Censuses," Economic History Review, ser. 2., v. 10
Helmholz, R.H., Marriage Litigation in Medieval England.
Herlihy, D., "Family Solidarity..." in Herlihy, Lopez and Slessarev, Society and
            Government in Medieval Italy
      "Mapping households in medieval Italy," Catholic Hist. Rev., v. 58, 1972.
Homans, George C., English Villagers of the 13th Century.
Hughes, Diane O., "Urban Growth and Family Structure..." Past and Present, 66, 1975.
"Marriage in the Middle Ages", Viator, 4 (1973) 416-501.
Miskimin, H., Herlihy and Udovitch, eds. The Medieval City
Noonan, J.T., "Marital Affection in the Canonists", Studia Gratiana, 12 (1967) 479-509.
Painter, S., "Family and Feudal System..." Speculum, 35 (1960), 1-17.
Raftis, J.A., Tenure and Mobility;
Renouard, Y., Les villes d'Italie de la fin du Xe Siècle...
Schneider, J., et al., Les structures sociales de l'Aquitaine, du Languedoc, et l'Espagne
Sheehan, M., "The influence of Canon Law on the property rights..." Medieval Studies, 23
            The Will in Medieval England
Strait, P., Cologne in the 12th Century.
Walker, Sue S., "Violence and the Exercise of Feudal Guardianship... American Journal
    of Legal History, 16, 1972, 320-33.

Part Four: The End of the Middle Ages: National Europe

1. Legal conflicts and economic threats.

2. The State in loco parentis
3. Protestantism and the Council of Trent.

Bibliography:

Aries, Philippe, Centuries of Childhood
Ashby, M.K., The Changing English Village, 1066-1914
Barton, J.L., Nullity of marriage and illegitimacy ...." Legal Hist. Studies
Bilton, D., The French Nobility in Crisis   1972, 28-49
Bois, Guy, Crise de feodalisme...
Bourdieu, P., "Marriage strategies" in Forster & Ranum, Family and Society.
Bücher, K., Die Bevölkerung von Frankfurt am Main im 14 und 15 Jahrhundert
Brissaud, Y.B., "L'infanticide..." Rev. Hist. Droit Francais & etranger, 50, 1972
Chojnacki, Stanley, "Dowries and Kinsman..." in Stuard, Women in   Middle Ag
de Camugliano, G.N., The Chronicles of a Florentine Family
Faith, R., "Peasant Family and Inheritance..." Agricultural Hist. Review, 14, 196
Flandrin, J-L., Les Amours Paysannes
_____, "Repression & change ..." Journal of Family History, vol. 2-3, 1077.
Girard, R., "Marriage in Avignon..." Speculum, 28, 1953, 485-498.
Goody, J., Thirsk, J., and Thompson, E.F., Family and Inheritance
Goubert, P.,"Historical Demography..." Jour. Interdisciplinary History, 1, 1970.
Heers, J., Le clan familial au moyen age
Herlihy, D., The Family in Renaissance Italy
Kellum, B.A., "Infanticide in England..." Hist. of Childhood Quarterly, 1, 1973
Kelly, H., Love and Marriage in the Age of Chaucer
Kent, F.W., Household and Lineage in Renaissance Florence
Klapisch, C., "Fiscalité et démographie..." Annales, 1969.
_____ & Demonet, M., A uno pane e uno vino..." in Forster & Ranum, Family & Soci
Lafon, J., Les époux bordelais, 1450-1550.
Leroy Ladurie, E., Montaillou, village occitane de 1294-1324.
Levine, D., Family Formation in an age of nascent capitalism.
McFarlane, K.S., The nobility of later medieval England
Niccolai, F., La formazione del diritto successorio
The Paston Letters
Pollock and Maitland, A History of English Law.
Postan, M.M., "Some Economic Evidence of Declining Population..." Economic Histor
                                                    2, 1950.
Pounds, N., "Overpopulation in France..." Journal of Social History, 3, 1970.
Rosenthal, J. Nobles and the Noble Life, 1295-1500.
Sabean, D.W., Landbesitz und Gesellschaft am Vorabend des Bauernkriegs.
Sheehan, M. M., "Formation and Stability of Marriage..." Medieval Studies, 33, 19
Stone, L., The Family Sex and Marriage in England, 1500-1800.
Trexler, R., The Foundlings of Florenge" Hist. of Cildhood Quarterly, I, 1973.

Spring 1979

Donald Queller
University of
Illinois, Urbana

History 331

Medieval Economic and Social History

The assigned readings are:

FONTANA ECONOMIC HISTORY OF EUROPE, ed. by Carlo Cipolla, vol. 1
Bloch, FRENCH RURAL HISTORY
Pirenne, MEDIEVAL CITIES
Power, MEDIEVAL WOMEN
White, MEDIEVAL TECHNOLOGY AND SOCIAL CHANGE
Sapori, ITALIAN MERCHANT IN THE MIDDLE AGES

You are responsible for having them read and prepared for discussion by the dates given in the syllabus. They are not assigned on a daily basis, so you must look ahead and get going.

In addition, I would like a short term paper on a limited topic, complete with bibliography and footnotes. It will be due on March 26, the day after spring vacation. I will accept them earlier, of course, but there will be a penalty for late papers.

We will have regular lectures on Mondays and Wednesdays. On Fridays we will have discussions of the assigned books when due, book reports by me, or something else. The Friday sessions should certainly not be considered peripheral or of less importance than the ordinary lectures.

I am in the habit of using what is called the "contract" system for students who find that the course does not quite fit their individual needs. You may propose to me in writing any variations on the set course which would be of more value to you. Usually this means a substitution of something else for the term paper, but it may be a more radical proposal. If I accept, then to that extent the course is individualized for you. Not many students choose to take advantage of this, and that is probably as it should be, but it is there if you think it valuable.

My office is 314A Gregory Hall. Office hours will be 3:00 P.M. Monday and 2:00 P.M. Thursday. If your schedule conflicts with this, I'll make other arrangements, but please try to make it during these times if you can.

SCHEDULE

Jan. 22 Climate, topography, tools and foods
24 Economic and social decline
26 Russell, LATE ANCIENT AND MEDIEVAL POPULATION (Queller); Cipolla, ch. 1
29 The Carolingian Age
31 The Economy and the New Invasions
Feb. 2 Duby, EARLY GROWTH OF THE EUROPEAN ECONOMY (Queller)
5 Medieval Economic Theory
7 Economies and societies in non-manorial areas; Cipolla, ch. 5
9 DISCUSS Bloch, FRENCH RURAL HISTORY
12 The manor
14 Village classes
16 DISCUSS White, MEDIEVAL TECHNOLOGY AND SOCIAL CHANGE; Cipolla, ch. 4
19 Life on the manor
21 Byzantium and Islam: the developed areas
23 Ashter, SOCIAL AND ECONOMIC HISTORY OF THE NEAR EAST IN THE MIDDLE AGES (Queller)
26 Beginnings of the revival of commerce; Cipolla, ch. 3
28 The Crusades and West European Expansion
Mar. 2 DISCUSS Pirenne, MEDIEVAL CITIES
5 The town: origins and appearances. Cipolla, "Origins"
7 Urban classes
9 Herlihy, MEDIEVAL AND RENAISSANCE PISTOIA (Queller)
12 Guilds
14 Town governments
16 DISCUSS Saperi, ITALIAN MERCHANT IN THE MIDDLE AGES
26 Impact of the commercial revolution upon agriculture; Cipolla, ch. 2
28 Mediterranean trade at its medieval peak
30 Heer, LE CLAN FAMILIAL AU MOYEN AGE (Queller)
Apr. 2 Non-Italian commerce, especially in the northern seas
4 Medieval transportation
6 Lane, ANDREA BARBARIGO (Queller)
9 Money
11 Credit and banking; Cipolla, chs. 7 & 8
13 De Roover, MONEY, BANKING AND CREDIT IN MEDIEVAL BRUGES (Queller)
16 Merchant capitalists and the putting-out system; Cipolla, ch. 6
18 Manufacturing
20 Thrupp, MERCHANT CLASS OF MEDIEVAL LONDON (Queller)
23 Social turmoil of the Late Middle Ages
25 Agriculture of the fourteenth and fifteenth centuries
27 DISCUSS Power, MEDIEVAL WOMEN
30 Industrial changes in the fourteenth and fifteenth centuries
May 2 Beginnings of the modern economy
4 Lane, VENICE (Queller)
7-9 Somewhere along here I'll be at a professional meeting, probably for only one day. On the other I'll likely give another book review

The Three Religions
Jewish-Muslim-Christian Contacts in the Middle Ages

Junior Seminar, Tuesday 1:30-3:320
John Boswell
Yale University

Requirements: readings, attendance at weekly discussions; two papers. First paper (due at 4th meeting): 3 pages maximum (pages beyond 3 will be discarded, unread, by instructor) on assigned topic: criticize one of the three religions from the perspective of an adherent of another. (Further details in class.)
Second paper (due last day of classes: extensions require at least one week prior approval): research paper on some aspect of the interaction of at least two of the three religions or their adherents. Topic to be chosen by student and approved by instructor. Minimum 10pp; no maximum, but brevity and high content>word ratio strongly encouraged. See p.4 for bibliographical assistance.

Weekly readings:

[a date in parentheses indicates a volume on reserve for this course in CCL or SML; the name of a press in parentheses indicates a book (also on reserve) you may wish to purchase for yourself at the Co-op; both together indicate an expensive book you could buy but might prefer to consult in the library]

1st week: **Jewish scriptures and lawcodes, Hellenization**
Genesis, Leviticus, Isaiah (use any translation not already familiar to you or the Masoretic or Septuagint text)
The Mishnah, trans. Herbert Danby (1933): Moed, Shabbath (pp.99-120); Nashim, Sotah (pp.293-307); Nezikin, Abodah Zarah (pp.437-46)
Philo Judaeus, "Selections," ed. H. Lewy, in Three Jewish Philosophers (1972), pp.27-51, 93-106

2nd week: **Christian scriptures and laws, Hellenization**
Matthew, John, Acts, Galatians (any translation not already familiar to you, or the Greek text or Vulgate translation)
Canons of the Councils of Elvira, trans. Laeuchli   , and Nicea, in C. Davis, The Eagle the Crescent and the Cross (1967) pp.23-28, or in H. Schroeder, Disciplinary Decrees of the General Councils (1937) pp.18-58 [with commentary]

3d week: Muslim scriptures and law; Hellenization
The Meaning of the Glorious Koran, trans. M.M. Pickthall
(Mentor): Surahs 2, 13, 17
A Manual of Hadith, ed. M.M. Ali (1977), pp.1-30, 41-67, 223-31,
268-81, 293-301, 344-58, 373-408
G. von Grunebaum, Medieval Islam (Univ. of Chicago) pp.142-69,
294-319

4th week: early interaction
J.R. Marcus, The Jew in the Medieval World (Atheneum) pp.3-9,
20-24, 101-15, 349-55
F. Talmage, Disputation and Dialogue; a Reader in the
Jewish-Christian Encounter (KTAV) pp.17-32, 89-99, 134-37
St John Damascene "On the Moslem Heresy," trans. J. Voorhis, The
Moslem World 24 (1934) 392-98 and idem, "The Discussion of a
Christian and a Saracen," ibid. 25 (1935) 266-73
'Abu 'Uthman 'Amr b. Bahr al-Jahiz, "Risala on the
Christians," trans. Joshua Finkel, Journal of the American
Oriental Society 47 (1927) 322-34
Gregory of Tours and creeds   {NB: less than 100pp.total}

5th week: Islam in Europe (and the Jews in Muslim Spain)
The Poem of the Cid, trans. W.S. Merwin (NAL)
R.W. Southern, Western Views of Islam in the Middle Ages
(Harvard) pp.1-33
N. Stillman, The Jews of Arab Lands (Jewish Publ.Soc.)
pp.152-167
Monroe, J. Hispano-Arabic Poetry (1974) pp.206-212, Stillman,
pp.211-25, and Goldstein, D. The Jewish Poets of Spain (1965)
pp.39-40, 60-71, 119-21, 137-39

6th week: the beginnings of dialogue
Talmage, Disputation, 9-13, 71-81, 117-19, 155-74
Abelard, Dialogue of a Philosopher with a Jew and a Christian,
trans. P.J. Payer (PIMS)
Joseph Kimhi, The Book of the Covenant, trans. F. Talmage (PIMS)
or J. Halevi, Kuzari, ed. I. Heinemann, in Three Jewish
Philosophers, pp.7-130.

**7th week: armed conflict--the Christian view of the
Crusades**
"Spurious Letter of Alexius Comnenus to Count Robert of Flanders
Imploring His Aid against the Turks"--
either The Deeds of the Franks, ed.R. Hill (1962)
or Fulcher of Chartres, A History of the Expedition to
Jerusalem, 1095-1127, trans. F. Ryan (1969) [or in E. Peters,
The First Crusade (1971)]
or Odo of Deuil, De profectione Ludovici VII in orientem (The
Journey of Louis VII to the East), ed. & trans. V. Berry (1948)
or Robert of Clari, The Conquest of Constantinople, trans. E.
McNeal (1964)

or The Song of Roland (any translation you have not read before)

8th week: **armed conflict—other views**
The Jews and the First Crusaders, ed. & trans. S. Eidelberg (U. of Wisconsin)
one account from F. Gabrielli, Arab Historians of the Crusades (1969)
or Usamah ibn Murshid Ibn Munquidh, Ibn Munqid, An Arab-Syrian Gentleman and Warrior in the Period of the Crusades, trans. P. Hitti (1929)
or Ibn al-Qalanisi, The Damascus Chronicle of the Crusades, trans. H.A.R. Gibb (1932)

9th week: **philosophical harmony and the appeal to reason**
Averroes [Ibn Rushd], On the Harmony of Religion and Philosophy, trans. G. Hourani (1976) pp.44-71
Maimonides, The Guide of the Perplexed, in I. Twersky, A Maimonides Reader (Behrman) pp.234-35, 251,259-65, 274-291, 335-39
Thomas Aquinas, Summa contra Gentiles, trans. the English Dominican Fathers (1923) or A. Pegis (Doubleday, 1955), Bk 1, chs.1-8, 11-13; Bk 2, chs. 32-38
creeds

10th week: writing a research paper
class discussion of methods of research, analytical techniques, varieties of historical approach, organizing and writing papers; historiographical and technical issues
each student will submit to the class an outline and preliminary bibliography of his second paper and to one other student a revision of the first paper

11th week: **sectarian responses: Judaism and Islam**
Maimonides, "Epistle to Yemen," in Maimonides Reader, pp.438-62
The Jewish-Christian Debate in the High Middle Ages: A Critical edition of the Nizzahon Vetus with an Introduction, Translation and Commentary, David Berger (Jewish Pub.Soc.) pp.167-230
Samua'al al-Maghribi, "Ifham al-Yahud," ed. & trans. M. Perlmann in Proceedings of the American Academy for Jewish Research 32 (1964) 31-93

12th week: **darkening clouds: the 13th century**
Marcus, pp.24-28, 34-42, 121-54, 368-69
Ibn Kammuna's Examination of the Three Faiths, trans. M. Perlmann (1971)
"The Disputation of Rabbi Moses Ben Nachman with Fra Paulo Christiani on the subject of the Jewish Faith," in O.S. Rankin, Jewish Religious Polemics (1956), pp.178-210 [or in M. Braude, Conscience on Trial (1952) pp.69-94]

13th week: **the final storm**
Marcus, pp.43-60
F. Machado, <u>The Mirror of the New Christians (Espelho de
Christãos novos</u>, ed. & trans. M. Vieira (PIMS, 1977)
pp.45-79, 231-83, 311-27

Although part of teaching is helping students to locate sources,
part of writing a paper is learning to locate materials on your
own. Use the notes and bibliographies of assigned texts to
pursue more specialized studies, or consult general
bibliographies for the areas which interest you. Ask the
instructor for bibliographical assistance only <u>after</u> you have
made some effort to familiarize yourself with relevant
bibliographical materials. For Western Europe in the Middle
Ages, e.g., see R.C. van Caenegem and F.L. Ganshof, <u>Guide to the
Sources of Medieval History</u> (1978) or L.J. Paetow, <u>Guide to the
Study of Medieval History</u> (1931), both of which will help you to
find more specialized references by topic. If you read only
English but wish to work with primary sources, it will help you
to consult C.P. Farrar and A. Evans, <u>Bibliography of English
Translations from Medieval Sources</u> (1946), updated by M.
Ferguson, <u>Bibliography of English Translations from Medieval
Sources 1943-67</u> (1967), to see what is available.
Materials relating to Jews under Christianity and Islam are
conveniently summarized in the essays and bibliographies in
<u>Bibliographical Essays in Medieval Jewish Studies</u> (The Study of
Judaism, II) (1976). J. Sauvaget, <u>Introduction to the History of
the Muslim East</u> (1965) and the <u>Index Islamicus</u> [ongoing] provide
bibliographical introductions and indices for Islam. For brief
historical background <u>The Cambridge Medieval History</u> and <u>The
Cambridge History of Islam</u> may prove useful, and for specific
topics quick assistance (and small bibliographies) are available
in <u>The Catholic Encyclopedia</u> (the 1908 edition is more detailed,
though also more biassed, than the new one), <u>The Jewish
Encyclopedia</u> and the <u>Encyclopedia Judaica</u>, and <u>The Encyclopaedia
of Islam</u> [2d edition complete only through "K"].

Some suggestions for paper topics, to be taken as food for
thought rather than as constraints:
Contrast the attitudes toward two religions evinced in the
work of an adherent of a third; e.g., attitudes toward Jews and
Muslims in <u>The Poem of the Cid</u>. Distinguish between personal
relations and attitudes and ideological responses to systems of
belief.
Using two specific sources from different periods, discuss
the effect on one of the three religions of one or both of the

others (e.g., show that although both Saadia Gaon and Maimonides were influenced by Islam, the influence of Christianity makes Maimonides' attitudes substantially different from Saadia's.)

Analyze the differential impact of some social issue--assimilation, secularization, intermarriage, church-state relations, etc.--on two religions. Limit your answer to a specific and reasonably short time period.

Contrast the polemical literature of one age or area (but not both) with that of another.

Differentiate among the attitudes of proponents of the three religions at a given time in regard to a social or moral issue such as divorce, business ethics, warfare, etc.

Try to account for differences in tolerance of other religions within one religious tradition over a period of time: e.g., why does Christian Europe seem so much less tolerant in the Later Middle Ages than in the early medieval period?

Compare the developments of one aspect of religious experience (eschatology, mysticism, orthodoxy, etc.) in two of the religious traditions during a given period and comment on the extent to which they can be explained by the particularities of the tradition itself or appear to be the result of broader historical trends affecting all religious systems of the time.

History 310, Winter, 1982
Prof. Penny Gold
Knox College
Home Phone: 342-0244
Office Hours: Thurs. 1:30-4:00 or
                appointment

MEDIEVAL RELIGION

"We should do away with things that lead to serious sin--that is to say, gluttony
too much rest, and too much contact with those who are self-indulgent." (Ailred
of Rievalux, d. 1167; Letter to his sister)

Books available for purchase (all except Russell also available on reserve)
J. B. Russell, A History of Medieval Christianity: Prophecy and Order
Augustine, Confessions
The Rule of Saint Benedict
Bede, A History of the English Church and People
Self and Society in Medieval France: The Memoirs of Abbot Guibert of Nogent
E. Mâle, The Gothic Image: Religious Art in France of the Thirteenth Century
E. Le Roy Ladurie, Montaillou

Other major readings available on reserve
New Testament
Monastic documents
The Mass, in Liturgies of the Western Church
Brenda Bolton, "Mulieres Sanctae"
The Life of Christina of Markyate: A Twelfth-Century Recluse

I   T   1/5   Introduction

     Th   1/7   Early Christianity   New Testament: Gospel According
                                                          Matthew; First Letter of Paul
                                                          the Corinthians
                                                       Russell, pp. 1-44

II   T   1/12   Conversion to Christianity: Russell, 45-59
                 Augustine of Hippo   Augustine, Confessions, 11-90 (In
                                                          duction and Bks. 1-4)

     W   1/13   (cont'd)   Film: Augustine of Hippo (showing
                                                          time to be arranged)

     Th   1/14   (cont'd)   Augustine, 91-205 (Bks. 5-9)

III T   1/19   Early Monasticism   Russell, 59-62
                                                       The Rule of St. Benedict (entire)

     Th   1/21   (cont'd)   Monastic documents (on reserve):
                                                       Plan of Durham Priory; winter and
                                                       summer horarium; Regularis Concor
                                                       Foreword and chps. 1, 7, 10, 12.
                                                       (Read chp. 1 not for the exact de
                                                       of liturgical practice, but for a
                                                       sense of the content and rhythm of
                                                       a monk's day.)

                                                       [Report on choice of topic for
                                                       oral report.]

1/26	Conversion to Christianity: The English	Russell, 63-81 Bede, A History of the English Church and People, pp. 33-35, 336-338, 36-40, 66-131 (Author's Preface; personal note on author; Bk I, chps. 1, 23-24; Bk II, chps. 1-15)
h 1/28	(cont'd)	Bede, pp. 203-269 (Bk 4) [Proposals for grade contracts due.]
2/3	The Liturgy	The Mass, in Liturgies of the Western Church, pp. 54-91 (on reserve)
h 2/5	no class	
2/6	Take-home Midterm Due	
2/9	The Church Hierarchy	Baldwin, The Mediaeval Church, pp. 5-24 (on reserve) Russell, 82-98
h 2/11	Conversion to Monasticism: Guibert of Nogent	Russell, 99-112 Self and Society in Medieval France: The Memoirs of Abbot Guibert of Nogent, pp. 4-117 (Introduction and Book I)
2/16	Monastic Reform Movements	Russell, 113-169 Brenda Bolton, "Mulieres Sanctae [Holy Women]" (on reserve)
2/18	Trip to New Melleray Abbey and Our Lady of the Mississippi Abbey	Knowles, Christian Monasticism, 183-204 (to 244 if you have time) pamphlet on New Melleray Abbey (both readings on reserve)
2/23	Eremeticism	The Life of Christina of Markyate: A Twelfth-Century Recluse, 35-193 (note chronology of her life, pp. 14-15). Microfiche text on reserve; must be read on machine in basement of the library. (This biography was written in the 12th century by a monk of St. Albans who knew Christina personally.)
2/25	Religious Expression in Art	Mâle, The Gothic Image, vii-xv 1-63, 131-151, 176-195, 231-281, 390-399 Russell, 170-180
3/2	Heresy and the Inquisition	Russell, 181-195 Le Roy Ladurie, Montaillou, Introduction and chps. 1-13 (Note the index of the main families of Montaillou at the end of the book.)
3/4	(cont'd) 163	Montaillou, chps. 14-21
3/9	Conclusion	Florilegia due

COLLEGE ATTENDANCE POLICY: "Students are expected to attend class regularly and to participate fully in class activities. Students who are absent from clas for whatever reason, are still responsible for all assigned work."

MIDTERM EXAM: The midterm will be a take-home essay exam, due Friday, February

FINAL EXAM: The final exam will also be a take-home essay exam, due at the normally scheduled exam time.

ORAL REPORT: Each student will present an oral report on a primary source not assigned for the class (maximum length of report: 20 minutes). Suggested texts will be on open reserve on the second floor of Seymour Library. Your oral repor should be an analysis of one or more interesting issues raised by the work. What does the text tell us about medieval religious beliefs and practices? (The report should not be a simple summary of the substance or narrative of the work. Where relevant and interesting, the text may be compared to material assigned in the course. I encourage you to schedule a conference with me before you give yo report. Topics and dates should be confirmed with me by Thursday, January 21.
    At the time of the report, you should hand in an outline of the report.   I material other than the one text has been used, a bibliography should be attache

FLORILEGIUM: Each student will compile a florilegium, choosing quotations from least seven of the eight texts listed below. Each quotation should illustrate s important aspect(s) of medieval religion. For each quotation, write a paragrap explaining the significance of the passage chosen. (The quotation may be as bri as one sentence, and should not be longer than one paragraph.) You may hand the quotations in at any time during the term and receive comments, or you can hand the whole collection in on March 9.
        Texts: Augustine, Confessions
                 The Rule of St. Benedict
                 Regularis Concordia
                 Bede, A History of the English Church and People
                 the Mass
                 The Memoirs of Guibert of Nogent
                 The Life of Christina of Markyate
                 Montaillou (quotation should be from the villagers themselves, no
                      from Le Roy Ladurie)
        (N.B.   Indicate text and page number for each quotation.)

PENALTY FOR LATENESS: Work handed in late will be graded down severely, with mor points taken off for each successive day late. If you have a legitimate reason for an extension without penalty (e.g., illness), discuss your situation with me as soon as possible, so that we can arrange an extension.

GRADE: Your grade will be based on the following:

	Standard	Negotiable range
Midterm	20%	0-25%
Oral report	20%	15-25%
Florilegium	10%	10-15%
Final exam	30%	10-50%
Class participation	20%	0-30%

If you would like to negotiate a grade base other than the standard, submit a proposal to me by Thursday, January 28.

Possible texts for oral reports
(available on 24-hour open reserve, 2nd floor Seymour Library)

This sign indicates that a portion, rather than the whole, of the book may be used for the report.

ıe First Crusade, ed. Edward Peters (D 161 P47)

ʋeryman and Medieval Miracle Plays (820.124 E93ev)

ɪtchcraft in Europe 1100-1700: A Documentary History, ed. Alan C. Kors and
    Edward Peters (1972) (BF 1566 K67)

ıe Birth of Popular Heresy: Documents of Medieval History, ed. R. I. Moore
    (1976) (BT 1319 B57 1976)

ıe Life of Ailred of Rievaulx by Walter Daniel, ed. and trans. Maurice Powicke
    (1950; repr. 1979) (BX 4700 E7 W3 1978)

ɪdmer, The Life of Saint Anselm, Archbishop of Canterbury, ed. and trans. R. W.
    Southern (1962; repr. 1972) (BX 4700 A58 E2 1972)

ıe Letters of Saint Boniface, tr. E. Emerton (1973) (BX 4700 B7 A43 1973)

ıe "Little Flowers, Life and "Mirror" of St. Francis (Everyman Library, 1910)
    (282.92 F818L)

ıe Letters and Poems of Fulbert of Chartres (Oxford, 1976) (BX 4705 F88 A4 1976)

ıe Correspondence of Pope Gregory VII, tr. E. Emerton (1932) (282 C 363g)

·dieval Handbooks of Penance: A Translation of the Principal "Libri poenitentiales"
    and Selections from Related Documents, ed. McNeill and Gamer (1938)
    (BX 2260 M3 1965)

ʰhe Anglo-Saxon Missionaries in Germany, Being the Lives of SS. Willibrord,
    Boniface, Sturm, Leoba, and Leguin, together with the Hodoeporicon of St.
    Willibald and a Selection from the Correspondence of St. Boniface (N.Y., 1954)
    (270.92 T138)

ıe Chronicle of the Election of Hugh, Abbot of Bury St. Edmunds and Later Bishop
    of Ely (Oxford, 1974) (BX 4705 H785 E413 1974)

ɪdung of Prüfening, Cictercians and Cluniacs: The Case for Citeaux. A Dialogue
    between Two Monks, An Argument on Four Questions (1977) (BX 3406.2 I3513)

ıe Chronicle of Jocelin of Brakelond, Monk of St. Edmundsbury: A Picture of
    Monastic and Social Life in the Twelfth Century (271 J63)

ɪbellus de diversis ordinibus et professionibus qui sunt in Aecclesia (The Orders
    and Callings of the Church) (Oxford, 1972) (BX 2430 L46)

ɪliana of Norwich, Revelations of Divine Love (242 J94r)

ɪrnard of Clairvaux, The Life and Death of Saint Malachy the Irishman (1978)
    (BX 4700 M23 B4613 1978)

ɪcobus de Voragine, The Golden Legend (London, 1941) (270.92 J17r)

ʋes of the Saints, trans. J. F. Webb (Penguin, 1965). Includes The Voyage of
    St. Brendan, Bede's Life of Cuthbert, Eddius Stephanus' Life of Wilfrid
    (personal copy, PSG)

the Tumbler of Our Lady and Other Miracles (N.Y., 1966) (840.17 W 439)

ıe Book of Margery Kempe (N.Y., 1944) (822 K32 XAb)

Penelope Johnson

CHRISTIAN MONASTICISM:
ITS HISTORY AND CULTURE
G57.2114
Penelope Johnson
New York University

1. Introduction(slides)

2. *The Fathers in the Desert
        David Knowles, Christian Monasticism, 7-24   (abbreviated
            as CM).
        Helen Wadell, The Desert Fathers, 1-129, 173-201,
            156-160.
        Cassian (xerox)

3. Early Institutional Efforts
        St. Augustine "Epistle CCXI" BR60.f3.A8 v.6, part 5
        Sulpicius Severus "The Life of St. Martin"
        Lina Eckenstein, Women Under Monasticism 48-50.
        CM 25-36.

4. Geographic Extremes: Celtic and Byzantine Monasticism (slides)
        Eleanor Duckett, The Gateway to the Middle Ages:
            Monasticism, chapter 2.
        "Life of St. Daniel," in Three Byzantine Saints, ed.
            Elizabeth Dawes.
        St. Basil, "An Ascetical Discourse," Fathers of the Church
            207-215. BR60.F3.B3

5. *St. Benedict: The Great Organizer
        The Rule of St. Benedict
        Gregory the Great, Life and Miracles of St. Benedict
        CM 212-223.

6. Carolingian Monasticism (slides)
        Walter Horn and Born, The Plan of San Gall,NA5851.S34.H6.
        Vol. I:xxi-xxvii, 24-5, 145-155, 241-292, 311-324, 330-54.
        Vol II:139-164, 168-188, 300-312.
        CM 37-53.

7. Reform Efforts (slides)
        Joan Evans, Monastic Life at Cluny
        David Knowles, The Monastic Order in England 16-56.
        CM 54-61

8. *Benedictine Learning and Education
        Jean Leclercq, <u>Love of Learning and Desire for God</u>

9. Women and the Monastic Ideal
        Lina Eckenstein, <u>Women Under Monasticism</u> 184-221
        <u>Letters of Abelard and Heloise</u>, (Penguin) 159-269.

10. *St. Bernard and the Cistercian Reform (slides)
        <u>Vita Prima Bernardi</u>
        <u>Letters of St. Bernarad</u> 1,8,105,112,118.
        CM 62-97.

11. The Monastic Arts (slides)
        Sample from the following:
            George Zarnecki, <u>The Monastic Achievement</u>
            Joan Evans, <u>Art in Medieval France</u>, chap. 2 & 3.
            _____ <u>Romanesque Architecture of the Order of
                Cluny</u>
            Whitney Stoddard, <u>Monastery and Cathedral in France,</u>
                chap. 32.
            Eckenstein, chap. 7.
        Listening assignment, Music Library, 2nd floor of Bobst
            Pange lingua, sixth century
            Liturgy, tenth century
            Mass of the Assumption of the Virgin
            Office for the Dead

12. *The Friars (slides)
        St. Francis, <u>The Little Flowers of St. Francis</u>
        H. G. Beck, "The Dispute over Franciscan Poverty,"
            <u>Am. Eccl. Review</u> (1943).
        CM 108-123.

13. Late Medieval Decay and the Reformation
        Eckenstein 398-476
        Luther, "An Answer to Several Questions," BR330.E5.1955
            v. 46.
        _____ "How God Rescued an Honorable Nun", v. 43.
        Evans, <u>Monastic Life</u>, 126-130.
        CM 135-164.

REQUIREMENTS:
    Regular class attendance.
    Class trip to the Cloisters.
    Five 2-page papers due in class on starred dates. Each paper
is to examine a central issue in that week's reading.
    Final Exam, date to be announced.

MEDIEVAL CHRISTIAN MYSTICISM
E. Ann Matter
University of Pennsylvania

This course covers a selection of writings from some of the great mystical and spiritual Christian writers of the 5th-16th centuries. The main focus will be on the primary sources. These have, however, been grouped according to Christian mystical themes; each section will be opened by a secondary reading, which will be available in xerox from the instructor. These secondary readings are meant to help us ask important questions of the texts: what distinguishes "mysticism" from "spirituality?", what are the sources of Christian mystical language?, what do the mystics say about personal experience, as distinguished from cosmology or theology?

Each student has a choice of writing:

1) Two 7-10 page papers (critical, exegetical work) on one of the primary texts, or a selection from one of the primary texts; or

2) One paper as described above, and one short research paper (10-15 pp.) on a mystical treatise by an author not covered by the course. A list of possible topics for this paper will be distributed the first week of classes.

COURSE OUTLINE

I. BIBLICAL THEMES: ALLEGORY / THE SONG OF SONGS
P. P. Parente, "The Canticle of Canticles in Mystical Theology," Catholic Biblical Quarterly 6 (1944) 142-158

1) Introduction, The Song of Songs, Parente

2) Origen of Alexandria and Hugh of Saint Victor on the Song of Songs

3) Bernard of Clairvaux, On the Song of Songs v.1

4) Hildegard of Bingen, Ordo Virtutum (a liturgical morality play) Alain of Lille, On the Six Wings of the Cherubim

II. THE DARK WAY
D. Knowles, "The Influence of Pseudo-Dionysius on Western Mysticism" Christian Spirituality, ed. P. Brooks (London, 1975) 80-94
and E. Underhill, "The Dark Night of the Soul," Mysticism, chapter 9.

5) Dionysius the Areopagite (Pseudo-Dionysius), Introduction and The Mystical Theology, Knowles, Underhill

6) Pseudo-Dionysius, The Divine Names

7) The Cloud of Unknowing

III.   THE TRINITY E.   Underhill,   "Mysticism   and   Theology,"
       Mysticism, chapt. 5
       or J. Leclerq, "Monastic Theology," The Love of Learning
       and the Desire for God, chapter 9.

8) Augustine, Confessions, books 1-9, Underhill, Leclerq

9) Augustine, Confessions, books 10-13, Bonaventure, The Mind's Road to God

IV.   INCARNATION AND CRUCIFIXION C. Talbot, "Christina of Markyate:
      A Monastic Narrative of the Twelfth Century," Essays and
      Studies 1962, pp. 13-26
      and E. McLaughlin, "'Christ My Mother': Feminine Naming
      and Metaphor in Medieval Spirituality," Nashotah Review 15
      (1975, no. 3) 230-248

10) Julian of Norwich, A Revelation of God's Love

11) Teresa of Avila, The Interior Castle

V.   THE TREMBLER BEFORE THE COSMOS / THE PILGRIM D.   T.   Suzuki,
     "Meister Eckhart and Buddhism," Mysticism Christian and
     Buddhist, chapter 1

12) Meister Eckhart, The Book of Divine Comfort, About Disinterest,
    Selected Sermons, Suzuki

13) The Way of a Pilgrim

Prof. JoAnn McNamara
Hunter College

History 250--The Age of the Crusades   M, W, Th, 10:10-11:05
Professor McNamara   Room 911

Text: Hollister: Medieval Europe: A Short History.

Midterm Examination: March 24

Two Book Reports: March 3
                  April 25

A final examination will be scheduled by the Registrar

The book reports are to be about five pages each, and must follow the instructions
accompanying the syllabus. One is to deal with a primary source (something written in ancient times) and the other with a secondary source. You are to follow
an essay form with the number of the question being considered to appear in the
margin. This will enable you to alter the order of the questions if you feel it
makes your meaning clearer but assures me that each question has been considered.

The Roots of the Crusade.
1. The Council of Clermont
2. Latin Christendom: an Augustinian world.
3. Islam and Byzantium
4. Early Medieval Christianity: Proprietors and Parishioners.
5. The Monastic Church and the Episcopal Church
6. The Papal Church
7. Peasant and Seigneury: the agrarian revolution.
8. An exploding Population: the urban movement.
9. The First Crusade and the Vision of Jerusalem.

Primary Sources:

Anna Comnena, The Alexiad
Christine of Markyates, Biography
Emerton, E. (ed.) Correspondence of Pope Gregory VII
Fulcher of Chartres, History of the Expedition to Jerusalem
    Letters and Poems
Downer, L.J. (ed.) Leges Henrici Primi
Pernoud, Regine (ed.) The First Crusade

Secondary Sources:

Atiya, Aziz, Crusade, Commerce and Culture
Bloch, Marc, Slavery and Serfdom in the Middle Ages
Chenu, M.D., Nature, Man and Society in the Twelfth Century
Chodorow, Stanley, Christian Political Theory and Church Politics in the mid-12th
Cheyette, Frederic L, Lordship and Community in Medieval Europe.
Cohn, Norman, The Pursuit of the Millenium
Duby, Georges, Rural Economy and Country Life in the Medieval West
Ennen, Edith, The Medieval Town
Erdmann, Carl, The Origin of the Idea of the Crusade
Hyde, J.K., Society and Politics in Medieval Italy
Power, Eileen, Medieval Women
Prawer, Joshua, The Crusaders Kingdom
Runciman, Steven, A History of the Crusades (3 vols.)
Russell, Frederick H., The Just War in the Middle Ages
Setton, Kenneth M., The Crusades
Tellenbach, Gerd, Church State and Christian Society at the time of the Investi-
    ture Conflice

II. Self and Society in Crusading Europe
   1. The Latin Kingdom and the Chivalric Ideal
   2. Bernard of Clairvaux and the Second Crusade
   3. Monastic Love and Courtly Love
   4. Twelfth Century Individualism
   5. Learning and Heresy
   6. Conflict of Church and State: Italy and England and Germany
   7. The Feudal Kingdom and the Third Crusade
   8. Richard the Lion Hearted's England
   9. Philip Augustus' France

Primary Sources:

Guibert of Nogent, <u>Autobiography</u> (Paper: Self and Society in Medieval Europe
Hall, G.D.G. (ed.) <u>The Treatise on the Laws and Customs of England</u>
James, Bruno, S. (ed.) <u>The Letters of Saint Bernard of Clairvaux</u>
<u>Letters of Abelard and Heloise</u>
Odo of Deuil, <u>The Journey of Louis VII to the East</u>
Otto of Freising, <u>The Deeds of Frederick Barbarossa</u>

Secondary Sources:
Bloch, Marc, <u>The Feudal Society</u> (vol. 2)
Brundage, James, <u>Canon Law and the Crusader</u>
Brundage, James, <u>Richard the Lion-Heart</u>
Bullough, Vern and Brundage, James, <u>Sexual Practices and the Medieval Church</u>
Cobban, Alan, <u>The Medieval Universities</u>
Douglas, David, <u>The Norman Fate, 1100-1154.</u>
Duby, Georges, <u>The Chivalrous Society</u>
Duby, Georges, <u>Medieval Marriage</u>
Kelly, Amy, <u>Eleanor of Aquitaine and the Four Kings</u>
Kibler, William W., ed., <u>Eleanor of Aquitaine, Patron and Politician</u>
LeGoff, Jacques, <u>Intellectuals of the Middle Ages.</u>
Lindsay, Jack, <u>The Troubadours and their World.</u>
MacFarlane, Alan, <u>The Origins of English Individualism</u>
Moore, John, <u>Love in Twelfth Century France</u>
Petit-Dutaillis, Charles, <u>The Feudal Monarchy in France and England</u>
de Rougemont, Denis, <u>Love in the Western World</u>
Seward, D., <u>Monks at War</u>
Ullmann, Walter, <u>The Individual and Society in the Middle ages</u>
Warren, W.L., <u>Henry II</u>
Weinstein, Donald and Bell, Rudolph, <u>Saints and Society</u>
Weintraub, Karl J., <u>The value of the Individual: Self and Circumstance in</u>
   <u>Autobiography.</u>

II. The Internalization of the Crusade
   1. The Fourth Crusade
   2. Economic Imperialism and the Rise of Italy
   3. Children's Crusades and the Cult of Poverty
   4. The Albigensian Crusade
   5. Intellectual Imperialism: Aristotelianism and the Rise of Universities
   6. Frederick II and the Heretic Crusade
   7. Spain and the Perpetual Crusade
   8. Henry III and the Cost of the Crusade
   9. Saint Louis' Holy Wars

Primary Sources:

Coulton, G.G. (ed.), From Saint Francis to Dante
Herrad of Landsberg, Hortus Deliciarum
Lopez and Raymond (eds) Medieval Trade in the Mediterranean World
Memoirs of the Crusade: Joinville's Life of St. Louis
                        Villehardouin's Chronicle of the Fourth Crusade
Origo, Iris (ed) The Merchant of Prato
Peters, Edward (ed.) Christian Society and the Crusades: 1198-1299.
Peters, Edward (ed.) Heresy and Authority in Medieval Europe
Robert of Clary, The Conquest of Constantinople
Thorndike, Lynn, University Records and Life in the Middle Ages
Wakefield, Walter, and Evans, Austin, Heresies of the High Middle Ages.

Secondary Sources:
Bynum, Caroline, Jesus as Mother
Hamilton, Bernard, The Medieval Inquisition
Boswell, John, Christianity, Social Tolerance and Homosexuality
Brentano, Robert, Rome before Avignon
Hampe, Carl, Germany under the Salian and Hohenstaufen Emperors
Homans, Goerge, C., English Villagers of the 13th Century
Hyams, Paul, King, Lords, Peasants in Medieval England
Kantorowica, Ernst, Frederick the Second.
Lambert, Malcolm, Medieval Heresy: Popular movements from Bogomil to Hus.
McDonnell, Ernest, Beguines and Behards in Medieval Culture.
Miller, E., and Hatcher, J., Medieval England: Rural Society ant change.
Mundy, John, Europe in the High Middle Ages
Noonan, John, Scholastic Analysis of Usury
Norwizh, John J., A History of Venice
Oldenbourg, Zoe, Massacre at Montségur
Queller, Donald, The Fourth Crusade
Strayer, Joseph, R., The Albigensian Crusade
Tillmann, Helene, Pope Innocent III

IV. The Secularization of the Crusade.
1. Christian xenophobia in Europe
2. The Angevin Crusades in Italy
3. The Papacy and the Age of the Holy Ghost
4. Edward I: the last crusader
5. The Fall of Acre
6. Marco Polo and a new venture
7. The Nation and holy war
8. Philip the Fair and the Destruction of the Templars
9. Visions of the Next Crusade.

Primary Sources:

Dante, Inferno
Dawson, Christopher, The Mongol Mission
Dubois, Pierre, The Recovery of the Holy Land
Marco Polo, Travels
Muldoon, James, ed., The Expansion of Europe, the First Phase.

Secondary Sources:

C.T. Allmand, Society at War
Fourquin, Gyy, Anatomy of Popular Rebellion in the Middle Ages
Heers, Jacques, The Family Clan in the Middle Ages
Heers, Jacques, Parties and Political Life in the Medieval West
Hillgarth, Joyce, The Spanish Kingdoms, 1250-1516.
Kedar, Benjamin, Merchants in Crisis.
Lane, Frederic C., Venice: A Maritime Republic
McLaughlin, Eleanor, Women in Medieval Theology.
Martines, Lauro, Violence and Disorder in Italian Cities, 1200-1500.
McKay, Angus, Spain in the Middle Ages.
Muldoon, James, Popes, Lawyers and Infidels
Raftis, Ambrose, Tenure and Mobility: Studies in the Social History of Enhlish
Synan, The Popes and the Jews in the Middle Ages
Szasa, Thomas, The Manufacture of Madness
Trexler, Richard, Public Life in Renaissance Florence
Waley, Daniel, The Italian City Republics
Weissman, Ronald, Ritual Brotherhood in Renaissance Florence

EASTERN CHRISTIANITY IN THE MIDDLE AGES
John Meyendorff
Fordham University

Requirements: Three short papers (no more than five pages) on
subjects announced at least one week in advance, and related to the
required readings. The final examination covering the whole
content of the course.

Required readings:
   The New Testament, esp. Mark 1-6; John 1-2, 18-21; Acts 1-5,
8-9; 1 Cor. and Gal.
   Henry Chadwick, The Early Church, Penguin Books, 1967.
   Colin McEvedy, The Penguin Atlas of Medieval History, 1969
   Alexander Schmemann, The Historical Road of Eastern Orthodoxy
1978.
   John Meyendorff, Byzantine Theology (particularly part I:
Historical Trends), Fordham Press, 2nd ed., 1978.
   Francis Dvornik, Byzantium and the Roman Primacy Fordham Press,
1966.

1.   Basic Acquaintance with Christian Origins
        New Testament. Chadwick, 9-73.

2.   The Early Church: intellectual life, persecutions.
        Chadwick, 74-124; Schmemann, 3-61.

3.   Emperor Constantine. The transfer of the imperial capital
     to Constantinople.
        Chadwick, 125-132; Schmemann, 62-80

4.   From Constantine to Theodosius: The establishment of
     Christianity. Paganism surviving. Monasticism. Arianism.
        Chadwick, 133-191; Schmemann, 80-112.

5.   The Controversy on the Identity of Jesus Christ: different
     trends in Alexandria and Antioch.
        Chadwick, 192-200.

6.   Church and State in Byzantium. The ecumenical councils.
        Schmemann, 113-134.

7.   The Council of Chalcedon and the Schism of the Monophysites.
        Chadwick, 200-205; Schmemann, 134-142.

8.   Emperor Justinian (527-565): The Roman dream of universality.
        Schmemann, 142-168; Chadwick, 205-210.

CHURCH AND STATE IN THE MIDDLE AGES   **Brian Tierney**
Cornell University

HISTORY 367

READING LIST   Fall 1981

aperbacks

B. Tierney, THE CRISIS OF CHURCH AND STATE, 1050-1300.
W. Ullmann, HISTORY OF POLITICAL THOUGHT (=MEDIAEVAL POLITICAL THOUGHT)
J. A. Watt, JOHN OF PARIS
G. Barraclough, THE MEDIEVAL PAPACY.
J. R. Strayer, ON THE MEDIEVAL ORIGINS OF THE MODERN STATE

her Assigned Readings

M. V. Clarke, MEDIEVAL REPRESENTATON AND CONSENT, Ch. 12, 13.
P. Hughes, HISTORY OF THE CHURCH, II, pp. 209-238.
E. Kantorwicz, THE KING'S TWO BODIES, pp. 143-164.
F. Kempf, "Die papstliche Gewalt in der mittelalterlichen Welt,"
     MISCELLANEA HISTORIAE PONTIFICIAE (1959). (English summary).
F. Kern, KINGSHIP AND LAW, pp. 149-205.
G. Post, STUDIES IN MEDIEVAL LEGAL THOUGHT, pp. 241-269, 301-309.
J. R. Powell, INNOCENT III
J. R. Strayer, "Laicization of Society in the Thirteenth Century,"
     reprinted in S. Thrupp, CHANGE IN MEDIEVAL SOCIETY.
G. Tellenbach, CHURCH, STATE, AND CHRISTIAN SOCIETY, Introduction
B. Tierney, "Some Recent Works on...the Medieval Canonists,"
     TRADITIO, 10 (1954).
B. Tierney, "Medieval Canon Law and Western Constitutionalism,"
     CATHOLIC HISTORICAL REVIEW, 62 (1966).
W. Ullmann, GROWTH OF PAPAL GOVERNMENT, pp. 1-31, 262-309, 340-343.

r Reference

R. W. and A. J. Carlyle, HISTORY OF POLITICAL THEORY (6 vols.)

l works listed above are on Reserve in Uris Library. The source **materials**
d other books mentioned on the following sheet of Term Paper Topics are
so on the Reserve shelf.

e paperbacks may be purchased at the Campus Bookstore.

1. **The Early Centuries** (to 800 A.D.)

       Introduction - Problems of Church and State
       Foundations - Scripture and the Early Church
       Rome and the Barbarians - St. Augustine
       The Papacy to Gelasius I
       Rome, Byzantium, and Gaul, 500-750
       Charlemagne - The Medieval Empire

       Readings: CRISIS OF CHURCH AND STATE, pp. 1-32; Ullmann, GROWTH OF
                 PAPAL GOVERNMENT, pp. 1-31; Ullmann, POLITICAL THOUGHT,
                 pp. 7-99; Kempf, Review of Ullmann (translated summary);
                 Barraclough, MEDIEVAL PAPACY, pp. 7-61.

2. **Empire and Papacy** (800-1150)

       Disintegration - Feudal Kingship
       Recovery - Theocratic Kingship
       The Papal Reform Movement
       Papacy versus Empire - Gregory VII and Henry IV
       End of the Conflict - Effects on Church and State

       Readings: CRISIS, pp. 33-95; Hughes, HISTORY OF THE CHURCH, II, pp.
                 209-238; Ullmann, GROWTH, pp. 262-309; Tellenbach, CHURCH,
                 STATE AND CHRISTIAN SOCIETY, INTRODUCTION: Barraclough,
                 MEDIEVAL PAPACY, pp. 63-101.

3. **The Revival of Law** (1150-1200)
       Law and Administration - the Church
       Law and Administration - England, France, Germany
       Empire versus Papacy - Frederick I and Alexander III
       Canonistic Theories of Church and State
       Canonistic Theories of Empire and Kingdoms

       Readings: CRISIS, pp. 97-126; Kern, KINGSHIP AND LAW, pp. 149-205;
                 Post, STUDIES, pp. 241-269, 301-309; Ullmann, GROWTH,
                 pp. 340-343; Tierney, "Some Recent Works on ... the
                 Medieval Canonists"; Strayer, MEDIEVAL ORIGINS, pp. 3-56.

4. **Papal Theocracy?** (1200-1250)

       Innocent III: Personality and Problems
       Innocent III: Political Theory
       Papal Sovereignty and its Limitations
       Royal Sovereignty and its Limitations
       Empire versus Papacy - Frederick II and Innocent IV

       Readings: CRISIS, pp. 127-157; Powell, INNOCENT III; Tierney, POPE
                 AND COUNCIL; SOME NEW DECRETIST TEXTS; W. Ullmann,
                 POLITICAL THOUGHT, pp. 100-158; Barraclough, pp. 101-140;
                 Kantorowicz, KING'S TWO BODIES, pp. 143-164.

5. <u>Aristotelianism, Nationalism, and the Constitutional State</u> (1250-1300)

        Thomas Aquinas
        Factors in Medieval Constitutionalism
        The Rise of Representative Government
        Church versus State - Boniface VIII and Philip IV
        Political Theory - Giles of Rome and John of Paris

        Readings: CRISIS, pp. 159-210; Ullmann, POLITICAL THOUGHT, pp. 159-
                    232; M. V. Clarke, REPRESENTATION AND CONSENT, Ch. 12, 13;
                    Tierney, "Western Constitutionalism and Medieval Canon
                    Law;" Strayer, "Laicization of Society;" J. A. Watt, JOHN
                    OF PARIS.

History 595

Medieval Crime

W. R. Jones
Department of History

University of New Hampsh
Semester I, 1982-3

The following bibliographical citations should be used both for
the definition of term paper topics and for the assembling of pertinent bibligraphical materials for them.

I. The Social and Economic Contexts of Medieval Crime

For a recent, but classic statement of the economic determinants
of crime in medieval and early modern England, see J. M. Beattie,
"The Pattern of Crime in England, 1600-1800," Past & Present,
62 (1974), 47-95. Compare with Michael Weisser's attempt to
fashion general societal models for explaining criminality in
Crime and Punishment in Early Modern Europe (Atlantic Highlands,
1979). Compare both with the older work of L. O. Pike, A History
of Crime in England, 2 vols.; London, 1893 and the popular treatment of the subject by Andrew McCall, The Medieval Underworld
(London, 1979). Note that different methodologies and models
produce quite different results. What are the weaknesses and
strengths of the methodologies and models employed by individual
authors?

II. Felony in Medieval England

A recent attempt to write legal and social history using the
records of criminal justice is Barbara Hanawalt's Crime and
Conflict in English Communities, 1300-1348 (Cambridge, MA and
London, 1979). Look up the critical reviews of this book in
the scholarly journals (Journal of Interdisciplinary History,
American Journal of Legal History, etc.) Compare Hanawlt's
description of homicide in medieval England with the similar
work of James Given, Society and Homicide in Thirteenth Century
England (Palo Alta, CA, 1977). Did they find any significant
differences between the thirteenth and fourteenth centuries?

III. Politics, Justice and Crime

Did the existence of an efficient criminal justice system
and of strong royal authority inhibit the incidence of criminal
disorder? Read John Bellamy, Crime and Public Order in England
in the Later Middle Ages (London and Toronto, 1973); W. R. Jones

Rex et ministri: English Local Government and the Crisis of 134?
Journal of British Studies, 13 (1973), 1-20; idem, "Keeping the
Peace: English Society, Local Government, and the Commissions
of 1341-44," American Journal of Legal History, 18 (1974), 307-
20; John Langbein, Torture and the Law of Proof (Chicago, 1977);
Alfred Soman, "Deviance and Criminal Justice in Western Europe,
1300-1800: An Essay in Structure," Criminal Justice History,
I (1980), 1-28. John Langbein, Prosecuting Crime in the
Renaissance (Cambridge1974).

IV. Organized Crime in the Middle Ages

See the articles of E. L. G. Stones, "The Folvilles of Ashby-Folville, Leicestershire, and Their Associates in Crime, 1326-1341," Transactions of the Royal Historical Society, 5th series, 7 (1957), 117-36, and J. G. Bellamy, "The Coterel Gang: An Anatomy of a Band of Fourteenth Century Criminals," English Historical Review, 74 (1964), 698-717; and the recent monograph of J. C. Holt, Robin Hood (London, 1982).

Can one speak of "professional criminals" in premodern Europe? Does Robin Hood conform to the "social bandit" described by Eric J. Hobsbawm in his classic work, Bandits?

V. The Criminal in Literature

In addition to Holt's Robin Hood, see M. H. Keen, The Outlaws of Medieval England (London, 1977).

VI. Cultural Determinants of Crime

W. R. Jones, "Violence, Criminality and Culture Disjunction on the Anglo-Irish Frontier: the Example of Armagh, 1350-1550," Criminal Justice History, 1 (1980), 29-47; Timothy Curtis, "Explaining Crime in Early Modern England," ibid., 117-37; I. A. Thompson, "A Map of Crime in Sixteenth Century Spain", Economic Hist. Review, 21 (1968) 244-67

VII. Changing Paterns of Crime

Joel Samaha, Law and Order in Historical Perspective: the Case of Elizabethan Essex (New York, 1974); E. P. Thompson, Albion's Fatal Tree (London, 1975); J. C. Cockburn, Crime in England: 1500-1800 (London, 1977); E. P. Thompson, Whigs and Hunters (London, 1975) V. A. C. Gatrell, B. Lenman, and G. Parker, Crime and the Law since 1500 (London, 1979); J. J. Tobias, Crime and Industrial Society in the Nineteenth Century (London, 1967); idem, Urban Crime in Victorian England (New York, 1972).

VIII. Imprisonment

Contrast the approaches of R. B. Pugh, Imprisonment in Medieval England (Cambridge, 1968) and Michel Foucault, Discipline and Punish, the Birth of the Prison (New York, 1977). What are the implications of Foucault's thesis?

FOUNDATIONS OF ANGLO-AMERICAN LAW
Professor Donald Sutherland
University of Iowa

A general familiarity with English history for the period 1150-1700 is essential. For those who have not studied English history before, this may be got from any of a number of books. These in particular may be mentioned as brief and reliable:

J. R. Lander, Ancient and Medieval England, chap. 5-8, together with Charles M. Gray, Renaissance and Reformation England.

G. M. Trevelyan, A Shortened History of England, Bk. II, III, IV chap. 1-5.

Goldwin Smith, A History of England, chapters 4-19.

The following books should be purchased. Purchase of the first of them, Pollock and Maitland, is essential, since it will be the textbook for the first half and more of the course. There will be copies of the other, Maitland's Forms of Action, on reserve in the Law Library and if you like you can work from these, but it will be more convenient if you buy it too.

F. Pollock and F. W. Maitland, The History of English Law, ed. S. F. C. Milsom, (1968) 2 vols., paperback.

F. W. Maitland, The Forms of Action at Common Law, eds. Chaytor and Whittaker, (1965).

Do the reading according to the following time-table.

THE BEGINNINGS OF THE COMMON LAW--Jan. 18-Feb. 4

Pollock and Maitland, The History of English Law Vol. I, bk. I, chap. 6-7, Vol. I, bk. II, chap. 1, pp. 229-383.

D. W. Sutherland, The Assize of Novel Disseisin, chap. 1.

F. W. Maitland, The Forms of Action, lectures 1-4.

THE NEW CRIMINAL LAW Feb.--5-Feb. 19

Pollock and Maitland, op. cit., Vol. II, chap. 8

Thomas A. Green, "The Jury and the English Law of Homicide, 1200-1600," Michigan Law Review, 74 (1976), 414-456, 472-499.

John H. Langbein, "The Criminal Trial before the Lawyers," University of Chicago Law Review, 45 (1978), 263-316.

Increase Mather, "Witchcraft in Massachusetts," in Stephen Botein, Early American Law and Society, 147-56.

THE EARLY COMMON LAW: LANDS AND TENEMENTS--Feb. 20-Mar. 13.

Pollock and Maitland, op. cit., vol. II, chap. 4, 1-149, chap. 6, 260-313.

Sutherland, op. cit., chap. 2, 3.

T. F. T. Plucknett, Legislation of Edward I, chap. 3-5.

THE EARLY COMMON LAW: OTHER DOCTRINES--Mar. 14-Ap. 7

Pollock and Maitland, op. cit., vol. II, chap. 6, 314-363, chp. 7, 364-447.
R. H. Helmholz, Marriage Litigation in Medieval England, intro, and chap. 1-3, chap. 6 and conclusion.

THE RESHAPING OF THE COMMON LAW--Ap. 8-Ap. 13

Sutherland, op. cit., chap. 4-5.
Maitland, Forms of Action, lectures 5-7.

EQUITY IN CHANCERY AND STAR CHAMBER--Ap. 14-Ap. 24

W. S. Holdsworth, A History of English Law
vol. I, pp. 395-423
Vol. V, pp. 278-338
Vol. IV, pp. 407-480
E. P. Cheyney, "The Court of Star Chamber," in American Historical Review, 18 (1912-13), 727-750.

THE LAW CROSSES THE ATLANTIC--Ap. 25-May 6

Stephen Botein, Early American Law and Society, entire except pp. 147-56, and 185-92.

MAGNA CARTA THROUGH THE AGES

Description: Approximately the first half of the term will be
spent on Magna Carta in its early thirteenth-century setting: its
causes, its contents, its meaning in its own day. The second half
of the term will trace the role which Magna Carta has played in
English and American constitutional and legal development from the
thirteenth century to the present and the interpretations and mis-
interpretations to which it has been subjected in the process.

Class mode: discussion seminar.

Grades will be based on:

   participation in class discussion (30%)

   two written book reviews, one also to be delivered orally (20%
   each). The instructions for these reviews are on a separate
   sheet.

   a final examination (30%). This examination will be given at
   the scheduled time, Thursday, June 6, 5:45-7:45; but the
   questions will be handed out in advance, probably in the last
   class. I invite any of you who might like to do so to submit
   possible questions for inclusion on the exam. I retain absolute discretion as to whether to include a question, but I
   shall be happy to explain why a question was rejected should
   I choose not to use one which you submit.

Office hours: Tuesdays and Thursdays, 1:15-2:45, and by appointment in 306A Morrill Hall (telephone: 353-9039). You may leave
messages in 301 Morrill Hall (telephone: 355-7500).

                           * * * * *

Background: Students who do not have some background in medieval
and early modern English history should read S. B. Chrimes, English
Constitutional History (any edition). You may also wish to consult
Alan Harding, A Social History of English Law. A copy of each book
is on 2-hour reserve for this course.

Reading assignments: The following pages contain the reading assignments for each class. They are followed by an alphabetical
listing of all the works assigned for the course, giving full citations for each and indicating where they are available. The order
in which required readings are listed in the class-by-class assignments is the order in which you should, if it is at all possible,
read them.

   Because this is a discussion seminar, the reading must be com-
pleted before the class for which it is assigned.

   All sources assigned are contained in the sourcebook which I
have compiled for the course. Most of the articles and excerpts
from books assigned are contained in the coursebook which I have
compiled for the course. Both the sourcebook and the coursebook
are on 2-hour reserve. Each is also available for purchase in
photocopy at Kinko's on Division Street.

Class # 1 (March 28): Introduction

    no reading assignment

                PART I: MAGNA CARTA IN ITS OWN DAY

Classes # 2-5 (April 2, 4, 9, 11): Reading the charter

Required reading:

    Sources: Magna Carta
             Coronation charters of Henry I, Stephen and Henry II
             "Unknown" Charter
             Articles of the Barons

    Secondary: Thorne, "What Magna Carta Was"
               Painter, "Magna Carta"
               Cam, Magna Carta—Event or Document?

Recommended reading: Davis, Magna Carta
                     Dickinson, The Great Charter
                     Galbraith, "Magna Carta"
                     Goodhart, "Law of the Land"
                     Howard, Magna Carta
                     Jennings, Magna Carta

Note: there are extended clause-by-clause commentaries on Magna
  Carta in:

    McKechnie, Magna Carta, pp. 191-480
    Swindler, Magna Carta, pp. 244-351

Class # 6 (April 16): The reign of John

Required reading: Jones, King John and Magna Carta

Recommended reading: Hollister, "King John and the Historians"

Books for review: Warren, King John
                  Painter, The Reign of King John
                  Powicke, The Loss of Normandy
                  Norgate, John Lackland

Class # 7 (April 18): Concepts behind Magna Carta

Required reading: Holt, "The Barons and the Great Charter"
                  Holt, "Rights and Liberties in Magna Carta"
                  Jolliffe, selections from Angevin Kingship

Books for review: Holt, Magna Carta
                  Young, The Royal Forests of Medieval England
                  Richardson, English Jewry under Angevin Kings

Class # 8 (April 23): The motives of the barons

Required reading: Stubbs, Constitutional History, section 155
Jenks, "The Myth of Magna Carta"
Petit-Dutaillis, "The Great Charter"
Holt, Magna Carta, Chapter VII

Books for review: Jolliffe, Angevin Kingship
Holt, The Northerners
Painter, William Marshal
Powicke, Stephen Langton

Class # 9 (April 25): Magna Carta, clause 34

Required reading: McKechnie, Magna Carta, commentary on c. 34
Hurnard, "Magna Carta, Clause 34"
Clanchy, "Magna Carta, Clause Thirty-Four"

Class # 10 (April 30): Magna Carta, clause 39

Required reading: McKechnie, Magna Carta, commentary on c. 39
McIlwain, "Due Process of Law in Magna Carta"
Powicke, "Per iudicium parium vel per legem terrae"
Keeney, Judgment by Peers, Chapter III
Holt, Magna Carta, pp. 226-29

Book for review: Keeney, Judgment by Peers

PART II: MAGNA CARTA IN ENGLAND AFTER 1215

Class # 11 (May 2): The Middle Ages

Required reading:

Secondary: Cam, Magna Carta, pp. 11-20 (review)
Dunham, "Magna Carta and British Constitutionalism," pp. 26-36
Stenton, After Runnymede

Sources: Charter of the Forest
Confirmation of the Charters
Articles on the Charters
The Six Statutes

Books for review: Thompson, The First Century of Magna Carta
Turner, The King and his Courts

Class # 12 (May 7): The Tudors

Required reading: Butterfield, The Englishman and his History, pp. 1-30
Radin, "The Myth of Magna Carta"
Butterfield, "Magna Carta in the Historiography of the Sixteenth and Seventeenth Centuries," pp. 3-14

Books for review: Thompson, Magna Carta: Its Role . . .
Shakespeare, King John
Bale, King Johan
Anonymous, The Troublesome Raigne of King John

ss # 13 (May 9): The early Stuarts

equired reading:

Secondary: Cam, Magna Carta, pp. 20-24 (review)
Dunham, "Magna Carta . . . ," pp. 36-42
Butterfield, The Englishman and his History, pp. 31-72
Ashley, Magna Carta in the Seventeenth Century,
pp. 3-33
Butterfield, "Magna Carta . . . ," pp. 15-25

Sources: Debates in Commons, 26 April 1628, on the Lords' Propositions of 25 April
The Petition of Right
Penn, The Excellent Priviledge of Liberty and Property

ooks for review: Pocock, The Ancient Constitution and the Feudal Law
Relf, The Petition of Right
White, Sir Edward Coke . . .

ss # 14 (May 14): Two seventeenth-century revolutions

equired reading:

Secondary: Dunham, "Magna Carta . . . ," pp. 42-46
Butterfield, The Englishman and his History, pp. 72-78
Ashley, Magna Carta . . . , pp. 33-62
Pallister, Magna Carta, pp. 1-42

Sources: Walwyn, Englands Lamentable Slaverie
Lilburne, Englands Freedome, Souldiers Rights
Brady, A Complete History of England, prefatory material
The Declaration of Rights

ooks for review: Gough, Fundamental Law . . .
Schwoerer, The Declaration of Rights

ss # 15 (May 16): Modern England

equired reading: Blackstone, Commentaries, IV, pp. 416-18
Pallister, Magna Carta, pp. 43-107

ok for review: Blackstone, The Great Charter, pp. i-lxxvi

PART III: MAGNA CARTA IN AMERICA

s # 16 (May 21): General

quired reading: Cam, Magna Carta, pp. 24-26 (review)
Hazeltine, "The Influence of Magna Carta"
Kurland, "Magna Carta and Constitutionalism . . ."

oks for review: Howard, The Road from Runnymede
Pound, The Development of Constitutional Guarantees of Liberty

Class # 17 (May 23): The colonial period

Required reading:

Secondary: Swindler, <u>Magna Carta</u>, Chapter VII
Colbourn, <u>The Lamp of Experience</u>, pp. 25-39
Howard, <u>The Road from Runnymede</u>, pp. 35-48, 133-38,
156-64, 188-202

Sources: Penn, <u>The Excellent Priviledge</u> (review)
The Massachusetts "Parallels" of 1646
Instructions of the Town of Braintree (1765)

Books for review: Colbourn, <u>The Lamp of Experience</u>
Mullett, <u>Fundamental Law</u> . . .
Schwartz, <u>The Great Rights of Mankind</u>

Class # 18 (May 28): Habeas Corpus and Magna Carta

Required reading:

Secondary: Meador, <u>Habeas Corpus and Magna Carta</u>

Source: Habeas Corpus Act of 1679

Book for review: Duker, <u>A Constitutional History of Habeas Corpus</u>

Class # 19 (May 30): Summary and review

no reading assignment

BIBLIOGRAPHY

Except as noted, all the works listed are on 2-hour or 7-day reserve
at Assigned Reading. Two asterisks indicate that a work should be
available for purchase in the bookstores. One asterisk indicates
that the work—or the part of it assigned—is in the coursebook.
Some of the books assigned for report are in print (some are even
paperbound) and may therefore be purchased, though they have not
been ordered for the course.

**Ashley, Maurice, <u>Magna Carta in the Seventeenth Century</u> (1965)
Bale, John, <u>King Johan</u> (Huntington Library edition, 1969)
Blackstone, William, <u>The Great Charter and the Charter of the
Forest</u> (1759). Available only in Special Collections.
*Butterfield, Herbert, <u>The Englishman and his History</u> (1944)
*_____, "Magna Carta in the Historiography of the Sixteenth and
Seventeenth Centuries," The Stenton Lecture, University of
Reading, 1968
**Cam, Helen Maud, <u>Magna Carta—Event or Document?</u> (1965)
Chrimes, S. B., <u>English Constitutional History</u>, 4th ed. (1967)
*Clanchy, M. T., "Magna Carta, Clause Thirty-Four," <u>English Histo-
rical Review</u>, LXXIX (1964), 542-48
*Colbourn, H. Trevor, <u>The Lamp of Experience: Whig History and
the Intellectual Origins of the American Revolution</u> (1965)
Davis, G. R. C., <u>Magna Carta</u> (1971)
Dickinson, J. C., <u>The Great Charter</u> (1955)
Duker, W. F., <u>A Constitutional History of Habeas Corpus</u> (1980)

*Dunham, William Huse, Jr., "Magna Carta and British Constitutionalism," in Thorne et al., The Great Charter, pp. 26-50

Galbraith, V. H., "Magna Carta," in his Studies in the Public Records (1948), pp. 122-50

Goodhart, Arthur L, "Law of the Land" (1966)

Gough, J. W., Fundamental Law in English Constitutional History (1955)

Harding, Alan, A Social History of English Law (1966)

*Hazeltine, H. D., "The Influence of Magna Carta on American Constitutional Development," in Malden, MCCE, pp. 180-225

Hollister, C. Warren, "King John and the Historians," The Journal of British Studies, I (1961), 1-19

*Holt, James C., "The Barons and the Great Charter," English Historical Review, LXX (1955), 1-24

*_____, Magna Carta (1965)

*_____, The Northerners (1961)

*_____, "Rights and Liberties in Magna Carta," Album Helen Maud Cam, I (1960), 57-69

Howard, A. E. Dick, Magna Carta: Text and Commentary (1964)

_____, The Road from Runnymede: Magna Carta and Constitutionalism in America (1968)

*Hurnard, Naomi D., "Magna Carta, Clause 34," in Studies in Medieval History presented to Frederick Maurice Powicke (1948), pp. 157-79

*Jenks, Edward, "The Myth of Magna Carta," Independent Review, IV (1904-5), 260-73

Jennings, Ivor, Magna Carta and its Influence in the World Today (1965)

Jolliffe, J. E. A., Angevin Kingship, 2nd ed. (1963)

_____, excerpts from Angevin Kingship, in Norman F. Cantor and Michael S. Werthman (edd.), The English Tradition, I (1967), pp. 45-52

Jones, J. A. P., King John and Magna Carta (1971)

Keeney, Barnaby C., Judgment by Peers (1949)

Kurland, Philip B., "Magna Carta and Constitutionalism in the United States: 'The Noble Lie,'" in Thorne et al., The Great Charter, pp. 51-75

McIlwain, Charles H., "Due Process of Law in Magna Carta" (1914), reprinted in Constitutionalism and the Changing World, pp. 86-126

McKechnie, William S., Magna Carta, 2nd ed. (1914)

Malden, H. E. (ed.), Magna Carta Commemoration Essays (1917)

Meador, Daniel John, Habeas Corpus and Magna Carta (1966)

Mullett, Charles F., Fundamental Law and the American Revolution, 1760-1776 (1933)

Norgate, Kate, John Lackland (1902)

Painter, Sidney, "Magna Carta," American Historical Review, LIII (1947), 42-49

_____, The Reign of King John (1949)

_____, William Marshal: Knight-Errant, Baron and Regent of England (1933)

Pallister, Ann, Magna Carta: The Heritage of Liberty (1971)

*Petit-Dutaillis, Charles, "The Great Charter," in <u>Studies and Notes Supplementary to Stubbs' Constitutional History</u> (1908), pp. 127-45

Pocock, J. G. A., <u>The Ancient Constitution and the Feudal Law</u> (1957)

Pound, Roscoe, <u>The Development of Constitutional Guarantees of Liberty</u> (1957)

Powicke, Frederick Maurice, <u>The Loss of Normandy, 1189-1204: Studies in the History of the Angevin Empire</u> (1913, 1961)

*_____, "Per iudicium parium vel per legem terrae," in Malden, <u>MCCE</u>, pp. 96-121

_____, <u>Stephen Langton</u> (1928)

*Radin, Max, "The Myth of Magna Carta," <u>Harvard Law Review</u>, LX (1947), 1060-91

Relf, Frances Helen, <u>The Petition of Right</u> (1917)

Richardson, H. G., <u>English Jewry under Angevin Kings</u> (1960)

Schwartz, Bernard, <u>The Great Rights of Mankind: A History of the American Bill of Rights</u> (1977)

Schwoerer, Lois G., <u>The Declaration of Rights, 1689</u> (1981)

Shakespeare, William, <u>King John</u> (any edition)

Stenton, Doris Mary, <u>After Runnymede: Magna Carta in the Middle Ages</u> (1965)

*Stubbs, William, <u>Constitutional History of England</u>, I (first edition, 1873)

*Swindler, William F., <u>Magna Carta: Legend and Legacy</u> (1965)

Tabuteau, Emily Z. (comp.), Sourcebook on Magna Carta

Thompson, Faith, <u>The First Century of Magna Carta</u> (1925)

_____, <u>Magna Carta: Its Role in the Making of the English Constitution</u> (1948)

*Thorne, Samuel E., "What Magna Carta Was," in Thorne et al., <u>The Great Charter</u>, pp. 11-25

_____ et al., <u>The Great Charter</u> (1965)

<u>The Troublesome Raigne of King John</u>, ed. J. W. Sider (1979)

Turner, Ralph V., <u>The King and his Courts: The Role of John and Henry III in the Administration of Justice, 1199-1240</u> (1968)

Warren, W. L., <u>King John</u> (1961)

White, Stephen D., <u>Sir Edward Coke and "The Grievances of the Commonwealth"</u> (1979)

Young, Charles R., <u>The Royal Forests of Medieval England</u> (1979)

OOKS:

1. Warren, <u>King John</u>. For class # 6.

2. Holt, <u>Magna Carta</u>. For class # 7.

3. Thompson, <u>The First Century of Magna Carta</u>. For class # 11.

4. Thompson, <u>Magna Carta: Its Role in the Making of the English Constitution</u>. For class # 12.

5. Pocock, <u>The Ancient Constitution and the Feudal Law</u>. For class # 13.

6. Howard, <u>The Road from Runnymede: Magna Carta and Constitutionalism in America</u>. For class # 16.

7. Colbourn, <u>The Lamp of Experience: Whig History and the Intellectual Origins of the American Revolution</u>. For class # 17.

8. Mullett, <u>Fundamental Law and the American Revolution</u>. For class # 17.

9. Gough, <u>Fundamental Law in English Constitutional History</u>. For class # 14.

10. Schwoerer, <u>The Declaration of Rights, 1689</u>. For class # 14.

11. Jolliffe, <u>Angevin Kingship</u>. For class # 8.

12. Keeney, <u>Judgment by Peers</u>. For class # 10.

13. Turner, <u>The King and his Courts: The Role of John and Henry III in the Administration of Justice, 1199-1240</u>. For class # 11.

14. Relf, <u>The Petition of Right</u>. For class # 13.

15. Blackstone, <u>The Great Charter and the Charter of the Forest</u>. For class # 15.

16. Painter, <u>The Reign of King John</u>. For class # 6.

17. Young, <u>The Royal Forests of Medieval England</u>. For class # 7.

18. Richardson, <u>English Jewry under Angevin Kings</u>. For class # 7.

19. Holt, <u>The Northerners</u>. For class # 8.

20. Painter, <u>William Marshal</u>. For class # 8.

21. White, <u>Sir Edward Coke and "The Grievances of the Commonwealth"</u>. For class # 13.

22. Pound, <u>The Development of Constitutional Guarantees of Liberty</u>. For class # 16.

23. Schwartz, <u>The Great Rights of Mankind: A History of the American Bill of Rights</u>. For class # 17.

24. Powicke, <u>The Loss of Normandy, 1189-1204: Studies in the History of the Angevin Empire</u>. For class # 6.

25. Powicke, <u>Stephen Langton</u>. For class # 8.

26. Shakespeare, <u>King John</u>. For class # 12.

27. Duker, <u>A Constitutional History of Habeas Corpus</u>. For class # 18.

28. Norgate, <u>John Lackland</u>. For class # 6.

29. Bale, <u>King Johan</u>. For class # 12.

30. <u>The Troublesome Raigne of King John</u>. For class # 12.

INSTRUCTIONS:

1. One book review is to be delivered orally in the class to which the book is most directly relevant.

   a. The correlation between books and classes is indicated both on the list above and on the syllabus.

   b. Each student must review a different book. Assignments of books to individual students will be made early in the term, probably on April 9. Before then, students should have familiarized themselves with the books sufficiently to be able to make an informed choice. All these books are on 7-day reserve at the Assigned Reading desk of the Library. Until the assignments have been made, however, please do not take one of these books out more than overnight, as the books must be available to all students in the class.

   c. An oral review should take about fifteen minutes and do three things:

      1. describe to the class the author's subject, approach and conclusions;

      2. explain the relevance of the book to the subject of the course and the particular class;

      3. evaluate the book (as explained below).

   The reviewer should be prepared, also, to add insights derived from the book in the course of general class discussion and/or to entertain questions after presenting the review.

   d. The written version of this review should be submitted within a week after the oral review is delivered. During the interim, the reviewer should have a conference with me about the review.

2. The other review, to be submitted in writing only, may be done on any of the books listed above. This review may be submitted at any time during the term. I advise you not to submit it before attending the class to which the book is relevant but also to submit it fairly soon thereafter. NO REVIEW WILL BE ACCEPTED LATER THAN THE LAST MEETING OF THE COURSE, that is, May 30.

. You may rewrite either or both of your reviews and resubmit the revised version(s) for reconsideration of grades. Pressure of time means that this opportunity will be available only for reviews initially submitted no later than May 16. Revised versions must be submitted no later than the last meeting of the course, that is, May 30.

. Each written review should aim to do two things:

    a. discuss the contents of the book in the context of this course. In other words: what is the subject of the book? what does it say about its subject? what are its theses? what light does it cast on the subject of this course in general and of the particular class for which the book is assigned? does it support or refute any other works which you have read for the course or any theses which we have developed in class?

    b. evaluate the book as a piece of historical investigation. In other words: what sources does the author use (the evidence)? how are the sources used (the methodology)? how well does the evidence support the author's thesis or theses? are there flaws in the methodology or the reasoning? does the author miss anything? do other conclusions (complementary or antithetical) emerge from the evidence? if the book differs in one or more conclusions from other works which you have read for the course or from a thesis developed in class discussion, which conclusion(s) seem to you more nearly correct, and why? In short, it the book, good, bad or indifferent? (Here, in effect, I am asking you to grade the book.)

For more guidance on how to approach these assignments, see the accompanying handout "How to Analyze a Book."

. Written reviews should be as long as you find necessary to say what you have to say. Between five and seven typed pages should be sufficient. Papers <u>must</u> be typed. For toher matters of form, see the attached sheet "Remarks concerning the Form of Papers."

. Note: I have read most but not all of the books available for review. Before writing your reviews, you should ascertain whether I have read the books on which you are writing, as you will have to describe what the books say at greater length if I have not than if I have. With regard to oral reviews, remember that most, if not all, of your audience will not have read the book.

. Please feel free to consult me, either in office hours or by appointment, at any stage in the production of these reviews.

MEDIEVAL DISCUSSIONS OF THE ETERNITY OF THE WORLD
Dr. Richard Dales
University of Southern California, Los Angeles

I. The sources: Loci classici of the Problem.
    Timaeus; Clacidius; Augustine, Confessions and City of
    God; Boethius, Consolation of Philosophy; Genesis I.

II. Eriugena and his Followers
     Eriugena, Division of Nature; Anonymous Commentator on the
     Consolation; Bernard of Chartres; Hugh of St. Victor;
     Didascalicon and Homilies on Ecclesiastes.

III. The Early Twelfth Century
      William of Conches; Anonymous On the Elements; Hermes, On
      the Six Principles of Things; Richard of St. Victor, On
      the Trinity; Bernard Silvestris, Cosmographia.

IV. The Re-assertion of the Traditional View
     Peter Lombard, Sentences.

V. A Different Presentation of the Question
    Aristotle, Decaelo, Metaphysics, Physics; Algazel,
    Metaphysics; Avicenna, Metaphysics; Maimonides, Dux
    dubitantium.

VI. The Initial Latin Response
     Gundissalinus, De processione mundi; Alexander of Hales,
     Summa theologiae and Questio utrum mundus sit eternus.

VII. The Alarm Sounded
      Robert Grosseteste, Hexameron and De finitate motus et
      temporis.

VIII. The Development of the Franciscan Position
       Thomas of York, Sapientiale; John Pecham, Utrum mundus sit
       eternus; William of Baglione, Utrum mundus sit eternus;
       Bonaventure, Commentary on the Sentences, II, I; Matthew of
       Aquasparta, Could the World Have Been Created from Eternity.

IX. The Position of the Philosophers
     Boethius of Dacia, The Eternity of the World; Ps.-Siger of
     Brabant, Questions on the Physics; Thomas of Aquino, The
     Eternity of the World; Siger of Brabant, The Eternity of
     the World.

X. The Condemnations of 1277

XI. The Aftermath of the Condemnations
     Anonymous, Could the World Have Been Created from Eternity;
     Arlotto of Prato, Utrum mundus sit eternus; Henry of
     Harclay, Could the World Have Been Created from Eternity;
     William of Alnwick, Determinations.

  **Prof. Dales has translated all the above texts which are generall
    only available in Latin.

RELIGIOUS STUDIES 236
CHRISTIAN THOUGHT TO THE REFORMATION
E. Ann Matter
University of Pennsylvania

This course will trace the development of normative
Christianity from the early church to the beginning of the age
of reform (200-1350). The focus will be on the interrelation
of institutional expressions ("The Church") with popular piety
("the people"). Topics considered will include
heresy/orthodoxy, the development of the clerical hierarchy,
and the place of women in the Christian tradition. Readings
will include primary sources, and both traditional and
"unorthodox" secondary interpretations.

Tuesday classes will be, for the most part, presentation
and explanation of the weekly theme by the instructor.
Thursdays will be given over to discussion of the readings,
especially the primary materials, assigned for the week.
Particiaption in the Thursday discussions is an important
requirement of the course.

Each student will write two 3-5 page "thought papers" on
one or more of the primary sources. The nature of these papers
will be discussed in class; their due-dates are given in the
class outline. There will also be a take-home midterm, given
out on October 20, due October 29, and a final exam during exam
week.

1. INTRODUCTION: THE VARIED BACKGROUND OF CHRISTIANITY
        Chadwick, The Early Church, 1-3.

2. HELLENISM AND CHRISITANITY
        Dodds, Pagan and Christian in an Age of Anxiety
        Apuleius, The Golden Ass, selections

3. CHRISTIAN PLATONISM
        Chadwick, 4-6;
        Knowles, The Evolution of Medieval Thought, I
        Justin Martyr and Origen of Alexandria, selections

4. THE QUESTION OF PERSECUTION AND THE IDEAL OF MARTYRDOM
        Chadwick, 7, 10
        Gibbon, Decline and Fall of the Roman Empire XVI
        The Martyrdom of Saint Polycarp
        The Passion of Perpetua and Felicitas

5. THE DIALECTIC OR ORTHODOXY/THE COUNCILS
        Chadwick, 8, 9, 11, 14
        Macmullen, Constantine, IV

        PAPER DUE

6. THE GREEK FATHERS, SPIRITUAL AND ASCETIC TRADITIONS
        Chadwick, 12, 13
        Basil the Great and John Chrysostom, selected homilies
        Gregory of Nyssa, The Life of Saint Macrina

7. THE LATIN FATHERS, DOGMA AND DISCIPLINE
        Chadwick, 15-16
        Augustine of Hippo, Enchiridion
        A. Yarborough, "Christianization in the Fourth Century"

        MIDTERM GIVEN OUT

8. MONKS AND MISSIONARIES

        Chadwick, 17-18
        Gibbon, XXXVII
        Gregory the Great, The Life of Saint Benedict
        Benedict of Nursia, A Rule for Monks
        The Venerable Bede, Ecclesiastical History of the
        English Church II, 1

        MIDTERM DUE

9. THE FRANKS AND THE BYZANTINES
        Knowles, VI-VII
        Pelikan, The Spirit of Eastern Christendom, 3-4
        Einhart and Notker, Two Lives of Charlemagne

10. SPECULATIVE THEOLOGY EAST AND WEST
        Knowles, VIII-XII
        Pelikan, 5
        Hroswitha, Paphnutius, Sapientia
        Anselm of Canterbury, Cur Deus Homs, selections

11. RELIGION AND HUMANISM IN THE TWELFTH CENTURY
        Knowles, III
        Peter Abelard, Historia calamitatum, letters to and
        from Heloise.
        Bernard of Clairvaux, De diligendo Deo

12. THE CRUSADES
        Peters, ed. Christian Society and the Crusades
        Marcus, The Jew in the Medieval World, selections
        Abrahams, Jewish Life in the Middle Ages, IV
        Cohn, The Pursuit of the Millennium, 3,2 (pp. 61-71)

13. THE SCHOLASTIC SYNTHESIS
        Knowles IV-V
        Pelikan, 6
        Thomas Aquinas, Summa Theologica, selections

        PAPER DUE

14. SPIRITUAL MOVEMENTS OF THE HIGH MIDDLE AGES
        The Little Flowers of Saint Francis
        Bolton, "Mulieres Sanctae"

Books to purchase:

Augustine of Hippo, The Enchiridion on Faith, Hope, and Love
    (Gateway)
R. Brown, tr., The Little Flowers of Saint Francis(Image)
Henry Chadwick, The Early Church (Penguin)
E. R. Dodds, Pagan and Christian in an Age of Anxiety(Norton)
Gregory of Nyssa, Life of Saint Macrina(Eastern Orthodox Bks)
Gregory the Great, Dialogues Book II: Saint Benedict, tr.
    Uhlfelder.(Bobbs-Merrill)
David Knowles, The Evolution of Medieval Thought(Vintage)
A. C. Meisel and M. L. del Mastro, eds., The Rule of Saint
    Benedict(Image)
Jaroslav Pelikan, The Christian Tradition 2: The Spirit of
    Eastern Christendom(Chicago)
Edward Peters, ed., Christian Society and the Crusades
    1198-1229l(Penn Press)
Betty Radice, ed., The Letters of Abelard and Heloise(Penguin)
Lewis Thorpe, tr., Einhard and Notker the Stammerer, Two Lives
    of Charlemagne(Penguin)

History 718
Dr. Spiegel

The Twelfth-Century Renaissance

Bibliographical Guides:

L. J. Paetow, Guide to the Study of Medieval History, NY 1931. New edition
   by Gray c. Boyce, Northwestern U. now out.

U. Chevalier, Repertoire des sources historiques du Moyen Age (to 1500 A.D.)
   Bio-bibliographie, 2 vols., 2nd ed. 1905 -07.
   Topo-bibliographie, 2 vols., 1894-1903

A. Potthast, Bibliotheca Historica Medii Aevi, 2nd ?d. 1896

Repertorium Fontium Historia Medii Aevii primum ab Augusto Potthast digestur,
   nunc... vol. 1, 1962

Wm. Wattenbach, Deutschlands Geschichtsquellen im Mittelalter bis zur Mitte
   des 13. Jahrhunderts.

Progress of Medieval and Renaissance Studies in the United States and Canada.
   ed. Williard, before , by S. Harrison Thompson. Boulder Colorado, 1923
   ff.

H. Pirenne, Bibliographie de l'Histoire de Belgique, 3rd. ed. 1931.

General Reference Works on Intellectual History:

Giles Constable, R. Benson, eds. The Twelfth-Century Renaissance, Los Angeles,
   1983

Max Manitius, Geschichte der Lateinische Literatur des Mittelalters 3 vols. 191]
   1930. Indispensable reference work.

E.R. Curtius European Literture and the Latin Middle Ages, trans. Willard
   Trask, New York, 1953.

Frederick B. Artz, The Mind of the Middle Ages, 3rd. rev. ed. 1967 (has
   fairly good, if somewhat outdated, bibliographies on various topics)

John W. Baldwin, The Scholastic Culture of the Middle Ages 1000–1300

Charles H. Haskins, The Renaissance of the Twelfth Century

H.O. Taylor, The Medieval Mind.

H. Rashdall, The Universities of Europe in the Middle Ages, 3. vols.

J. Leclercq, The Love of Learning and the Desire for God.

M. Grabmann, Die Geschichte der Scholastischen Methode, 2 vols. (required reading on scholasticism)

B. Geyer, Die Patristische und Scholastische Philosophie.

A. Forest, F. Van Steenberghen, M. de Gandillac, Le Mouvement doctrinal de XIe au XIVe siècle (Histoire de l'Eglise, vol 13)

M. Chenu, La Théologie au XIIe siècle (There is a partial English translation of this important book by Lester K. Little and Jerome Taylor entitled, Nature, Man and Society in The Twelfth Century, Chicago).

E. Gilson, History of Christian Philosophy in the Middle Ages.

F. Copleston, History of Philosophy, vol. II.

R.R. Bolger, The Classical Heritage and its Beneficiaries.

Christopher Brooke, The Twelfth-Century Renaissance.

E. Gilson, Heloise and Abelard.

C.H. Haskins, The Rise of Universities.

David Knowles, The Evolution of Medieval Thought.

Gordon Leff, Medieval Thought from Augustine to Ockham.

Gordon Leff, Paris and Oxford Universities in the Thirteenth and Fourteenth Centuries.

Émile Mâle, The Gothic Image.

Robert Branner, Gothic Architecture.

E. Panofsky, Gothic Architecture and Scholasticism.

General Reference works on Intellectual History cont:

Otto von Simpson, The Gothic Cathedral.

Helen Waddell, Wandering Scholars.

Beryl Smalley, The Study of the Bible in the Middle Ages.

H. Wieruszowski, The Medieval University.

Some available Texts to be read in this course:

Abelard, The Story of Abelard´s Adversity (J.T. Muckle, trans).

Abelard, Christian Theology (J.R. McCullum, trans).

Anselm of Bec, Monologium and Proslogion, in Deane, St. Anselm:Basic Writings
    (Open Court).

John of Salisbury, Metalogicon, (D.D. McGreary, trans).

John of Salisbury, Historia Pontificalis (M. Chibnall, trans.)

Hugh of St. Victor, Didascalion (J. Taylor, Trans).

Otto of Freising, The Deeds of Frederick Barbarossa (contains important
    philosophical excursi on the development of philosophy in the 12th
    century).

Guibert de Nogent, Self and Society in Medieval France (John Benton, trans.).

Suger, Abbot Suger On the Building of the Abbey Church (trans. E. Panofsky).

Bernard of Clairvaux, The Steps of Humility

--On Consideration

-- On the Song of Songs

-- Treatises I: Apologia to Abbot William

Most of the works of Bernard are translated into English and available from
the Cistercian Fathers Series published by the Cistercian Institute at Western
Michigan U. Kalamazoo

Aelred of Rievaux, Spiritual Friendship (Cistercian Fathers Series

Lynn Thorndike, University Records and Life in the Middle Ages

OUTLINE OF TOPICS

I. The Problem of the Twelfth-century Renaissance: Its Social and Political Setting

II. Schools and Education in the 12th Century

III. Chartres and Medieval Humanism

    Bernard of Clairvaux
    John of Salisbury
    Bernard Silvestris
    Thierry of Chartres
    William of Conches
    Alain de Lille

IV. Theologians and Philosophers: The First Generation

    Anselm of Bec
    Anselm and Ralph of Laon
    Abelard
    Gilbert de la Poirée

V. Mystics: Cistercians and Victorines

    Bernard of Clairvaux
    Aelred of Rievaux
    Hugh of Saint-Victor
    Andrew and Ralph of Saint-Victor

VI. The Discovery of the Individual: Self and Society in the 12th Century

    Guibert de Nogent
    Goliards

VII. The Aristotelian Reception: The Age of Translations

    The New Logic
    Salerno and the Beginnings of Medical Science

VIII. The Beginnings of Law: Romanists and Canonists at Bologna

IX. The Rise of Universities: Paris and Bologna

XI. Gothic Architecture: Saint-Denis and its Successors

12th Century Renaissance

Week I

I. The Problem of the Renaissance of the Twelfth Century

C.H. Haskins, The Renaissance of the Twelfth Century
Erwin Panofsky, "Renaissance and Renascences,"
Kenyon Review, vol VI (1944). Now available in expanded form in
Renaissance and Renascences in Western Art

II. Social Setting: Population Trends in the 12th century

L. Genicot, "On the Evidence of growth of population in the West
from the 11th to the 13th century," in Sylvia Thrupp, ed. Change
in Medieval Society
Marc Bloch, French Rural History, p. 5-17.
J. C. Russell, Late Ancient and Medieval Populations (Transactions
of the American Philosophical Society, n.s., vol 48, part III).
C. Cipolla, J. Dhondt, M. Postan, and P. Wolff, "Rapport sur la
démographie au Moyen Age," in Rapports of the 9th International
Congress of Historical Sciences, vol. I, p. 55ff. (Paris, 1950)
J.C. Russell, "Population in Europe, 500-1500," in C. Cipolla,
ed., The Fontana Economic History of Europe: The Middle Ages, p. 25
ff.

III. Political Developments

Marc Bloch, Feudal Society, vol I, part. II. The Two Ages of Feudalism,
vol II. Towards the Reconstruction of States.
E. Bournazel and J-P Poly, Les Mutations Féodales
J. R. Stryaer, "The Development of Feudal Institutions," in M. Clagett,
G. Post, R. Reynolds, eds. Twelfth-Century Europe and the Foundations
of Modern Society.
Georges Duby, La Société aux XI et XII siècles dans la région Mâonnaisse
F. Ganshof, Feudlaism

IV. The Rise of Towns

H. Pirenne, Medieval Cities
J. Mundy and P. Riesenberg, The Medieval Town
C. Petit-Dutaillis, Les Communes Francaises
F. Ganshof, Etude sur le développement des villes entre Loire et
Rhin au Moyen Age
J. LeGoff, Les Intellectuels au Moyen Age, chapter one.

<u>Schools and Education in the 12th Century</u>

<u>Week II</u>

I. Schools and Education in the Twelfth Century:

Pierre Delhaye, "l'Organisation scolaire au XIIe Siècle,"
   <u>Traditio</u>, 5 (1947-48), pp. 211-268
Paré, Brunet et Tremblay, <u>La renaissance au XIIe Siècle: Les Ecoles
   et L'Enseignement</u>, Paris, 1933
Gaines Post, "Alexander III, the <u>Licentia docendi</u> and the Rise of the
   Universities," in <u>Anniversary Essays for Charles Homer Haskins,</u>
   pp. 255-277
P. Abelson, <u>The Seven Liberal Arts</u>
James Stuart Beddie, "Libraries in the Twelfth Century: Their Catalogues
   and Contents," also in <u>Haskins Anniversary Essays</u>

II. Relevant Texts:

Hugh of Saint-Victor, <u>Didascalion A Medieval Guide to the Arts</u>
   ed. James Taylor; and read Taylor's introduction
John of Salisbury, <u>Metalogicon</u>, on Logic; especially section on manner
   of teaching of Bernard of Chartres
Abelard, <u>The Story of My Misfortunes [Historia Calamitatis]</u> - story
   of earlier combative career symptomatic of the disorganized nature
   of the schools in early twelfth century

III. Points:

Organization of "curriculum," i.e. what books are reading
Method of teaching: <u>lectio</u> and its applications

The School of Chartres in the 12th Century

Week III

I. Standard Works

A. Clerval, *Les Ecoles de Chartres au Moyen Age*
Raymond Kiblansky, "The School of Chartres," in *Twelfth Century Europe and the Origins of Modern Society*
Reginald L. Poole, "The Masters of the Schools at Paris and Chartres in John of Salisbury's Time," in Poole, *Studies in Chronology and History*, pp. 223-247
R.W. Southern, "Humanism and the School of Chartres," in *Medieval Humanism and other Studies*, pp. 61-85.
N. Haring, "Chartres and Paris revisited," *Essays in honor of A. C.Pegis*, ed. J. Reginald O'Donnell (Toronto, 1974): 268-329.
Peter Dronke, "New Approaches to the School of Chartes," *Annuario de estudios medievales*, 6 (1971): 117-40.
R.W. Southern, "The Schools of Paris and the School of Chartres," in *Renaissance and Renewal in the Twelfth Century*, ed. Benson .

Relevant Chapters in:

David Knowles, *The Evolution of Medieval Thought*
Gorden Leff, *Medieval Thought from Augustine to Ockham*
E. Gilson, *History of Christian Philsophy in the Middle Ages*

Also important are:

M.D. Chenu, "The Platonisms of the Twelfth Century," in *Nature Man and Society in the Twelfth Century*, eds. J. Taylor and I. Little.
Adolf Katzenellenbogan, "The Representation of the Seven Liberal Arts," (on, among others, the west portal of Chartres), in *Twelfth-Century Europe and the Foundations of Modern Society*
Winthrop Wetherbee, *Platonism and Poetry in the Twelfth Century: The Literary Influence of the School of Chartres.*

II. On Individuals:

Brian Stock, *Myth and Science in the Twelfth Century: A Study of Bernard Sylvester*
Hans Liebeschutz, *Medieval Humanism in the Life and Writing of John of Salisbury* (Studies of the Warburg Institute, vol 17)
Mille d'Alverny, *Alain de Lille*

N.M. Haring, "The Creation and Creator of the World According to Thierry of Chartres and Clarembaldus of Arras," in *Archives d'Histoire doctrinale et littéraire du Moyen Age*, 30 (1955), p. 137-216

Week IV

Theologians and Philosophers: The First Generation

I. General Works with Relevant Chapters:

David Knowles, The Evolution of Medieval Thought
Gordon Leff, Medieval Thought
E. Gilson, History of Christian Philosophy in the Middle Ages
F. Coppleston, History of Philosophy
A. Forest, F. Van Steenberghen, M. de Gandillac, Le Mouvement
    Doctrinal de XIe au XIVe Siècle (Histoire de L'Eglise)

II. On Individuals:

St. Anselm of Canterbury:

R.W. Southern, Saint Anselm and his Biographer
R.W. Southern, on Cur Deus Homo, Medieval and Renaissance Studies,
3 (1953)

Anselm and Ralph of Laon:

Beryl Smalley, The Study of the Bible in the Middle Ages

Gilbert de la Poirée:

Gammersbach, Gilbert von Poitiers
Nicholas Haring, "The Case of Gilbert de la Poirée," Medieval Studies,
    13 (1951)
Otto of Freising, The Deeds of Frederick Barbarosa, pp. 82-101

This philosophical excursus by Otto should be read by everyone together with
Abelard: Historia Calamitatis The Story of Abelard's Adversities

Also: Bruno S. James, ed., The Letters of Bernard of Clairvaux, letters
236-249 deal with Bernard's controversy with Abelard.

John of Salisbury, Historia Pontificalis, trans. M. Chibnall, pp. 15-41;
account of the trial of Gilbert de la Poirée

Peter Abelard

I. Reference Works:

J. Sikes, Peter Abailard

J. Cotiaux, "La Conception de la Théologie chez Abelard,"
Revue d´Histoire Ecclésiastique, (1932)

John F. Benton, "Fraud, Fiction and Borrowing in the Correspondence
of Abelard and Heloise," repirnt in my office

Mary McLaughlin, "Abelard as Autobiograher: The Motives and Meaning
of his ´Story of Calamities´," Speculum, 43 (1967), pp. 463-89

R. W. Southern, "The letters of Abelard and Heloise," in
Medieval Humanism

Etienne Gilson, Abélard and Heloise

II. Texts

Abelard, Story of Abelard´s Adversities (Historia Calamitatum) trans.
J Muckle, Pontifical Institute

-- Glosses on Porphyry ed. Richard McKeon, in Selections from Medieval
Philosophers, vol. I, p. 208-58

Bernard of Clairvaux, Letters of Benard of Clairvaux, trans. Bruno S. James
Letters 236-249

Abelard, Christian Theology, trans. J.R. McCallum, pp. 45-94

Otto of Freising, The Deeds of Frederick Barbarosa, pp. 82-101

In addition, might want to consult chapters in Leff , Knowles, Gilson etc
on problem of Universals and on Abelard

Mystics

Cistercians:

   Bernard of Clairvaux:

      E. Gilson, The Mystical Theology of St. Bernard of Clairvaux

      Jean Leclercq, Bernard of Clairvaux and the Cistercian Spirit

      Bernard, On the Steps of Humility

. Victorines:

   Hugh of Saint-Victor:

      Beryl Smalley, The Study of the Bible in the Middle Ages

      J. P. Kleinz, The Theory of Knowledge of Hugh of Saint-Victor
         Catholic University of America Philosophical Studies, vol. LXXXVII

      Jerome Taylor, intro. ed, The Didascalion of Hugh of Saint-Victor

      R. J. Deferrari, Hugh of Saint-Victor on the Sacraments of the
         Christian Faith

I. General Reading:

   M. D. Chenu, "Monks, Canons, and Laymen in Search of the Apostolic Life,"
     and "The Evangelical Awakening,: chapters 6 and 7 of Man Nature
     and Society in the Twelfth Century

Week VII

The Discovery of the Individual: Self and Society in the 12th Century

I. General Reading:

    Colin Morris, The Discovery of the Individual 1050-1200

    R.W. Southern, The Making of the Middle Ages, chapter: "From Epic to Romance."

    J.F. Benton, "Individualism and Conformity in Medieval Western Europe," in Individualism and Conformity in Classical Islam, ed. Amin Banani and Speros Vyronis (Weisbaden, 1977) pp. 145-48

II. Goliards:

    Helen Waddell, The Wandering Scholars
    Helen Waddell, Medieval Latin Lyrics [texts]
    Hubert Creekmore, Lyrics of the Middle Ages [texts]
    Peter Dronke, Poetic Individuality in the Middle Ages
    Peter Dronke, The Medieval Lyric

III. Courtly Love:

    Andreas Capellanus, The Art of Courtly Love
    Denomy, The Heresy of Courtly Love
    C.S. Lewis, The Allegory of Love
    H. Moller, "The Social Causation of the Courtly Love Complex," Comparative Studies in Society and History 1 (1959), pp. 1137-63
    Joan Ferrante, ed. The Pursuit of Perfection
    Francis X. Newman, Courtly Love: A Symposium [title?]

IV. Autobiography:

    John F. Benton, Self and Society in Medieval France The Memoirs of Abbot Guibert de Nogent

    Cf. Mary McLaughlin, "Survivors and Surrogates" [on medieval chilhood] in Lloyd DeMause, History of Childhood

    Abelard, Historia Calamitatum etc

    Georg Misch, Geschichte der Autobiographie

The Aristotelian Reception – Salerno and the Beginnings of
Medical Science

I. The Aristotelian Reception:

C.H. Haskins, The Renaissance of the Twelfth Century: "The Translators"

Van Steenberghen, Aristotle in the West

David Knowles, The Evolution of Medieval Thought: Chapter XV:
The Rediscovery of Aristotle

II. Salerno:

C.H. Haskins, Studies in the History of Medieval Science

Rashdall, The Universities of Europe in the Middle Ages

C. Singer, and D. Singer, "Origin of the mediecal school of Salerno,
The First University," in Essays on the History of Medicine,

ed. F. Garrison, pp. 121-38

B. Lawn, The Salernitan Questions: An Introduction to the History of
Medieval and Renaissance Problem Literature. Oxford, 1963

G. Sarton, Introduction to the History of Science, vol. II, part I.

Scholastic Culture

I. Peter Lombard and the Followers of Abelard

    D.E. Luscombe, <u>The School of Peter Abelard</u> (includes chapter on Lombard)

    Delhaye, <u>Pierre de Lombard</u>

II. Peter the Chanter and the Biblical Moralists

    John W. Baldwin, <u>Masters, Princes, and Merchants The Social Views of Peter the Chanter and His Circle</u>

III. Lothario de Segni --Innocent III

    A. Luchaire, <u>Innocent III</u>

History 210, Spring 1983
Prof. Penny Gold
Knox College
Home phone: 342-0244
Office hours: Tu 5th period
Th 4th & 5th periods
or by appointment

MEDIEVAL CULTURE

BOOKS AVAILABLE FOR PURCHASE (books marked with an asterisk are also
available on reserve)
Denys Hay, The Medieval Centuries
*William, Count of Orange: Four Old French Epics
*Medieval Romances, ed. R. S. Loomis and L. H. Loomis
*The Death of King Arthur
Baldwin, Scholastic Culture of the Middle Ages
Introduction to St. Thomas Aquinas
*E. Le Roy Ladurie, Montaillou

Goal: To come to an understanding of medieval world-views. What shape did human
life have, as looked at by medieval people? What principles ordered relationships
between people, between people and their natural environment, between people and
God? Through what values were these relationships maintained? What forces
were potentially most destructive to these relationships? I hope that in this
study of medieval culture we will both come to appreciate the meaning and
integrity of lives far removed from us in space and time, and also come to a
better understanding of our own contemporary principles and values, as we see
them compared and contrasted to medieval ones.

M 3/21 Introduction

RNS OF THOUGHT

W 3/23 Order

> Hay, Medieval Centuries (read entire book
> quickly for background; don't worry
> about details)

F 3/25 Symbolism

> The Bestiary (on reserve)
> Lion (pp. 7-11)
> Unicorn (20-21)
> Elephant (24-28)
> Crocodile (49-51)
> Dog (61-67)
> Viper (170-73)
> Stages of man's life (219-27)
> Gesta Romanorum (on reserve)
> v-xiii, 73-92 (Tales I-X)

M 3/28 The Supernatural

> Caesarius of Heisterbach, Dialogue on
> Miracles (on reserve): vol. 1, pp. 1-3;
> vol. 2, pp 171-98
> Jacobus de Voragine, The Golden Legend
> (on reserve): vol. 1, v-xvi, 1-2,
> 88-90 (St. Paul the Hermit), 157-61
> (St. Agatha); vol. 2, 347-51 (St.
> Alexis), 539-43 (St. Theodora)

W 3/30 Sense of Time

> Le Goff, "Merchant's Time and Church's Time
> in the Middle Ages," in Time, Work and
> Culture in the Middle Ages, pp. 29-42
> (on reserve)
> handout (The Chronicle of St. Evroult
> and Orderic Vitalis, The Ecclesiastical
> History

211

	F 4/1	Epic Literature	no reading assignment
III	M 4/4	"	The Crowning of Louis (in William, Cou of Orange), pp. 1-30
	W 4/6	"	The Crowning of Louis, pp. 31-59
	F 4/8	Instructor out of town	SHORT PAPER DUE
IV	M 4/11	Lyric poetry	. handout
	W 4/13	Romance literature	Chrétien de Troyes, Perceval (in Medie Romances, pp. 3-87)
	F 4/15	"	no reading assignment
V	M 4/18	"	The Death of King Arthur, pp. 1-133 (Intro. and chps. 1-106)
	W 4/20	"	The Death of King Arthur, pp. 133-235 (chps. 107-204)
	F 4/22	Fabliaux	Gallic Salt (on reserve): 219-55, 307-41, 381-97
VI	M 4/25	MIDTERM	

LEARNED CULTURE

	W 4/27	The Production of Medieval Manuscripts	no reading assignment; class will meet in the library
	F 4/29	Universities	Baldwin, Scholastic Culture, 1-77 Readings in the History of Education. 55-75, 107-116 (on reserve)
VII	M 5/2	Theology	Baldwin, 79-97 Introduction to St. Thomas Aquinas (see attached sheet for assignment
	W 5/4	"	(see attached sheet)
	F 5/6	"	(see attached sheet)
VIII	M 5/9	"	(see attached sheet)

POPULAR CULTURE

	W 5/11	Popular Culture: A Case Study	Le Goff, "The Historian and the Ordina Man," in Time, Work, and Culture i the Middle Ages, pp. 225-36 (on re Le Roy Ladurie, Montaillou, vii-68
	F 5/13	"	Montaillou, 69-102, 120-203
IX	M 5/16	"	Montaillou, 218-250, 277-356

| 5/18 | Early Medieval Art | Treasures of Early Irish Art (on reserve)
SHORT ASSIGNMENT DUE (see note below) |
|------|-------------------|---|
| 5/20 | Instructor out of town; no class | |
| 5/23 | Romanesque Art | Duby, The Making of the Christian West, 980-1140
(on reserve)
SHORT ASSIGNMENT DUE |
| 5/25 | Gothic Art | Duby, The Europe of the Cathedrals, 1140-1280
Aubert, The Art of the High Gothic Era
(on reserve)
Baldwin, 99-118
SHORT ASSIGNMENT DUE |
| 5/27 | Conclusion | |

GRADE: Your grade will be based on the following:

Short paper (4/8)	10%
Oral report (Thomas Aquinas)	10
Midterm exam	25
Art assignments	10
Class participation	20
Final exam	25

COLLEGE ATTENDANCE POLICY: "Students are expected to attend class regularly and to participate fully in class activities. Students who are absent from class, for whatever reason, are still responsible for all assigned work."

PENALTY FOR LATENESS: Exams or papers handed in late will be graded down, with more points taken off for each successive day late. If you have a legitimate reason for an extension without penalty (e.g., illness), discuss your situation with me as soon as possible so that we can negotiate an extension.

SHORT ART ASSIGNMENTS: For each of the three classes on art, xerox one illustration from the book(s) assigned for that day. (Note on the xerox the source of the plate.) Choose an object that typifies some central aspect of art in the given period. Write a paragraph or two analyzing the attitudes/values expressed in the work of art you have chosen, as seen in its style and subject matter.

M.5/2 <u>On Sacred Doctrine (Theology)</u>
            Q 1, articles 1, 2, 4, 5, 7, 10 (between pp. 3-19)

Read these articles in their entirety. Consider the method of argument
as well as the substance of the argument.

W 5/4 For today and Friday, read for substance rather than method. Try not to
get bogged down in the technicalities of the philosophical arguments; look
instead for the major point being made in each article. Rather than reading
each article in its entirety, I suggest you read the statement of the
question at the beginning of the article, Objection 1, the "on the contrary,"
and "I answer that." Skip the rest of the objections and the replies
unless you are particularly confused or particularly interested.

<u>God</u> (between pp. 24-232)
      Q 2, art. 3
      Q 6, art. 1-3
      Q 7, art. 1
      Q 11, art. 3
      Q 12, art. 1, 7, 11-13
      Q 14, art. 1
      Q 19, art. 1, 4, 9
      Q 22, art. 1, 2
      Q 25, art. 1-3

            Choices for five minute oral report (these <u>quaestiones</u> are in the
            unabridged <u>Summa Theologicae</u> on reserve):
            Part I, Q 31 (vol. 1): "Of what belongs to the unity or
                                      plurality in God" [on the Trinity]
            Part III, Q 1 (vol. 2): "Of the fitness of the Incarnation"
                                      [on Christ]
            Part III, Q 28 (vol. 2): "Of the virginity of the mother of God"

F 5/6 <u>Creation, Man, and the End of Man</u>
            Q 44, art. 1, 4
            Q 46, art. 2
            Q 48, art. 3   between pp. 233-79
            Q 49, art. 1-3
            Q 18, art. 1 (pp. 520-22)
            Q 75, Intro. and art. 1
            Q 76, art. 1, 3   between pp. 280-370
            Q 83, art. 1
            <u>Summa contra Gentiles</u>, chps. 37-40, 47, 48 (pp. 453-67)
            Q 57, art. 5
            Q 58, art. 2
            Q 61, art. 1-2   between pp. 575-603
            Q 62, art. 1-3
            Q 63, art. 3

            Choices for oral report (see next page)

5/6 (cont'd)

Choices for oral report:
First Part of Second Part, Q 81 (vol. 1) and Second Part of
the Second Part, Q 163 (vol. 2): "Of the cause of sin, on
the part of man" and "Of the first man's sin"
Second Part of the Second Part, Q 153 (vol. 2): "Of lust"
First Part of the Second Part, Q 82 (vol. 1): "Of original
sin, as to its essence"
Part 1, Q 50 (vol. 1): "Of the substance of angels absolutely
considered"
Part 1, Q 63 (vol. 1): "The malice of angels with regard
to sin" [on the fall of the angels]
Part 1, Q 114 (vol. 1): "Of the assaults of the demons"

5/9 Law and Grace (between pp. 616–81)
Q 91, art. 1-4
Q 93, art. 2
Q 94, art. 3
Q 109, art. 1-5, 8
Q 112, art. 1-3, 5

AL REPORT: Prepare a five minute oral report on your chosen quaestio , covering
e following:
1) Briefly describe the subject of the quaestio and the major questions
(articles) into which Thomas has subdivided the subject.
2) What are Thomas' answers to these questions? (Rather than going through
each article one after another, summarize the basic conclusions reached
in the quaestio.)
3) What interesting issues arise from the arguments presented in this quaestio?

MEDIEVAL CULTURE: THE AGE OF SPIRITUALITY

INDS 293, ENGL 287, FNAR 159, HIST 239
Drs. Brauner, Masi, Rosenwein

Patricia Brauner
Michael Masi
Barbara Rosenwei
Loyola Universit
Chicag

Required books:
William Cook and R. Herzman, *The Medieval World View: an Introduction*
   (Oxford University Press)
Geoffrey of Monmouth, *History of the Kings of Britain* (Penguin)
Anon., *Quest of the Holy Grail* (Penguin)
Chrétien de Troyes, *Arthurian Romances* (Everyman)
St. Benedict, *Rule of St. Benedict* (Liturgical Press)
Peter Abelard, *The Letters of Abelard and Heloise* (Penguin)
Macaulay, David, *Cathedral* (Houghton Mifflin)
Selected readings, marked below with an *;   copies will be available.

Recommended Books:
W.T.H. Jackson, *Medieval Literature, A History and a Guide* (Collier) [out of
   print; see copy on reserve]
Bernard of Clairvaux, *On the Song of Songs*, I (Cistercian Fathers series,
   no.4)
E. Holt, *A Documentary History of Art*, vol.1 (Doubleday)
A. Seay, *Music in the Medieval World* (Prentice-Hall)
   [All books ordered at Loyola Bookstore and Beck's. Copies of recommended
   texts are on reserve]

Syllabus and Assignments

Jan.15   Introduction to the course

Jan.17- **Cook and Herzman**   (4 classes)
   Jan.29   [Jan.17, chs.1-3; Jan.22, chs.4-5; Jan.24, chs.6-7; Jan.29, chs.8-9]

         TOPIC I: THE COURT MILIEU
Jan.31- **Princes, kings, lords, and vassals**
   Feb.5   ***Suger, *Life of Louis the Fat***
            Begin reading Geoffrey of Monmouth, *History of the Kings* , pp.166-
            261, and Chrétien de Troyes, *Lancelot*

Feb.7-   Geoffrey of Monmouth: historical context and sources for Arthurian
   12   literature
            Geoffrey of Monmouth, *History*, pp.166-261

Feb.14- FIRST PAPER DUE
   19   Troubadours: lyric poetry and medieval song
            Troubadour poems (to be distributed)

Feb.21- Chrétien de Troyes: the court at Troyes; Arthurian literature between
   26   Geoffrey and Chrétien; Chrétien's other poetry
            Chrétien de Troyes, *Lancelot*

Feb.28   MID-TERM EXAM

Mar.4-   SPRING VACATION
  8
                   TOPIC II: THE MONASTIC MILIEU
Mar.12   Monasticism: video tape: *Life in a Medieval Monastery*

Mar.14   Monastic architecture

Mar.19   *The Rule of St. Benedict*

Mar.21-   Gregorian chant: The Liturgy of monastic life.
  26   Begin reading *The Quest of the Holy Grail*

Mar.28   St. Bernard and Suger
          Bible, *The Song of Songs*
          St. Bernard, *Sermons* 1, 7, 20 (on reserve)
          St. Bernard, "Apologia to William of St. Thierry," and Suger, "The
             Book of Suger," in Holt, *Documentary History of Art*, pp.18-48 (on
             reserve

Apr.2- **Anon., *The Quest of the Holy Grail***
  4

          TOPIC III: THE URBAN MILIEU
Apr.9   The rise of cities

Apr.11   SECOND PAPER DUE
          Realism/Nominalism; Peter Abelard: life
          Abelard, *Story of My Misfortunes*

[Apr.15, 2:30-4:30 p.m. Lester K. Little, "Words and Violence: the Medieval
          Clamor." Crown Hum. Center, Rm.530]

Apr.16   ***Abelard, *Sic et Non***

Apr.18   Gothic architecture and the mysticism of light: Suger and St. Denis

Apr.23-   Chartres
  25

May 2 (Thurs.), 10:45-12:45: *FINAL EXAM*

Ground Rules

You are expected to do the readings assigned for each class and to participate in class discussions. One-third of your grade is based on class participation.

Examinations will combine short answer and essay questions. The final exam will be comprehensive. Cheating will result in a grade of F on that examination. There will be no make-up exams unless the student calls an instructor *on the day* of the exam with his or her excuse and *arranges for the make-up at that time.* Otherwise, a missed exam will result in a grade of F. Exams count one-third of your grade.

There are two papers. The first paper is to be a discussion of the themes expressed in the troubadour poems. This will be made clearer in class. The second topic is to be chosen in consultation with a professor. Included here is a list of suggested topics to start you thinking. Papers should be typewritten or computer-printed, double-spaced, with one inch margins, **proofread**; each should be 5-7 pages long, not counting footnotes and bibliography (both to be attached to the back of the paper). Plagiarism will result in a grade of F on that paper; there will be no chance to rewrite it. Plagiarism means not only simply quoting another person's work without acknowledgment but also paraphrasing without acknowledgment. It also means not stringing together *acknowledged* quotes or paraphrases. Consult a professor if you have questions. Late papers will be downgraded 1/2 grade for every class day late (e.g. A- one day late will be B+). Papers count one-third of the grade.

Grades for papers, exams, and the course are given by the three instructors in consultation.

MEDIEVAL INSTITUTIONS
Donald Queller
University of Illinois, Urbana

Introduction

The Germans and the Germanic Kingdoms

The Carolingians

Feudalism

Early Medieval Monarchy

Manorialism

Medieval Towns

Commerce and Industry

The Crusades

The Angevin Empire

France in the Thirteenth Century

The Disintegration of the Empire

Italy in the Late Middle Ages

Parliamentary Institutions

Medieval Administration

THE GERMANS AND THE GERMANIC KINGDOMS

<u>Topics</u>:

The Anglo-Saxons
Sources for the Early Germans*
Peaceful Germanization of the Roman Empire
Visigoths
Vandals
Huns
Ostrogoths*
Lombards
Salian Franks
Social and Political Structure

<u>Bibliography</u>:

Bury, J.B., THE INVASION OF EUROPE BY THE BARBARIANS. 940.1-B975i
Lot, F., THE END OF THE ANCIENT WORLD AND THE BEGINNING OF THE MIDDLE AGES. 841.09-L882e
Tacitus, GERMANIA. 870 - T118- tG.E7
Gregory of Tours, HISTORY OF THE FRANKS (Dalton translation) 944.01 - G821h-1927
Hodgkin, T., ITALY AND HER INVADERS. 945 - H689i
Moss, H. St. L. B., THE BIRTH OF THE MIDDLE AGES
Dill, S., ROMAN SOCIETY IN GAUL IN THE MEROVINGIAN AGE. 914.401 - D598r
Drew, Katherine Fisher, comp., THE BARBARIAN INVASIONS
THE BURGUNDIAN CODE, D. Fischer translation
Cassiodorus, LETTERS, Hodgkin translation. 879 - C345 - d.E4
Hodgkin, T., THEODORIC THE GOTH. 92 - T388h
Villari, P., THE BARBARIAN INVASIONS OF ITALY
Arragon, R.F., THE TRANSITION FROM THE ANCIENT TO THE MEDIEVAL WORLD. 937.09 - A.773t
Wallace-Hadrill, J.M., THE BARBARIAN WEST, 400-1000. 940.1 - W1956 - 1961
Pirenne, Henri, MOHAMMED AND CHARLEMAGNE. 940.1 - P666mo - paper
Bark, Wm., ORIGINS OF THE MEDIEVAL WORLD. 330 - S785p - V.14 - paper
Thompson, E.A., THE EARLY GERMANS
Sullivan, Richard E., HEIRS TO THE ROMAN EMPIRE
Latouche, Robert, CAESAR TO CHARLEMAGNE
Thompson, E.A., THE GOTHS IN SPAIN
Duckett, E.S., GATEWAY TO THE MIDDLE AGES
Thompson, E.A., THE VISIGOTHS IN THE TIME OF ULFILAS
_____, A HISTORY OF ATTILA AND THE HUNS
Wallace-Hadrill, J.M., THE LONG-HAIRED KINGS AND OTHER STUDIES IN FRANKISH HISTORY
_____, EARLY GERMANIC KINGSHIP IN ENGLAND AND ON THE CONTINENT
Maenchen-Helfen, J. Otto, THE WORLD OF THE HUNS
Paul the Deacon, HISTORY OF THE LOMBARDS
Musset, Lucien, THE GERMANIC INVASIONS
Bachrach, Bernard, FRANKISH MILITARY HISTORY

THE CAROLINGIANS

Topics:

Carolingian Sources
The Carolingians before Charlemagne
Charlemagne's Conquests
The Coronation of Charlemagne
Government of Charlemagne
Louis the Pious
Wars of Lothair, Louis the German and Charles the Bald
The Division of the Middle Kingdom
Charles the Bald

Bibliography:

THE CORONATION OF CHARLEMAGNE (Problems in European Civilization)
Einhard, LIFE OF CHARLEMAGNE
Davis, H.W.C., CHARLEMAGNE
Duckett, Eleanor S., ALCUIN, FRIEND OF CHARLEMAGNE
Fichtenau, Heinrich, THE CAROLINGIAN EMPIRE
Cabaniss, Allen, SON OF CHARLEMAGNE; A CONTEMPORARY LIFE OF LOUIS THE PIOUS
Easton, Stewart, THE ERA OF CHARLEMAGNE
Boussard, Jacques, THE CIVILIZATION OF CHARLEMAGNE
Seelinger, G., Chaps. on Carolingian Empire in CAMBRIDGE MEDIEVAL HISTORY, II, 19 and 21
Thompson, James Westfall, THE DISSOLUTION OF THE CAROLINGIAN FISC
Ganshof, Francois Louis, FRANKISH INSTITUTIONS UNDER CHARLEMAGNE
Thorpe, Lewis G.M., TWO LIVES OF CHARLEMAGNE
CAROLINGIAN CHRONICLES, trans. by Bernhard Walter Scholz
Munz, Peter, LIFE IN THE AGE OF CHARLEMAGNE
Duckett, E.S., CAROLINGIAN PORTRAITS
Ganshof, Francois Louis, THE CAROLINGIANS AND THE FRANKISH MONARCHY
Cabaniss, James A., CHARLEMAGNE
Folz, Robert, THE CORONATION OF CHARLEMAGNE, 25 DECEMBER 800
Barruclough, Geoffrey, THE CRUCIBLE OF EUROPE
Folz, Robert, THE CONSTITUTION OF CHARLEMAGNE
Loyn, H.R., and John Percival, THE REIGN OF CHARLEMAGNE: DOCUMENTS ON CAROLINGIAN ADMINISTRATION

Mr. Queller

FEUDALISM

Topics:

Origins
The Combination of the Elements of Feudalism under the Carolingians
The Feudal Contract
Homage and Fealty
Subinfeudation and the Demesne
The Feudal Nobility
Military Training and Equipment
The Castle and Castle Life
Chivalry

Bibliography:

RAOUL DE CAMBRAI, trans. by Jessie Crosland
THE SONG OF ROLAND
University of Pennsylvania Translations and Reprints, Vol. IV, No. 3 (Documents
    Illustrative of FEUDALISM)
Stephenson, Carl, MEDIEVAL FEUDALISM
_____, AMERICAN HISTORICAL REVIEW, Vol. XLVI (1941), pp. 788-812
Bloch, Marc, FEUDAL SOCIETY
Stenton, Sir Frank, THE FIRST CENTURY OF ENGLISH FEUDALISM, 1066-1166
Seignobos, Charles, THE FEUDAL REGIME
Painter, Sidney, STUDIES IN THE HISTORY OF THE ENGLISH FEUDAL BARONY
Ganshof, Francois L., FEUDALISM, trans. by Philip Grierson
Vinogradoff, Sir Paul, "Feudalism," CMH, III, Ch. 18
White, Lynn, MEDIEVAL TECHNOLOGY AND SOCIAL CHANGE
Coulborn, Rushton, FEUDALISM IN HISTORY
Painter, S., FRENCH CHIVALRY
Strayer, Joseph R., FEUDALISM
Herlihy, David, ed., THE HISTORY OF FEUDALISM
Lewis, Archibald R., KNIGHTS AND SAMURAI: KNIGHTS IN NORTHERN RANCE AND
    JAPAN
Brown, R. Allen, ORIGINS OF ENGLISH FEUDALISM
Brown, Elizabeth A.R., "The Tyranny of a Construct: Feudalism and Historians of
    Medieval Europe," AHR, LXXIX (1974), 1063-1800"
Round, J.H., FEUDAL ENGLAND
Critchley, J.S., FEUDALISM

EARLY MEDIEVAL MONARCHY

<u>Topics</u>:

Sources
Theory of Feudal Monarchy
East Frankland
    Sources of royal strength
    The Stem Ducies
    The Ottonians
West Frankland
    Early Capetians
    Deterioration of the Demesne
    Capetian Government
    The Great Baronies
Anglo-Saxon England
    Before the Danes
    The Danes and the Rise of Wessex
    Anglo-Saxon Monarchy
    Local Government

<u>Bibliography</u>:

THE WORKS OF LUIDPRAND OF CREMONA, trans. by F.A. Wright
Barraclough, Geoffrey, MEDIEVAL GERMANY, 2 vols.
_____, THE ORIGINS OF MODERN GERMANY
_____, THE MEDIEVAL EMPIRE
Johnson, Edgar N., SECULAR ACTIVITIES OF THE GERMAN EPISCOPATE
Thompson, James Westfall, FEUDAL GERMANY
Hill, Boyd, ed., RISE OF THE FIRST REICH
Heer, Friedrich, THE HOLY ROMAN EMPIRE
Fawtier, Robert, THE CAPETIANS
Haskins, Charles Homer, THE NORMANS IN EUROPEAN HISTORY
Petit-Dutaillis, Charles, FEUDAL MONARCHY IN FRANCE AND ENGLAND
ENGLISH HISTORICAL DOCUMENTS, ed. by David Douglas, vol. I, ed. by Dorothy
    Whitelock
Blair, Peter Hunter, ANGLO-SAXON ENGLAND
Kirby, D.P., THE MAKING OF EARLY ENGLAND
Larson, L.M., CANUTE THE GREAT
Oman, Charles, ENGLAND BEFORE THE NORMAN CONQUEST
Stenton, Sir Frank M., ANGLO-SAXON ENGLAND
Whitelock, Dorothy, THE BEGINNINGS OF ENGLISH SOCIETY
Duckett, Eleanor Shipley, ALFRED THE GREAT
Deanesly, Margaret, THE PRE-CONQUEST CHURCH IN ENGLAND
Hollister, C.W., ANGLO-SAXON MILITARY INSTITUTIONS
Plummer, Christopher, LIFE & TIMES OF ALFRED THE GREAT
Cheney, C.R., THE CULT OF ANGLO-SAXON KINGSHIP

MANORIALISM

Topics:

The Manorial Village
The Open Fields
The Organization of Land and Labor
The Three Field System
Cottar and Borders
Serfdom
Free Peasants
Manorial Courts
Decline of Manorialism
Non-Manorial Medieval Agriculture

Bibliography:

Bennett, H.S., LIFE ON THE ENGLISH MANOR
Boissonade, P., LIFE AND WORK IN MEDIEVAL EUROPE
CAMBRIDGE ECONOMIC HISTORY, Vol. I
Kosminsky, E.A., STUDIES IN THE AGRARIAN HISTORY OF ENGLAND
Nielson, Nellie, MEDIEVAL AGRARIAN ECONOMY
Power, Eileen, "Peasant Life and Rural Conditions," CAMBRIDGE MEDIEVAL HISTORY,
    Vol. VII, Chap. XXIV
Ernle, R.E. Prothero, ENGLISH FARMING, PAST AND PRESENT
Orwin, C.S. & C.S., THE OPEN FIELDS
Lennard, Reginald, RURAL ENGLAND, 1086-1135
Bloch, Marc, FRENCH RURAL HISTORY
Raftis, James, TENURE AND MOBILITY
Ault, Warren, OPEN-FIELD HUSBANDRY AND THE VILLAGE COMMUNITY
Duby, Georges, RURAL AND COUNTRY LIFE IN THE MEDIEVAL WEST
Hilton, R.H., THE DECLINE OF SERFDOM IN MEDIEVAL ENGLAND
LeRoy Ladurie, E., THE PEASANTS OF LANGUEDOC
Bloch, Marc, SLAVERY AND SERFDOM IN THE MIDDLE AGES
Vinogradoff, Paul, VILLEINAGE IN ENGLAND
Ault, Warren, OPEN-FIELD FARMING IN MEDIEVAL ENGLAND
Homans, George, ENGLISH VILLAGERS IN THE THIRTEENTH CENTURY
Vinogradoff, Paul, GROWTH OF THE MANOR
_____, ENGLISH SOCIETY IN THE ELEVENTH CENTURY
Duby, Georges, THE EARLY GROWTH OF THE EUROPEAN ECONOMY
White, Lynn, MEDIEVAL TECHNOLOGY AND SOCIAL CHANGE

MEDIEVAL TOWNS

Topics:

Origins
The Middle Class
Town Charter & Urban Government
Social and Political Unrest in Medieval Towns
The Rise of Despots
Any Particular Town

Bibliography:

Pirenne, Henri, MEDIEVAL CITIES
_____, ECONOMIC AND SOCIAL HISTORY OF MEDIEVAL EUROPE
Stephenson, Carl, BOROUGH AND TOWN
Boissonade, P., LIFE AND WORK IN MEDIEVAL EUROPE
Lipson, E., INTRODUCTION TO THE ECONOMIC HISTORY OF ENGLAND
Pirenne, Henri, EARLY DEMOCRACIES IN THE LOW COUNTRIES
CAMBRIDGE ECONOMIC HISTORY, vol. II
Schevill, Ferdinand, HISTORY OF FLORENCE
Butler, W.F., THE LOMBARD COMMUNES
Hill, J.W., MEDIEVAL LINCOLN, 942.53-H646W
Thompson, James Westfall, ECONOMIC AND SOCIAL HISTORY OF THE MIDDLE AGES
_____, ECONOMIC AND SOCIAL HISTORY OF EUROPE IN THE LATTER MIDDLE AGES
   1300-1530
Power, Eileen, MEDIEVAL PEOPLE
Benson, E., LIFE IN A MEDIEVAL CITY
Evans, J., LIFE IN MEDIEVAL FRANCE
Salzman, L.F., ENGLISH LIFE IN THE MIDDLE AGES
Bland, A.E., P.A. Brown & R.H. Tawney, ENGLISH ECONOMIC HISTORY: SELECT
   DOCUMENTS (part I)
Mundy & Riesenberg, THE MEDIEVAL TOWN
Thrupp, Sylvia, THE MERCHANT CLASS OF MEDIEVAL LONDON
Herlihy, David, PISA IN THE EARLY RENAISSANCE
Waley, Daniel P., MEDIEVAL ORVIETO
Espinas, George, LA VIE URBAINE DE DONAI AU MOYEN AGE
Herlihy, David, MEDIEVAL & RENAISSANCE PISTOIA
Waley, Daniel, THE ITALIAN CITY-REPUBLICS
Baker, Timothy, MEDIEVAL LONDON
Williams, Gwyn A., MEDIEVAL LONDON: FROM COMMUNE TO CAPITAL
Schevill, Ferdinand, SIENA
Brucker, Gene, RENAISSANCE FLORENCE
Brooke, Christopher N.L. & Gillian Kerr, LONDON, 800-1216
Lane, Frederic C., VENICE
Platt, Colin, THE MEDIEVAL ENGLISH TOWN
Reynolds, Susan, AN INTRODUCTION TO THE HISTORY OF ENGLISH MEDIEVAL TOWNS
Beresford, Maurice, NEW TOWNS IN THE MIDDLE AGES
Holmes, Urban T., DAILY LIFE IN THE TWELFTH CENTURY

COMMERCE AND INDUSTRY

Bibliography:
Lopez, Robert S., THE COMMERCIAL REVOLUTION OF THE MIDDLE AGES, 950-1350
CAMBRIDGE ECONOMIC HISTORY, vol. II-III
Pirenne, Henri, ECONOMIC AND SOCIAL HISTORY OF MEDIEVAL EUROPE
Power, E., MEDIEVAL PEOPLE
Thompson, J.W., ECONOMIC AND SOCIAL HISTORY OF EUROPE IN THE LATER MIDDLE
    AGES
Boissonade, P., LIFE AND WORK IN MEDIEVAL EUROPE
Thompson, J.W., ECONOMIC AND SOCIAL HISTORY OF THE MIDDLE AGES
Byrne, E.H., GENOESE SHIPPING IN THE XII-XIII CENTURIES
Lane, F.C., VENETIAN SHIPS AND SHIPBUILDERS
De Roover, Raymond, THE RISE AND DECLINE OF THE MEDICI BANK
Reynolds, Robert L., EUROPE EMERGES
Cipolla, Carlo, MONEY, PRICES & CIVILIZATION IN THE MEDIEVAL WORLD
Salzman, L.F., ENGLISH TRADE IN THE MIDDLE AGES
_____, ENGLISH INDUSTRIES IN THE MIDDLE AGES
Renard, Georges Francis, GUILDS IN THE MIDDLE AGES
Dollinger, Philippe, THE GERMAN HANSA
Miskimin, Harry A., THE ECONOMY OF EARLY RENAISSANCE EUROPE, 1300-1460
Postan, M.M., MEDIEVAL TRADE AND FINANCE
De Roover, Raymond A., BUSINESS, BANKING AND ECONOMIC THOUGHT IN LATE
    MEDIEVAL AND EARLY MODERN EUROPE
Lane, Frederic C., ANDREA BARBARIGO
Sapori, Armando, ITALIAN MERCHANT IN THE MIDDLE AGES
Power, Eileen, THE WOOL TRADE IN ENGLISH MEDIEVAL HISTORY
Lloyd, Terence, THE ENGLISH WOOL TRADE IN THE MIDDLE AGES
De Roover, Raymond, THE MEDICI BANK
_____, MONEY AND BANKING IN MEDIEVAL BRUGES
Usher, Abbot Payson, THE EARLY HISTORY OF DEPOSIT BANKING
Lopez, R.S. & I.W. Raymond, MEDIEVAL TRADE IN THE MEDITERRANEAN WORLD

THE CRUSADES

<u>Topics</u>:

The Reconquista   Relations of Latins with the Byzantine Empire
First Crusade
Second Crusade   Latin States in the East
Third Crusade
Fourth Crusade   Later Crusades

<u>Bibliography</u>:

Strayer, Joseph R., THE ALBIGENSIAN CRUSADES
Anna Comnena, THE ALEXIAD
Fulcher of Chartres, CHRONICLE OF THE FIRST CRUSADE
Krey, A.C., THE FIRST CRUSADE
William of Tyre, HISTORY OF THE CRUSADES
LaMonte, J.L., FEUDAL MONARCHY IN THE LATIN KINGDOM OF JERUSALEM
Munro, D.C., THE KINGDOM OF THE CRUSADERS
Newhall, R.S., THE CRUSADES
Paetow, L.J., ed., THE CRUSADES AND OTHER ESSAYS PRESENTED TO D.C. MUNRO
Stevenson, W., THE CRUSADERS IN THE EAST
Robert of Clari, CONQUEST OF CONSTANTINOPLE
Runciman, S., A HISTORY OF THE CRUSADES
Hitti, P.K., AN ARAB-SYRIAN GENTLEMAN AND WARRIOR IN THE PERIOD OF THE
  CRUSADES
Archer, T.A., THE CRUSADE OF RICHARD I
Duncalf, F., and Krey, A.D., PARALLEL SOURCE PROBLEMS IN MEDIEVAL HISTORY,
  pp. 95-133
Joinville, Jean de, LIFE OF ST. LOUIS
Villehardouin. THE CONQUEST OF CONSTANTINOPLE
Setton, Kenneth, et al., HISTORY OF THE CRUSADES
Andressohn, J.C., ANCESTRY AND LIFE OF GODFREY OF BOUILLON
Yewdale, R.B., BOHEMOND I OF ANTIOCH
Nicholson, R., TANCRED
Southern, Richard W., WESTERN VIEWS OF ISLAM IN THE MIDDLE AGES
Brand, Charles, BYZANTIUM CONFRONTS THE WEST, 1180-1204
Riley-Smith, Jonathan, THE KNIGHTS OF ST. JOHN IN JERUSALEM AND CYPRUS
Brundage, James, CANON LAW AND THE CRUSADES
Prawer, Joshua, THE CRUSADERS' KINGDOM: MEDIEVAL COLONIALISM IN THE MIDDLE
  AGES
Mayer, Hans Eberhard, THE CRUSADES
Riley-Smith, Jonathan, THE FEUDAL NOBILITY AND THE KINGDOM OF JERUSALEM,
  1174-1277
Nicolson, R.L., JOSCELIN III AND THE FALL OF THE CRUSADER STATES, 1134-1199
Smail, R.C., CRUSADING WARFARE
  _____, THE CRUSADERS IN SYRIA AND THE HOLY LAND
Brundage, James A., RICHARD LION-HEART
Urban, William L., THE BALTIC CRUSADE
Queller, D.E., THE FOURTH CRUSADE
Erdmann, Carl, THE ORIGINS OF THE IDEA OF CRUSADE
Grousset, René, THE EPIC OF THE CRUSADES

THE ANGEVIN EMPIRE

<u>Topics</u>:

Formation of the Angevin Empire
Eleanor of Aquitaine
Judicial and Administrative Reforms of Henry II
Magna Carta

<u>Bibliographical suggestions</u>:

Morris, W.A., THE MEDIEVAL ENGLISH SHERIFF TO 1300
Pollock, F., and F.W. Maitland, THE HISTORY OF ENGLISH LAW BEFORE THE TIME OF
    EDWARD I
McKechnie, W.S., MAGNA CARTA
Poole, R.L., THE EXCHEQUER IN THE TWELFTH CENTURY
Powicke, F.M., STEPHEN LANGTON
_____, THE LOSS OF NORMANDY
Barlow, F., THE FEUDAL KINGDOM OF ENGLAND, 1042–1216
Stubbs, W., CONSTITUTIONAL HISTORY OF ENGLAND
Petit-Dutaillis, C., FEUDAL MONARCHY IN FRANCE AND ENGLAND
ENGLISH HISTORICAL DOCUMENTS, ed. by D.C. Douglas and G.W. Greenway, Vol. 2
Norgate, Kate, ENGLAND UNDER THE ANGEVIN KINGS
_____, RICHARD THE LION HEART
_____, JOHN LACKLAND
Painter, S., THE REIGN OF KING JOHN
Salzman, L.F., HENRY II
Ramsay, J.J., THE ANGEVIN EMPIRE, 1154–1216
Maitland. F.W.. CONSTITUTIONAL HISTORY AND ENGLAND
MAGNA CARTA COMMEMORATION ESSAYS
Warren, W.L., KING JOHN
Kelly, Amy, ELEANOR AND THE FOUR KINGS
Lyon, Bryce, CONSTITUTIONAL HISTORY
Davis, R.H.C., KING STEPHEN
Holt, J.C., MAGNA CARTA
Jolliffe, John E.A., ANGEVIN KINGSHIP
Knowles, David, THOMAS BECKETT
Cronne, H.A., THE REIGN OF KING STEPHEN
Caeneghem, R.C. Van, THE BIRTH OF THE ENGLISH COMMON LAW
Sutherland, Donald W., THE ASSIZE OF NOVEL DISSEISIN
_____, QUO WARRAUTO
Warren, W.L., HENRY II
Lloyd, Alan, KING JOHN
Bennetts, Pamela, THE BARONS OF RUNNYMEDE
Thompson, Faith, FIRST CENTURY OF MAGNA CARTA

MEDIEVAL HISTORY

France in the Thirteenth Century

Topics:

The Extension of Royal Power
  under Philip Augustus
Blanche of Castile
The Character of St. Louis
Royal Authority under St. Louis

National Assemblies
Brothers of St. Louis
Philip III
Philip IV

Bibliography:

Jordan, W.C., LOUIS IX AND THE CHALLENGE OF THE CRUSADE
Luchaire, Achille, SOCIAL FRANCE IN THE AGE OF PHILIP AUGUSTUS
Petit-Dutaillis, C., FEUDAL MONARCHY IN FRANCE AND ENGLAND FROM THE 10th TO THE 13th CENTURY
Strayer, J., ADMINISTRATION OF NORMANDY UNDER ST. LOUIS
Hutton, W.H., PHILIP AUGUSTUS
Perry, F., ST. LOUIS
Walker, Williston, ON THE INCREASE OF ROYAL POWER IN FRANCE UNDER PHILIP AUGUSTUS
Joinville, Jean de, LIFE OF ST. LOUIS
Strayer, Joseph R., "The Crusade Against Aragon," SPECULUM, Jan., 1953
Strayer, J.R., "Philip the Fair - A Constitutional King," AMERICAN HISTORICAL REVIEW, Oct., 1956
Fawtier, Robert, THE CAPETIAN KINGS OF FRANCE
Pegues, Frank, LAWYERS OF PHILIP IV
Labarge, Margaret Wade, ST. LOUIS
Strayer, Joseph R., THE MEDIEVAL ORIGINS OF THE MODERN STATE
Wood, Charles T., THE FRENCH APPANAGES & THE CAPETIAN MONARCHY, 1224-1328
Powicke. F.M., THE LOSS OF NORMANDY. 1189-1204
Hollister, C.Warren & John Baldwin, "The Rise of Administrative Kingship: Henry I & Philip Augustus," AHR, LXXXIII (1978), 867-905

THE DISINTEGRATION OF THE EMPIRE

Topics:

Frederick II
The Fall of the Hohenstaufens
The Interregnum
The German Constitution in the Later Middle Ages
Reasons for the Failure of the Holy Roman Empire

Bibliography:

Barraclough, Geoffrey, MEDIEVAL GERMANY
_____, ORIGINS OF MODERN GERMANY
Thompson, J.W., FEUDAL GERMANY
Kantorowicz, Ernst, FREDERICK II
Bayley, C.C., THE FORMATION OF THE GERMAN COLLEGE OF ELECTORS
Bryce, James, THE HOLY ROMAN EMPIRE
Henderson, E.F., A HISTORY OF GERMANY IN THE MIDDLE AGES
Stubbs, William, GERMANY IN THE EARLY MIDDLE AGES
_____, GERMANY IN THE LATER MIDDLE AGES
Einstein, D., EMPEROR FREDERICK II
Dollinger, Philippe, THE GERMAN HANSA
Heer, Friedrich, THE HOLY ROMAN EMPIRE
Van Cleve, Thomas, FREDERICK II
Hampe, K., GERMANY UNDER THE SALIAN & HOHENSTAUFEN EMPERORS

ITALY IN THE LATE MIDDLE AGES

Topics:

The Communes	Venice
Naples and Sicily	The Lesser States
The Papal States	Machiavelli's Prince
Florence	The Triumph of Despotism
Milan	

Bibliography:

Armstrong, E., LORENZO DE' MEDICI

Baron, H., THE CRISIS OF THE EARLY ITALIAN RENAISSANCE

_____, HUMANISTIC AND POLITICAL LITERATURE IN FLORENCE AND VENICE AT THE BEGINNING OF THE QUATTROCENTO

Brown, H., VENICE, AN HISTORICAL SKETCH

Burckhardt, J., THE CIVILIZATION OF THE RENAISSANCE IN ITALY

De Roover, Raymond, THE MEDICI BANK

Emerton, E., HUMANISM AND TYRANNY

Herlihy, David, PISA IN THE EARLY RENAISSANCE

Hodgson, F.C., VENICE IN THE FOURTEENTH AND FIFTEENTH CENTURIES

Mattingly, Garrett, RENAISSANCE DIPLOMACY

Molmenti, Pompeo, VENICE

Scheville, F., A HISTORY OF FLORENCE

_____, THE MEDICI

_____, SIENA

Symonds, J.A., THE RENAISSANCE IN ITALY

Young, George F., THE MEDICI

Waley, Daniel, THE PAPAL STATE IN THE THIRTEENTH CENTURY

Martin, Alfred von, SOCIOLOGY OF THE RENAISSANCE

Gilbert, Felix, MACHIAVELLI & GUICCIARDINI

Rubinstein, Nicolai, THE GOVERNMENT OF FLORENCE UNDER THE MEDICI, 1434-1494

Herlihy, David, MEDIEVAL AND RENAISSANCE PISTOIA

Martines, Lauro, LAWYERS AND STATECRAFT IN RENAISSANCE FLORENCE

Becker, Marvin B., FLORENCE IN TRANSITION

Goldthwaite, Richard, PRIVATE WEALTH IN RENAISSANCE FLORENCE

FLORENTINE STUDIES, ed. by Nicolai Rubinstein

Smith, Denis Mack, MEDIEVAL SICILY

Brucker, Gene, RENAISSANCE FLORENCE

Molho, Anthony, SOCIAL AND ECONOMIC FOUNDATIONS OF THE ITALIAN RENAISSANCE

Butler, William F.T., THE LOMBARD COMMUNES

Bowsky, William, FINANCE OF THE COMMUNE OF SIENA

Chambers, D.S., THE IMPERIAL AGE OF VENICE, 1380-1580

Garin, Eugenio, PORTRAITS FROM THE QUATTROCENTO

Hale, John R., ed., RENAISSANCE VENICE

Lane, Frederic C., VENICE

Pullan, Brian S., A HISTORY OF EARLY RENAISSANCE ITALY

Ferguson, Wallace, THE RENAISSANCE IN HISTORICAL THOUGHT

Jones, P.J., THE MALATESTA OF RIMINI AND THE PAPAL STATE

Partner, Peter, THE LANDS OF ST. PETER

Hyde, John Kenneth, SOCIETY & POLITICS IN MEDIEVAL ITALY; THE EVOLUTION OF THE CIVIL LIFE, 1000-1350

Brentano, Robert, ROME BEFORE AVIGNON

Kedar, Benjamin Z., MERCHANTS IN CRISIS: GENOVESE AND VENETIAN MEN OF AFFAIRS & THE 14th C. DEPRESSION

PARLIAMENTARY INSTITUTIONS

Topics:

Origins

English House of Commons

Estates General

Cortes

Roman and Canon Law and Parliamentary

Institutions

Principle of Consent

Bibliography:

SPECULUM, April, 1954, part 2- Given over to essays on Medieval Representation in
Theory and Practice

Madden, M.R., POLITICAL THEORY AND LAW IN MEDIEVAL SPAIN

Adams, G.B., COUNCILS AND COURTS IN ANGLO-NORMAN ENGLAND

Baldwin, J.F., THE KINGS' COUNCIL IN ENGLAND DURING THE MIDDLE AGES

Wilkinson, B., STUDIES IN CONSTITUTIONAL HISTORY OF THE XIII AND XIV CENTURIES

Haskins, G.L., THE GROWTH OF ENGLISH REPRESENTATIVE GOVERNMENT

McIlwain, C.H., THE HIGH COURT OF PARLIAMENT

Pollard, A.F., THE EVOLUTION OF PARLIAMENT

Gray, N.L., THE INFLUENCE OF THE COMMONS ON EARLY LEGISLATION

Pasquet, D., AN ESSAY ON ORIGINS OF OF THE HOUSE OF COMMONS

Clarke, M..W., MEDIEVAL REPRESENTATION AND CONSENT

Weske, D.B., CONVOCATION OF THE CLERGY

McIlwain, THE GROWTH OF POLITICAL THOUGHT IN THE WEST

Lyon, Bruce, A CONSTITUTIONAL & LEGAL HISTORY OF MEDIEVAL ENGLAND

Wilkinson, Bertie, THE CONSTITUTIONAL HISTORY OF ENGLAND, 1216-1399, 3 v.

Jolliffe, J.E.A., CONSTITUTIONAL HISTORY OF MEDIEVAL ENGLAND

Tierney, Brian, FOUNDATIONS OF THE CONCILIAR THEORY

Wilkinson, Bertie, CONSTITUTIONAL HISTORY OF ENGLAND IN THE FIFTEENTH
CENTURY

Post, Gaines, MEDIEVAL LAW AND POLITICAL THOUGHT

O'Callaghan, Joseph, "The Beginnings of the Cortes of Leon-Castile," in AMERICAN
HISTORICAL REVIEW, LXXIV (1969), pp. 1503-1537

Marongiu, Antonio, MEDIEVAL PARLIAMENTS

McKisack, May, THE PARLIAMENTARY REPRESENTATION OF THE ENGLISH BOROUGHS
DURING THE MIDDLE AGES

Bisson, Thomas W., ASSEMBLIES AND REPRESENTATION IN LANGUEDOC

Powicke, Michael R., THE COMMUNITY OF THE REALM, 1154-1485   942.03
P8753c

Sayles, G.O., THE KING'S PARLIAMENT IN ENGLAND

Fryde, E.B., and Edward Miller, eds., HISTORICAL STUDIES OF THE ENGLISH
PARLIAMENT

Harris, G.L., KING, PARLIAMENT AND PUBLIC FINANCE

Stubbs, William, CONSTITUTIONAL HISTORY OF ENGLAND

Petit-Dutaillis, Charles, STUDIES SUPPLEMENTARY TO STUBBS CONSTITUTIONAL
HISTORY

MEDIEVAL ADMINISTRATION

Topics:

Household Administration
Chancellor
Curia regis (or ducis or comitis)
Financial administration
Sheriffs
Baillis and Clerks

Bibliography:

Petit-Dutaillis, Charles, FEUDAL MONARCHY IN FRANCE AND ENGLAND
Luchaire, A., HISTOIRE DES INSTITUTIONS MONARCHIQUES DE LA FRANCE
Strayer, J., ADMINISTRATION OF NORMANDY UNDER ST. LOUIS
Taylor, C.H., and J.R. Strayer, STUDIES IN EARLY FRENCH TAXATION
Adams, G.B., COUNCIL AND COURTS IN ANGLO-NORMAN ENGLAND
Baldwin, J. F., THE KINGS' COUNCIL IN ENGLAND DURING THE MIDDLE AGES
Round, J.H., KINGS' SERJEANTS
Tout, T.F., CHAPTERS IN THE ADMINISTRATIVE HISTORY OF MEDIEVAL ENGLAND
Cuttino, C.P., ENGLISH DIPLOMATIC ADMINISTRATION, 1259-1339
Willard, J.F., and W.A. Morris, ENGLISH GOVERNMENT AT WORK, 1327-1336
Ramsey, J.H., THE REVENUES OF THE KINGS
Ballard, A., THE DOMESDAY INQUEST
Morris, W.A., THE MEDIEVAL SHERIFF TO 1300
Poole, R.L., THE EXCHEQUER IN THE TWELFTH CENTURY
Haskins, C.H., NORMAN INSTITUTIONS
Lunt, W., PAPAL REVENUES IN THE MIDDLE AGES
Chrimes, S.B., AN INTRODUCTION TO THE ADMINISTRATIVE HISTORY OF MEDIEVAL
    ENGLAND thru Chap. IV
Luchaire, Archille, MANUEL DES INSTITUTIONS FRANCAISES
    PERIOD DES CAPETIENS DIRECTES
Monier, Raymond, LES INSTITUTIONS FINANCIERES DU COMPTE DE FLANDRE DU XI
    SIECLE A 1384
Nowe, Henri, LES BAILLIS COMTAUX DE FLANDRE
Monier, Raymond, LES INSTITUTIONS CENTRALES DU COMPTE DE FLANDRE DE LA FIN
    DU IXE S. A 1384
Morris, W.A. THE EARLY ENGLISH COUNTY COURT
Lyon, Bryce, CONSTITUTIONAL AND LEGAL HISTORY OF MEDIEVAL ENGLAND
Wilkinson, Bertie, CONSTITUTIONAL HISTORY OF ENGLAND, 1216-1399
_____, STUDIES IN THE CONSTITUTIONAL HISTORY OF THE 13TH & 14TH CENTURIES
Lyon, Bryce, and Adriaan Verhulst, MEDIEVAL FINANCE
Strayer, Joseph R., ON THE MEDIEVAL ORIGIN OF THE MODERN STATE
BRITISH GOVERNMENT AND ADMINISTRATION: STUDIES PRESENTED TO S.B.CHRIMES,
    ed. by H.Mearder & H.R. Loyn

Penelope D. Johnson
New York University

Introduction

The Shaping of Attitudes
The Bible Genesis 1-3
Leviticus 12, 15:19-32; 20:10-21.
1 Corinthians 5-7; 11:1-15; 14:34-6.
Galatians 3:26-29.
1 Timothy 2:9-15; 5:3-16.
Aristotle, Politics, Bk. 1, Ch. 12-13.
Jerome, Letter 22 to Eustochium.
Rosemary Ruether, "Misogynism and Virginal Feminism in the
Fathers of the Church," Religion and Sexism ed. R. Ruether
(1974), 150-183.
Vern Bullough,"Medieval Medical and Scientific Views of
Women," Viator 4 (1973), 484-501.

The Early Middle Ages
A Lost Tradition: Women Writers of the Early Church, ed.
Patricia Wilson-Kastner et al. (Washington, D.C.:1981).
Elaine Pagels, The Gnostic Gospels (N.Y.:1981) intro., ch. 1-3
Rosemary Rader, Breaking Boundaries (N.Y.:1983).

The Barbarian Period
Suzanne Wemple, Women in Frankish Society (Philadelphia:1981).
Janet L. Nelson, "Brunhild and Balthild in Merovingian
History," in Medieval Women, ed. Derek Baker (1978),
103-118.
Hroswitha, in Medieval Women Writers ed. Katharina Wilson
(Athens, GA:1984), 30-63.

Life, Death, and Influence
David Herlihy, "Life Expectancies for Women in Medieval
Society," in The Role of Woman in the Middle Ages
ed. Rosmarie Morewedge (Albany:1975), 1-22.
_____, "Land, Family, and Women," Women in
Medieval Society, ed. Susan Stuard (Philadelphia:1976),
13-45.
Vern Bullough, "Female Longevity and Diet," Speculum
55 (1980).
Emily Coleman, "Infanticide in the Early Middle Ages", in
Stuard 47-70.
Jo Ann McNamarie and Suzanne Wemple, "The Power of Women
through the Family in Medieval Europe: 500-1000,"
in Clio's Consciousness Raised, ed. Mary Hartmann and
Lois Banner (N.Y.:1976), 103-118.

Education, Political Involvement, and Family
Joan Ferrante "The Education of Women in the Middle Ages
in Theory, Fact, and Fantasy," in Beyond Their Sex
Learned Women of the European Past ed. Patricia Labalme
(N.Y.:1980), 9-42.

Elizabeth Brown, "Eleanor of Aquitaine: Parent, Queen, and
Duchess", in Eleanor of Aquitaine, ed. Wm. Kibler.
(Austin, TX:1976), 9-34.
Frances & Joseph Gies, "A Reigning Queen: Blanche of Castile,"
in Women in the Middle Ages (N.Y.:1978), 97-119.
Penelope Johnson, "Agnes of Burgundy: An Eleventh-Century
Woman Seen in the Matrix of Gender, Class, and Family"

rriage

Georges Duby, Medieval Marriage: Two Models from
Twelfth-century France tr. E. Forster (Baltimore:1978).
Emily Coleman, "Medieval Marriage Characteristics: A
Neglected Factor in the History of Medieval Serfdom,"
Journal of Interdisciplinary History 2 (1971), 205-219.
John Noonan, "Power to Choose," Viator 4 (1973), 419-434.
Michael Sheehan, "The Influence of Canon Law on the Property
Rights of Married Women in England," Medieval Studies
25 (1963), 109-124.
_____, "The Formation and Stability of Marriage in
Fourteenth Century England: Evidence of an Ely Register,"
Medieval Studies 33 (1971), 228-263.
The Marriage Ceremony from the Old Sarum Missal, (my
translation and xerox)

Cloister: The Alternate for Women

The Correspondence of Abelard and Heloise, ed. Betty Radice
(Harmondsworth:1974).
Brenda Bolton, "Mulieres Sanctae" in Stuard, 141-158.
F. and J. Gies, "Hildegarde of Bingen", in Women in the Middle
Ages 63-96.

rtly Love and Social Reality

Marie de France in Medieval Women Writers, 64-89.
Castelloza in Medieval Women Writers, 131-152.
John Benton, "Clio and Venus," in The Meaning of Courtly Love,
ed. Francis Newman (Albany:1968).
Herbert Moller, "The Social Causation of the Courtly Love
Complex," Comparative Studies in Society and History, 1
(1959), 137-63.

Mystical Route

Julian of Norwich, Revelations of Divine Love tr. Clifton
Wolters (Harmondsworth:1966).
Casey Miller and Kate Swift, "Women and the Language of
Religion", The Christian Century 93 (1975), 353-58.
Hadewijch, Medieval Women Writers, 186-203.

en Active in Society

Christine de Pizan, The Book of the City of Ladies tr. Jeffrey
Richards (N.Y.:1982).
"The Case of a Woman Doctor in Paris," The Portable Medieval
Reader ed. James B. Ross and Mary McLaughlin
(Harmondsworth:1977), 635-40.
F. and J. Gies, "A City Working Woman: Agnes li Patiniere of
Douai; Women and the Guilds," in Women in the Middle Ages, 53-75.

Class Meeting for Reports

Class Meeting for Reports

Conclusions
     PAPERS DUE IN CLASS.

Requirements: Attendance in class is required.   One unexcused
          absence is allowed.
                    A seminar research paper of about 30 pages is due at
          the last class meeting.

SUPPLEMENTARY READING

Important bibliographic tools:

Erickson, Carolly and Kathleen Casey. "Women in the Middle Ages: a
     Working Bibliography." Medieval Studies 37 (1975).
Frey, Linda, Marsha Frey, and Joanne Schneider. Women in Western
     Europe and History: A Select Chronological, Geographical, and
     Topical Bibliography from Antiquity to the French Revolution.
     Westport, CT: 1982.
Kelly, Joan, et. at. Bibliography in the History of European
     Women. 5th ed. A Sarah Lawrence College Women's Studies
     Publication: 1982.

Bibliographic and Historiographic Essays:

Davis, Natalie. "Women's History in Transition: The European Case."
     Feminist Studies 3 (1976), 83-103.
Hartman, Mary and Lois Banner, ed. Clio's Consciousness Raised: New
     Perspectives on the History of Women.   N.Y.: 1974.
Kelly, Joan. Women, History and Theory: The Essays of Joan Kelly.
     Chicago: 1984.

General Bibliography:

Atkingon, Clarissa. Mystic and Pilgrim: The Book and the World of
     Margery Kempe. Ithaca: 1983.
Boyd, Catherine. A Cistercian Nunnery in Mediaeval Italy: The
     Story of Rifreddo in Saluzzo, 1220-1300. Cambridge: 1943.
Bynum, Caroline. Jesus as Mother: Studies in the Spirituality of
     the High Middle Ages. Berkeley: 1982.
Eckenstein, Lina. Women under Monasticism. Cambridge, Eng.: 1896,
     reissued 1963.
Flandrin, Jean-Louis.   "Contraception, Marriage, and Sexual
     Relations in the Christian West." Biology of Man in History,
     ed. Robert Forster and Orest Ranum.

Gazeau, R. "La cloture des moniales au XIIe siècle en France."
Revue Mabillon 58 (1974).

Gold, Penny. The Lady and the Virgin: Image and Attitude, and
Experience in 12th-Century France. Chicago: 1985.

Goodrich, Michael. "The Contours of Female Piety in Later Medieval
Hagiography." Church History 50 (1981), 20-32.

Herlihy, David. Women in Medieval Society. Houston, TX: 1971.

Hughes, Diane. "Urban Growth and Family Structure in Medieval
Genoa." Past and Present 66 (1975).

Hughes, Muriel. Women Healers in Medieval Life and Literature.
Reissued Freeport, N.Y.: 1968.

Jordan, William. "Jews on Top: Women and the Availability of
Consumption Loans in Northern France in the Mid-Thirteenth
Century." Journal of Jewish Studies 29-30 (1978-9).

Klinck, Anne. "Anglo-Saxon Women and the Law." Journal of
Medieval History 8 (1982).

Kraus, Henry. "Eve and Mary: Conflicting Images of Medieval
Women." in The Living Theatre of Medieval Art. Bloomington:
1967.

Leclercq, Jean. "Medieval Feminine Monasticism: Reality versus
Romantic Images." Benedictus: Studies in Honor of St. Benedict
of Nursia. Ed. Rozanne Elder (1981).

Lucas, Angela. Women in the Middle Ages: Religion, Marriage and
Letters. N.Y.: 1983.

McDonnell, Ernest. The Beguines and Beghards in Medieval Culture.
New Brunswick, NJ: 1954.

Milsom, S. F. C. "Inheritance by Women in the Twelfth and Early
Thirteenth Centuries." On the Laws and Customs of England:
Essays in Honor of Samuel E. Thorne. Chapel Hill: 1981.

Nichols, John and Lillian Shank, eds. Distant Echoes: Medieval
Religious Women. Kalamazoo, MI: 1984.

Otis, Leah. Prostitution in Medieval Society: History of an Urban
Institution in Languedoc. Chicago: 1985.

Pernoud, Regine. Blanche of Castile. N.Y.: 1972.

_____. La femme au temps des cathédrales. Paris: 1980.

Power, Eileen. "The Position of Women." The Legacy of the Middle
Ages. Ed. C. G. Crump and E. F. Jacob. Oxford: 1926.

Reilly, Bernard. The Kingdom of Leon-Castilla under Queen Urraca,
1109-1126. Princeton: 1982.

Searle, Eleanor. "Seigneurial Control of Women's Marriage: The
Antecedents and Function of Merchet in England." Past and
Present 82 (1979).

Shahar, Shulamith. The Fourth Estate: A History of Women in the
Middle Ages. Tr. Chaya Galai. London: 1983.

Walker, Sue Sheridan. "Free Consent and Marriage of Feudal Wards
in Medieval England." Journal of Medieval History 8 (1982).

Warner, Marina. Joan of Arc: The Image of Female Heroism. N.Y.:
1982.

_____. Alone of all her Sex: The Myth and Cult of the
Virgin Mary. N.,Y.:1976.

Wood, Charles T. "Queens, Queans, and Kingship: An Inquiry into
Theories of Royal Legitimacy in Late Medieval England and
France." Order and Innovation in the Middle Ages. Ed. William
C. Jordan, Bruce McNab, Teofilo F. Ruiz. Princeton: 1976.

THE MOTHERS OF THE CHURCH: WOMEN IN THE CHRISTIAN TRADITION

E. Ann Matter
University of Pennslyvania
243-8614

This course is intended to fill in the gaps left by traditional histories
of Christianity by looking at the roles women played in the development of the
Christian tradition. We will examine accounts by and about women in a chronological
period ranging from the early church to the Reformation. The organization will
be roughly topical within the mold of historical development.

Tuesday classes will feature lectures on the background of the readings,
intended to raise the major questions for discussion on Thursdays. Regular
attendance and class participation are essential for the success of the course.
In addition, each student will write two 4/5 page papers: the first on units I and
II, due one week after the completion of unit II, the second on units VI and VII,
due one week after the completion of unit VII. There will also be a final
examination, for which students may substitute a research paper on any topic
relating to the course and cleared with the instructor.

BOOKS ORDERED FROM THE UNIVERSITY BOOK STORE:

E. Clark and H. Richardson, eds., WOMEN AND RELIGION: A FEMINIST SOURCEBOOK OF
        CHRISTIAN THOUGHT (New York 1977) [abbreviated as WR]
J. Engelsman, THE FEMININE DIMENSION OF THE DIVINE (Philadelphia 1979)
Heloise, LETTERS, in B. Radice, trans., THE LETTERS OF ABELARD AND HELOISE (Penguin 1
R. Pernoud, ed., JOAN OF ARC: BY HERSELF AND HER WITNESSES (New York 1969)
R. Ruether, NEW WOMAN, NEW EARTH (New York 1975) [abbreviated NW]
_____, ed., RELIGION AND SEXISM: IMAGES OF WOMEN IN THE JEWISH AND CHRISTIAN
        TRADITIONS (New York 1974)   [abbreviated RS]
K. Stendahl, THE BIBLE AND THE ROLE OF WOMEN (Philadelphia 1966)
Teresa of Avila, AUTOBIOGRAPHY (Doubleday edition, trans. A. Peers)
S. Undset, KRISTEN LAVRANSDATTER III: THE CROSS (Bantam edition)

OPTIONAL (also on reserve):

R. Bainton, WOMEN OF THE REFORMATION IN GERMANY AND ITALY
Gregory the Great, DIALOGUES
E. Power, MEDIEVAL WOMEN, ed. M. Postan
S. Stuard, WOMEN IN MEDIEVAL SOCIETY

All other assigned readings will be on reserve. [abbreviated as R]

I. INHERITED IMAGES OF WOMEN
   A)   The Biblical Perspectives:
JAN. 15 LECTURE
Readings: Bible passages suggested in WR (3/4)
                P. Bird, "Images of Women in the OLd Testament" (RS)
                P. Trible, "Depatriarchalizing in Biblical Interpretation," JAAR 41
                   (1973) 30-48 (R)
                C. Parvey, "The Theology and Leadership of Women in the New Testament" (RS)
                K. Stendahl, THE BIBLE AND THE ROLE OF WOMEN

   B)   The Theological Question:
JAN. 22 LECTURE
Readings: J. Engelsman, THE FEMININE DIMENSION OF THE DIVINE

II. THE IDEAL WOMAN: THE BLESSED VIRGIN MARY
JAN. 29 LECTURE
Readings: R. Ruether, "Mistress of Heaven " (NW)
                _____, "Misogynism and Virginal Feminism" (RS)
                Selections from Infancy and Marian Pseudepigrapha (R)

III. THE IDEAL WOMAN: VIRGINITY, SERVICE, AND MARTYRDOM
FEB. 5 LECTURE
Readings: Clement of Alexandria, Augustine, Jerome (WR 5/7)
                Tertullian(?), THE PASSION OF SAINTS PERPETUA AND FELICITY (R)
                Gregory of Nyssa, THE LIFE OF SAINT MACRINA (R)
                A. Yarbrough, "Christianization in the Fourth Century: The Example
                   of Roman Women," CH 45 (1976) 1-17 (R)

V. SERVING AND RULING: WOMEN IN CHRISTIAN LEADERSHIP
   A) The Church
FEB. 12 LECTURE
Readings: R. Ruether, "Guarding the Sanctuary" (NW)
                E. McLaughlin, "Equality of Souls, Inequality of Sexes: Women in
                   Medieval Theology" (RS)
                Thomas Aquinas selections in WR (8)
                F. Cardman, "The Medieval Question of Women and Orders," The Thomist
                   42(1978) 582-99 (R)

   B) The State
FEB. 19 LECTURE
Readings: E.A.R. Brown, "Eleanor of Aquitaine: Parent, Queen and Duchess," in
                   ELEANOR OF AQUITAINE ed. W.W. Kibler (R)
                R. Pernoud, ed. JOAN OF ARC (1-6)
                V. Scudder, ed. SAINT CATHERINE OF SIENA AS SEEN IN HER LETTERS, sel. (R)

   THE TRIUMPHANT INSTITUTION: MONASTICISM
   A) Origin and Development
FEB. 26 LECTURE
Readings: Caesarius, RULE FOR NUNS, selections (R)
                E. Power, "Nunneries," in MEDIEVAL WOMEN
                B. Bolton, "Mulieres Sanctae," in WOMEN IN MEDIEVAL SOCIETY

B) Individual Self-Expression
MARCH 4 LECTURE
Readings: Gregory the Great, DIALOGUES, selections
               P.A. Crusack, "ST. Scholastica: Myth or Real Person?" DOWNSIDE REVI
                  92(1974) 145-59 (R)
               J.H. Wansbrough, "St. Gregory's Intention in the Stories of St.
                  Scholastica and Sy. Benedict," REVUE BÉNEDICTINE 75 (1965) 145-51
               Hroswitha of Gandersheim, SAPIENTIA, PAPHNUTIUS, DULCITIUS (R)
               Heloise, LETTERS

VI. THE TRIUMPHANT TRADITION: MYSTICISM
   A) Traditional Feminine Spirituality
MARCH 18 LECTURE
Readings: E. Underhill, MYSTICISM, selections (R)
          C.H. Talbot, THE LIFE OF CHRISTINA OF MARKYATE (R)
          Butler, LIVES OF THE SAINTS, lives of Gertrude the Great, Elisabeth of
             Schönau, Mechtilde of Hackeborn, Teresa of Avila, Catherine of
             Genoa, Brigid of Sweden, Lydwine of Schiedam

   B) The Mystical and the Saintly
MARCH 25 LECTURE
Readings: Julian of Norwich, Margery Kempe in WR (9)
               Mechtilde of Magdeburg, THE FLOWING LIGHT OF THE GODHEAD, tr. L. Me
                  selections (R)

VII THE QUESTION OF WITCHCRAFT
APRIL 1 LECTURE
Readings: MALLEUS MALEFICARUM, selections in WR (10)
               R. Ruether, "Witches and Jews: the Demonic Alien in Christian Cultu
               R. Pernoud, JOAN OF ARC (7-9)

VIII. THE DAWN OF THE MODERN ERA
APRIL 8 LECTURE
Readings: Luther and Milton, selections in WR (11/12)
               J. Irwin, "Anna Maria von Schurman: From Feminism to Pietism" CH (1
               Teresa of Avila, AUTOBIOGRAPHY, selections
               R. Bainton, WOMEN OF THE REFORMATION IN GERMANY AND ITALY, selection
               J.D. Douglas, "Women and the Continental Reformation" (RS)

IX. AN ORDINARY LIFE
APRIL 15 LECTURE
Reading: S. Undset, KRISTIN LAVRANSDATTER III: THE CROSS

APRIL 22 SUMMARY AND OVERVIEW

WOMEN IN EARLY EUROPEAN SOCIETY
Professor JoAnn McNamara
Hunter College

Textbook: Edward Peters, _Europe: The World of the Middle Ages_

There will be a take home mid-term given out on October 23 and
due a week later; the final exam will be scheduled in class
by the Registrar.

A term paper, approximately 20 pages, following the attached
instructions will be due on December 23.

Part I.   Primitive Europe

    1. Pre-Christian Society
    2. Christian Attitudes
    3. Christian Institutions
    4. The Conversion of Europe
    5. Germanic Laws and Institutions
    6. Personal Wealth and Public Power

Suggested Readings:

    The writings of the Christian fathers which have broad
    application to the study of women are available in several
    English translations. The most important series are: The
    Ante-Nicene _Fathers_ and the _Post-Nicene_ _Fathers_: _The_
    Fathers _of_ _the_ _Church_; _Ancient_ _Christian_ _Writers_ and
    (French translations) _Sources_ _Chretienne_. Nearly all the
    writers of the church to about the mid-12th century are
    included in the Latin collection of Migne, _Patrologia_
    Latina.

Some general collections include,

    Morwedge, Rosemary, _Women_ _in_ _the_ _Middle_ _Ages_
    Dunbar, Agnes, _A_ _Dictionary_ _of_ _Saintly_ _Women_
    Erickson, Carolly and Casey, Kathleen, "Women in the
        Middle Ages: a working Bibliography," _Medieval_
        Studies, 37, 1975, 340-59.
Several journals deal with subjects of interest to us:

    Medieval journals, dominated by _Speculum_
    Journals of social history, principally, the _Journal_ _of_
        Interdisciplinary _History_; the _Annales,_ _Econames,_
        socials _et_ _culturels_; _Journal_ _of_ _Family_ _History_.

Some secondary sources for part I:

Bachofen, J., _Myth, Religion and Mother Right: Selected writings of J. J. Bachofen_

Briffault, R., _The Mothers_

Corbett, Percy E., _The Roman Law of Marriage_

Dudley, D. R. and Webster, G., _The Rebellion of Boudicca_

Eckenstein, Lina , _The Women of Early Christianity_

Gough, Kathleen, _The Origins of the Family_

James, E. O., _The Cult of the Mother Goddess_

Laeuchli, S. _Power and Sexuality: the emergence of Canon Law at the Synod of Elvira_

Levy, Rachel, _The Gate of Horn_

Neumann, E. _The Great Mothers_

Phillpotts, B. _Kindred and Clan in the Middle Ages and After_

Reuther, ed., _Religion and Sexism_

Schneider, D. M. and Gough, K., _Matrilineal Kinship_

Tavard, G. H., _Women in Christian Tradition_

McNamara, J. "The Virginity Cult and Sexual Equality in Early Christian Thought" in _Feminist Studies_, vol. 3, 1976.

Part II: The Age of Family Power

1. Carolingian Society and Government
2. The Peasantry and Social Mobility
3. Divisions of Labor in field and fief
4. Medicine and Witchcraft
5. The Propietary Church
6. Family and seigneurial power

Roman and Germanic Law Codes of various peoples of Europe exist in translation. Other primary sources are indicated by an asterisk.

*Anna Comnena, _The Alexiad_

Bateson, M., "The Origin and Early History of Double Monasteries," _Royal Historical Society Transactions_, vol. 13 (1899), 137-198

*Bede, _Ecclesiastical History of the English People_

Besta, E., _La famiglia nella storia del diritto italiano_

*Le _Manuel de Dhuoda_, ed. P. Riche

Cornuey, L. M. A., _Le Regime de la dos aux epoques merovingiennes et carolingiennes_

Eckenstein, L., _Women under Monasticism, 500-1500_

Esmein, A., _Le mariage en droit canonique_

*Gregory of Tours, _History of the Franks_

Heinrich, M., _Canonesses and Education in the Early Middle Ages_

Herlihy, D., "Land, Power and Women" in Stuard, _Women in Medieval Society_

Lewis, Archibald, _The Development of Southern French and Catalan Society_

*Liutprand of Cremona, _Works_

*McNeill, J. and Gamer, H., _Medieval Handbook of Penance_

McNamara, J. and Wemple, S., "Marriage and Divorce in the Frankish Kingdoms" in Stuard, _Women in Medieval Society_

Noonan, John, _Contraception: A History of its Treatment by Catholic Theologians and Canonists_

*Roswitha, _Collected Works_

Stenton, D., _The English Woman in History_

*Talbot, C., _The Anglo-Saxon Missionaries in Germany_

Part III: The High Middle Ages

1. Reform and Restriction
2. Family solidarity and economic power
3. Feudalism and Bureaucracy
4. Courtly and Romantic Love
5. Heresy and Nonconformity
6. Scholars and Mystics

*Aquinas, _Summa Theologica_, and other works as well as treatises by various other theologians are available in translation.

Brooke, C.N.L., "Gregorian reform in action," in S.L. Thrupp, _Change in Medieval Society_

Facinger, Marion F., "A Study of Medieval Queenship," _Nebraska Studies in Medieval and Renaissance_, 5

Graham, R., _Gilbert of Sempringham and the Gilbertines_

Guibert de Nogent, _Self and Society in the Twelfth Century_

Hill, Georgina, _Women in English Life from Medieval to Modern Times_, 2 vols.

*Heloise and Abelard, _Letters_

*Bogin, M., _The Women Troubadours_

de Fontette, M., _Les religieuses a l'age classique du droit canonique_

Helmholtz, R.H., _Marriage Litigation in Medieval England_

Kibler, W.W., ed., _Eleanor of Aquitaine, Patron and Politician_

Koch, G., _Fraunfrage und Ketzerdum im Mittelalter_

McNamara, J., and Wemple, S., "The Power of Women through the Family, in _Clio's Consciousness Raised_

Newman. F-X., _The Meaning of Courtly Love_

Power, Eileen, _Medieval Women_

243

Receuils Jean Bodin, vols. 11-12, La Femme
*Trotula, The Diseases of Women
Weinhold, K., Die deutschen Frauen in dem Mittelalter.

Part IV: The Late Middle Ages

1. The household: wives, servants and mothers
2. Saints and femmes fatales
3. Wage earners
4. Prostitutes, beggars, thieves and foundlings
5. The pressures of nationalism

*The fifteen joys of marriage, tr. Abbot
Abram, A., "Women traders of medieval London," Economic
    Journal, vol. 28, 276-85
*Caxton, W., ed., The Book of the Knight of the Tower
Dale, Marion, "The London Silk Women of the 15th
    Century," Economic History Review, 4, 324-35
*The trial of Joan of Arc
Forbes, T., The midwife and the witch
*The Goodman of Paris, ed. E. Power
*Julian of Norwich, Revelations of Divine Love
*The Book of Margery Kempe, ed. Bowdon
McDonnell, E.W. Beguines and Beghards in Medieval
    Culture
*The Paston Letters
Power, E., Medieval English Nunneries
Power, E., "Women Traders in Medieval London," Economic
    Journal, 1916, 276 ff.
Ragg, L., The Women Artists of Bologna
Russell, J.B., Witchcraft in the Middle Ages
Sheehan, M.M., "The Formation and Stability of Marriage
    in Fourteenth Century England," Medieval Studies,
    33, 1971
*Ulrich von Liechtenstein, Frauendiesnt
Warner, M., Alone of All Her Sex.

THE JEWS IN THE MIDDLE AGES

ıdaic Studies 325
›of. Judith Baskin

University of Massachusetts
Amherst

is course surveys Jewish history and civilization under Islam
d in the Christian world from the fourth to the fifteenth century.
ncentration is on both Judaism's internal development, and external
sponses to the medieval civilizations of Islam and Christianity.
e first half of the course considers the Islamic sphere, the
cond the Christian.

urse requirements are a midterm, a final exam based on the last
lf of the course, and two short papers (4-6 pages), to be submitted
any two or four possible due dates. Paper due dates are indicated
an asterisk. Topics for each paper due date will be suggested,
t students may also write in an area of special interest (with
e Instructor's permission). A helpful collection of bibliographical
formation for these papers is Bibliographical Essays in Medieval
wish Studies. The Study of Judaism vol. 2 (published by KTAV for
e Anti-Defamation League of B'nai B'rith, New York, 1976).

quired Texts:	Robert Seltzer, Jewish People, Jewish Thought	JPJT
	Norman Stillman, The Jews of Arab Lands	JAL
	Jacob Marcus The Jew in the Medieval World (a sourcebook)	JMW
	Jacob Neusner Understanding Rabbinic Judaism URJ (a collection of essays by major scholars on important medieval ideas, trends and personalities)	
	Leon Poliakov The History of Antisemitism vol I	HA
	Israel Abrahams Jewish Life in the Middle Ages	JLMA

ongly Recommended: Jacob Katz   Exclusiveness and Tolerance
                                                     Tradition and Crisis

(currently out of print in paperback)

Schedule of Readings

Jan. 13:   Rabbinic Backgrounds of Medieval Judaism. URJ 39-70.

Jan. 18:   Judaism and Islam. JPJT 323-334; JAL 3-21, 113-151.

Jan. 20:   Baghdad and the Achievements of the Geonim. JPJT 334-
           337; JAL 22-39, 152-182; JMW 185-188.

Jan. 25:   The Karaite Movement and Saadia Gaon. JPJT 337-342, 373-
           381; URJ 149-171; JMW 233-240, 287-292.

Jan. 27:   Jewish Life under Islam: The Genizah Documents and
           Merchant Activity. JAL 40-53, 64-87, 183-209, 247-
           251; JMW 293-296.

* Feb. 1:   The Jews in Muslim Spain I: Social and Political Life.
           JPJT 342-348; JAL 53-63, 210-230; JMW 297-300.

  Feb. 3:   The Jews in Muslim Spain II: Creative and Artistic Life.
           Shalom Spiegel, "On Medieval Hebrew Poetry," in J. Goldin,
           The Jewish Expression (on reserve in Cross Campus Library).

  Feb. 8:   Achievements in Jewish Philosophy I: Ibn Gabirol and
           Judah Halevi. JPJT 382-392; URJ 135-145, 175-186.

  Feb. 10: Achievements in Jewish Philosophy II: Maimonides.
           JPJT 393-408; URJ 187-214.

  Feb. 15: The Jews in Christian Spain I. JPJT 364-370; URJ 215-237;
           JMW 34-40.

  Feb. 17: The Jews in Christian Spain II. JPJT 370-372; JMW 51-55,
           173-178.

  Feb. 22: Jewish Mysticism I. URJ 279-300; JPJT 419-422 425-450.

* Feb. 24: Jewish Mysticism II: Lurianic Mysticism. JPJT 454-467;
           S. Shechter, "Safed in the Sixteenth Century: A City of
           Light and Mystics," in Goldin, The Jewish Expression.

  Mar. 1:   MIDTERM EXAM

  Mar. 3:   The Jews in Western Europe in the Early Middle Ages.
           JPJT 350-355; JMW 3-7, 227-232, 349-352, 355-359; JAL 163-16

  Mar. 22: Medieval Christendom and the Jews. HA, ch. 1,2;
           J. Huizinga, The Waning of the Middle Ages, chs. 1,3,12 (on
           reserve in CCL); JMW 101-114, 353-354.

* Mar. 24: Franco-German Jewry before 1100. HA, ch.3; URJ 101-115;
           JMW 360-363.

  Mar. 31: The Crusades and Their Aftermath I: External Reactions.
           JPJT 355-360; HA ch. 4; JMW 115-131, 301-305.

pr. 5:   The Crusades and their Aftermath II: Internal Responses.
          HA, ch.5; JPJT 422-425; URJ 303-313.

pr. 7:   Church, State and Jews 1200-1400. JPJT 360-364; HA, chs. 6,7;
          JLMA, chs. 4,16,23.

pr. 12:   Daily Life. Economic Activity and Community Organization.
          JMW 28-33, 189-191, 364-365, 373-377; JLMA, chs. 1,2,3,11,12.

pr. 14:   Daily Life. Women and Family. JLMA, chs. 7-10; JMW 311-
          316, 389-393, 443-445.

pr. 19:   Medieval Jewish Creativity. I. Twersky, "The Shulkan
          Aruch: Enduring Code of Jewish Law," in Goldin, The Jewish
          Expression; B. Narkiss, Hebrew Illuminated Manuscripts;
          J. Gutmann, Jewish Manuscript Painting (all on reserve in
          CCL).

pr. 21:   The Jews at the End of the Middle Ages: Expulsions;
          Population Shifts; The Ghetto. JPJT 348-349, 467-482;
          JLMA, ch. 19.

   Further readings on Jewish women and family life

. D. Goitein, A Mediterranean Society vol. 3 (The Family)

. A. Agus, The Heroic Age of Franco-German Jewry, 277-309.

. Epstein, "The Jewish Woman in the Responsa," in Leo Jung, The
  Jewish Library, vol. 3, 123-152.

. Rabinowitz, The Social Life of the Jews of Northern France in the
  XII-XIV Centuries as Reflected in the Rabbinic Literature of the
  Period, 137-165.

. C. Jordan, "Jews on Top: Women and the Availability of Consumption
  Loans in Northern France in the Mid-Thirteenth Century," Journal
  of Jewish Bibliography, History and Literature in Honor of E. I.
  Kiev 347-355.

Prof. Jochanan Wijnhoven

SMITH COLLEGE
DEPARTMENT OF RELIGION
NORTHAMPTON, MASSACHUSETTS 01063

SYLLABUS   RELIGION 235 A : THE JEWS IN THE MIDDLE AGES   FALL 1983

The course will highlight important features of Jewish life in the Middle Ages
the interaction of Jews and Christians, and Jews and Muslims; Jewish social
and religious life, leadership, literary productivity, and influence on general
culture.
   The first four weeks will focus on Jews in Christian countries; the next
four weeks on Jewish life in Muslim countries, while the final four weeks
will consist of reading and discussing medieval Jewish philosophical and
religious texts, poetical and mystical.

General Historical Background

For general historical background on the Jews in the Middle Ages, the
students are urged to read the chapters in Jewish standard works that pertain
to the period from 600-1600.
   Such general histories can be found in the library, and several of the
following are available in paperback:

1. Hayim Ben-Sasson, A History of the Jewish People
2. Solomon Grayzel, A History of the Jews
3. Max Margulis and Alexander Marx, A History of the Jewish People
4. Cecil Roth, A History of the Jews
5. Abram Sachar, A History of the Jews
6. Leo Schwarz, ed., Great Ages and Ideas of the Jewish People

Multivolume Works

The following works deal with Jewish history in greater detail. Events and issues
are dealt with in greater depth:

1. Salo W. Baron, A Social and Religious History of the Jews (so far 17 vols.
   including the medieval period)
2. Semen M. Dubnov, History of the Jews (5 vols.)
3. Heinrich Graetz, History of the Jews (6 vols.)

All can be found in the Smith College Library.

Monographs

There is a plethora of monographs on Jews in specific countries, such as
England (Cecil Roth), Germany (Guido Kisch), Spain (F. Baer and E Ashtor),
Italy (Cecil Roth), France (Blumenkranz), Poland (Weinryb) etc.
   Of great help in research and preparation are the various Jewish Encyclopedies
which can be found in the reference room of the Library. Smith has three
different multivolume encyclopedies on Jews and Judaism, all of them useful
for the study of this course.
   Placed on reserve for this course will also be Bibliographical Essays in
   Medieval Jewish Studies, which contains a rich bibliography and topical
issues which students may wish to work on for a research paper.

Note

It should be pointed out that virtually all works and monographs on Jewish
history are done by Jews. It underscores the sad fact that general historical

248

scholarship has notoriously overlooked the presence and importance
of the Jews in Western culture. In standard works on medieval history and
culture passing references or few pages are devoted to the Jews,
frequently stressing pejorative aspects of their presence. It is
only in the last few decades that interest and knowledge of the
Jewish contribution to Western civilisation in the post-biblical era
has come to general academic attention.

Required Books for the Course

1. David Blumenthal, <u>Understanding Jewish Mysticism</u>
    vols 1-2

2. Lenn E. Goodman, <u>Rambam: Readings in the Philosophy of Moses
    Maimonides</u>

3. Jacob Katz, <u>Exclusiveness and Tolerance</u>

4. Norman Stillman, <u>The Jews of Arab Lands</u>

Other material will be prepared for handouts in class or placed on
reserve for specific reading assignments.

Course requirements

Evaluation of the students will be based on 1) class participation
and preparation, 2) a final examination at the end of the course,
3) a research paper on a subject of personal interest of the student to be determined in consultation with instructor.

The paper

The research paper will be a demonstration of personal research.
The perimeters are that the subject ought to deal with Jews and
should fall within the chronological limits from 600-1600.

A rough draft, containing <u>minimally</u> the outline, the definition of
the subject and a detailed bibliography, is due on the last class
<u>before</u> fall recess. The final draft is due on the last day of class.

Preview of Subject Matter

I. Week 1-4:   Jews and Christendom

The "medieval quality" of Jewish life between 600-1600.

Settlement and migrations of the Jews in medieval Europe.

Church and Synagogue: Jews and Christians: Social contact.

Jewish Life and Leadership. Rashi (11th cent.).

Spirituality and Mystics.

Persecutions and Expulsions.

Reading assignments: Jacob Katz, Exclusiveness and Tolerance (in toto)

Gavin Langmuir, "Majority History and Post-Biblical Jews"
(article handout)

Salo W. Baron, "The Jewish Factor in Medieval Civilization" (article
(handout)

H. Liebeschuetz, "Relations between Jews and Christians in the
Middle Ages" (article handout)

James Parkes, The Conflict of the Church and the Synagogue (on reserve)

I. B. Agus, "Rashi and his School" (on reserve)

B. Blumenkranz, "The Roman Church and the Jews" (on reserve)

II. Week 5-8:   Jews and Islam

Settlement and migrations in Muslim countries.

Mohammed, the Qur'an, and the Jews.

Karaites: the Schism in Judaism.

Jewish Leadership and poetry in Spain.

The Jewish Philosophers: Solomon ibn Gabirol; Judah Halevi; Moses
Maimonides

Kabbalah.

Reading assignments: Norman Stillman, The Jews in Arab Lands (selections
will be assigned in class)

David Blumenthal, Understanding Jewish Mysticism
(The General Introductions in both vols.)

Harry Wolfson, "Maimonides and Halevi: A Study in Typical Jewish
Attitudes towards Greek Philosophy in the Middle
Ages" (handout in class)

III. Weeks 9-12:   <u>Reading and Discussion of Philosophical and Mystical Texts</u>

Selections will be assigned and discussed in class from:

E. Goodman, ed., <u>Rambam: Readings in the Philosophy of Moses Maimonides</u>
David Blumenthal, <u>Understanding Jewish Mysticism</u> Vols I-II

For background reading:

Leo Straus, "<u>The Law of Reason in the Kuzari</u>"
(handout in class)

H. Liebeschuetz, "Judaism and Jewry in the Social Doctrine
of Thomas Aquinas" (article: handout in class)

Instructor: Jochanan H. A. Wijnhoven
Neilson Library 3/12   X660

Harold Garrett-Goodyear
Mount Holyoke College

Women's Studies 102 (History 114/Anthro 102)
Spring Semester, 1982-83

Women, Spirituality and Power:
Cross-Cultural Comparisons

How are the changing and varied experiences of women related
to notions of the sacred? How are the very distinctions between
"women" and "men" affected by such notions? In what ways is
spirituality a source of power for women, or a limit to their
power? Can we develop a vocabulary for understanding women's
experience in worlds which know no distinction between sacred and
profane? Case studies from several cultures, and from several
periods, will be used to address these questions. The critical
and self-reflective use of analytical and interpretative
approaches of anthropology and History will be central to this
inquiry into the rleationships between women's experiences and the
boundaries between sacred and profane in various cultures.

   Joan Cocks, Politics (603 Library,x2334: Thurs, 3-5)
   Anne Edmonds, Librarian
   Harold Garrett-Goodyear,History (205 Lib,x2377: Thurs,1:30-3:30)
   Eugenia Herbert,History (616 Lib, x2094: Mon & Wed, 4-6)
   Andrew Lass, Anthropology/Sociology (204 Merrill,Mon & Wed, 1-3)

     Books recommended for purchase are available from the College
Bookstore. In each unit of the syllabus, some, perhaps most,
reading assignments will be found in packets of multilithed
materials, also available for puchase from the bookstore. One
copy of each packet will also be found on Library Reserve.

     Classes will ordinarily meet Tuesday and Thursday mornings
from 10:00 a.m. until 12:15, in Skinner 214. In addition, hour
sections will meet Tuesday afternoons at 2:00 and 3:00 in Library
203 and Thursday afternoons, also at 2:00 and 3:00, in places to
be announced. During the first week, you will choose one section
to which you will belong for the remainder of the semester.

     Each section will divide itself further into four cells, of 2
or 3 students apiece, for collective projects important to class
meetings and section discussions. Such projects will include
finding and supplying your colleagues with background information
on people, events, or issues, and also framing questions or theses
for analysis and debate in sections.

                  Schedule of Classes and Assignments:

Feb. 1.   An Introduction to people, sources, and approaches.

Feb. 3.   An Introduction to topics, issues, and the course format.

I.Christianity and Women in Late Medieval Europe

In late medieval Europe, Christianity offered both men and women a source of meaning and purpose to their lives; indeed, it was perhaps the principal source of meaning. But Christian women did not find the same meaning and purpose in the worship of the Christian God that men found there , and their experiences as Christains were by means identical to those of Christian men. By examining the teachings and institutions of the Christian Church in the 14th and 15th centuries, we shall try to understand ways in which women were offered different choices and subjected to different restraints than those offered, or imposed upon, men; and by examining evidence from or about several women prominent in the history of late medieval Christianity, we shall try to understand te distinctive features of women's experiences within the observance of Christianity and discover the distinctive contributions that women made to the shaping of Christian faith and practice. On the one hand, we shall be looking at the ways in which Christianity, as a central, even dominant institution and ideology within medieval society, assigned different roles and possibilities for women as opposed to men; on the other hand, we shll attempt to discover how differences between men and women in medieval society shaped Christianity , and the way in which Christianity interpreted for human beings the meaning of their lives.

(Please note that Library Reserve holds not only one copy of the two books recommended for purchase and one copy of the packet of multilithed materials for this unit, but also, for many of the selections assigned below, a copy of the full work from which passages were taken. Should you wish to read further in any of the works mentioned below, you may find it or related works on Reserve. Remember, however, that these works are only a fraction of those to be found in our library and other libraries in the Valley.

Feb. 8.   Guest Lecture: Caroline Walker Bynum (History, University
          of Washington, and author of Jesus_as_Mother
               "The Importance of Perspective: A Medievalist
                 Looks at Gender and Religion"
          New York Room, 10:00 a.m. Following her lecture on
          "Perspective", Prof. Bynum will give an informal
          introduction to Christianity and mysticism in the high
          and late middle ages for students and faculty in WS-102.

          Reading: Julian of Norwich, Revelations_of_Divine_Love
                   Richard Rolle, The_Fire_of_Love
                   "From the Sarum_Missal" and other readings from
                      Chaucer:Sources_and_Backgrounds*

Prepare for February 10 a 2-3 page essay in which you analyse the language of a passage which you choose from Julian of Norwich's Revelations. Julian is not "typical," and we cannot generalize from her experience to that of all medieval mystics, nor can we generalize about all medieval women.on the basis of her

meditations on a series of visions. If, however, we work with
care but imagination from her language, from the terms and images
that she used, to her (often unarticluated) convictions and
assumptions about reality, we can begin to understand the
distinctive features of her experience and the world of conduct
and consciousness in which such experience occurred. Your essay
should lay out for a reader at least one feature or aspect of
Julian's world that, once understood or grasped, would give us a
fuller understanding of what she said, how she said it, and why
she said it; but you should also rely on what she said, and how,
to support your point about Julian's world. (This is not, let us
emphasize, a research paper; use Julian herself to understand
Julian.)

Feb.10. Late Medieval Society and Women's Choices.

> Reading: David Herlihy,"The Natural History of Medieval
> 111   Women" and "Women in Medieval Society." *
>   "Life of St. Umilta"*
>   Selections from The Book of Margery Kempe*

During class on Feb. 10, Anne Edmonds will introduce us to
some of the strategies and tactics of research on women,
spirituality, and power, and give us some pointers on using the
Library to teach ourselves about medieval people -- or any other
people, for that matter. After her introduction, cell groups in
each section should divide up responsibility for finding and
sharing information on the individual mystics or other persons
whom we are reading, and for identifying good books or articles o;
people or issues pertinent to our present discussions. As soon as
possible, each section should have someone able to tell her
colleagues what scholars know or have surmised about the women and
men whose lives we are trying to understand.

Feb.15. Women's Responsibilities and Men's Dependence

> Reading: Selections from Letters of St.Catherine of Siena*
>   Selections from The book of the Knight of La Tour
>   Landry*
>   Selections from The Paston Letters*
>   R.H.Hilton, "Women in the Village"*

Feb.16. (Optional) Film: Robert Bresson,"The Trail of Jeanne d'Arc"
    at 4:00 and 7:00 p.m., Library 210.

Feb.17. Warfare and Visions, Holiness and Witchcraft

> Reading: Joan of Arc by Herself and Her Witnesses*
>   Christine de Pisan, "Ditie de Jehanne D'Arc"*
>   "The Confession of Prous Boneta"*
>   "The Inquisition of Toulouse"*
>   "Trial of Giovanna Monduro of Salussola"*

Feb.22. The Meaning of Power

Reading: Eleanor McLaughlin, "Women, Power and the Pursuit
         of Holiness"*
         Elizabeth Petroff, "Seven Stages to Power"*

    Written Assignment: Relying on readings and classes to
date, write a short essay (max: 5 pages) in which you explain the
meaning of "power" for women in the late middle ages. You should
read McLaughlin and Petroff before writing this essay, but base
your own explanation on the sources that we have read and
discussed during the past three weeks.

****

                   II. Women, Spirituality and Power.
             Spirituality and the Idea of Women's Culture:
             Radical Feminism in the Contemporary Period

Our purpose in this section of the course is to explore the connection between women, spirituality and power as they have taken
form within the feminist movement in the United States. We will
trace the path that has led some women beyond the boundaries of
traditional religions into women centered religious experience.
We will give special attention, however, to the current prominence
of spiritual motifs in the "secular" radical feminist movement. We
will then take a critical look at the notion of a separate women's
culture, the radical feminist celebration of organic nature, and
the feminist attempt to fuse spirituality and sensuousness.Finally
we will compare the concerns of a spiritual feminism with those of
its more single-mindedly political counterparts and predecessors,
and with other forms of critical attack on science, technology and
militarism in advanced industrial society.

Schedule of Readings and Lectures

Feb.24. "The Radical Feminist Critique of Patriarchy and the
          Route out of Traditional Religion": Mary Daly, Beyond God
          The Father

Mar. 1. "The Radical Feminist Critique Continued": Naomi
          Goldenberg, Changing of the Gods

Mar.3.   "Curious Comrades: Critical Social Theory, The New Age
          Movement, and Cultural/Spiritual Feminism": Charlene
          Spretnak, ed., The Politics of Women's Spirituality.
             Spretnak, "Introduction";
             Starhawk, "Witchcraft as Goddess Religion," p.49
             Sojourner, "From the House of Yemanja...",p.57
             Christ, "Why Women Need the Goddess," p. 71
             Starrett,"The Metaphors of Power," p.187
             Inglehart, "Expanding Personal Power...",p.294
             Antonelli, "Feminist Spirituality...", p.399
             Appendix, "Two Debates." p.530

Mar.8.   "Spiritual Feminism Standing Alone": Susan Griffin,
          Woman and Nature

                            255

Mar.10. "Antimonies, Unities and Contradictions": Carolyn Merchant
The Death of Nature: Women, Ecology and the Scientific
Revolution

Written Assignments:

III. Deconstructing Gender

The degree to which sexual identity and genderization are
primarily cultural constructs rather than natural objects provides
the key problem around which this part of the course will be organized. What "male" and "female" means in different societies
requires that one first explore how a particular culture arti-
culates various domains of experience; the distinction between
culture and nature, the concept of the human body as well as the
related conceptualizations and expressions of morality and power,
sickness and ehalth, ghost and spirit, sacred and profane, all of
which exist in concrete, culturally specific ways.
    By looking at how some of the cultures of Papua New Guinea
construct their world through social and symbolic action, you will
be introduced to the basics of the anthropological analysis of
kinship, social and political organization, to some of the methods
involved in the cross-cultural understanding of symbolic systems,
and finally--and most importantly--to some of the controversies
that the anthropological enterprise leads to as we, in the process
of trying to understand others, confront ourselves (e.g. the
'straw men' of feminist anthropology).
    Lectures and discussion will incorporate the assigned reading
material (the READER containing all the articles will be available
at the college bookstore). There are also books of interest on
library reserve, including introductory textbooks to cultural
anthropology.

BOOKS ON LIBRARY RESERVE:

Foucault, M.: The History of Sexuality
Herdt, G. H.: Guardians of the Flutes
MacCormack & Strathern: Nature, Culture and Gender
Ortner 6 Whitehead: Sexual Meanings
Reiter, R. R.: Toward an Anthropology of Women
Rosaldo & Lamphere: Women, Culture & Society
Nanda: Cultural Anthropology; Introductory textbook

Schedule of Classes and assignments:

Mar.15. Discussion.
            Reading: P.Webster,"Matriarchy: A Vision of Power"
         Lecture on Basic Concepts of Anthropology.

Mar.17. Continuation of Lecture on Basic Concepts: Anthropology
                in the Highlands of Paua New Guinea.
         Discussion.

Reading: S. Ortner, "Is Female to Male as Nature is to Culture?"

Mar.29. Lecture: Self, Body and Society in Mt. Hagen.
Reading: Strathern, M.&A., "Popokl: The Question of Morality"; "The Female and Male Spirit Cults in Mount Hagen"; and " Sickness and Frustration in Two New Guinea Highland Societies."

Mar.31. Continuation of Lecture on Self, Body and Society.
Discussion.
Reading: M. Strathern, "No Nature, No Culture: The Hagen Case"
Assignment no. 1 due: An essay in which you apply Anthropological conceptualizations and approaches from readings and discussions of the past two weeks to any topic addressed earlier in this course. 3-5pp

Apr. 5. Discussion.
Reading: J.S. La Fontaine, "The Domestication of the Savage Male"; M. Strathern, "Culture in a Netbag: The Manufacture of a Subdiscipline in Anthropology"

April 7. Assignment no. 2 due: An essay in which you identify an issue, concept, argument, or theme in one of the articles read during this unit, and then use the library to find another article or further material relevant to that issue, etc. References in footnotes may be used to lead you to further material. With the additional material in hand, write a critical essay on the issue, etc. 5-7 pp.

****

IV. Women, Spirituality and Power
AFRICA AND AFRO-AMERICA

April 7. Introduction to women in African cultures.

Reading: Evans-Pritchard, "The Position of Women in Primitive Societies and in our own,"(1955)
Edwin Ardener, "Belief and the Problem of Women" (N.B., the Ardeners will speak at Mount Holyoke in early April, inshallah.)
The class on April 7 will include an introduction to research on Women in Africa by Anne Edmond. A Case Study: Women and Power among the Senufe. A model of equilibrium?

April 11 Monday   Lecture: Anita J. Glaze: "Women, Creativity
8.00 p.m . Gamble   and Power in Africa"

April 12   Discussion with Anita Glaze
Reading: Glaze, A. Art and death in a Senufo Village as much as you can but concentrate on Ch 2 and 3.

Glaze, A. "Women Power and Art in a Senufo
Village." African Arts. VIII: 3 (Spring,1975)
on reserve

April 14   Cults of Possession, Affliction and Healing in
Africa.
Readings: Iris, Berger, "Rebels or Status Seekers?
Women as Spirit Mediums in East Africa
Martha, Binford, "Julia: An East African
Diviner"
Anita, Spring, "Epidemology of Spirit
possession among the Luvale of Zambia"
Susan, Middleton Keurn, "Convivial Sister
hood: Spirit Mediumship and Client-Core
Networks among Black South African Women."

April 19   Cults of Possession, Affliction and Healing in Afro-
America.
Guest Lecturer, Monica Gorden.
Readings: Leonard Barret, "Healing and Medicine in
Jamaica," and "Witchcraft and Psychic Phenomena
in Jamaica" (From the Sun and Drum. African Roots
in Jamaica)
Monica, Schuler, "Central Africans in St.
Thomas-in-the East" (from Alas Alas Kongo.)
Maureen Warner Lewis, "The Nkuyu: Spirit
Messengers of the Kumina"
Yvonne Daniel, "The Potency of Dance: A
Haitian Examination"
W.F. Bradford, "Puerto Rican Spiritism:
Contrasts in the Sacred and the Profane"
Film: "To Serve the Gods"

April 21   Change in African and Afro-American Religions

Reading: John Q. Anderson," The New Orleans Voodoo Ritual
Dance and its Twentieth-Century Survivals"(1960)
Molly Dougherty, "Southern Lay Midwives as
Ritual Specialists" (1978)
Toni Cade Bambara, The Salt Eaters (excerpt)

Written Assignment: A 5-6 page paper on a specific cult or
religious movement and the position of women in it.
Use bibliographies and refence librarians to find
material.

V. Final Reflections and Generalizations

April 26 and 28. How are we to analyze and explain what appears
to be the universal phenomenon of women's subordination to men?
For most of this semester, our readings and discussions have
emphasized those ways in which women have enjoyed access to power.
But is Ortner perhaps correct, in thinking that it is necessary to
account for universal occurrence of men's dominance of women?

As a starting point, we should identify the constraints under which women live in our own world; from there, we can turn to late medieval, AFrican, and Melpa people, to ask what patterns of dominance and subordination appear in the evidence and readings that we have examined earlier this semester.

May 3 and 5. We have been asking questions about women, power and spirituality -- but central to all of our discussions have been the distinctive experience and vision of women themselves. Why are we and others asking questions about women today, and why have people not asked such questions before?

Is it indeed appropriate to ask questions of this sort within the academy? What difference will it, or should it make to the academy, when we ask them. Finally, is there yet, or can there be, a feminist history? a feminist anthropology? (Marilyn STrathern's work may be usefully reconsidered at this point, along with Edwin Ardener's essay; so also might we look back at Caroline Bynum's lecture.)

DANTE AND HIS WORLD
Professor Robert Raymo and Staff
New York University

The purpose of this course is to provide a comprehensive introduction to late medieval culture, using Dante, its foremost literary artist, as a focus. Its orientation is strongly interdisciplinary. Attention will be given not only to the literature, art and music, but also to the political, religious and social developments of the time, as well as to new philosophical and scientific currents. Particular emphasis will be placed on the continuity of the western tradition, especially on the classical backgrounds of medieval culture and its transmission to the modern world. Cinematic recreations, documentaries, and other visual aids will be used, and field trips to museums will be taken, as appropriate.

Lectures

September 14: Introduction
          16: Dante: His life and Work
              (Prof. Raymo)
          21: Dante: His life and Work (Raymo)
          23: Florence in Dante's Time: A guided tour by
              Giovanni Villani (Prof. Hicks)
          28: Florence in Dante's Time: Merchants and Bankers:
              The Economic Background (Hicks)
          30: Florence in Dante's Time: Magnati e Popolani:
              The Social and Political Background (Hicks)
October   5: Florence in Dante's Time: Medieval Christianity
              Urbanized: Religion in Politics and Popular Culture
              (Hicks)
           7: Art and Architecture in Florence (Prof. Bober)
          12: Art and Architecture in Florence (Bober)
          14: Dante's Political Theory (Prof. Claster)
          19: Dante's Political Theory (Claster)
          21: Dante and Medieval Learning: The Classical
              Tradition (Claster)
          26: The Christian Tradition and the Philosophy of
              Man: Augustine (Raymo)
          28: Boethius and the Tradition of Fame (Raymo)
November   2: Election Day: Holiday
           4: Modes of Mysticism and the Theology of the Soul
              (Raymo)
           9: The Ethical System of Aquinas (Raymo)
          11: Art, Music, and Scholasticism (Prof. Roesner)
          16: Music and Lyrics in Dante's Florence (Roesner)
          18: The Rise of Humanism: Transition to Modern World
              (Prof. Weinapple)
          23: Vision and Voyage (Weinapple)
          25: Thanksgiving: Holiday
          30: Symbol and Allegory (Weinapple)

December 2: Love and Literature (Weinapple)
7: God and Knowledge (Raymo)
9: Dante and Contemporary Literature (Raymo)
14: Dante's Influence (Raymo)
16: Scholasticism and Science (Prof. Bornstein)
21: Dante and Science (Bornstein)
23: Resume

Readings and Assignments

Readings will be assigned from the following texts:
1. Portable Dante
2. Dante, On World Government
3. D. Waley, The Italian City Republic
4. A. P. Entreves, Dante as Political Thinker
5. Boethius, The Consolation of Philosophy, De institutione musica, De institutione arithmetica
6. E. Panofsky, Renaissance and Renascences
7. J. LeClerq, The Love of Learning and the Desire for God
8. Giorgio Vasare, Lives of the Painters
9. John Pope-Hennesy, Italian Gothic Sculpture
10. James Stubblebine, ed., Giotto: The Arena Frescoes
11. E. Auerbach, Figura
12. C. Singleton, Dante Studies I, Dante Studies II

Listening:

1. Perotin (ca. 1200). Sederunt principes (organum: beginning portion only)
2. Philippe de Vitry (1315). In nova fert--Garrit gallus--Neuma (motet)
3. Anonymous (ca. 1275). Mout me fu grief--Robin m'aime--Portare (motet)
4. Anonymous (ca. 1275) Lai de Kievrefuel (Trouvere lai)
5. Francesco Landini (ca. 1350). Donna s'i' t'o fallito (ballata)
6. Francesco Landini (ca. 1350). Gran piant' agli ochi (ballata)
7. Francesco Landini (ca. 1350). Chosi pensoso (caccia)

Supplementary materials will be distributed or placed on reserve. All students will write two short essays on topics approved by the Director and take a final examination.

THE DEVELOPMENT OF HUMAN CONSCIOUSNESS AND INTELLIGENCE:
EXPLORATIONS IN HISTORIOGRAPHY AND THE PHILOSOPHY OF HISTORY
Elizabeth A. R. Brown
Brooklyn College

How have human consciousness, perception, and
intelligence developed and changed through the centuries?
What explanations have been and can be offered for the
modifications that have occurred? What relationship exists
between these changes and modifications in human
sensibilities and emotions? These are the chief questions
with which this seminar will be concerned. Particular
attention will be paid to the writings of Michel Foucault,
but, in order to understand and assess his point of view,
the seminar will also study, compare, and analyze the
writings of a number of important thinkers who, since early
modern times, have confronted and wrestled with the problems
he discusses. The stands these thinkers take will be
related to the life histories of the individuals who
developed them and to the milieus in which they were
formulated.

The seminar is planned as an essay in exploration and
investigation, as an opportunity for students and faculty
who are interested in these problems to meet together, read
a body of common texts, and discuss and analyze them.
Scholars working on the problems will be invited to attend
meetings of the seminar to discuss their own work and to
participate in our discussions, and I hope that some of the
authors whose works we are reading will be able to be with
us.

REQUIREMENTS

Each student will be asked to write an essay examining
an idea, a thinker, or a group of thinkers: the essay is
not to exceed ten pages in length and must be prepared in
conformity with the MLA Style Sheet. Students will present,
orally, their initial hypotheses and research designs and,
in the final meetings of the seminar, the results of their
investigations. These presentations and the research paper
will be the most heavily weighted components of the course.
Another important requirement of the course will be that
students read the assigned material in advance of each
seminar and participate in class discussion: for reasons
that will be apparent to anyone surveying the list of
readings, this seminar will not and cannot be a lecture
course, and the quality of the results we achieve will
depend on the participation and cooperation of each member
of the seminar. There will be a take-home final examination

which will count for approximately 25% of the final grade.

Copies of the books and ariticles to be assigned will be available on reserve in the Brooklyn College library, although most of the books are available in paperback and have been ordered through the College Bookstore: assigned articles will be available in xeroxed copies. Many participants will have read one or more of the assigned readings, and I encourage them to re-read them as well as to explore additional material related to the topics of the seminar. If you have not investigated the subjects we will be considering, do not be discouraged, and, above all, do not be overwhelmed by the list of readings, since, as you will see, the core of required readings will be manageable. I hope that you will want to do some of the reading before the seminar begins. Particularly appropriate as background are S. I. Hayakawa, Language in Thought and Action; Myron P. Gilmore, Humanists and Jurists: Six Studies in the Renaissance; James D. Watson, The Double Helix, and Francis Crick, Life Itself: Its Origin and Nature (see also the reveiw of this book by Gunther S. Stent in The New York Review of Books, December 3, 1981, pp. 34-36).

MASTER READING LIST
The asterisked readings will constitute the core reading
for the seminar

*The New Science of Giambattista Vico, abridged and tr. from the third edition by T. G. Bergin and M. H. Fisch

Julian Jaynes, The Origin and Consciousness in the Breakdown of the Bicameral Mind, and

for those who have not recently read them, the Iliad and the Odyssey are strongly recommended--either or both.

*Jean Piaget, The Child's Conception of the World, and

*The Moral Judgment of the Child.

*Charles M. Radding, "Evolution of Medieval Mentalities: A Cognitive-Structural Approach," American Historical Review 83 (1978) 577-597, and

*"Superstitions to Science: Nature, Fortune, and the Passing of the Medieval Ordeal," American Historical Review 84 (1979) 945-969.

*F.   Edward Cranz, two unpublished papers discusssing the reorientation of thought and consciousness in the Twelfth Century.

*Elizabeth A. R.   Brown, Review Essay of R.   Howard Bloch, <u>Medieval</u> <u>French</u> <u>Literature</u> <u>and</u> <u>Law</u> (Los Angeles and London, 1977), <u>History</u> <u>and</u> <u>Theory</u> 19 (1980) 319-338, and

*"The Tyranny of a Construct: Feudalism and Historians of Medieval Europe," <u>American</u> <u>Historical</u> <u>Review</u> 79 (1974) 1063-1088, and

"Feudalism Five Years Later," unpublished essay.

*Michel Foucault, <u>The</u> <u>Order</u> <u>of</u> <u>Things:</u>   <u>An</u> <u>Archaeology</u> <u>of</u> <u>the</u> <u>Human</u> <u>Science,</u> and

*<u>The</u> <u>Birth</u> <u>of</u> <u>the</u> <u>Clinic:</u>   <u>An</u> <u>Archaeology</u> <u>of</u> <u>Medical</u> <u>Perception,</u> and

*Discipline and Punishment: The Birth of the Prison, and

*<u>Madness</u> <u>and</u> <u>Civilization,</u> and

*<u>A</u> <u>History</u> <u>of</u> <u>Sexuality,</u> vol. 1, INTRODUCTION.

264

Penelope D. Johnson
New York University

THE CRUSADES: A REASSESSMENT

spring, 1985   G57.2219

This course is designed as a colloquium to explore in great depth the phenomenon of the medieval crusades, attempting to weigh and balance the different perspectives of those involved.

Each student is to assume a _perspective_, for instance, that of a geographic area: France, Spain, the Germanies, Byzantium; or of a power: the papacy, the Holy Roman Empire; or of an ethnic group: the Jews, the Arabs; or of a problem: the crusade as economic event. Whatever the perspective adopted, that student is to read particularly in that area from the general reading list and attempt to bring an acute sensitivity to the class discussions. I hope that we can have at a minimum, people to represent the key positions of:

                        western Christendom,
                        Byzantium,
                        the Jews,
                        the Arabs.

The requirements are to do the designated reading and participate in each class discussion. Students will be expected to attend all classes with one unexcused absence. There will be no lectures. In addition, each student will close the course with one of three options:

            a paper of between 12 and 20 pages.
            an oral presentation of 30 minutes.
            a final exam.

Further reading and research to prepare for this project can come from the general reading list or from other sources tracked down by the student.

Graduate Colloquium
New York University
Penelope Johnson
19 University Place
Room 410
598-3322/3

WEEKLY TOPICS AND ASSIGNMENTS FOR
THE CRUSADES: A REASSESSMENT

Feb. 5 INTRODUCTION

Feb. 12 THE OVERVIEW
+Hans Mayer, The Crusades tr. John Gillingham, Oxford
(1972). Read the whole book, and then reread the
appropriate sections each week.

Feb. 19 EPIC REFLECTIONS OF CRUSADING FERVOR
+The Song of Roland, tr. Sayers, Penguin pb.
+The Cid, tr. W. S. Merwin, NAL pb. (1975).
G. E. von Grunebaum, "The World of Islam: The Face of the
Antagonist," Twelfth Century Europe and the
Foundations of Modern Society, ed. M. Clagett et
al.

Feb. 26 "DEUS VULT." THE LAUNCHING OF THE FIRST CRUSADE
+Fulcher of Chartres, A History of the Expedition to
Jerusalem Norton (1969).
+Anna Comnena, The Alexiad, tr. E. R. Sewter, Penguin (1969)
pp. 333-469.

Mar. 5 JEWS AND ARABS DURING THE FIRST CRUSADE
+F. Gabrieli, Arab Historians of the Crusades U. of Ca.
Press (1978) pp. 3-55.
+The Jews and the Crusaders ed. Shlomo Eidelberg, U.
Wisconsin Press (1977).
+Robert Chazan ed. Church, State, and Jew in the Middle
Ages Behrman pb (1980) pp. 57-63, 113-4.
S. D. Goitein, "Contemporary Letters on the Capture of
Jerusalem," Journal of Jewish Studies 3 (1952).

Mar. 12 ARAB CULTURE
+Usamah Ibn, Memoirs of an Arab-Syrian Gentleman ed. Philip
Hitti AMS Press (1964).
Norman Daniel, "The Developmnent of the Christian
Attitude to Islam," Dublin Review 231 (1957).
W. M. Watt, "Islamic Conceptions of the Holy War," in
The Holy War, ed. Thomas Murphy (1976) pp. 141-156.

Mar. 19 ST. BERNARD AND THE SECOND CRUSADE
+Odo of Deuil, De profectione Ludovici VII in orientem ed.
Virginia Berry, Norton (1948).
Gabrieli, pp. 56-84.
Chazan, pp. 100-8, 114-117.
Constable, "The Second Crusade as Seen by Contemporaries,"
Traditio 9 (1953).

Mar. 26   THE CRUSADE OF THE KINGS
          Gabrieli, pp. 87-252.
          Chazan, pp. 157-165, 309-312.
          Chazan, "Emperor Frederick I, the Third Crusade, and the
               Jews," Viator 8 (1977).
          Gavin Langmuir, "The Jews and the Archives of Angevin
               England: Reflections on Medieval Anti-Semitism,"
               Traditio 19 (1963).
          Amboise, Crusade of Richard Lion-Heart pp. 31-53.

April 9   THE IDEAL ASTRAY: THE FOURTH CRUSADE
          +Villehardouin, in Chronicles of the Crusades, tr. Shaw,
               Penguin (1963).
          +Donald Queller, The Fourth Crusade, U. Pa. Press (1978).

April 16 WOMEN AND CHILDREN
          James Brundage, "The Crusader's Wife," and "The Crusader's
               Wife Revisited," Studia Gratiana 12 & 14 (1967).
          Peter Raedts, "The Children's Crusade of 1212," Journal of
               Medieval History 3 (1977).
          Maureen Purcell, "Women Crusaders: A Temporary Canonical
               Aberration?" In L. O. Frappell Principalities, Powers
               and Estates (1979).
          Hans Mayer, "Queen Melisende of Jerusalem," Dumbarton Oaks
               Papers 26 (1972).

April 23 ST. LOUIS AND THE CRUSADE.
          +Joinville in Chronicles of the Crusades ed. Shaw.
          Gabrieli, pp. 284-304.
          Chazan, pp. 213-220, 283-287.

April 30 THE LAST STAGES
          Gabrieli, pp. 307-350.
          Chazan, pp. 319-322.
          H. A. R. Gibb, "The Influence of Islamic Culture on Medieval
               Europe," Bulletin of the John Rylands Library 38
               (1955).
          A. Luttrell, "The Crusade in the Fourteenth Century," Europe
               in the Late Middle Ages, ed. John R. Hale (1965).

May 7   ORAL PRESENTATIONS

May 14 ORAL PRESENTATIONS

    All books and articles are on reserve in Bobst (books under the
authors' names, and copied articles under P. Johnson).
    All books designated + have been ordered at the Book Center.
    All   articles are also in my box in the history department
where they can be read in the department lounge, or signed out for a
brief time only to be copied. Please be considerate of each other.

THE CRUSADES: A REASSESSMENT
G57.2219

PRIMARY SOURCES:

ISLAM:

Anonymous Syriac Chronicle. "The First and Second Crusades from an
  Anonymous Syriac Chronicle," tr. A. S. Tritton, notes H. A. R.
  Gibb, Journal of the royal Asiatic Society (1933) (1st & 2nd)
Ayyubids, Mamlukes and Crusaders: Selections from the Tarikh al-Duwal
  we'l-Muluk of Ibn al-Furat, tr., U. and M.C. Lyons 2 vols.,
  (1971).
Beha ed-Din ibn Shedad, Life of Saladin, tr. C. W. Wilson, Palestine
  Pilgrim's Texts Society (1897) (3rd).
The Autobiography of Ousâna, 1095-1188, ed. G.R. Potter (1929).
**Gabrieli, Francesco, ed., Arab Historians of the Crusades U. of
  California Press (reprinted 1978) (all crusades).
Ibn-al-Qualanisi, The Damascus Chronicle of the Crusades Extracted
  and tr. by H. A. R. Gibb, "University of London Historical
  Series," no. 5, (1932).
Ibn Battuta, The Travels of Ibn Battuta, a.d. 1325-1354 tr. H. A. R.
  Gibb, 2 vols. ser. 2, nos. 110, 117, (1958 & 1962).
Ibn Jubayr, The Travels of Ibn Jubrayr, tr. R. Broadhurst, (1952)
Nâsir-i-Khusrau, Diary of a Journey through Syria and Palestine in
  1047 tr. G. le Strange, PPTS (1893) (pre-crusades).
**Usamah Ibn, Munqidh, Memoirs of an Arab-Syrian Gentleman or An
  Arab Knight in the Crusades ed. Philip K. Hitti, (1964)(2nd)

THE JEWS:

Abu'l Faraj, The Chronography of Gregory Abuy'l Faraj, The Son of
  Aaron, The Hebrew Physician Commonly Known as Bar Hebraeus, tr.
  Ernest A. Wallis Budge, vol. 1, (1932). (1st)
**Chazan, Robert ed., Church, State, and Jew in the Middle Ages
  (1980).
Marcus, Jacob R. ed., The Jew in the Medieval World; A Source Book:
  315-1791 (1975).
**The Jews and the Crusaders: The Hebrew Chronicles of the First and
  Second Crusades ed. Shlomo Eidelberg U. of Wisconsin hb.,
  (1977)(1st & 2nd).

THE CHRISTIANS: edited collections

Bedier, J. P. Aubry, Les chansons de croisade (1909)
Brundage, James ed., The Crusades: A Documentary Survey (1962) (all
  crusades).
Krey, August ed., The First Crusade: The Accounts of Eye-Witnesses
  and Participants (1921) (1st)
Munro, Dana C. ed., Letters of the Crusaders (1894) (all crusades).
Pernoud, Regine ed., The First Crusade (1st)

THE CHRISTIANS:

**Amboise, The Crusade of Richard Lion-Heart tr. M. J. Hubert.(repr. 1976) (3rd)
**Anna Comnena, The Alexiad Penguin pb., (1969), (1st)
Archer, T. ed., The Crusade of Richard I, (1889), (3rd).
De expugnatione Lyxbonensi, tr., D. W. David, (1936)
Emerton, E. ed., Correspondence of Pope Gregory VII (1st)
**Fulcher of Chartres, A History of the Expedition to Jerusalem, 1095-1127, tr. F. R. Ryan, ed. Harold Fink Norton pb., (1969). (1st)
Helmold, The Chronicle of the Slavs, tr. F. J. Tschan, (1935).
**Joinville and Villehardouin, Chronicles of the Crusades tr. M. R. B. Shaw (1963) Penguin pb., (4th, 7th & 8th)
Kohler, Charles ed. "Un sermon comméemoratif de la prise de Jérusalem par les croisés, attributé à Foucher de Chartres," Revue de l'Orient latin 7 (1901), 158-64. (1st)
**Odo of Deuil, De profectione Ludovici VII in orientem: The Journey of Louis VII to the East ed. Virginia Berry, Norton pb., (1948) (2nd)
Otto of Freising and his continuator, Rahewin, The Deeds of Frederick Barbarossa Norton pb. (1956) (3rd).
"Pèlerinage en Palestine de l'Abbesse Euphrosyne, Princesse de Polotsk" tr. de Khitrowo Revue de l'Orient Latin 3 (1896).
Raymond of Aguilers, Raymond of Aguilers, Historia Francorum qui ceperunt Jerusalem, tr. J.; H. and L. L. Hill (1968).
Richard of Devizes, Chronicle of Richard of Devizes of the Time of King Richard the First, tr. J. T. Appleby (1963) (3rd).
**The Poem of the Cid, tr. W. S. Merwin, (1975) NAL pb. (reconquista).
Tudebode, Peter, Peter Tudebode, Historia Hierosolymitano itinere, tr. J. H. and L. L. Hill (1974).
William of Tyre, William of Tyre: A History of the Deeds done beyond the Sea, tr. E. Babcock and A. C. Krey, 2 vols. (repr. 1971) (1st).

**Designates a work which is required to be read for this course and is on reserve in Bobst.
*Designates a work which is optional, but is on reserve in Bobst.

SECONDARY SOURCES:

Alphandery, P., and A. Dupront, La chrétienté et l'idée de croisade 2 vols, (1954-59).

Atiya, A. S., Crusade, Commerce, and Culture (1962).

Barber, Malcolm, "Lepers, Jews and Moslems: The Plot to Overthrow Christendom in 1321," History 66 (1980).

_____, The Trial of the Templars (1978).

Beebe, B., "The English Baronage and the Crusade of 1270," Bulletin of the Institute of Historical Research 48 (1975).

Blake, E. O., "The Formation of the 'Crusade Idea'", Journal of Ecclesiastical History 21 (1970).

Brundage, James, "'Cruce Signari': The Rite for Taking the Cross in England," Tradition 22 (1966).

_____, Canon Law and the Crusader.

** _____, "The Crusader's Wife," and "The Crusader's Wife Revisited," Studia Gratiana 12 (1967) and 14 (1967).

_____, "The Army of the First Crusade and the Crusade Vow: Some Reflections on a Recent Book," Medieval Studies 33 (1971).

Bulliet, Richard W., Conversion to Islam in the Medieval Period: An Essay in Quantitative History (1979).

Burns, Robert I., Islam under the Crusaders. Colonial Survival in the Thirteenth-Century Kingdom of Valencia (1973).

_____, Muslims, Christians, and Jews in the Crusader Kingdom of Valencia (1984).

Cahen, Claude, "Une lettre d'un prisonnier musulman des Francs de Syrie," in Melanges Edmond-René Labande (1974).

Christiansen, E., The Northern Crusades (1980).

**Constable, Giles, "The Second Crusade as Seen by Contemporaries," Traditio 9 (1953).

Cowdrey, H. E. J., "Pope Urban II's Preaching of the First Crusade," History 55 (1970).

Crocker, Richard L., "Early Crusade Songs," in T. P. Murphy, ed., The Holy War (1976).

Daniel, Norman, Islam and the West: The Making of an Image (1962).

** _____, "The Development of the Christian Attitude to Islam," Dublin Review 231 (1957).

Delaville le Roulx, J., La France en Orient au XIVe siècle: Expéditions du maréchal Boucicaut 2 vols. (1885-6).

Duncalf, F. "The Peasants' Crusade," AHR 26 (1920-1).

Erdmann, Carl, The Origin of the Idea of Crusade, tr. of 1935 ed. notes by Baldwin and Goffart (1977).

Favreau, M.-L., Studien zur Fruhgeschichte des Deutschen Ordens (1974).

**Gibb, H. A. R., "The Influence of Islamic Culture on Medieval Europe," Bulletin of the John Rylands Library 38 (1955).

Hehl, E.-D., Kirche und Kreig im 12. Jahrhundert (1980).

Housley, Norman, The Italian Crusades: The Papal-Angevin Alliance and the Crusades Against Christian Lay Powers 1254-1343 (1982).

Jacoby, D. "Crusader Acre in the Thirteenth Century: Urban Layout and Topography," Studi Medievali 3rd ser., 20 (1979).

Jordan, William, Louis IX and the Challenge of the Crusade (1979).

Kedar, Benjamin Z., "The Passenger List of a Crusade Ship, 1250: Towards the History of the Popular Element on the Seventh Crusade," _Studi Medievali_, 3rd ser. 13 (1972).
_____, _Crusade and Mission: European Approaches toward the Muslims_ (1984).
Lomax, D. M., _The Reconquest of Spain_ (1978).
_____, _La Orden de Santiago, 1170-1275_ (1965).
**Luttrell, A., "The Crusade in the Fourteenth Century," _Europe in the Late Middle Ages_, ed. J. A. Hale et al. (1965).
Martin, M. E., "The Venetian-Seljuk Treaty of 1220," _EHR_ 95 (1980).
Moorhead, J., "The Earliest Christian Theological Response to Islam," _Religion_ 2 (1981).
**Mayer, Hans, _The Crusades_, tr. John Gillingham (1965).
Munro, D. C. , "The Children's Crusade," _AHR_ 19 (1914).
_____ "A Crusader" _Speculum_ 7 (1932).
*_____ _The Kingdom of the Crusaders_ .
Murphy, Thomas, ed., _The Holy War_ (1976).
Nesbitt, J. W., "The Rate of March of Crusading Armies in Europe: a Study and Computation," _Traditio_ 19 (1963).
O'Callaghan, J. F., _The Spanish Military Order of Calatrava and its Affiliates_ (1975).
Pennington, Kenneth, "The Rite for taking the Cross in the Twelfth Century," _Traditio_ 30 (1974).
**Purcell, Maureen, "Women Crusaders: A Temporary Canonical Aberration?" in Frappell, L. O. ed., _Principalities, Powers and Estates_,
Pflaum, H., "A Strange Crusaders' Song," _Speculum_ 10 (1935).
Pissard, H., _La guerre sainte en pays chrétien_ (1912).
Prawer, Joshua, _The Crusaders' Kingdom_ (1972).
_____, _The Latin Kingdom of Jerusalem 1099-1291_ (1947).
Prutz, H., _Die geistlichen Ritterorden_ (1908).
Purcell, M., _Papal Crusading Policy 1244-1291_ (1975).
Porges, Walter, "The Clergy, the Poor, and the Non-Combatants on the First Crusade," _Speculum_ 21 (1946).
Queller, Donald E. and Susan Stratton, "A Century of Controversy on the Fourth Crusade," _Studies in Medieval and Renaissance History_ 6 (1969).
**Queller, Donald E., _The Fourth Crusade_ (1978).
**Raedts, Peter, "The Children's Crusade of 1212," _Journal of Medieval History_ 3 (1977).
Richard, Jean, "An Account of the Battle of Hattin, Referring to the Frankish Mercenaries in Oriental Moslem States," _Speculum_ 27 (1952).
Riley-Smith, Jonathan, "Peace Never Established: The Case of the Kingdom of Jerusalem," _Trans. Roy. Hist. Soc.,_ 5th ser., 28 (1978).
_____, "Crusading as an Act of Love," _History_ 65 (1980).
_____, "An Approach to Crusading Ethics," _Reading Medieval Studies_ 6 (1980).
_____, _The Knights of St. John in Jerusalem and Cyrprus, c. 1050-1310_ (1967).
Riley-Smith, Louise and Jonathan, _The Crusades: Idea and Reality 1095-1274_ (1981).
Robinson, I. S. "Gregory VII and the Soldiers of Christ," _History_ 58 (1973).

Roscher, H., Papst Innocenz III und die Kreuzzuge (1969).
Rouche, Michel, "Cannibalisme sacré chez les croises populaire," in
    Yves-Marie Hilaire, ed., La religion popularie (1981).
Roussett, P. "La notion de Chrétienté aux XIe et XIIe siècles," Moyen
    âge 69 (1963).
*Runciman, Steven, A History of the Crusades 3 vols. (1951-54).
Schmandt, R. H., "The Fourth Crusade and the Just-War Theory,"
    Catholic Historical Review 61 (1975).
Setton, Kenneth Meyer, A History of the Crusades 6 vols., (1955-).
_____, The Papacy and the Levant 1204-1571 2 vols. (1976-8).
Sivan, E., L'Islam et la croisade (1968).
Smail, R. C., Crusading Warfare (1097-1193) (1956).
Somerville, Robert, "The Council of Clermont and the First Crusade,"
    Studia gratiana 20 (1976).
Southern, R. W., Western Views of Islam in the Middle Ages (1980).
Spence, Richard, "Pope Gregory IX and the Crusade in the Baltic," EHR
    69 (1983), 1-19.
Sumberg, L. A. M., "The Tafurs and the First Crusade," Medieval
    Studies 21 (1959).
Synan, The Popes and the Jews in the Middle Ages.
Throop, Palmer A., Criticism of the Crusade: A Study of Public
    Opinion and Crusade Propaganda (1940).
Villey, M. La croisade: Essai sur la formation d'une théorie
    juridique (1942).
_____, "L'idée de croisade chez les juristes du moyen âge,"
    Relazioni del X congresso internazionale di scienze storiche:
    III, Storia del medio evo (1955).
**Watt, W. M., "Islamic Conceptions of the Holy War," in Murphy, Holy
    War.
_____, Islam and the Integration of Society (1961).
_____, The Influence of Islam on Medieval Europe (1972).

THE JEWS:

Abrahams, Israel, Jewish Life in the Middle Ages (1969).
Baron,Salo, A Social and Religious History of the Jews 2nd ed. Vols
    3-8 (1957).
_____, Ancient and Medieval Jewish History (1972).
**Chazan, Robert, "Emperor Frederick I, the Third Crusade, and the
    Jews," Viator 8 (1977).
Dunlop, D. M. The History of the Jewish Khazaqrs (1954).
Goitein, S. D., A Mediterranean Society: The Jewish Communities of
    the World as Portrayed in the Documents of the Cairo Geniza vol
    1, Economic Foundations (1968); vol. 2, The Community (1971).
** _____, "Contemporary Letters on the Capture of Jerusalem,"
    Journal of Jewish Studies 3 (1952).
Grant, Michael, The Jews in the Roman World (1973).
**Langmuir, Gavin, "The Jews and the Archives of Angevin England:
    Reflections on Medieval Anti-Semitism," Traditio 19 (1963),
    183-244.
_____, "From Ambrose of Milan to Emicho of Leiningen: The
    Transformation of Hostility against Jews in Northern
    Christendom," Settimane di studio del Centro italiano di studi
    sull' alto medievo (Mar.-Apr., 1978) 26 (1980).

Roth, Cecil and I. H. Levine eds. The Dark Age: Jews in Christian
    Europe 711-1096, vol. 2 of Cecil Roth gen. ed., The World History
    of the Jewish People, Second Series; The Medieval Period (1966).
Starr, Joshua, The Jews in the Byzantine Empire, 641-1204 (1970).
Trachtenberg, Joshua, The Devil and the Jews: The Medieval Conception
    of the Jew and its Relation to Modern Antisemitism (1943).
**von Grunebaum, G. E., "The World of Islam: The Face of the
    Antagonist," in Twelfth Century Europe and the Foundations of
    Modern Society ed. M. Clagett, G. Post, R. Reynolds (1966).

ISLAM:

Andrae, Tor, Mohammed: The Man and his Faith (1960).
Bell, R. Introduction to the Qu'ran (1970).
Daniel, Norman The Arabs and Medieval Europe (1974).
Dunlop, D. M. Arab Civilization to 1500 (1971).
Gabrieli, Francesco, Muhammad and the Conquests of Islam (1968).
Jourani, A. H. and S. M. Stern, eds., The Islamic City (1970).
Ketton, K. M., ed. A History of the Crusades vols. 1 & 2 (1969).
Lewis, Bernard, The Arabs in History (1960).
Lane, E. W. Arabian Society in the Middle Ages (1971).
Lombard, Maurice, The Golden Age of Islam (1975).
Rosenthal, F.I. J., Political Thought in Medieval Islam (1962).
Richards, D. S. ed. Islam and the Trade of Asia (1971).
von Grunebaum, G. E., Medieval Islam (1961).

BYZANTIUM:

Baynes, Norman and H. St. L. B. Moss, eds., Byzantium: An
    Introduction to East Roman Civilization (1961).
Geanakoplos, D. J., Interaction of the Sibling Byzantine and Western
    Cultures in the Middle Ages and Italian Renaissance (300-1600)
    (1976).
Haussig, H. W., A History of Byzantine Civilization (1971).
Hussey, Joan M., The Byzantine World (1961).
_____,ed., The Byzantine Empire in The Cambridge Medieval
    History vol. 4, (1966).
Kempt, Friedrich, ed al., eds., The Church in the Age of Feudalism
    chaps. by Hans-Georg Beck on religion (1969).
Obolensky, Dimitri, The Byzantine Commonwealth (1971).
Ostrogorsky, George, A History of the Byzantine State, 2nd ed.,
    (1968).
Runciman, Steven, The Byzantine Theocracy (1977).

BIBLIOGRAPHY:
Atiya, Azia, The Crusade: Historiography and Bibliography (1976).

NB: Bobst has an excellent collection on the crusades. Look in
the D150-D182, and DS90-135 stacks. You may be able to take out
library books for some of the required reading.

FINAL EXAM
THE CRUSADES: A REASSESSMENT

"This concept of holy war could be exploited or perverted by
colonialists, merchants, and freebooters, kings, popes and republics
only because it retained some meaning in the Latin conscience."
                                        Anthony Luttrell
                            "The Crusade in the Fourteenth Century"

Write a carefully constructed essay which defends or attacks this
statement, being careful to undergird your position with evidence and
sound arguments.

SEMINAR IN MEDIEVAL EUROPE

HISTORY 724
SPRING 1984

JOHN A. NICHOLS
SLIPPERY ROCK UNIVERSITY

I.   TEXTBOOK:

    Norman F. Cantor and Michael S. Werthman (eds.), Medieval Society 400-
1450 (New York: Thomas Crowell, 1972).

II. COURSE SCOPE:

    The intention of this seminar is to offer a survey of the institutional
and cultural developments in Europe from 400 to 1450 by means of selective
readings on persons and events in the medieval civilization. Ideally the
student should already have had some introduction to this time in history
thanks to a Western Civilization survey course, but some association with
the discipline of history and a desire to learn would be sufficient pre-
requisites for the student to comprehend the material covered in this upper
division graduate course.

II. GRADING:

    There will be no examinations in this class. Rather than conduct the
class on a normal lecture/test/research paper method, I want to introduce you
to the medieval civilization by way of a reading seminar. As a consequence,
your final grade will be the average of grades given for short papers written
every other week for the duration of the semester, oral reports and class participation based on common reading assignments.

IV. INDIVIDUAL ASSIGNMENTS:

    Every other week each student will be assigned an individual assignment
which relates to the common reading material in the textbook. The assignments
will be chosen by all students in turn so that everyone will have read approximately the same number of pages of reading and have the opportunity to select
preferential assignments. Once the assignment is read the student will report
on that assignment orally to the class per questions posed by the instructor.

    In addition the student will prepare a three to five page typed paper
answering the following questions for each individual reading assignment:

1) What is the major aim, theme, or intent of the author?

2) What is the nature of the material (give a brief synopsis of the assigned
   pages)?

3) Was the presentation clear and organized?

4) Was the conclusion acceptable given the material?

5) What relationship, if any, did the assignment have to the common reading?

V. CLASS SCHEDULE:

        January 18 – Course Introduction

        January 25 – Lecture/Carolingian Prelude, pp. 4-32

        February 1 – Reports/Written Assignment #1

        February 8 – Lecture/Feudal World, pp. 33-82

        February 15 – Reports/Written Assignment #2

        February 22 – Lecture/Christian Society, pp. 84-122

        February 29 – Reports/Written Assignment #3

        March 14   – Lecture/Commerce & Urban, pp. 124-165

        March 21   – Reports/Written Assignment #4

        April 4   – Lecture/Byzantine, pp. 167-201

        April 11   – Reports/Written Assignments #5

        April 18   – Lecture/Church & State, pp. 203-229

        April 25   – Reports/Written Assignments #6

        May 2   – Lecture/Science & Technology, pp. 230-258

        May 9   – Reports/Written Assignment #7

VI. BREAKDOWN OF GRADES:

The seven written reports will represent 42% of your final grade or 6% per report. The seven oral reports will represent 42% of your final grade or 6% per report. The class discussion from the common reading assignments will represent 16% of your final grade.

VII. ATTENDANCE:

Since sixty percent of your final grade is based on class participation and oral reports, it is necessary for each student to attend every class meeting. If an absence occurs the student will receive no credit for participation unless an individual makeup is scheduled with the instructor.

VIII. EXTRA CREDIT:

Slippery Rock University, along with other Universities, is sponsoring a Conference on Medieval and Renaissance Cultures on April 6 and 7 at Duquesne University in Pittsburgh. Students may add 10 points (10% of the final grade to their final average by attending either one day or both days of the Conference, listening to the major papers presented by the speakers, and writing a three to five page typed paper answering the five questions as posed above in IV except instead of relating the talk to a common reading, relate the talk or talks to the Conference theme: The Courtly Tradition. The program for the Conference will be distributed in class when they become available.

IX. OFFICE HOURS:

        Office: Room 212-K, SWCB
        Hours: 10:30-11:30 M,W,F
                  2:15- 3:15 T, Th

In addition, I will be pleased to meet you by appointment; see me at the break, after class or call (412) 794-7189, 794-7317 for an appropriate day and time.

X. COURSE OBJECTIVES:

The hope of organizing the course in the above way is to familiarize the student with the major themes of the Middle Ages, to expose the student to the diversities of opinion about events which transpired during that era in history, to develop a critical manner of evaluating secondary material, to improve the student's written and oral presentations, to acquaint the student with the major scholars and works of this field of study, and last, but not least, to satisfy those requirements each of you may have in taking this course.

SEMINAR IN MEDIEVAL EUROPE

(Carolingian Prelude)

UNIT I
JOHN A. NICHOLS

HISTORY 724
SPRING 1984

COMMON READING:

Robert Lopez, "The Carolingian Prelude" in Medieval Society (New York:
Thomas Y. Crowell, 1972), pp. 4-32.

INDIVIDUAL ASSIGNMENTS:

Pierre Riche, "Cults and Culture" in Daily Life in the World of Charlemagne trans. by Jo Ann McNamara (Phila.: Univ. of Pennsylvania Press, 1978),
pp. 181-229.   49

Peter Lasko, "The Frankish Church" in Kingdom of the Franks (New York:
McGraw, 1971), pp. 71-129.   59

Lynn White, "Stirrup, Mounted Shock Combat, Feudalism, and Chivalry"
in Medieval Technology and Social Change (Oxford: University Press, 1962),
pp. 1-38.   39

Suzanne Wemple, "Carolingian Marriages" in Women in Frankish Society
(Phila.: University Press, 1981), pp. 75-123.   49

Peter Munz, "King, Government, and Army" in Life in the Age of Charlemagne (New York: Capicorn Books, 1971), pp. 40-79.   40

Archibald Lewis, "The Carolingian Era, 781 to 840," in Emerging Medieval
Europe (New York: Knopf, 1967), pp. 76-109.   34

Eleanor Duckett, "Saints Boniface, Lull, and Leoba" in Wandering Saints
of the Early Middle Ages (New York: Norton, 1964), pp. 193-228.   36

QUESTIONS TO CONSIDER:

1. What are the important facts in your assigned reading?

2. In what way, if any, does your assignment relate to the common reading?

3. Did you find any differences between the facts or interpretations of
   your reading with the common reading?

SEMINAR IN MEDIEVAL EUROPE

(The Feudal World)

UNIT II   HISTORY 724
JOHN A. NICHOLS   SPRING 1984

COMMON READING:

Marc Block, "The Feudal World" in <u>Medieval Society</u> (New York: Thomas Crowell,
1972), pp. 33-82.

INDIVIDUAL ASSIGNMENTS:

C. Stephen Jaeger "The Courtier Bishop in Vitae from the Tenth to the
Twelfth Century" <u>Speculum</u> 58 (April 1983), 291-325.   35

Norman Cantor and Michael S. Werthman, "The Dimensions of Popular Religious
Life" in <u>Popular Culture</u> (New York: Macmillan, 1968), pp. 100-121.   22

Eileen Power, "The Peasant Bodo" in <u>Medieval People</u> (New York: Barnes and
Noble, 1924), pp. 18-38.   21

Ralph Turner, "The Judges of King John: Their Background and Training"
<u>Speculum</u> 51 (July 1976), 447-461.   15

Eileen Power, "The Working Woman" in <u>Medieval Women</u> (Cambridge: University Press, 1975), pp. 53-75.   23

Joseph and Frances Gies, "Small and Big Business" <u>Life in a Medieval City</u>
(New York: Apollo, 1973), pp. 76-108.   33

Michael Mitterauer and Reinhard Sieder, "The Young in the Family" <u>The</u>
<u>European Family</u> (Chicago: Univ. Press, 1982), pp. 93-117.   25

INSTRUCTIONS:

1. After reading your assignment, create a medieval character that you
    can tell the class about.

2. Your character should have a name, dates of birth and death, place
    of inhabitation, responsibilities, obligations, and life-style as
    seen in your reading.

3. You will report your assignment using the first person single
    pronoun and the present verb tense to give a feeling of who you
    are and what your life is like.

4. Details are important as is your ability to answer questions at
    reports end.

SEMINAR IN MEDIEVAL EUROPE

(Persons in the English Aristocracy)

COMMON READING:

Richard W. Southern, "The Bonds of Christian Society" in Medieval Society, pp. 84-112.

INDIVIDUAL READING:

David C. Douglas, William the Conqueror (Berkeley: Univ. of Calif. Press, 1964), pp. 15-30, 181-209, 247-264.

Edward J. Kealey, Roger of Salisbury (Berkeley: Univ. of Calif. Press, 1972), pp. 1-81.

R.H.C. Davis, King Stephen 1135-1154 (Berkeley: Univ. of Calif. Press, 1967), pp. 1-55.

W.L. Warren, Henry II (Berkeley: Univ. of Calif. Press, 1973), pp. 54-149.

William W. Kibler, Eleanor of Aquitaine (Austin: Univ. of Texas Press, 1976), pp. 9-24.

David Knowles, Thomas Becket (Stanford: Standford Univ. Press, 1971), pp. 1-20, 30-70, 135-155.

Sidney Painter, William Marshall (Baltimore: John Hopkin's Press, 1933), pp. 1-81.

INSTRUCTIONS:

1. Introduce your person to the class with a brief summary of their life as given in your assignment.

2. Report on the personality of your character: strengths, weaknesses, etc. by using appropriate illustrations/examples.

3. How did your individual become who they became: education, family, friends, chance.

4. Judge your person's impact on their own time period, as well as for future generations.

SEMINAR IN MEDIEVAL EUROPE

(Medieval Cities)

UNIT IV
JOHN A. NICHOLS

HISTORY 725
SPRING 1984

COMMON READING:

Henri Pirenne, "The Impact of Commerce and Urbanization", in Medieval Society (New York: Thomas Crowell, 1972), pp. 124-166.

INDIVIDUAL ASSIGNMENTS:

Timothy Baker, Medieval London (New York: Praeger Pub., 1970), pp. 27-49. 23

Michael Winch, "Bruges", in Introducting Belgium (London: Methuen, 1964), pp. 25-64. 35

Glanville Downey, Constantinople (Norman, Okla.: Oklahoma Press, 1960), pp. 14-42 and Dean Miller, Imperial Constantinople (New York: John Wiley, 1969), pp. 43-77. 62

Margaret Lebarge, "Paris: The King's Capitol", in Saint Louis (London: Eyre and Spottiswoode, 1968), pp. 155-178. 23

Philip Strait, Cologne in the Twelfth Century (Gainesville, Florida Univ., 1974), pp. 3-43. 40

John Davis, Venice (New York: Newsweek, 1973), pp. 14-47. 33

QUESTIONS TO CONSIDER:

1. Describe your city with reference to demographic data, physical appearance, noted buildings and/or structures, and time period your reading relates to.

2. Describe the major economic characteristics of your city, how money was made, who made it, major goods produced in the city, traded by the city, or imported to the city.

3. Who were the persons with the wealth/power/influence? Who were the persons with the skills/trades? Who were the persons with the poorest/worst chance for economic/social success?

4. What importance did your city have on the economic/political/social/intellectual history of medieval Europe?

SEMINAR IN MEDIEVAL EUROPE

(Heritage of Byzantium)

UNIT V   HISTORY 725
JOHN A. NICHOLS   SPRING 1984

COMMON READING:

   Deno Geanakoplos, "The Heritage of Byzantium," in Medieval Society
(New York: Thomas Crowell, 1972), pp. 167-201.

INDIVIDUAL ASSIGNMENTS:

   Philip Whitting, "Justinian and his Successors" in Byzantium
(New York: New York University Press, 1971), pp. 17-35.   18

   Charles Diehl, "Theodora" in Byzantine Empresses (New York:
Alfred Knopf, 1963), pp. 44-64.   20

   Peter Arnott, "The Church . . . Missionaries and Monks" in The
Byzantines (New York: St. Martin's, 1973), pp. 137-185.   48

   Joan M. Hussey, "Learning and Literature" in The Byzantine World
(London: Hutchinson Univ. Library, 1961), pp. 145-155.   11

   Anna Comnena, The Alexiad (Baltimore Penguin Books, 1969), pp.
frontpiece and 11-21, 73-101, 505-515.   49

   Philip Sherrard, "A Glittering Culture" in Byzantium (New York
Time-Life, 1966), pp. 134-159.   25

DISCUSSION BY YOU:

   1. Report on your reading assignment by giving the important
      information found therein.

   2. How, if at all, does your assignment relate to the common
      reading?

   3. What is the heritage of Byzantium as found in your assign-
      ment?

SEMINAR IN MEDIEVAL EUROPE

(Medieval Religious Life)

UNIT VI   HISTORY 724
JOHN A. NICHOLS   SPRING 1984

COMMON READING:

    Friedrick Heer, "Church and State," in Medieval Society (New York:
Thomas Crowell, 1972), pp. 203-229.

INDIVIDUAL ASSIGNMENTS:

    Wolfgang Braunfels, "The Beginnings" in Monasteries of Western Europe
(Princeton: University Press, 1972), pp. 9-36.   27

    Louis J. Lekai, The Cistercians (Kent: Kent State Press, 1977),
pp. 1-51.   51

    David Knowles, "The Charterhouse of Witham," in Monastic Order in
England (Cambridge: University Press, 1966), pp. 375-391.   17

    Richard Southern, "The Friars," in Western Society and Church in
Middle Ages (New York: Penguin, 1970), pp. 272-299.   27

    Brenda M. Bolton, "Mulieres Sanctae," in Women in Medieval Society
(Phila.: Penn. Press, 1976), pp. 141-158.   17

POINTS TO CONSIDER:

    1. Describe your assignment with reference to the important facts, names,
        dates, etc.

    2. What contributions did the religious orders make to the medieval
        church in particular and medieval society in general?

SEMINAR IN MEDIEVAL EUROPE

(Science and Technology)

UNIT VII
JOHN A. NICHOLS

HISTORY 725
SPRING 1984

COMMON READING:

A.C. Crombie, "Medieval Science and Technology" in Medieval Society
(New York: Thomas Crowell, 1972), pp. 230-258.

INDIVIDUAL ASSIGNMENTS:

Charles H. Gibbs-Smith, The Bayeux Tapestry (London: Phaidon, 1972),
pp. 4-15, plus figures, 52 slides, 1 tray.   30

Allan Temko, Notre Dame of Paris (New York: The Viking Press, 1952),
pp. 3-14, 114-153, ____ slides.   52

Hans Jantzen, "The Exterior of Cathedrals" High Gothic (Hamburg:
Minerva Press, 1962), pp. 98-156, ____ slides.   58

Ronald Sheridan and Anne Ross, Gargoyles and Grotesques (Boston:
Graphic Society, 1975), pp. 11-22, plus figures, 12 slides.   31

June Osborne, Stained Glass in England (London: Frederick Muller,
1981), pp. 7-41 and James R. Johnson, The Radiance of Chartres (New
York: Random House, 1965), pp. 67-79, ____ slides, 1 tray.   48

INSTRUCTIONS:

1. You will receive two grades for this assignment.

2. Your first will be a summary of your individual reading with
   the focus on the technique and meaning behind what they did
   rather than exactly what they did.

3. The second grade will be your discussion of the slides given
   to you using the individual reading assignments as your guide.

   a. You may use other books to help with your description,
      other slides too.

   b. You need not use all the slides I gave you, pick the ones
      you want to talk about and give them to me before your oral
      report.

   c. I want a concise, creative 5 to 10 minute description not a
      dissertation.

BEGINNING AND ORGANIZING RESEARCH TOPICS IN WOMEN'S STUDIES
Elizabeth Petroff
University of Massachusetts

Phase One: Topic and primary sources. Documents.

Step 1: Acquire a small notebook to carry with you in which you will write down everything you look up, take notes on readings, etc. Later you will transfer this information to notecards, outlines. etc.

Step 2: Identify your topic. Examples of topics:
a. an individual woman, eg. Margery Kempe of Lynn, England, wrote 1st autobiography in English.
b. a movement founded by women or participated in by women collectively, eg. beguines in Belgium in 12th century, Marie d'Oignies and her followers in 12th century France.
c. a critical problem in interpretation, eg. literacy of women especially nuns, in the 13th century the role of women in the Christianization of Roman culture in the 4th century. Define for yourself the poles of the argument: women were highly educated/women were almost illiterate; women's influence in converting Rome was indispensible/negligible. Keep your eyes open for evidence used to support these positions.
A topic is elastic—you can shrink or expand it depending on how much information you learn is available. Limits in time, geography, numbers of people, etc.

Step 3: Learn where the primary sources are for your topic. Identify area or type.

a. biography
b. literature
c. history of religion
d. social history
e. arts

Step 4: Check out bibliographies that will give names and locations of collections of primary sources or documents. Begin with Bibliographies on bibliographies, and Paetow, Guide to the Study of Medieval History.

a. biography—start with Dictionary of Christian Biography and Dictionary of Saintly Women. Other collections, esp. hagiographical, in Paetow.
b. literature. Consult Fisher, The Medieval Literature of Western Europe. Fisher is organized according to national literature; useful to get an overview of how a writer fits into general literary picture.
c. history of religion. Consult Paetow, Eckenstein, Women Under Monasticism.
d. social history. Consult Paetow.
e. arts. Check art and architecture section in reference room.

285

Step 5: Getting your hands on the primary sources.

    a. After you have identified the editions of primary
sources you want, consult the card catalog.
    b. Go to National Union Catalog. Look up volume you want.
This is a catalog of all printed books that exist somewhere
in libraries in the US; below each entry for a book, there
is a code which tells you which US libraries own the book.
This is what you need to order the book through interlibrary
loan. If the book is relatively near, and you think you can
go to the library to use it, ask the reference librarian for
a letter of reference to that library. This will introduce
you as a serious student and will simplify using their
resources.

Phase Two: Secondary Sources. Locating, reading, assessing
scholarship; building a useful bibliography.

Step 1: back to the bibliographies to locate journals in your
field, recent monographs and books on you topic, and so on.

Basic categories of bibliographies:

    a. medieval. _International Medieval Bibliography,
Quarterly Checklist of Medievalia, International Guide to
Medieval Studies_. Journals: _Medieval Studies, Speculum,
Viator, Medium Aevum_.
    b. Women's Studies annual bibliographies.
    c. literature. _Modern Language Association Annual
Bibliography_.
    d. religion. _Index to Religious Literature_. Journals of
religious orders, _Church History_.

Step 2: Getting Started on Your Reading.

By now you should know four or five journals that publish in
your topic area, and you will have a short list of books and
articles that deal with your topic in some way, often rather
peripherally. Now—work backwards chronologically, from
most recent publications to older ones, and beginning with
articles, then going to books. Begin with articles because
they are more up-to-date, get published much faster then
books, smaller journals will have more recent material and
will take more risks in what they publish than will large
respectable journals. Your real bibliography begins in the
footnotes to interesting articles and books. One or two
good recent articles will give you clues concerning debates
on your topic, will summarize available evidence and how
that evidence has been interpreted. Articles can tell you
what is worth reading in books written decades ago, and will
prepare you for the bias in a particular scholar's work.

Step 3: Recording Your Progress. Write down everthing you encounter, even dead ends, in your notebook. You may need this information to retrace your steps. Do not worry about organizing your notebook--it's just a catch-all.

Notecards: I put bibliography on notecards, and I try to use different size cards for books and articles, and different colors for different topics.

Notes on Reading: summaries of articles can go on a large notecard or on a separate piece of paper. What you want is something you can file and find later. File folders for general categories are useful at this point. So are xeroxes of articles if you can afford them.

Step 4: Evaluating Your Information.

a. historical/biographical data: dates, countries, history of person or movement. Where does this historical/biographical evidence come from? Reliable source?
b. sources for further information?
c. How is information used? Basis of argument? Do different scholars interpret same bit of evidence differently? How can you make an argument?

Professor Gabrielle Spiegel
University of Maryland

HISTORICAL WRITING IN THE MIDDLE AGES

This course is an undergraduate seminar. No one actually reads all
These texts, but we do cover quite a few in the first part of the
course, and then each student writes a fairly lengthy paper on a single
text selected from the genres outlined in the syllabus. Each student
presents his/her paper to the class and all students are responsible for
reading each other's papers, which are handed out the week before any
given presentation.

Week I: Introduction: Principles of Greek and Roman Historiography

      read: Collingwood, <u>The Idea of History</u>

Week II: The Bible: The Historicity of Sacred Life

      read: <u>New Testament:</u>

         The Gospel according to St. Matthew

         St. Paul, I Corinthians

         Collingwood, The Idea of History, pt. II, pp. 46-56

         Erich Auerbach, "The Arrest of Peter Valomeres," in <u>Mimesis,</u>
           pp. 50-76

Week III: History as Ancilla to Christian Apologetics: The Chronology of
               Sacred Life

      read: Eusebius, <u>The History of the Church from Christ to Constantine</u>
         Bks. 1-3; pp. 31-153; Bks. 8-10, pp. 327 -414

Week IV: God and His Nation Elect: The Ecclesiastical Histories of Western
            European Peoples

      read: Bede, A History of the English Church and People

                   or

         Gregory of Tours, <u>History of the Franks</u>

                   or

         Paul the Deacon, <u>History of the Lombards</u>

288

Part Two: Evolution of Historical Genres

Biography in the Classical Style:

Einhard, The Life of Charlemagne

Biography in the Christian Style:

Gesta Stephani,The Deeds of Stephen, King of England,
ed. K.R. Potter (Medieval Texts, 1955)

Helgaud, Life of Robert the Pious, trans. into French by R.-H. Bautier

History as Epic:

The Song of Roland

Snorri Sturluson, Helmskringla: History of the Kings of Norway

The Song of Igor's Campaign

Guillaume d'Orange, The Coronation of Louis

History and Romance:

Wace, Roman de Rou,

Geoffrey of Monmouth, History of the Kings of Britain [as a source
of later romance themes, rather than a romance histroy]

Gaimar, L'Estoire des Engles in Rolls Series, vol 91 (Part two
contains an English translation)

Chronicles of the Crusades:

Villehardouin, Conquest of Constantinople

Joinville, The Life of Louis IX

Both of the above texts can be found in English in: Chronicles of
the Crusade (Penguin)

Chronicles of the Crusades cont.

>   Odo of Deuil, De Profectione Ludovici Septimi in Orientem
>   Engl. Translation Virginia Berry [Columbia Records of
>   Civilization]

History and Politics in the 12th Century: The Dignity of the Secular World:

>   Otto of Freising, The Deeds of Frederick Barbarosa

>   Ordericus Vitalis, The Ecclesiastical History of England trans.
>   Majorie Chibnall

>   Suger, Life of Louis the Fat (transcript available from me; also
>   available in French)

>   William of Malmesbury, Historia Novella (New History) trans. K.R. Potter

>   Nelson, 1955

>   William of Newburgh, The History of William of Newburgh trans. Appleby

Hagiography in a Secular Mode:

>   The Chronicle of Jocelyn of Brakelond concerning the acts of Samson
>   Abbot of Bury St. Edmunds, trans. Butler, 1949

>   Daniel Walter, The Life of Allred of Rievaulx, trans. Powicke,
>   1950

>   Adam of Eynsham, The Life of Saint Hugh of Lincoln, trans. Doule
>   and Farmer, 2 vols. 1961-2

Autobiography:

>   Abelard, Historia Calamitatum The Story of Abelard's Adversities
>   trans. Muckle

>   Christina of Maryate, The Life of Christina of Markyate, trans.
>   C.H. Talbot, 1959 [not exactly an autobiography, but useful
>   in comparison with Abelard, as in Hanning, The Individual
>   in 12th Century Romance]

>   Guibert de Nogent, Self and Society in medieval France, the Memoires
>   of Abbot Guibert de Nogent, trans. J. Benton

About the editor

Penelope D. Johnson is a graduate of Yale College and received her M.Phil. and Ph.D. from Yale University. She is an Associate Professor of History at New York University where she teaches courses in Medieval History and the History of Women. She is currently director of the graduate program in Women's History at NYU. Her publications include Prayer, Patronage, and Power: The Abbey of la Trinité, Vendôme, 1032-1187 (N.Y., 1981), and articles published in Revue bénédictine, The Dictionary of Christian Spirituality, Bulletin de la société, archéologique, scientifique et littéraire du Vendômois and Augustinian Studies. She is currently at work on a study of monastic women in France during the central Middle Ages.

other titles:

Selected course outlines and reading lists in history as reference books for faculty members, librarians and graduate students.

ANCIENT HISTORY
0-910129-11-8

MEDIEVAL HISTORY
0-910129-09-6

EARLY MODERN EUROPEAN HISTORY
0-910129-10-X

MODERN EUROPEAN HISTORY I & II
Vol. I, Chronological & National Courses
0910129-07-X
Vol. II, Topical & Thematic Courses
0-910129-08-8

AMERICAN HISTORY I, II & III
Vol. I, Survey & Chronological Courses
0-910129-04-5
Vol. II, Selected Topics in Cultural, Social & Economic
History 0-910129-05-3
Vol. III, Selected Topics in 20th Century History
0-910129-06-1

WOMEN'S HISTORY (American)
0-910129-12-6

WOMEN'S HISTORY (European & Third World)
0-910129-32-0 (May '85)

WORLD HISTORY
0-910129-23-0

For information, write to
Markus Wiener Publishing, Inc.
2901 Broadway, New York, NY 10025